PSYCHOLOGY and INDUSTRY TODAY

PSYCHOLOGY and INDUSTRY TODAY

Second Edition

An Introduction to Industrial and
Organizational Psychology

DUANE P. SCHULTZ

The American University

Macmillan Publishing Co., Inc.
New York

Collier Macmillan Publishers
London

Macmillan Publishing Co., Inc.
866 Third Avenue, New York, New York 10022
Collier Macmillan Canada, Ltd.

Library of Congress Cataloging in Publication Data

Schultz, Duane P
  Psychology and industry today.

  Includes bibliographies and index.
  1. Psychology, Industrial. I. Title.
HF5548.8.S356 1978   158.7   77–4950
ISBN 0–02–408160–4

Printing: 2 3 4 5 6 7 8   Year: 8 9 0 1 2 3 4

To Sydney Ellen

PREFACE

The second edition of *Psychology and Industry Today* retains the basic theme and approach that seems to have been responsible for the gratifying reception accorded the first edition. The book is written as an introduction to the field of industrial/organizational psychology and is designed as a text for courses in industrial, business, applied, or personnel psychology.

My purpose in this book is not to train people to become industrial psychologists, but rather to acquaint students—most of whom will work for some kind of organization—with the principles, practices, problems, and occasional pretenses of industrial/organizational psychology. In addition, I believe that it is important to show students how psychology will aid them in their careers, and how the findings of industrial/organizational psychologists will directly influence their everyday lives as job applicants, employees, managers, and consumers.

Research methods and findings are discussed within the framework of actual work problems rather than as academic or theoretical exercises. The focus throughout the book is on contemporary, practical, and on-the-job situations. Research studies using workers rather than college students as subjects have been used.

Because *Psychology and Industry Today* is intended for undergraduate classroom use, it is written expressly for students. They are the ones who must read, underline, and study the text, and I would like them not only to learn about industrial/organizational psychology but also to enjoy reading about it. I have attempted to combine readability with thorough, accurate coverage.

The level of the discussion in this edition is particularly suitable for students who are not psychology majors, who often constitute a large portion of those enrolled in this course. It is appropriate for use by departments of psychology and schools of business administration at the four-year college and university level, and at junior and community colleges.

The second edition contains significant changes. Much of the book has been rewritten to increase clarity and to eliminate sex-biased language (in recognition of the fact that women now constitute nearly 48 per cent of the work force), and the entire book has been substantially updated to reflect current practices, problems, and trends.

The thirteen chapters have been grouped in five sections, with introductory remarks providing a meaningful framework for the chapters in each section. A new chapter on organizational psychology points out the impact of the style of the organization on working life. The chapters on leadership and motivation in the organizational psychology section have been revised to reflect the importance of organizational psychology. Overall, the general quality of working life, especially the trend toward the humanization of work, is stressed. Also, increased use is made of studies and applications of industrial/organizational psychology in countries other than the United States.

Two changes are introduced specifically to aid students in learning the material. First, chapter summaries have been added that emphasize important topics, issues, and studies. Second, the suggested readings for each chapter have been greatly expanded to provide guidance for students who wish to pursue particular topics.

In addition to these broad changes in the second edition, many new topics are discussed. These include, among others, behavior modification in industry, organizational development (OD), participatory democracy at work, classic and modern theories of organization, effects of worker participation and organizational climate on the role and status of the leader, the role of power in leadership, harmful effects of merit pay plans and salary secrecy, work space design for the handicapped worker, environmental psychology and office design, selection techniques such as job previews, videotape interviewing, forced-choice reference checks, and assessment centers, computer-assisted testing and instruction, reactions of children to television commercials, and the effects of price on buying behavior.

A manual of multiple choice and essay examination questions is available for the instructor, along with a list of multimedia instructional aids for each chapter.

I wish to thank the students and instructors who used the first edition of the book and who took the time to tell me their reactions to it. Their comments were of great help in preparing the second edition. It is also a pleasure to record my gratitude to my wife, Sydney Ellen, whose bibliographic skills were responsible for securing the research materials required for this edition, and whose editorial skills sharpened its style. From the beginning of the book to the end, each page testifies to her abilities, patience, and dedication.

Duane P. Schultz

CONTENTS

INTRODUCTION

1

Principles, Practices, and Problems

SCOPE AND IMPORTANCE OF INDUSTRIAL PSYCHOLOGY

The field of industrial psychology exerts a tremendous influence on the quality of our lives. No matter where and how we live and work, or at what level of society we function, what we do with our lives is affected by this vital part of psychology.

Since the influence of industrial psychology is so pervasive, this may be one of the most personally important and relevant courses of your college career. Since our behaviors and attitudes are shaped, directly and indirectly, by the principles and practices of industrial psychology, you should be aware of the nature of this powerful influence.

Most of you, upon completion of college training, will work for some sort of organization—a business corporation, a manufacturing concern, the federal or state government, a hospital or university, or the military. No matter where you work, your entire career—from the day you approach the personnel office for your first interview until your retirement dinner—will be shaped and guided by the findings of industrial psychologists. Indeed, second to your own ability, industrial psychology will help determine the job you perform and the manner in which you perform it, your ultimate rank, responsibilities, and remuneration, and, most important, the kind of personal satisfaction you derive from your work.

We spend the greatest portion of our adult lives at some sort of employment and the nature of our working career determines not only how well we live financially but also our emotional security and happiness. Our work provides us with a sense of identity; it tells us, and others, who and what we are. It contributes to our sense of self-esteem, affiliation, and belonging. If we are frustrated or dissatisfied

3

in our job, we are also likely to be unhappy when we go home to our family at the end of the workday.

Unhappiness at work can also affect our physical and emotional health. A fifteen-year study of the aging process [1] found that the single greatest predictor of longevity was work satisfaction. Heart disease, ulcers, arthritis, psychosomatic illnesses, anxiety, worry, and tension have also been shown to be related to stress and dissatisfaction at work. Consequently, finding the appropriate kind of work may be the single most important decision you make in your life.

Industrial psychologists aid you initially in making that difficult decision because of their prominent role in job selection. Your first formal contact with industrial psychology will probably be the psychological tests and the other selection measures used by a potential employer to determine if you are the right person for the job and, of equal importance, if the job is the right one for you.

After you have satisfied a company and yourself about the appropriateness of the job, the contribution of industrial psychology to your work life continues. Your advancement in the organization depends on several criteria including your actual job performance (which will be periodically evaluated using techniques devised by psychologists), and your performance on additional psychological tests. In many businesses today, high-level promotions are never made without the recommendation of the company psychologist about a person's potential for handling increased responsibilities.

Because of your college training, you may assume a management position at some level within the corporate hierarchy. This means that you must be aware of and sensitive to the diverse motivational and emotional factors influencing the people who work for you. To learn how best to lead and motivate your subordinates, you may turn profitably to the findings of industrial psychologists. Indeed, you will probably find yourself in a training program that was established by psychologists to teach you how to motivate your subordinates and how to be an effective manager of the work of others.

Even if you do not assume leadership responsibilities—if you are an engineer, an accountant, a technician, for example, working in a staff capacity with no subordinates—you will still encounter problems of interpersonal relations. Whatever your job, most likely you will be working with other people and a knowledge of human relations skills (how to get along with others) is important. Awareness of the research findings of industrial psychologists can spell the difference between success and failure. The importance of getting along with others was recognized in one psychological study of several thou-

[1] *Work in America* (Cambridge, Mass.: MIT Press, 1973), pp. 76–96.

sand white-collar workers. Investigating the reasons why people were fired from their jobs, the researchers learned that only 10 per cent were dismissed for lack of appropriate technical ability. A staggering 90 per cent were fired because they could not get along with their fellow workers or with their supervisors. Organizations today devote a great deal of effort to improving their employees' interpersonal and human relations skills, training that you may well undergo yourself.

You will certainly be interested in seeing your employer grow and prosper since the more your company expands, the more opportunities there will be for you to advance within the organization. The company's output must be produced with as much efficiency and quality as possible. Therefore, the plant, equipment, and working conditions must foster a productive working climate. This is another responsibility of industrial psychologists; they participate in the design of machinery, the layout of assembly lines, and the arrangement of the working environment to assure maximum high-level production. The finished product of a manufacturing concern must be advertised and attractively packaged to entice people to buy it. Industrial psychologists play a role in these activities too.

At all levels of modern organizational life, industrial psychologists provide essential services to you and your employer. Psychology as applied to the world of work serves two masters—the individual and the company. It cannot benefit one without benefiting the other.

A note of caution. As vital as the field of industrial psychology is, as influential as it will be in your career, it is primarily a tool. And any tool is only as valuable as the skill of the person who uses it. Improperly used by management, inadequately understood by employees, the findings of industrial psychologists can do more harm than good. Proper use of this tool by competent managers and employees will profit everyone.

But there is more to industrial psychology. It also affects your daily life away from the job; its effects are not limited to the factory or office. Industrial psychology influences your role as a consumer. We noted the use of industrial psychology in packaging, marketing, and advertising a company's products. Whether we like it or not, advertising is an integral part of our society and a necessary cornerstone of our multibillion-dollar economy. On radio and television, in magazines and newspapers, on billboards and even in the sky, we are continually bombarded by messages urging us to buy this and try that.

What governed your choice of a toothpaste, breakfast cereal, or car? Most likely it was the psychological image created for the product, the attractiveness of the package, or the emotional need satisfied by a particular brand. Advertising has told us, successfully, that we will be more popular, nicer to be near, or more kissable if we wear these

5

jeans or use that after-shave lotion. And many of the professionals who create our needs, and design the packages and slogans to satisfy them, are psychologists.

The same kinds of psychological techniques designed to rid us of bad breath and heartburn are also used to sell political candidates. Psychology has entered the political arena to create images for candidates that will induce you to vote for them. Also, public opinion polls are widely used to inform political leaders about how people feel on various issues. Polling techniques are used by psychologists in other areas. For example, the ratings that determine the television programs we watch are based on scientifically conducted polls of cross-sectional samples of television viewers.

If you have an automobile, your driving behavior is influenced by the industrial psychologists who assisted design engineers in the layout of the instrument panel so that knobs and controls are easy to use and visual displays (such as the speedometer) are easy to see and interpret. The shape and color of road signs are a result of research by psychologists on highway safety.

The list of contributions of industrial psychologists to daily living both on and off the job is a long one, but I think the point has been made. Since you are so affected by this field, no matter where you are or what you do, you should try to learn something about it, if only for self-defense!

DEFINITION AND METHOD OF INDUSTRIAL PSYCHOLOGY

We can define industrial psychology quite simply as *the application of the methods, facts, and principles of psychology to people at work.* As such, industrial psychology is one of many fields of the discipline of psychology. Now, as so often happens with definitions, we must define the term *psychology* in order to adequately understand our initial definition.

Psychology is the science of human and animal behavior. As a rule, however, industry is not overly concerned with animal behavior (except in those rare but delightful instances where chimpanzees have been trained to work on assembly lines and pigeons trained to inspect pills). Although much useful knowledge in psychology has come from animal research, some of which is applicable to the world of work, industrial psychologists are little concerned with animal behavior.

Industrial psychology, then, involves *the application of the methods, facts, and principles of the science of human behavior to people at work.*

6

The fact that industrial psychology is a science tells us a great deal about its manner of operation. A science deals only with observable fact—that which can be seen, heard, touched, measured, and recorded. Hence, science is empirical; that is, it relies on observation and experience, not on opinions, intuitions, pet notions, or private prejudices. It follows that science is objective in its approaches and results. The observed facts must be public; that is, capable of being seen and confirmed by other scientists working independently. Chapter 2 examines the methods by which the science of psychology gathers and analyzes its facts or data.

One point to remember throughout this book is that industrial psychology, in its methods and procedures, is just as scientific as physics or chemistry; a science is known by its methods not by its subject matter. When industrial psychologists observe the behavior of people at work, they do so in the best time-honored traditions of science—objectively, dispassionately, and systematically.

Since the method of the science of industrial psychology is objective, so must be the focus of its observation—human behavior. Overt behavior—our movements, speech, and creative works—are the only aspects of human existence that can be objectively seen, heard, measured, and recorded. Therefore, psychologists concentrate on overt behavior in order to understand and analyze the people they are studying. However, something more must be involved since psychology also deals with intangible human aspects such as motivations, emotions, thoughts, and wishes. These facets of our inner or subjective life cannot be observed directly.

For example, motivation. We cannot see motivation—it is an internal driving force inaccessible to observation. How can psychologists know anything about motivations or drives? While it is true that motivation itself cannot be seen, the *effects* of motivation can be observed. An angry person may openly exhibit this motivation in overt behaviors such as a flushed face, rapid breathing, or clenched fists.

We cannot see intelligence directly but we can see the overt behavioral manifestations of various levels of intelligence. Psychologists can observe objectively that one person performs (or behaves) at a higher level on an intelligence test than does another person. From these facts it can be inferred that the first person possesses greater intelligence than the second.

Inference based on observed behavior enables us to draw conclusions regarding various human states or conditions even when these aspects cannot be seen directly.

This is how industrial psychologists function. They observe the behavior of the worker on an assembly line, the secretary at a desk, or the executive at a meeting, under well-controlled and systematic conditions. They record the person's behavioral responses—the number of parts produced each hour, the number of words typed per minute, the quantity and quality of decisions made. They vary the conditions under which the job is performed and look for any resulting differences in performance. They use these and other techniques to seek a better understanding of human behavior but, over all, the essence of the scientific method is simply that psychologists *observe*. They look, listen, measure, and record with objectivity, precision, and dispassion.

A BRIEF HISTORY OF INDUSTRIAL PSYCHOLOGY

Industrial psychology was born of, and is nurtured on, necessity. The urgency of a practical problem needing a solution gave the initial impetus to the field, and the continuing demands of crisis and need have stimulated its growth and influence.

Psychology itself is approximately one hundred years old and industrial psychology had its formal beginning only in the early years of the twentieth century. It is difficult to determine the precise origin and founder of any field of study but many accord the honor in this case to Professor Walter Dill Scott who, in 1901, spoke out on the potential uses of psychology in advertising. Responding to the urgings of the advertising industry, Scott wrote additional articles and, in 1903, *The Theory of Advertising,* a book generally considered to be the first dealing with psychology and an aspect of the world of work. In 1913, a second book appeared: *The Psychology of Industrial Efficiency* by Hugo Münsterberg, a German psychologist teaching at Harvard University. This work dealt more broadly with the field of industrial psychology. These books generated a modest degree of interest, but it was the request of the U.S. Army for help during World War I that marked the emergence of industrial psychology as an important and useful discipline. Faced with the necessity of screening and classifying millions of recruits, the army commissioned a number of psychologists to devise a general intelligence test so that persons of low intelligence could be identified and eliminated from training programs. Two tests were developed: the Army Alpha for literates and the Army Beta for nonliterates.

Success in that endeavor quickly led to the development of other tests for use in selecting candidates for officer and pilot training, and for other military classifications requiring special abilities. The formulation of these tests was an extremely difficult task since there were no precedents, but the psychologists of the day successfully met the challenge.

This military experience provided the basis for a dynamic proliferation of industrial psychological activities following the war. The public, businesses, school systems, and other organizations requiring classifying and screening techniques, became aware of the successful use of tests and eagerly clamored for more and better testing techniques. The tests that had been used by the army were adapted for civilian use and new ones were designed for a variety of situations. A widespread and intensive program of psychological testing in the public schools, in industry, and in the military, to which we are now routinely exposed (perhaps overexposed), began.

Thus, the initial contributions of industrial psychologists centered around what is usually called *personnel psychology*—the proper selection and placement or matching of the right individual for the right job.

The scope of the field broadened considerably in 1924 with the commencement of the most famous series of studies ever conducted in industrial psychology. Called the Hawthorne studies (because they were conducted at the Hawthorne, Illinois, plant of the Western Electric Company),[2] these research programs took industrial psychology beyond the selection and placement of workers to the more complex problems of human relations, morale, and motivation.

The research began as a reasonably straightforward investigation of the effects of the physical aspects of the work environment on worker efficiency. The researchers asked such questions as: What is the effect on production of an increase in the level of illumination? Do temperature and humidity affect production? What happens if rest periods are introduced?

The results of the Hawthorne studies were astounding to both the investigators and the Hawthorne plant managers. It was found that social and psychological conditions of the work environment were of potentially greater importance than the physical work conditions. For example, changing the level of illumination from very bright to nearly dark did not diminish the level of efficiency of a group of workers. Other, more subtle, factors were operating to cause these workers to maintain their original production levels under almost dark conditions.

In another case, illumination was increased and production levels rose. Other changes were then introduced—rest periods, free lunches, a shorter workday—and with the introduction of each change, production increased. But the most startling result occurred when all the improvements were eliminated: production still increased! It was con-

---

[2] F. J. Roethlisberger and W. J. Dickson, *Management and the Worker—An Account of a Research Program Conducted by the Western Electric Company, Chicago* (Cambridge, Mass.: Harvard University Press, 1939).

cluded that the physical aspects of the work environment were not as important as had been supposed.

These research studies opened up whole new areas of exploration, lasting more than a decade, into such factors as the quality and nature of supervision, informal groups among workers, employees' attitudes toward their jobs, communication, and a host of other social-psychological forces now recognized as capable of influencing, even determining, a worker's efficiency, motivation, and job satisfaction.

World War II brought more than two thousand psychologists directly into the war effort. Their major contribution, as in World War I, was the testing, screening, and classifying of millions of recruits in various branches of the service. More complex human skills were required to operate the new and sophisticated planes, tanks, and ships, and the necessity of identifying persons who possessed the ability to learn these skills resulted in the development of many refinements in selection and training procedures.

The increasingly complex weapons of war also led to the development of an entirely new area of industrial psychology: *engineering psychology* (also called human engineering, or human factors engineering). Working closely with engineers, engineering psychologists supplied information on human capacities and limitations for operating sophisticated equipment such as high-speed aircraft, submarines, and tanks, and therefore influenced their design.

Industrial psychology achieved even greater stature and recognition as a result of its successful contributions to the war effort. Government and industry leaders were made aware that psychologists were well equipped to solve pressing practical problems. The experience also demonstrated to many psychologists, who before the war had worked in the isolation of their laboratories, that there were important and challenging problems in the real world and that they could effectively contribute to finding solutions to them.

The growth of industrial psychology since 1945 has paralleled the phenomenal growth of American business and technical enterprise. The size and complexity of modern business and government organizations have placed additional demands on the skills of psychologists to maintain and increase levels of industrial efficiency. New techniques and manufacturing processes mean that workers must be trained to develop new skills. In many cases, technical advances have led to entirely new occupations. The advent of computers, for example, generated the insistent need for computer programmers, and psychologists had to determine the abilities needed to successfully perform this job, the kind of person possessing these abilities, and the best methods for selecting and training him or her.

The demands made upon engineering psychology today are more

critical than ever before. Planes fly at supersonic speeds and weapons are so complex and dangerous that efficient and safe operation is of paramount importance. Engineering psychologists have also been called upon to assist in the design of industrial equipment and consumer items such as the dashboard of your automobile or your push-button telephone.

Human relations skills are becoming more significant as industry leaders are made increasingly aware of the influence of motivation, leadership, and other psychological factors on job performance. The human relations aspect of management has assumed greater importance in the world of work along with the recognition of the impact of the organizational setting in which work takes place. Psychologists now study the structure or climate of different types of organization, their patterns and styles of communication, and the formal and informal social structures they produce, in order to determine their effect on employee behavior.

So significant has been this stress on organizational variables that the Division of Industrial Psychology of the American Psychological Association changed its name in 1970 to the Division of Industrial and Organizational Psychology to reflect this recent awareness. Indeed, the field is often referred to as industrial/organizational psychology (see Chapters 7–9). The term *industrial psychology* can still be used as long as we recognize that the field now encompasses organizational psychology. Also, not all industrial psychologists are also organizational psychologists; some are personnel psychologists, consumer psychologists, or engineering psychologists, and thus are not directly concerned with the variables of interest to organizational psychologists.

In sum, industrial psychology influences virtually every facet of organizational life—it touches upon everything we do in the world of work.

THE PROFESSION OF INDUSTRIAL PSYCHOLOGY

The Professional Association

The success of industrial psychology in its contributions to business and government organizations has led to the development of a widely recognized and respected profession. The primary organization to which most members of this profession belong is the American Psychological Association, the stated purpose of which is "to advance psychology as a science and profession and as a means of promoting human welfare" (APA Bylaws, 1975). In 1976, there were approximately

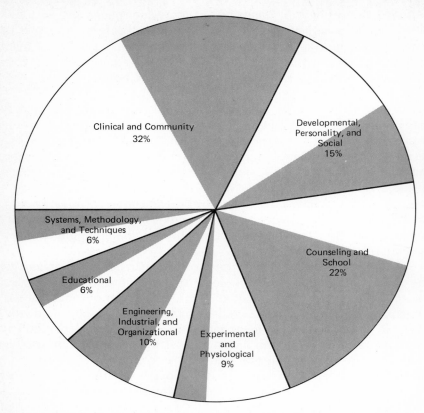

Figure 1–1. Fields of psychology. Data from survey of APA-member psychologists in U.S. and Canada, 1972 (*Careers in Psychology*, Washington, D.C.: American Psychological Association, 1975), p. 17. White areas represent scientific specialties of PhD psychologists; shaded areas represent scientific specialties of Master's-level psychologists. Copyright 1975 by the American Psychological Association. Reprinted by permission.

forty-two thousand members of the APA and it is predicted that membership will exceed sixty-two thousand, five hundred by 1985.

The various areas or fields of psychology and the percentage of psychologists in each field are shown in Figure 1–1. The primary places of employment of psychologists are presented in Figure 1–2. It must be noted that some of the psychologists who are employed by colleges and universities are also industrial psychologists engaged in research or part-time consulting to industry.

The interests of psychologists as a group are so diverse that the APA includes thirty-four divisions representing various scientific and professional interests. Four of these divisions represent the bulk of

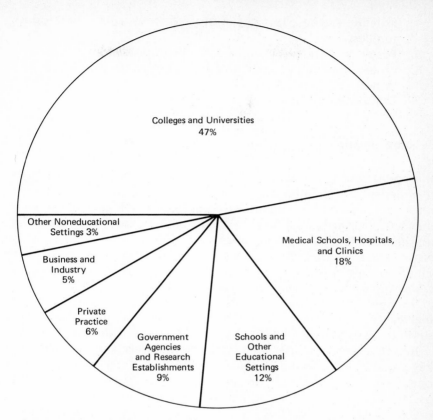

Figure 1–2. Employers of psychologists. Data from survey of APA-member psychologists in U.S. and Canada, 1972 (*Careers in Psychology,* Washington, D.C.: American Psychological Association, 1975), p. 17. Copyright 1975 by the American Psychological Association. Reprinted by permission.

industrial psychologists: Industrial and Organizational Psychology; Military Psychology; the Society of Engineering Psychologists; and Consumer Psychology. Of these divisions, Industrial and Organizational Psychology has the largest membership and represents most of the APA-affiliated psychologists working in industry. The division is concerned with scientific, professional, and ethical issues and specifies several goals that all industrial psychologists should strive to satisfy (Division 14 Bylaws, 1971).

1. Establish and maintain high standards of practice.
2. Stimulate research and publication.
3. Facilitate exchange of information and experience among themselves as well as the general public.

4. Expedite the development of professional standards and opportunities.
5. Foster cooperative relations with allied professions.
6. Protect the public from untrained and/or unethical practioners.
7. Contribute to the broad advancement of psychology.

Training Requirements for Industrial Psychologists

It is an interesting phenomenon that though few feel themselves to be qualified physicists after taking one or two courses in that subject, many people consider themselves expert psychologists, even when they have had no formal training. Unfortunately, some individuals feel that the practice of psychology requires nothing more than common sense and a lot of experience with people. Merely interacting with others, however, will no more make one a psychologist than years of taking medicines will qualify one as a physician.

Modern psychology is a complex and demanding profession requiring years of concentrated university work and a lifetime of continuing study to keep abreast of rapidly unfolding modern developments.

Industrial psychologists are, first, psychologists and as such must have a solid background in the discipline before specializing in any one area. The four years devoted to an undergraduate degree in psychology are not at all sufficient to qualify one as an industrial psychologist, since the B.A. or B.S. degree in psychology carries no professional recognition. Those possessing only this level of training find themselves in low-level jobs as apprentices or technicians. A minimal requirement for any position of potential responsibility in industrial psychology is the M.A. or M.S. degree, but the person who intends a career in the field might consider obtaining the PhD. As a rule, the higher positions (in terms of rank in the corporate hierarchy and salary) go to those with the highest advanced degree. However, as shown in Figure 1–1 more people with master's degrees than with doctorates were working in industrial psychology. Employment opportunities for master's-level persons are very good in this area.

In addition to graduate degrees, industrial psychologists may also aspire to professional recognition for achievement. Members of the APA may be nominated to the status of Fellow on the basis of professional accomplishments and five years of experience beyond the PhD. A further level of recognition is the Diplomate in Industrial Psychology, awarded by the American Board of Professional Psychology to those who are particularly well trained and competent.

The training and preparation of the industrial psychologist is long and difficult but the rewards in terms of stimulating work, challenging responsibility, and continuing intellectual growth can be great.

Employment of Industrial Psychologists

Industrial psychologists usually work as full-time members of business, government, or industrial organizations, as members of firms of consulting psychologists offering their services to a variety of organizations, or as faculty members of universities, perhaps serving as consultants to industry on a part-time basis.

Most psychologists who work full-time in industry are employed by large organizations of practically every type of business operation—insurance, manufacturing, advertising, retailing, and so on. To give you an idea of the scope of employment opportunities for industrial psychologists, Table 1–1 contains examples of the companies that employ psychologists and their specific job titles. As you can see, the range of job responsibilities and titles is broad and impressive.

As to the specific activities performed by industrial psychologists, one researcher interviewed seventy-five psychologists and found that their work could be divided into six general categories.

1. Personnel Selection—the selection and continuing evaluation of all levels of employees.
2. Personnel Development—the measurement of performance and attitudes, training, and counseling.
3. Engineering Psychology—design of equipment, vehicles, and consumer products.
4. Efficiency in Production—research on physical and psychological conditions of the work environment.
5. Supervision—identification and development of leadership abilities.
6. Miscellaneous—counseling, labor relations, safety.

As this list indicates, psychologists are actively involved in just about every activity that concerns people in an organization.

Many smaller organizations cannot afford a full-time psychologist and must rely on the services of consulting firms whenever they are faced with problems requiring an industrial psychologist. These consulting organizations operate on a contract basis and perform activities such as assessing candidates for employment, developing a piece of equipment or an assembly line, setting up a training program, conducting a study on consumer acceptance of a new product, or finding out why production efficiency is slipping. The value of consulting lies not

15

TABLE 1–1

PLACES OF EMPLOYMENT AND JOB TITLES OF SELECTED INDUSTRIAL PSYCHOLOGISTS

American Telephone and Telegraph
　Public Relations Effectiveness Opinion and Marketing
　　Research Statistician
Bell Telephone Laboratories
　Business Systems Supervisor
City Government
　Assistant Personnel Director
Columbia Broadcasting System
　Director of Compensation
Continental Oil
　Director of Advertising
Dow Chemical
　Manager of Consumer Research
Executronics
　Vice President
General Dynamics
　Head of Human Factors Laboratory
General Electric
　Senior Staff Specialist
Harcourt Brace Jovanovich
　Executive Editor of Test Department
International Harvester
　Manager of Corporate Marketing Research
International Multifoods
　Director of Management Development
McGraw-Hill
　Regional Manager
Metropolitan Life Insurance
　Staff Psychologist
Port Authority of New York and New Jersey
　Supervisor of Test Development and Evaluation
Reynolds Metals
　Manager of Personnel Research
Sears Roebuck
　National Director of Training and Development
Self-Employed
　Management Consultant
Standard Oil
　Manager of Psychological Services
State Department of Health and Welfare
　Program Planner, Bureau of Research and Training

TABLE 1–1 (continued)

Texas Instruments
  Personnel Director of Worldwide Operations
U.S. Naval Personnel Research and Development Center
  Research Engineering Psychologist
U.S. Steel
  Staff Supervisor of Testing and Counseling
Westinghouse Electric
  Manager of Employee Relations
Xerox
  Manager of Information and Planning Services

only in the technical skills that can be applied to a problem but also in the freshness of approach and objectivity that an outside organization may possess. The number of such firms is increasing and they are filling a vital need in business and government organizations.

PROBLEMS OF INDUSTRIAL PSYCHOLOGY

No field of study is free of internal or external difficulties. Industrial psychology as a science and profession has several problem areas, all of which are aggravated by the very factor that has made it so successful—the demand for its services.

The Charlatan

Certainly more than any other science, psychology has been bothered by quackery—the illicit and invalid practice of "psychology" by persons with little or no professional training. This is particularly crucial in clinical and counseling psychology where untrained charlatans can do great harm to emotionally disturbed persons seeking help.

Quackery has also been practiced in industrial psychology; an uninformed business organization can be just as gullible as an individual. Unfortunately, there have been unethical consulting firms and individuals who have sold their services to industry and made quick money (and a quicker getaway) before the company realized it had been duped.

Not only is unethical behavior potentially dangerous to industry—consider, for example, the number of competent people who might not be hired because they did not perform well on the quack's phony test—but it is also harmful to psychology. If the company is damaged by the charlatan's services, psychology as a whole will frequently be blamed. The executives of a company that has been "taken" in the past may be reluctant to consider any psychological services or advice in the future.

The problem of the charlatan is lessening, however, because many states now license psychologists in the same way that professionals such as physicians are licensed. In these states it is illegal for persons to call themselves psychologists, or use any of the tools of psychology, unless they have met the licensing requirements.

Other states have developed certification requirements that, though not as strong a control as licensing, do at least prevent unqualified persons from representing themselves as certified psychologists. However, a person or an organization must exercise care when seeking the services of a psychologist. It is not enough to consult the telephone directory. The educational and professional qualifications of anyone called a psychologist must be considered.

Communication

All sciences develop a specialized technical jargon which its members use to communicate with one another. Unfortunately, this very specific vocabulary is not usually understood by those outside the discipline. Since industrial psychologists must work closely with foremen, executives, workers, and other nonpsychologists, it is imperative that they be able to communicate with all these people. The research results and recommendations of industrial psychologists will be of no value to a company if its executives cannot understand the language of the reports; they will be filed in the nearest wastebasket. Psychologists must know the terminology used by the organizations employing them and, in turn, must be able to present contributions in a form that will be easily understood.

The Reluctance to Try Something New

This section might be called, "I've always done it this way and I'm not about to change now!" Psychologists who work in industry often come across this attitude—an unwillingness to "rock the boat," a resistance to change.

Frequently, a change in the usual way of performing a job is viewed as a threat to a worker's personal well-being. Employees who are told to change their work patterns to the more efficient system recommended by the psychologist may actively resist the change because they feel that the company is just trying to get them to work harder for no additional pay. If the workers are insecure, they may feel that the company is criticizing their past job performance. Whatever the reason, this resistance to change is a serious problem at all levels of industry, from the assembly line worker to the company president.

If the recommendations of psychologists are to have any value, they must have the active support of those who are affected. Psychologists must, in a sense, "sell" their suggestions in such a way that those involved fully appreciate the reasons for the change, and accept the fact that the change is not a threat to their jobs. Consequently, psychologists must possess considerable human relations skills and patience, in addition to a high level of technical competence.

Research Versus Application

The question of research versus application continues to plague industrial psychology in its relations with management. It is a problem that can often lead to unfortunate consequences for both the psychologist and the executive.

The ideal (indeed necessary) relationship between the two functions is research *and* application. Without research, there would be no knowledge to apply to the practical situation on the job. This point is often overlooked by organization leaders who want immediate answers to highly specific questions and cannot understand the hesitation of the psychologist who tells them that the answer can come only from research on the problem.

Executives want immediate answers because production schedules and contract deadlines won't always wait for the design and execution of a research study. Frequently harried managers become very impatient when the company psychologist, "our expert on human behavior," can't provide a quick answer.

The difficulty is that virtually every human problem in industry is unique to a particular company or department or section within that company. The results of a research study conducted on absenteeism of spot welders at Company A may be irrelevant when applied to spot welders at Company B. Of course, there occasionally are comparable situations where research results from one organization may be applied to another, but it is impossible to predict this transferability. An invalid solution applied to an industrial problem can be just as damaging as attempting no solution at all.

This is not to suggest that whenever industrial psychologists are asked a question, they run to the laboratory to undertake a two-month experiment. The one hundred-year history of psychology provides us with a wealth of data about human behavior in a variety of situations, and well-trained psychologists can often apply this information to the specific problems of industry. The value of these data depends on the similarity of the settings of the past research and the current problem.

For example, learning studies conducted on chimpanzees or college sophomores have less relevance for a learning problem in a chemical company than will a learning study conducted in a steel company. The steel company research will provide the more useful results. But a learning study conducted in another chemical company might be even more applicable. And a study conducted on the very workers about whom the question was asked will be the most useful of all.

Compromise, patience, and understanding on both sides—the management and the psychologist—are called for. As an example of how one company handled the research versus application issue, consider the experience of the General Electric Company. Faced with a lack of applicability of social and behavioral science data to the company's problems, General Electric organized the Behavioral Research Service to conduct studies on their unique situations in their own work environment. The management and researchers at General Electric have been pleased with the effort, primarily because of the accuracy and high degree of relevance of the research findings. Several features of the research approach are responsible for its success.

First, since research is conducted only on problems generated by specific company needs, employees and executives give their full interest and cooperation because they recognize the importance of the research for their own jobs. Such cooperation is vital since research efforts can be easily frustrated by executives who think the studies are a waste of time or by employees who may not understand how the research will benefit them.

Second, research is conducted only on problems for which a substantial body of data already exists, and which are generating current research in industrial and academic laboratories. The greater the amount of available data that can be applied to the problem, the more directly and quickly that problem can be solved.

Finally, the Behavioral Research Service conducts its studies on the job—in the office or on the assembly line—rather than devising an artificial laboratory setting in which to pursue its investigations. Research conducted in the actual context of the problem stands a much greater chance of providing meaningful and useful results.

The experiences of General Electric and other business concerns demonstrate the necessary compatibility of research and application. When the problem of research and its application is approached in this enlightened manner, with both management and psychologist recognizing the other's needs and problems, the entire worker-management-corporate structure will benefit. Properly devised research can be of immense value to the productive efficiency of an organization as long as it is recognized that the fundamental question is not research versus application, but research plus application.

AREAS OF INDUSTRIAL PSYCHOLOGY

Industrial psychology influences all levels and phases of the relationship between people and their work. We briefly note specific aspects of this relationship—the professional interests of industrial psychologists—which are discussed in detail in the following chapters.

The Scientific Method

In every area in which industrial psychology has an impact on human behavior, it does so through the judicious use of the tools and techniques of science. So pervasive is this application of the scientific method that we might consider it an area of specialization.

The valuable contributions of industrial psychology are offered within the context of observation and experimentation—the cornerstones and the bases of industrial psychology. It would be difficult to comprehend fully the work of industrial psychologists without some understanding of the ways in which they perform their services. In Chapter 2, we consider the methods of science as they are used by industrial psychologists.

Employee Selection

Perhaps the most important problem faced by any organization is to select qualified persons to perform the various jobs required in our complex society. The success or failure of any organization depends in large measure on the caliber of its employees. It was the critical nature of this problem for the U.S. Army in World War I, noted earlier, that gave such an impetus to the growth of industrial psychology.

Despite the opinion of some executives and personnel managers who still think they can judge job applicants by the strength of their handshakes, the steadiness of their gazes, or their clothing, employee selection is a complicated issue requiring detailed psychological knowledge and sound research.

Even before applicants reach the personnel office, considerable work must be done to determine the nature, requirements, and demands of the position for which employees are being sought. It is impossible to know who will be successful in a job without knowing exactly what the job entails—what skills, aptitudes, interests, or personality characteristics are basic to successful performance of the job.

Once the details of the job are known and methods of selection have been chosen, it is necessary to determine if these selection measures are picking the best people. Employees selected and hired must be evaluated, after they have been working for a period of time, and their job performance compared with their earlier performance on the selection devices. Only through such long-term research can selection procedures be evaluated objectively.

Selection and evaluation of employees continue long after the initial hiring. Throughout one's career, questions of promotion (or demotion) must be considered. Many of the same selection devices used in hiring (for example, psychological tests) are also used in making subsequent career decisions.

Properly executed, selection and evaluation procedures are of great value to an organization. Poor design and misuse of these techniques is costly, however, in terms of time and money.

Not only is appropriate selection important to the organization but it is also vital to you as an employee. Your initial job and subsequent advancement (or lack of it) will be determined in part by your performance in the selection situation. It has been suggested that one of the most momentous days of your life is the day you apply for a job and are given a battery of psychological tests. Your performance at that time influences the direction of your career.

It is beneficial, then, as you approach your first full-time job, to understand the selection techniques currently in use. It is also to your advantage that a potential employer use the most valid techniques possible. Improper matching of the person and the job brings unhappiness and dissatisfaction to you, your family, and your employer.

Performance Evaluation

One activity that will continue throughout your working career is the evaluation of the quality of your job performance. As with other areas of industrial psychology, performance evaluation is important to you and to your employer. How much responsibility should you be given?

Should you be promoted? How great a salary increase should you get next year? Should you be fired?

These questions will be determined on the basis of the quality of your work. Such decisions should be made as fairly, objectively, and precisely as possible. It is the responsibility of industrial psychologists to devise adequate means of work evaluation for all levels of employment.

For some jobs this is a straightforward task. The efficiency of workers on an assembly line can be assessed quantitatively by determining how many units they produce each hour or each day, how much spoilage they cause, or how many accidents they are involved in, as compared with co-workers. A typist can be evaluated in similar quantitative terms.

But other jobs defy such easily determined estimates of job performance. How should we evaluate the work of executives—by counting the number of ideas they have each day? Obviously not. The scope of an executive's job is so broad that it cannot be evaluated in simple terms. Yet, it is necessary that the work be appraised periodically and with as much fairness and objectivity as that of the lathe operator. Industrial psychologists devote considerable effort to all levels of performance evaluation.

Training

At any level of the organization for which you work—as apprentice, management trainee, or middle-aged executive—the training opportunities provided for you are important. Just as poorly selected individuals can cause frustration for themselves and their employers, so can poorly trained workers.

The goal of training programs in industry is to develop specific skills, attitudes, and capacities in order to maximize the individual's job performance. Virtually every new employee in an organization undergoes some degree of training, either formal or informal. Inexperienced production workers must be taught the specific operations they are expected to perform. Experienced workers must learn, at the very least, the policies and procedures of a new employer.

Highly structured training programs are offered by many companies for new college graduates who often spend up to two years in classroom instruction as well as on-the-job performance and training. Also, some organizations send their experienced executives to special institutes and seminars, usually at universities, to learn the latest techniques of management and administration.

Industrial psychologists assume a large part of the responsibility for establishing, conducting, and evaluating training programs in industry. As the machinery of production and the dynamics of organizational life become more complex, the demands made on employees to learn and employers to teach increase in scope and significance.

Leadership

A key aspect of the worth of any organization is the quality of its leadership, from foreman to president. One of industry's greatest challenges is selecting, training, and developing effective leaders at all levels. This problem is of concern to you for two reasons: (1) as an employee you will work under a supervisor and your efficiency and satisfaction will be affected by the style and nature of this leader, and (2) since most business leaders today come from the ranks of the college-educated, you will most likely find yourself, in time, at some level of leadership.

Psychologists have conducted much research on leadership in all kinds of organizational situations. They are concerned not only with the personal characteristics and abilities associated with effective leadership but are also continually experimenting with various styles of supervision (for example, democratic versus authoritarian) to determine their differential effects on subordinates. Another area of interest is the kind of leadership that best inspires and motivates workers to produce at their optimal level in diverse work situations.

It is necessary to the continued growth and survival of any organization that the most competent people be placed in positions of leadership and that, once there, they exercise their influence in the most effective manner.

Motivation and the Quality of Working Life

Factors that exert a considerable impact on the efficiency of any organization are the motivations of the employees and the kinds of satisfaction they receive from their membership in the organization. Motivation and satisfaction are strongly influenced by various aspects of the work environment—for example, the quality of leadership, advancement opportunities, level of job security, and physical and psychological work climate.

Since these factors can be manipulated to optimize motivation and satisfaction, the employing organization should arrange them so that workers are efficient and content in their jobs. This is yet another task of industrial psychologists—to determine, through careful, on-the-job research, what contributes to positive worker motivation and satisfaction.

Intensive studies of the workers are required, through personal interviews and questionnaires, to elicit their concerns, gripes, and recommendations about how the job and work environment might be improved. If approached with consideration, openness, and fairness, the worker on the job is the best, and sometimes the only, source of such information.

This research requires a high level of technical competence from the psychologist, and the willingness of management to invest the time and money necessary to support the research. Negative aspects of a job environment can produce effects such as increased absenteeism, reduced production, higher accident rates, and grievances to the union. It is vital, therefore, that the company, through the work of its psychologists, find and correct factors that can impair the quality of working life before they have serious economic consequences.

Organizational Psychology

Few people work in isolation. Whether our work is in a classroom, a department store, or a steel mill, it takes place within the context of formal and informal organizational factors. The organization for which we work fosters a certain climate that includes, for example, the formal chain of command and the centralization or decentralization of power. These factors influence the way in which we perform our jobs and the satisfactions we may or may not find. The structures, policies, and resulting climate differ from one organization to another. Organizational psychologists study the impact of these structural aspects on productivity, motivation, and morale. Another dimension of the organizational structure, leadership, is part of the work climate as well, and the style and nature of leadership can have dramatic effects on the lives of the employees.

Since organizational psychology includes motivation, leadership, and the quality of working life, these topics, as well as a chapter entitled *The Organization of the Organization,* are discussed in the *Organizational Psychology* section.

There is more to organizational psychology than the formal structural characteristics of an organization; informal climates develop that reflect the nature and characteristics of cliques or small groups of workers. Sometimes these informal groups set norms and standards of behavior that are at variance with those imposed by the organization, a situation that obviously affects production.

At all levels—from informal to formal—the organization of the

25

organization represents a powerful source of influence on the worker, one that is receiving a great deal of attention from organizational psychologists.

Conditions of Work

The physical aspects of a job are obvious and visible and, consequently, were the first to be studied by psychologists in industry. Many research studies have been conducted on lighting, temperature, humidity, noise level, location of equipment, and working hours to determine their effects on production levels. Because of this vast amount of research, numerous guidelines are available to aid in the design and layout of the physical work environment. Additional research is needed, however, as new jobs and new methods of production are created.

Since the late 1940s it has come to be recognized that the physical environment would have to undergo a drastic change in order to have any significant effect on production. Note the matter of temperature levels, for example. In most work environments, the temperature would have to become extremely cold or extremely hot in order for the workers' output to be greatly affected. The widespread use of air conditioning, as well as improvements such as soundproofing, have reduced the extreme variations that used to mark many jobs. Modern technology has thus produced relatively stable physical conditions of work.

Attention has shifted therefore to less tangible and more complex social and psychological conditions of the work environment. The psychological climate of a job, including fatigue and boredom, is now recognized as more important than the physical climate because psychological conditions are subject to greater variation. However, just as features of the physical environment can be manipulated to produce more efficient and satisfying work, so can the psychological environment be controlled for optimum results, once research has determined the desirable aspects of a job's psychological environment.

Engineering Psychology

The design of the equipment, tools, and vehicles used in work is directly related to the physical work environment, to motivation and morale, and to accidents. The machinery of the manufacturing and transportation industries has become increasingly complex and, consequently, greater demands are placed on the human operator of this equipment.

Pilots of commercial jet airliners, for example, have only a limited time period in which to react in an emergency situation. Their equipment (the cockpit instruments and controls) must be designed and arranged so that information needed (altitude and speed, for example) can be read quickly and accurately and appropriate responses made as rapidly as possible. Operators of semiautomated rotary shears in a steel mill must be able to respond with as little delay as possible when something happens to the sheets of steel moving through the machine at forty miles per hour. In your automobile, you want to be able to know as quickly as possible when your engine overheats.

All of these are examples of man-machine systems; it is the job of the engineering psychologist to provide the best functional relationship between the person and the machine. This is accomplished through proper design of the machine so as to compensate for the human operators' weaknesses and to capitalize on their strengths.

This area of industrial psychology has widespread application to consumer products such as washing machines and lawnmowers.

Accidents, Alcohol, and Drugs

Industry is very concerned about the safety records of its employees because accidents on the job cause suffering (sometimes death) to employees and cost the company money. Economic losses resulting from industrial accidents run into billions of dollars every year from lost hours of work, employee compensation, and the costs of training replacement workers.

Industry today devotes considerable energy and funds to accident prevention. Part of this effort is research by industrial psychologists to attempt to identify job-related factors and individual personality characteristics that may contribute to accidents. Their research results have led to the development and installation of safety devices on potentially dangerous equipment, the selection and training of employees for safety awareness, and information programs designed to keep safety prominent in the minds of the employees.

Since the majority of accidents are caused by the human element, and not by equipment failure or bad luck, the application of psychology is crucial in reducing society's staggering accident toll—not only in industry but also in the home and on the highway. Psychologists are conducting considerable research on the personalities of those involved in an unusual number of accidents.

Alcoholism has long been a problem among employees at all levels and in all kinds of organizations. It leads to excessive absenteeism, reduced productivity, poor quality of work, and increased accidents. Many companies are recognizing and accepting their responsibility for trying to help employees who have drinking problems, and psychologists, both in the company and in outside clinics, are called upon to rehabilitate alcoholic workers.

A more recent problem in the world of work is the use of drugs on the job. Previously centered in high schools, colleges, and the military, the use of drugs has expanded into the organization as young drug users leave school or the army and begin a working career. Companies are forced to screen for drug use as part of their selection programs, educate their employees on the effects of drugs, and deal with those who are found using drugs while at work.

Psychology and the Consumer

Consumer psychology is important to you for two reasons: (1) throughout your life you will be bombarded with advertising appeals to buy certain products, some of which you will purchase, and (2) if you work for a company that sells consumer products or services, its ability to do so successfully affects your economic well-being. Millions of dollars are spent annually by business organizations in an attempt to get you to notice their product, to want it, and, of course, to purchase it.

The psychologist makes a unique contribution to the marketing of goods and services in terms of the carefully controlled experimental determination of the size and nature of the potential market for a product, the effectiveness of various advertising appeals and campaigns, customer reactions to different products, and the motivations and needs of the buying public.

THE FUTURE OF INDUSTRIAL PSYCHOLOGY

The continuing growth of the U.S. economy, together with technological advances and an increasing population, will probably dictate certain changes in the nature of our work in the future. And any changes in the way people work will mean new demands and responsibilities for industrial psychologists.

One significant change that is already in evidence is in the characteristics of the work force. In general, workers today tend to be younger, more educated, and more resistant to authority than those in the past. This means that workers may no longer respond to traditional incentives and leadership styles. Modern workers are demanding more challenging and stimulating jobs, and the opportunity to participate in decisions that affect their working lives. Also, they resist supervisors who behave in a dictatorial fashion. As a result, many jobs and organizational structures are being redesigned to incorporate autonomy, challenge, and satisfaction into work.

Another change has to do with the job opportunities for the unskilled and poorly educated workers, which seem to decrease each year. Greater demands are thus being placed on the selection and training functions of industrial psychologists to identify new abilities and training methods in order to upgrade the skills of the disadvantaged.

Industrial organizations of the future will most likely be larger and more impersonal to the individual employee. Psychologists will be challenged to devise ways of decreasing this sense of depersonalization and alienation, and to make employees feel that each of them is an integral part of the organization.

New and more complex equipment and manufacturing procedures present challenges to engineering psychologists who must find ways to design and adapt this equipment for efficient and safe human use. Much modern equipment is automated, requiring skillful maintenance although less attention to its daily operation. Means will have to be developed to alleviate the boredom and inattention that inevitably accompany the monitoring of automated machinery.

Workers are now retiring at an earlier age, and many are working fewer hours or days each week as reduced or flexible working schedules are introduced. The use of this new leisure time requires careful planning, research, and possibly even training—a responsibility that industry may have to assume and psychologists may have to direct.

Probably the most persistent challenge facing industrial psychologists today is to improve the quality of working life. The movement to humanize work is strong in Western Europe and is growing in the United States as individual workers, labor unions, and some congressional committees fight for an end to work that is boring, routine, and degrading. Workers and their representatives are demanding that jobs be changed so that workers may find satisfaction and fulfillment. A bigger paycheck is no longer an effective inducement for greater productivity; employees want meaning in their working lives as well. In the coming years, this movement to humanize work may be as revolutionary a change in the workplace as the assembly line was in an earlier time. It seems an idea whose time has come.

As the economy expands and new demands are made by the work

force, the problems faced by industrial psychologists will increase in scope and urgency. It seems safe to predict that psychology is destined to play an even more vital role in the organizational life of the future than it has in the past.

SUMMARY

Industrial psychology influences every aspect of your life at work and much of your life outside of work as well. It affects your initial hiring and training, the way in which your work is performed and evaluated, your motivations and the satisfactions you derive, and a host of other factors that determine your level of advancement and personal growth as well as the efficiency and vitality of the organization for which you work. As such, industrial psychology may be one of the most personally important courses of your college career.

Industrial psychology is defined as **the application of the methods, facts, and principles of the science of human behavior to people at work.** As a science, industrial psychology relies on the use of **observation** and **experimentation,** and deals only with overt human behavior, that which can be <u>observed objectively</u>.

empirical

Industrial psychology began in the early years of the twentieth century and grew rapidly, particularly under the impetus of the two world wars, which gave the field unique opportunities to demonstrate its value. A major change in industrial psychology was the recognition of the influence of social-psychological variables on worker behavior as demonstrated by the Hawthorne studies in the 1920s and 1930s. A new area of industrial psychology, engineering psychology, emerged out of the development of increasingly sophisticated weapons in World War II. In recent years, another new area has developed—organizational psychology—which is concerned with the setting or climate in which work takes place.

Most industrial psychologists are members of the American Psychological Association, which contains among its thirty-four divisions four that are devoted to the interests of industrial psychologists: Industrial and Organizational Psychology, Military Psychology, the Society of Engineering Psychologists, and Consumer Psychology. In order to work professionally as an industrial psychologist, a person needs at least a master's degree, and will find a position of higher responsibility with a PhD. Diverse employment opportunities are available for industrial psychologists.

Industrial psychology faces several problems that were brought about, in part, by the continuing demand for its services. These include

(1) **the charlatan,** the practice of industrial psychology by persons not professionally trained; (2) **communication,** the translation of technical jargon so that it can be understood by business personnel; (3) **the reluctance to try something new,** the resistance to change on the part of executives and workers often faced by industrial psychologists; and (4) **research versus application,** the necessary relationship between acquiring knowledge and applying it to specific problems.

Specific areas of industrial psychology are discussed in the following chapters. These include employee selection; performance evaluation; training; leadership; motivation and the quality of working life; organizational psychology; conditions of work; engineering psychology; accidents, alcohol, and drugs; and consumer psychology.

The future of industrial psychology calls for continued growth and new challenges brought about by the changing nature of the work force, the increasing size of organizations, more complex equipment and procedures, and increased leisure time. The greatest challenge facing industrial psychologists today is the movement to humanize work and to improve the quality of working life by introducing challenge, autonomy, and worker participation.

SUGGESTED READINGS

American Psychological Association. *Careers in Psychology.* Washington, D.C.: American Psychological Association, 1975. (Single copies free to students; write APA, 1200 17th St., N.W., Washington, D.C. 20036.)

American Psychological Association, Division of Industrial and Organizational Psychology. *A Career in Industrial Psychology.* Washington, D.C.: American Psychological Association, undated.

APA Task Force on the Practice of Psychology in Industry. Effective practice of psychology in industry. *American Psychologist,* 1971, **26,** 974–991.

Argyris, C. Problems and new directions for industrial psychology. In M. Dunnette, Ed., *Handbook of Industrial and Organizational Psychology.* Chicago: Rand McNally, 1976. Pp. 151–184.

Barrett, G., and Bass, B. Cross-cultural issues in industrial and organizational psychology. In M. Dunnette, Ed., *Handbook of Industrial and Organizational Psychology.* Chicago: Rand McNally, 1976. Pp. 1639–1686.

Clark, K. Survey of the behavioral and social sciences: Psychology. *American Psychologist,* 1970, **25,** 464–468.

Ghiselli, E. E. Some perspectives for industrial psychology. *American Psychologist,* 1974, **29,** 80–87.

Klaw, S. The management psychologists have landed. *Fortune,* 1970, **81** (April), 106–109, 116.

Meltzer, H., and Nord, W. The present status of industrial and organizational psychology. *Personnel Psychology,* 1973, **26,** 11–29.

Meyer, H. The future for industrial and organizational psychology: Oblivion or millennium? *American Psychologist,* 1972, **27,** 608–614.

Muchinsky, P. Graduate internships in industrial psychology: A success story. *Professional Psychology,* 1976, **7,** 664–670.

Parsons, H. M. What happened at Hawthorne? *Science,* 1974, **183** (8 March), 922–932.

Purcell, T. et al. What are the social responsibilities for psychologists in industry? A symposium. *Personnel Psychology,* 1974, **27,** 435–453.

Rice, R., and Keleman, K. Ten years of industrial/organizational psychology. *Professional Psychology,* 1976, **7,** 117–119.

Roethlisberger, F. J., and Dickson, W. J. *Management and the Worker —An Account of a Research Program Conducted by the Western Electric Company, Chicago.* Cambridge, Mass.: Harvard University Press, 1939.

Schein, V. The woman industrial psychologist: Illusion or reality? *American Psychologist,* 1971, **26,** 708–712.

2

Techniques, Tools, and Tactics

WHY STUDY RESEARCH METHODS?

In Chapter 1 we gained some appreciation of the importance of industrial psychological research to industry. Indeed, it can be said that psychology would be of little, if any, value to industry without the continuing application of research methods to the problems of people and their work.

Its value to industry, then, is beyond question, but what is its value to you in your future working career? How will you benefit from a knowledge of the methods used by psychologists to collect and analyze their research data?

Even though you may not be working as an industrial psychologist, most of you will be working directly or indirectly with the findings of industrial psychologists. As potential managers, you no doubt will find yourselves calling upon psychologists to solve particular management problems and you will be faced with decisions based in part on the results and recommendations of your company's psychologists.

The problems confronting business managers and executives today are so complex and difficult that answers can no longer be made on the basis of "common sense," pet ideas, or past procedures. Imagine that you are responsible for implementing a new manufacturing process in your department. A modern production facility must be developed and part of your problem will be to facilitate the changeover from the old process to the new. How will the workers react to such an abrupt change in their jobs? Will they be able (and, more important, willing) to operate the new machinery so as to maintain high production levels? How will the new process affect morale, absenteeism, and safety? These are just a few of the questions you would be expected to answer. If you make an incorrect decision, the cost will be high to both you and your company.

Using information based on sound research, psychologists may be able to help you in this situation. However, if you are to evaluate properly their advice and recommendations, you must be aware of the methods they use to study the problems.

As a manager, you may also be called upon to decide whether or not the research program recommended by the company psychologist is worth the time and money required. Again, a knowledge of the methods of research will enable you to make such a decision more wisely.

The purpose of this chapter is not to train you to do research yourself, but to acquaint you with the requirements, limitations, and methods of the scientific approach. The importance of understanding this information cannot be stressed too strongly. The application of the scientific method to problems too often dealt with by intuitive or subjective means may be psychology's most important contribution to better management and work practices. If you understand these research tools, you will be able to ensure their proper use.

REQUIREMENTS OF PSYCHOLOGICAL RESEARCH

One of the basic requirements and defining characteristics of scientific research in any discipline is *objective observation*. Researchers base their conclusions only on the objective evidence at hand and they view that evidence without preconceived ideas or biases.

It is well known in psychology that our perception of the world around us is subjective; that is, what we see is determined by our fears, values, attitudes, or prejudices. Thus, our observations are shaped not so much by what we are looking at as by our own psychological and emotional conditions at the time.

This is not the case with scientists. They must look upon the data in an open and unbiased manner. The facts of the situation must speak for themselves and determine the conclusion. A psychologist's choice of a particular test, method of training, or job environment layout cannot be determined by private hunches, by the recommendations of prestigious authorities, or even by past research. Rather, the decision must be based on an objective evaluation of the facts at hand.

A second requirement of psychological research is that observation be *well controlled and systematic*. The conditions under which objective observations are made must be determined in advance so that every factor that could possibly influence the responses of the subjects is known to the researcher. If, for example, we are studying the effect of music on the typing efficiency of secretaries, the situation must be arranged so that no factors other than the music can affect typing efficiency.

The systematic control of objective observation also allows for the fulfillment of a third research requirement—*duplication and verifiability*. With careful control of conditions, a scientist working at another time and place can duplicate the conditions under which the earlier experiment was conducted. We can have more confidence in research findings if they have been verified by another investigator, and this verification is possible only under thoroughly controlled experimental conditions.

Psychological research in any setting, then, requires full and careful systematic planning, control of the total experimental situation so that findings can be duplicated and verified, and objective observation of the data. How these requirements are implemented by industrial psychologists is discussed in the following pages.

LIMITATIONS OF RESEARCH IN INDUSTRIAL PSYCHOLOGY

There are many challenges to the proper design and execution of psychological research when it is conducted in a university research laboratory. But, when a study is undertaken in the real-life setting of a factory or office, the problems are magnified in scope and intensity.

One obvious limitation of psychological research in general is that its methods cannot be applied to every problem. In the area of social psychology, for example, psychologists cannot conduct carefully controlled observations of the behavior of people in riots—the situation is too complex and dangerous to prearrange. Similarly, in industry, it is not feasible to conduct systematic research on some procedures or devices designed to prevent accidents since subjects might be exposed to possible injury. There is a limit to what human beings can be exposed to in the interest of scientific research.

A second problem is that the act of observation may interfere with or change that which the psychologist is trying to observe. If, for example, workers are given personality tests as a part of research into job satisfaction, they may fake or distort their test responses simply because they are aware that their personalities are being investigated.

Consider the matter of research on the effects of jet engine noise on the efficiency of engine mechanics. The mechanics, aware that they are part of a psychological study, may perform quite differently than they normally would on a routine workday when they are not being observed. Often, people will behave in a changed manner when they know their behavior is being observed, and ethical and technical considerations frequently dictate that subjects be informed that they are participating in a research study.

A third weakness of psychological research is that some studies must be conducted in an artificial setting. For example, the management of a company may not allow the psychologist to disrupt production schedules by experimenting with various work procedures. As a result, the research may have to be conducted in a simulated job environment elsewhere in the plant. The research results, then, are based on performance in a setting that is not identical with the job environment in which the findings are to be applied. This artificiality can reduce the level of generalizability of the research findings.

Recognizing that there are weaknesses and difficulties in psychological research does not mean that research should not be attempted. For all its limitations, the results of carefully controlled and systematic research are infinitely superior to problem solving and decision making on purely subjective considerations. Properly conducted research is better than no research at all. The questions and problems investigated by industrial psychologists must be answered and only through objective observation can we have confidence in those answers.

METHODS OF DATA COLLECTION

Several procedures are available to the industrial psychologist to aid in conducting research. The problem of selecting the most effective technique is one of the first questions asked in any research program, and the answer is determined by the nature of the problem to be investigated.

The Experimental Method

The experimental method is simple in its basic concepts but difficult in its detailed operations. The purpose of an experiment is to determine the effect or influence of one variable upon the performance or behavior of a group of subjects (the people being studied).

We are constantly bombarded by a wide range of stimuli in our environment, all of which may influence our behavior in one way or another. When psychologists want to investigate the effect of just one of these stimuli, they must arrange a situation in which only that stimulus is allowed to impinge on the subject. The operation of all the other stimuli in the environment must be eliminated or kept constant. Only in that way can we conclude that any change in the behavior of the subject is attributable to the stimulus in question.

Thus, two factors or variables are of importance in the conduct of an experiment: (1) the stimulus variable, the effect of which we are interested in determining, and (2) the resulting behavior of the subject. Both of these variables can be objectively observed, measured, and recorded.

The stimulus variable is called the *independent variable,* and the subject's behavior or response is called the *dependent variable.* The latter is called dependent for an obvious reason—it depends upon the independent variable.

Consider the following experiment. The management of a company is concerned about the production level of a group of drill press operators who perform a vital job in the total production process. The company psychologist is asked to find out how output could be increased. Many factors may be responsible for the workers' lowered production—low pay, poor training, an unpopular foreman, or faulty equipment. The psychologist, however, after inspecting the room in which the drill press operators work, suspects that the problem is insufficient lighting.

The two variables in this experiment are easy to identify and measure precisely. The independent variable is the level of illumination (which will be increased in the experiment), and the dependent variable is the workers' resulting production rate.

The psychologist arranges for the lighting level in the workroom to be increased and compares the production level before the experiment with the production level two weeks after the lighting increase. Prior to changing the lighting, the workers each produced an average of eight units per hour. Two weeks later, the individual production rate averaged fourteen units per hour—a considerable increase.

Surely we can conclude that the change in the independent variable (the increase in the level of illumination) brought about a change in the dependent variable (the increase in production). **Wrong!** We cannot draw this conclusion on the basis of the experiment described. How do we know that some factor other than the increased lighting did not bring about the higher production levels? Perhaps the usually grouchy foreman was nicer to the workers during the two-week experiment because he knew the company psychologist was around. Maybe the workers purposely produced more because they thought the presence of the psychologist meant that their jobs were in jeopardy. Or possibly it was because the weather turned better during that period.

Many other factors could account for the increase in production, but the important point is that the psychologist must be certain that nothing operated to influence the subjects' behavior except the stimulus being manipulated; that is, the level of illumination.

An essential ingredient of the scientific method was omitted from our experiment—the element of *control*. Controlling the experimental conditions properly would assure us that any change in the behavior or performance of the subjects was solely because of the independent variable.

To provide this necessary control, two groups of subjects must be used in an experiment. The *experimental group* is exposed to the independent variable; the group discussed in our drill press operator experiment is an experimental group. The group that provides the element of control is called, not surprisingly, the *control group*.

In an experiment, the experimental and control groups are as similar as possible in every respect except that the control group is *not* exposed to the independent variable. Measures of productivity are taken from both groups at the beginning and end of the experimental period.

To conduct the drill press operator experiment properly we must divide the workers into these two groups. Their performance is measured before and after the experiment and the production level of the control group serves as a standard against which the resulting performance of the experimental group is compared.

If the groups of workers are similar, and if the performance level of the experimental group at the end of the experiment is higher than that of the control group, we can conclude that the increased illumina-

TABLE 2–1

EFFECTS OF INCREASED ILLUMINATION ON
PERFORMANCE OF DRILL PRESS OPERATORS

Experimental Group		Control Group
8	Average individual pre-experiment production (units/hour)	8
Experimental treatment		No treatment
14	Average individual post-experiment production (units/hour)	8

tion (the independent variable) was indeed responsible for the increased production. Extraneous factors such as the weather or the foreman's temper could not have influenced the subjects' behavior—if they had, the performance of both groups would have changed in the same manner.

The experimental design and results of this research study are shown in Table 2–1.

Composition of Control Groups

The control group must be as similar as possible to the experimental group. There are two ways to bring this about.

One method, the *random group design,* involves the random assignment of the subjects to the experimental and control groups. In our experiment, if there had been fifty drill press operators, they would have been assigned at random to the two groups—twenty-five to each condition.

Since the basis for dividing the subjects into the experimental and control conditions is random assignment, we may assume that the two groups are essentially similar. Any possible influencing variables such as age or length of job experience should be evenly distributed over the two groups since these factors were not allowed to influence the assignment of the subjects.

Another method of assuring similarity between experimental and control groups uses the *matched group design.* In this approach, the subjects in one group are evenly matched with the subjects in the other on the basis of characteristics that could influence the dependent variable. For example, in our drill press operator experiment, we could determine pairs of subjects who are identical in terms of length of job experience, age, level of intelligence, or supervisor's ratings, and assign one member of each pair to each group. In this way, the experimental and control groups will be evenly matched.

This approach, while desirable, is costly and difficult to put into practice. In order to find large enough numbers of evenly paired subjects, we need an even larger number of potential subjects from whom to choose. Further, it becomes extremely complex to equate pairs of subjects on more than one factor. Matching subjects on length of job experience alone presents little problem, but equating them on several factors at the same time becomes cumbersome. Finally, since many experiments in psychology involve more than one experimental group (such as studying the effects on production of several different levels of illumination), matching subjects becomes virtually impossible.

A Typical Industrial Experiment

This experiment, conducted in a factory that produces lingerie, was concerned with the influence of different levels of training on the turn-over rate and productivity of sewing machine operators.[1] The management had asked a consulting industrial psychologist to determine why 68 per cent of the workers had quit in one year. Based on the results of an attitude survey of the employees, and questioning of supervisors, the psychologist suspected that insufficient training for the job accounted for the high turnover.

Accordingly, it was decided to investigate the effects of increased training on both turnover and productivity. Note that the initial problem leading to the research was the high rate of job terminations. In the process of designing a study to investigate this factor, the psychologist saw that with little extra effort data could also be secured on another dependent variable—the level of production.

The subjects were 208 female employees hired in one year by the factory as trainees. The dependent variables were (1) job turnover, defined as the percentage of workers who quit in their first forty days on the job; and (2) productivity, defined in terms of daily production figures in the first forty days on the job. The psychologist chose the first forty-day period because the records of the company showed that most of the previous terminations had occurred within that length of time. The dependent variables are easy to observe, measure, and record with precision.

The independent variable is the level of training, and the consulting psychologist chose to investigate four different training periods. The company's standard practice was to provide one day of training for new employees, conducted in a training facility and not on the job. Thus, one-day training was the control condition against which longer training periods would be compared.

Trainees assigned to Group I received the standard one-day training, Group II received two days of training, Group III had three days of training, and Group IV also received three days of training but part of it was conducted on the job whereas all the other training took place in the company's training facility. Table 2–2 shows the independent and dependent variables.

The subjects were assigned to each of the four conditions on the basis of the date of their initial employment with the company. Those hired during the first month of the study were placed in Group I, those hired during the second month in Group II, and so on, repeating the

[1] J. Lefkowitz, "Effect of training on the productivity and tenure of sewing machine operators," *Journal of Applied Psychology*, **54** (1970), 81–86.

TABLE 2–2

DESIGN OF THE SEWING MACHINE OPERATOR STUDY

Independent Variable:	Dependent Variables:	
Level of Training	Turnover	Productivity
Group I (control group)	—	—
Group II	—	—
Group III	—	—
Group IV	—	—

cycle throughout the year the study was in progress. Statistical comparisons of the groups' initial performance levels demonstrated their similarity.

The results of the study concerned with turnover revealed that the longer the training received in the training facility (Groups I–III), the lower the rate of turnover, as shown in Figure 2–1.

The three-day training period combining on-the-job experience with the training facility (Group IV), did not reduce the turnover rate compared to the three-day training period in the training room alone (Group III). Comparing Groups I and III, however, clearly shows that the two additional days of training greatly reduced the turnover rate from 53 per cent to 33 per cent.

The second part of the study, the effect of training on productivity, produced some unexpected complications. The data indicated that the longer a new employee remained in the training facility, the lower was the resulting level of production. Figure 2–2 shows this surprising finding. The three days of integrated training (Group IV) led to a

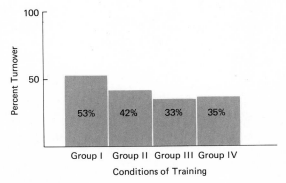

Figure 2–1. Turnover rates of four training conditions.

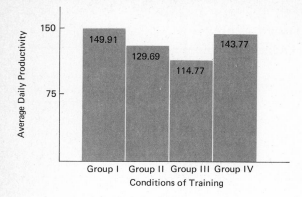

Figure 2–2. Production levels of four training conditions.

higher level of productivity than the three days of training solely in the training facility (Group III).

This study demonstrates that the independent variable (different levels of training) produced conflicting results on the two dependent variables: greater time spent in the training room resulted in a lower turnover rate but it also yielded a lower level of productivity.

It is at this point—the interpretation of the research results—that the training, wisdom, and experience of the psychologist are put to their most severe test. Experiments do not always, or even often, turn out as the researcher would like. Research results are not always clear-cut or consistent, and considerable interpretive skill is necessary to relate the data to the job or problem in question.

The psychologist in this study concluded that, considering both productivity and turnover, the three-day integrated training condition (Group IV) was the most profitable. It yielded a close second highest level of production and a close second lowest rate of turnover.

As we can see from this example, the research process proceeds at two levels of complexity: (1) designing the experiment; and (2) understanding, interpreting, and implementing the results. Both steps depend on the cooperation of managers who are sensitive to the intricate nature of psychological research.

Naturalistic Observation

In the complicated study of human behavior, it is not always possible to bring the relevant variables under the precise control required by the experimental method. Also, it may be more appropriate to study some human behaviors as they occur naturally in real-life situations. We mentioned that one of the weaknesses of the experimental method is the artificiality it might introduce into the study of human behavior. To avoid this artificiality, it is sometimes preferable to observe behavior in its normal setting.

For these reasons, psychologists may be forced (and sometimes prefer) to observe behavior without introducing any manipulation of the independent variable. This is the essence of another method of data collection—naturalistic observation. As we shall see, however, not manipulating variables directly does not mean that the psychologist has no control over them.

One advantage of naturalistic observation is that the behavior being observed, and the situation in which it is observed, are more representative of what occurs in everyday life. Our ordinary daily activities take place in situations that are not under the stringent control necessary in the experimental method. Hence, advocates of this method argue that the results of naturalistic observation can be more readily generalized and applied to real life, for that is where the results were obtained.

This advantage is also a major source of weakness. Since researchers do not manipulate the independent variable, it is often difficult for them to conclude with any assurance just what brought about the resulting change in the subjects' behavior or performance. Another limitation is that the observation cannot be repeated; it is impossible to duplicate the exact conditions that prevailed during the initial observation.

The experimental method is not without its own limitations. Nevertheless, when it can be used, it is preferred over the method of naturalistic observation because the experimenter can control and systematically manipulate the independent variable. However, both tools—used with precision and interpreted with caution and understanding—are valuable means of studying human behavior.

Sample Observational Studies

A classic example of the naturalistic observation approach is provided by a study of automobile driver behavior at intersections.[2] The problem of the researchers was to determine whether a stop sign or a red blinking light was more effective in getting drivers to come to a full stop.

This problem could have been investigated in a laboratory setting

[2] C. F. Hummel and G. R. Schmeidler, "Driver behavior at dangerous intersections marked by stop signs or by red blinker lights," *Journal of Applied Psychology*, **39** (1955), 17–19.

by having the subjects "drive" automobile simulators in which the road ahead is presented on film. A laboratory study would have controlled factors such as age and driving experience of the subjects, condition of car and brakes, and the weather. The independent variables (the stop sign and blinking light) could have been presented as frequently as, and in whatever sequences, the experimenter considered appropriate. However, the subjects in such a laboratory study would have known that their behavior was being observed, and they might have responded quite differently than if they were actually driving on the street. Also, "driving" a simulated vehicle in a laboratory is obviously an artificial setting.

The naturalistic observation of driver behavior was conducted in a well-controlled fashion. Two intersections—one with a stop sign and the other with a red blinking light—in the same neighborhood were chosen as observation sites. The observers were hidden from view in a doorway. The independent variables were the signals—the stop sign and the red blinking light. The dependent variable was the behavior of the drivers in response to the signal. Even though the experimenters did not manipulate the independent variables, they did control for the influence of other factors that might have affected the drivers' reactions.

First, the experimenters made sure that the drivers did not know they were being observed. Had the drivers seen that someone was watching them, their behavior might have been different.

The second element of control was that both sets of observations were made in the same neighborhood. Neighborhoods exhibit differences in respect for and obedience to the law, and conducting the study in a single neighborhood helped to control that possible influence on driver behavior.

A third variable under control was that of inducements to stop at the intersection, in addition to the stop sign or light. For instance, if the police regularly patrolled one intersection but not the other, more people at the patrolled intersection might have stopped; this would have biased the results.

A final control was to eliminate from the data those drivers who slowed down or stopped at the intersections because another car was directly in front of them.

Thus, taking a research study out of the laboratory and placing it in the real world still allows the researcher to control the relevant variables so that objective observations of behavior can be undertaken.

You might be interested in the results of this study the next time you approach an intersection. No more than half the drivers came to a complete stop for either the stop sign or the red blinking light. Many more drivers stopped too late (past the intersection line) when confronted with the stop sign than with the blinking light. The researchers concluded that the light could be seen from a greater distance.

Another example of naturalistic observation can be drawn from the work of an engineering psychologist for a company producing missile systems. The missile—a small surface-to-surface type launched from a truck—had already been built and the customer, the U.S. Army, wanted to know if the procedures that had been established to assemble, aim, and fire the missile were the most efficient ones possible.

The launching of the missile required a sequence of several hundred small operations performed by a ten-person launching crew. These included aiming, assembling (attaching wings and fins), electronically checking out all components, and firing. The operating procedures were dictated by the engineering requirements of the system and the purpose of the study was to determine if all the steps were necessary, if the sequence was correct, if there were possibilities of error, and if the total time taken could be shortened.

This study could have been conducted in a laboratory by having the subjects perform one operation, and evaluating their performance before proceeding to the next step. However, if the research were conducted in as realistic a setting as possible, the results would be more directly applicable to the use of the missile in combat.

The observations were carried out under the naturally stressful conditions of the White Sands Proving Ground in New Mexico where, in the summer, the temperature often reached 120° F. The primary element of control was in the nature of the subjects used. Army troops trained in missile operation (the same kind of soldier who would eventually operate the system) followed the prescribed operating procedure. The subjects wore full military gear and worked under the pressure of time.

Observers with stopwatches carefully recorded each task, looking for potential sources of error and slowdown. Periodically, the soldiers were interviewed about their own suggestions for improving the operation of the missile system.

The subjects in this study knew that their performance was being observed and evaluated; they knew they were participating in an experiment. It would have been desirable if they could have been observed without their awareness but the detailed nature of the required observations did not allow for this refinement.

The results of the research were an improvement in the procedures for launching the missile system and a considerable reduction in the time necessary to do so.

In both of these examples, the behavior being observed was not as well controlled as it could have been under laboratory conditions.

However, the greater realism afforded by the use of real-life situations may offset this disadvantage. The nature and complexity of the phenomena under investigation often determine the most appropriate method. In other cases, the psychologist must decide on the relative merit of sacrificing some degree of control for greater realism, or vice versa.

Survey Methods of Research

Closely related to the method of systematic observation is the conduct of surveys and public opinion polls. These rely on the observation of behavior as revealed in the subjects' responses to personal interviews and questionnaires. Thus, the focus in the survey method is not on what subjects do (as in the experimental or naturalistic observation methods), but rather on what they say.

Questionnaires and interviews to determine what people think, feel, like, and dislike have many uses in industrial psychology. Within a company, psychologists use survey methods to ascertain those factors that contribute to job satisfaction and employee morale. Advertising and motivation research firms conduct surveys to discover consumer preferences for specific products. Public opinion polls determine the popularity of political candidates and the issues most important to the voters.

Regardless of the use to which survey data eventually are put, the methods of gathering the information remain essentially the same. The three basic data-collecting techniques are personal interviews, telephone surveys, and mail surveys.

The *personal interview,* the most expensive and time-consuming technique, is widely used for all purposes of survey research. It requires a face-to-face meeting with the respondents who are asked not only to divulge information about themselves but also to give up to an hour or more of their time. Obviously this requires cooperation and patience on the part of the persons being questioned and great skill in human relations on the part of the interviewers.

Finding and training capable interviewers is vital because their appearance, manner, dress, and general behavior can influence the way in which respondents will answer the questions put to them. For example, black interviewers asking white persons about their attitudes toward blacks might get different responses than would white interviewers asking the same questions.

There are more subtle interviewer variables that can bias the results. If, for example, in asking questions about the use of drugs, interviewers show (by frowning or smiling) their agreement or disagreement with what respondents are saying, the respondents may modify their subsequent answers because of their perception of the interviewer's opinion on drugs.

Assuming a competent, well-trained interviewer, this method offers several advantages over telephone and mail surveys. It yields the highest percentage of returns—80 to 95 per cent—and it can obtain greater accuracy of responses because the face-to-face situation establishes a rapport and encourages the respondent to answer more honestly. Also, it is usually possible to obtain more information in a personal interview than through the mail or over the telephone.

The major disadvantage of the personal interview survey method is the high cost, in both time and money, of training interviewers and conducting the interviews. It is far more expensive and time-consuming to contact five hundred individuals in person than to telephone them or mail them a questionnaire. Additional problems involve the safety of interviewers in some neighborhoods, the difficulty of finding people at home, and the possible bias of the interviewer on the topic in question. Also, interviewers are generally not paid very well and some have been known to make up answers to the interview questions rather than go to the time and trouble of actually conducting the interview.

A *mail survey* is a cheaper and more convenient method of obtaining information from large numbers of people over a wide geographical area. Those being questioned are able to remain anonymous and this often encourages them to respond more freely and openly on sensitive or personal topics. Another advantage is that respondents are given more time in which to formulate their answers than in a personal interview situation.

The major disadvantage of mail surveys is the relatively small number of replies that are usually obtained. In one mail survey of five hundred U.S. corporations having business operations in Europe, the companies could remain anonymous, the questionnaire was brief (one page), and a postage-paid return envelope had been included. However, only 45 per cent of the companies responded.

Follow-up procedures can be used to secure additional returns. A second letter can request cooperation and explain the importance of the survey. Letters sent by registered mail and follow-up telephone calls can also be used to solicit returns.

Since there is no way to determine how those who did respond might differ on the issues from those who failed to respond, it becomes unwise to generalize too broadly on the basis of limited returns.

Telephone surveys offer the advantages of a low cost per interview and the possibility of a single interviewer contacting several hundred people in the course of a day. Also, with perseverance, it is usually possible to reach almost every person in the sample by continuing to telephone until the person answers.

The major disadvantage of this technique is that it does not allow the researcher to contact a fully representative sample of the general public. There are still some people who do not have telephones, particularly in rural areas, and others who have unlisted telephone numbers.

With any survey method, two problems must be resolved: (1) the questions to be asked, and (2) the people to be questioned.

In general, there are two basic types of question used in surveys—open-end questions and fixed alternative questions. With the *open-end question,* respondents are allowed to freely present their answer in their own words, without any limitations imposed by the interviewer or by the phrasing of the question. They are encouraged to answer in their own terms and to take as much time as needed.

An example of an open-end question is: What do you think about the proposed city bond issue? Since this kind of question has the advantage of eliciting answers in the respondents' own words, their complete thoughts on the issue can be recorded. Of course, this can also be a disadvantage; if there are many questions, the survey will be very time-consuming. Also, the usefulness of the reply depends on how well respondents are able to verbalize or articulate their thoughts and feelings. Finally, this kind of question places pressure on the interviewer to be accurate and complete in recording the answers.

The *fixed alternative question* limits a person's answer to a fixed number of alternatives. The sample question might be phrased as follows: How do you feel about the proposed city bond issue? In favor ———— Opposed———— Undecided————. The person is faced with a finite number of possible answers.

This type of question greatly simplifies and speeds up the survey being taken. More questions can be asked in a given period of time and the answers can be recorded more easily. A disadvantage is that the limited number of choices may not reflect accurately a person's feelings on the topic. For example, a person might be in favor of the proposed bond issue under certain circumstances and opposed to it under others. When he or she is restricted to "yes," "no," or "undecided," these circumstances cannot be made known to the interviewer. If enough of the people questioned have such unexpressed qualifications, the results of the poll will be misleading.

No matter which type of question is used, it is desirable to pretest the questions on a small number of people to make sure they understand them. If respondents fail to understand a word that has been used in the question, or if they interpret a question in a way that is different from what the interviewer intended, the results of the survey could be misleading. This happened with opinion surveys taken in 1973 about the impeachment of the then President Nixon. Many of the people questioned did not know the meaning of the word *impeachment,* and interpreted the word in various incorrect ways. This misunderstanding obviously affected the responses as well as the usefulness of the results of the survey.

The second problem in surveys is the selection of the sample of people who will be polled or questioned. This requires a great deal of careful attention.

Suppose that a researcher is assigned the task of determining the attitude of all automobile owners in the state of California toward a proposed change in the license fee. To question every car owner would be laborious and difficult, even if sufficient time and money were provided. It would not be feasible to locate and personally interview each automobile owner in the state.

Fortunately, it is not necessary to question every person in the population in which we are interested. With proper care, a representative sample of this population can provide the needed information. A sample of only several hundred, if it is truly representative of the larger population, can be used to accurately predict the responses of the total population.

To select a sample of automobile owners in California, we could question people wherever they are found—at a shopping center, a service station, or a busy intersection. However, this procedure would not guarantee that those questioned are representative of all automobile owners in the state; people found at a particular shopping center, for example, might only be from a suburban upper income bracket.

Two methods of constructing representative samples of the total population are probability sampling and quota sampling.

In the *probability sampling* technique, each individual in a population has a known probability or chance of being included in the sample. By securing from the state department of motor vehicles a list of all automobile owners, the researcher could select every tenth or twenty-fifth name, for example, depending on how large a sample was needed. Thus, every person in the population would have the same chance (one in ten, or one in twenty-five) of being included in the sample.

This method is satisfactory as long as there is a list of everyone in the population of interest. If you wanted to study every *eligible* voter in the United States, however, this method could not be used; only *registered* voters are listed.

In *quota sampling,* the researcher tries deliberately to construct a duplicate, in miniature, of the larger population. If it is known from

49

census data that in California 10 per cent of all automobile owners are college graduates, 64 per cent are male, 4 per cent are Mexican-American, and so on, then these proportions must be included in the sample.

Interviewers are given quotas for people to interview in the various categories (level of education, sex, age, income, ethnic background) and must find appropriate respondents. Since the persons actually questioned are chosen by each interviewer, there is some opportunity for personal bias to enter into the selection of the sample. The interviewer may prefer to talk to those who live in nicer neighborhoods or who seem friendlier.

A Typical Survey

Three psychologists employed by a large business concern wanted to determine those factors that employees considered important to their own job satisfaction and work motivation.[3] Cooperating with the firm's management, the researchers compiled a list of seventeen variables thought to be relevant to job satisfaction and motivation. A questionnaire was developed that consisted of several questions related to employment history, the list of seventeen variables, and a request to rank these factors in accordance with how much the worker thought they contributed to (1) job satisfaction and (2) motivation.

Constructing a sample did not present a problem here since the population—two thousand, three hundred scientists and technicians employed by the company—was not too large to be reached with mailed questionnaires. Even though the responses were anonymous, only 41 per cent of the employees returned completed questionnaires. Anonymity also meant that it was not possible to use follow-up procedures to increase the rate of response; it could not be determined who had responded and who had not.

This low response rate is one disadvantage of surveys conducted by mail. There is no way of knowing if those who failed to respond did so because they were more or less satisfied or motivated in their jobs than those who did respond. In either case, the results would be biased and of limited value. Other reasons for not responding include carelessness or laziness—factors not necessarily related to the variables under study.

Another problem encountered by the psychologists with this survey

[3] P. F. Wernimont, P. Toren, and H. Kapell, "Comparison of sources of personal satisfaction and of work motivation," *Journal of Applied Psychology*, **54** (1970), 95–102.

was incomplete or incorrectly filled out questionnaires. More than one hundred fifty of the returned forms could not be used for that reason, lowering the effective response rate to 34 per cent.

If this survey had been conducted on a personal interview basis, it would not necessarily have yielded more useful results. Although a larger number of workers could have been sampled, they would not have been able to reply anonymously. They might not have answered as freely and honestly for fear that management might use their responses against them. Also, personal interviews would have been time-consuming and disruptive of the work of many employees.

Keeping in mind these limitations, the researchers found that certain factors were considered important by the employees in contributing to job satisfaction and work motivation. With information of this nature, the management was in a better position to arrange the working conditions so as to facilitate both satisfaction and motivation.

For any question that can be asked about the nature of human behavior at work, there is a psychological research technique available to explore the answer. The methods are not infallible—they have recognized weaknesses and limitations—but for all their shortcomings they do represent the best approach. Research can be difficult, expensive, and time-consuming but, properly performed, it can provide results that will, if wisely applied, enhance the efficiency of any organization. The alternative to scientific research is a decision based not on facts, but on opinion, prejudice, or habit.

METHODS OF DATA ANALYSIS

In research in psychology, as in any other science, data collection is merely the first step in the scientific approach to problem solving. If we have conducted a study on the production levels of two hundred employees, we are left with two hundred numbers—the *raw data*. It is necessary to evaluate and interpret these data, and that is the purpose of statistics.

The principles and concepts of the statistical analysis of data are not difficult to grasp. Statistics is a tool to help us summarize and describe large masses of data and to enable us to draw inferences or conclusions about the meaning of those data. The purpose of this discussion is to acquaint you with the nature and importance of statistical tools, not to teach you how to perform them.

Descriptive Statistics

Let us examine some research data and see what statistical analysis can do. To evaluate a new test designed to predict the success of persons in life insurance sales jobs, a company psychologist administered the test to ninety-nine applicants. The test scores are shown in Table 2–3.

Just looking at this swarm of numbers should give you an understanding of why a method to summarize and describe them is so important. It is difficult to make any meaningful interpretation of these data as they now stand. You cannot get any useful idea about the performance of these job applicants as a whole by looking at the table of individual numbers.

One convenient way of describing the data is to present them in graphic form in a *frequency distribution*. To construct a frequency distribution, we plot on a graph the number of times each score

TABLE 2–3

RAW SCORES OF NINETY-NINE JOB APPLICANTS ON
LIFE INSURANCE SALES TEST

141	91	92	88	95
124	119	108	146	120
122	118	98	97	94
144	84	110	127	81
151	76	89	125	108
102	120	112	89	101
129	125	142	87	103
128	94	94	114	134
102	143	134	138	110
117	121	141	99	104
107	114	67	110	124
112	117	144	102	126
127	79	105	133	128
87	114	110	107	119
156	79	112	117	83
99	98	156	108	143
96	145	120	127	133
113	120	147	122	114
123	90	114	121	99
89	118	128	118	

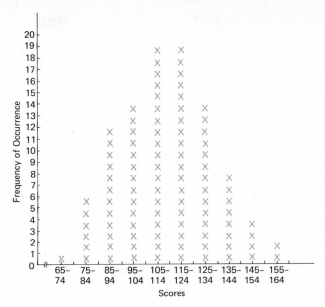

Figure 2–3. Frequency distribution of life insurance sales test scores (grouped data).

occurs. For convenience in dealing with many scores, we can group them into equal intervals. Grouping the data is not necessary, but it does make them easier to work with. Figure 2–3 shows the frequency distribution of the ninety-nine raw scores grouped into intervals, each interval comprising ten possible scores.

By examining the frequency distribution we can get a much clearer idea of the performance of the job applicants than we can by inspecting the individual raw scores in Table 2–3.

Two other ways of graphically portraying the raw data of a group of subjects are the *histogram* or bar graph (Figure 2–4) and the *frequency polygon* (Figure 2–5).

All three of these graphic descriptions of the data enable us to see pictorially the performance of the group as a whole. Scientific analysis of the data, however, requires that the raw scores be summarized and described quantitatively; that is, we must be able to represent or summarize all the data with a single number. We must find the typical or average score on this test by measuring the *central tendency* of the distribution.

The most common measure of central tendency is the average or the arithmetic *mean*. The mean is found by adding up all of the raw

53

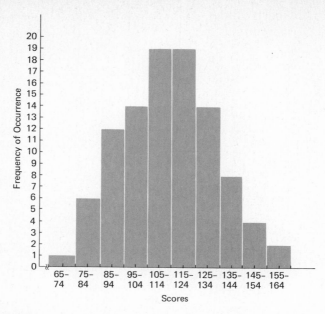

Figure 2–4. Histogram of life insurance sales test scores (grouped data).

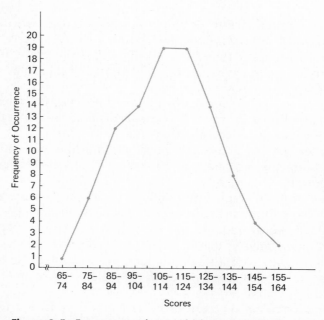

Figure 2–5. Frequency polygon of life insurance sales test scores (grouped data).

scores and dividing the resulting sum by the total number of scores. The formula for the mean is

$$\overline{X} = \frac{\Sigma X}{N}$$

where $\overline{X}$ is the mean, X is the individual raw score, Σ is the process of adding, and N is the number of scores with which we are dealing. The mean of the raw scores in Table 2–3 is

$$\overline{X} = \frac{11251}{99} = 113.6$$

We now know that the average score for this group of 99 job applicants is 113.6. Our raw data have been reduced to and can be described by this single number. The mean is the most useful measure of central tendency and provides the basis for many higher-level statistical analyses.

Two other ways of measuring central tendency are the median and the mode.

The *median* is the score obtained by the person who stands at the midpoint of the distribution. If we arrange our 99 scores in ascending order, the median is the score of the fiftieth person—half of the job applicants scored higher than this person and half lower. In our sample of scores, the median is 114, which is quite close to the mean. The median is particularly useful when dealing with skewed distributions, as discussed in the following section.

The *mode* is the most frequently obtained score in the distribution. (A distribution may have more than one mode if two or more scores occur with the same highest frequency.) With our data, the mode is 114. The mode is seldom applied in analyzing data but is useful in certain practical situations. For example, a plant supervisor concerned with stocking an adequate inventory of machine parts would be interested in knowing which part was used more frequently than any other.

The Normal Curve of Distribution

In the three graphs showing the scores on the life insurance sales test, we can see that most of the applicants achieved scores in the middle of the distribution of scores, and only a few scored at either extreme end. Many measurements approximate this same kind of distribution. In general, it occurs when a large number of measurements are taken

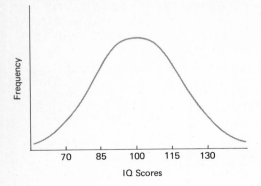

Figure 2–6. Normal curve of IQ scores.

of a psychological or physical characteristic. Whether we are measuring height or weight or intelligence, a sample of sufficient size will produce a distribution in which most scores fall near the middle and very few fall at the extreme low or high ends.

This bell-shaped distribution is called the *normal curve.* Figure 2–6 depicts the normal curve of a distribution of a large number of scores on an IQ test.

The normal curve is predicated upon the random nature and size of the sample tested. If the sample is not truly representative of the population, but is biased in one direction or another, the distribution will not approximate the normal curve.

Suppose, for example, that we gave an IQ test to a group of advanced medical school students and to a group of high school drop-

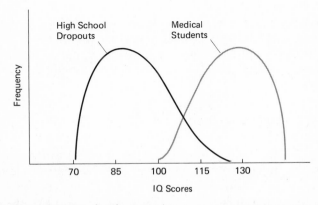

Figure 2–7. IQ distribution of two nonrepresentative samples.

outs. Neither group is representative of the general population so the distribution of the test scores will not look like the normal curve (see Figure 2–7). When measurements are taken from specially selected groups of individuals, the distribution of their scores will most likely be *skewed* or asymmetrical.

In dealing with skewed distributions, the median is the most useful measure of central tendency. The mean (the arithmetic average) is seriously affected by a few extreme scores in either direction and may thus be misleading when dealing with skewed distributions. The median is less affected by such extreme scores.

A Note of Caution

You have no doubt heard someone say, "Statistics lie!" Although it is true that statistics can be misleading, this is the fault of the person who misuses them and not of the techniques themselves.

Consider the following example. A union is trying to organize the only textile plant in a small southern town. The union organizer claims that the average salary in the company is only $8,000, and that, consequently, the workers need the union to upgrade their salaries. In reply, the company president reports that the average salary is really $10,500, and that the union organizer is lying. It is possible that neither person is lying but that each chose a statistic to best fit his or her own purpose. The distribution of salaries for all company employees, including executives, is given in Figure 2–8.

The union organizer is using the median as the average figure; the company president is citing the mean. Both are technically correct although, as noted, the median is the better measurement to use with

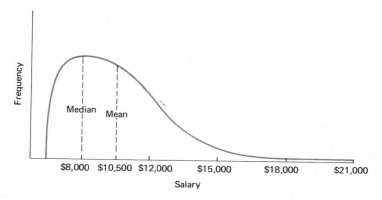

Figure 2–8. Salary distribution.

a skewed distribution. The few high executive salaries affect the mean much more than the median.

It pays to be skeptical when reading about "average" figures. Ask which average is being used—the mean or the median.

The Variability of a Distribution

Having proceeded to measure, pictorially and numerically, the central tendency of a distribution, you may not be happy to learn that still more analysis is needed to provide a comprehensive description of a distribution of scores. It is not sufficient to know only the central tendency of a distribution, we must also have a numerical indication of the spread of scores around the measure of central tendency. This spread is called *variability*.

Consider the two normal distributions in Figure 2–9. If we take the mean or the median as a measure of these distributions, we would conclude that the distributions are identical since the means and medians are the same for both curves. As you can see, however, the two distributions of scores are not identical—they differ greatly in their spread or variability.

There are two measures of variability, the range and the standard deviation, but the *range* (the difference between the highest and lowest scores) is of so little value that it is seldom used.

Far more important as a numerical measure of variability is the *standard deviation,* a precise distance along the baseline of the frequency distribution. Once we determine this distance, we can obtain a great deal of useful information about the data.

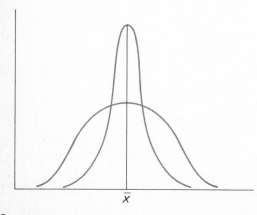

$\overline{x}$

Figure 2–9. Normal curves with the same central tendency but different variability.

Let us examine the distribution of IQ scores of adult white males in the United States. The data form a normal curve with a mean of 100 and a standard deviation of 15, as represented in Figure 2–10.

Knowing that the standard deviation (σ or SD) is 15 tells us that an IQ of 115 is 1σ distance above the mean of 100; an IQ of 130 is 2σ units or distance above the mean. Similarly, IQ scores below the mean can be identified in terms of their σ equivalents. An IQ of 85 is 1σ distance below the mean, or −1σ.

With the standard deviation we can easily determine the percentage of scores in the distribution that fall above or below any particular raw score. Tables based on the mathematical formula for the normal curve give us the percentage of cases (or frequency of scores) that lie between standard deviation units or between a standard deviation unit and the mean.

For example, in Figure 2–10, 68 per cent of the sample scores fall between −1σ and +1σ, 95.4 per cent between −2σ and +2σ, and 99.7 per cent between −3σ and +3σ. These percentages hold for any variable measured where the distribution of the data follows the normal curve. Thus, if we know the standard deviation of a distribution, we can determine precisely the meaning of any score; that is, we can tell where it falls in terms of the performance of the group as a whole.

Suppose we have developed a new aptitude test and a job applicant obtains a score of 60 on it. By itself, this figure tells us nothing about the aptitude level of this individual relative to all the others who applied for the job and took the same aptitude test. However, if we know that the mean of this distribution of test scores is 50 and the standard deviation is 10, the applicant's score of 60 (a distance of +1σ from the mean) informs us that only 16 per cent of the applicants in

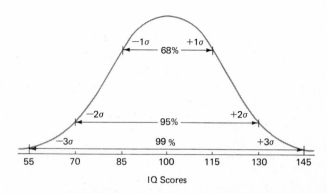

Figure 2–10. Distribution of IQ scores.

the sample scored higher than this person and 84 per cent scored lower. This can be verified by looking at Figure 2–10 and noting the percentage of cases above and below $+1\sigma$.

There is a method by which any raw score in a distribution can be converted to a standard deviation score. In that way we can interpret each raw score in the distribution. Also, the standard deviation allows us to compare the performance of individuals on two or more tests that utilize different scoring systems. By converting the distributions on all tests to standard deviation units, we can compare directly a person's performance on one test with performance on another, since the sets of scores will be expressed in the same terms.

The Relationship Between Two Variables

Thus far, we have been concerned with the statistical treatment of one variable at a time, for example, a set of test scores from a group of job applicants. In psychological research in industrial and academic settings, the researcher is often concerned with the relationship between two or more variables. For instance, to determine if a particular test is of value in predicting the job success of crane operators, the psychologist would have to know how the test scores corresponded to a quantitative measure of success on the job. The statistical measure used to determine this relationship is the *correlation coefficient*.

The application of this statistical procedure tells the researcher two things about the relationship between variables: (1) the direction of the relationship and (2) the magnitude or strength of the relationship.

The direction of the relationship may be positive or negative, depending on whether high scores on one variable are accompanied by high or low scores on the other variable. To determine direction, both variables are plotted on a *scattergram*. The scattergram in Figure 2–11 shows the relationship between test scores of job applicants and their supervisor's ratings after some time on the job.

Figure 2–11 shows that as the test scores increased, so did the ratings; that is, those who had higher test scores as applicants consistently received higher ratings from their supervisors on actual job performance. This example illustrates a perfect positive correlation (an inflexible relationship between the two measures). A test score of 20 will always be accompanied by a rating of 1, a test score of 100 by a rating of 5. By obtaining an applicant's test score, the personnel manager could accurately predict the rating that person would later receive from the supervisor.

Through the use of the formula for the product-moment correlation coefficient it is possible to calculate in numerical terms the direction

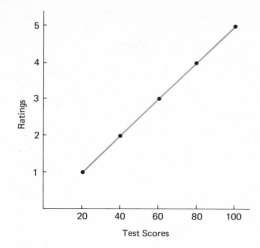

Figure 2–11. Scattergram of relation between test scores and ratings.

and the intensity or strength of this relationship. The correlation co-efficient from the data in Figure 2–11 is +1.00, indicating a perfect positive correlation. Positive correlations never exceed the value of +1.00. Thus, the magnitude of a positive relationship can be expressed by a number ranging anywhere from 0 to +1.00.

Not all relationships are perfect or positive. Consider the scatter-grams in Figures 2–12 and 2–13.

The negative correlation shown in Figure 2–12 indicates that as the test scores increase, job ratings decrease. Negative correlation co-

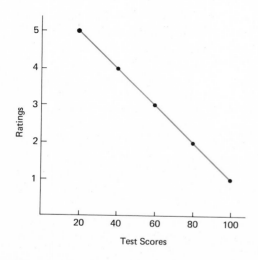

Figure 2–12. Negative correlation.

61

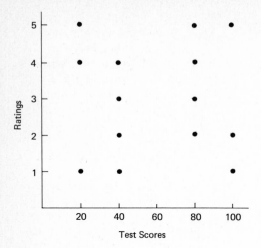

Figure 2–13. Zero correlation.

efficients range from 0 to −1.00. It is important to remember that a correlation coefficient of −1.00 indicates just as strong a relationship or correspondence as a coefficient of +1.00—only the direction is different. In both cases, performance on one variable (for example, job ratings) can be predicted from performance on the other variable (for example, applicants' test scores).

Figure 2–13 depicts data with a correlation coefficient of zero; there is no predictive relationship between the two variables. Some people with low test scores received high ratings, and some with high test scores received low ratings.

The closer the correlation coefficient is to +1.00 or −1.00, the more accurately we can predict performance on one variable from performance on the other. Correlation is a valuable and widely used tool in psychology and its applications in industrial psychology are numerous.

Inferential Statistics

In the typical psychological experiment, researchers are interested in comparing the performance levels of at least two groups—the experimental and the control groups. For example, in an experiment to test the value of a new method of training, the experimental group, which has had the training, is compared with the control group, which has not been exposed to the new method of training. An important decision rests on the basis of this comparison: should this training method be introduced in the entire plant? The decision hinges upon the size of the difference between the two groups on the dependent variable (job performance).

But how do psychologists know when the difference between the two groups is large enough to justify the cost of setting up a new training program? They can answer this question by determining the level of *statistical significance* of the difference between the means of the two groups. The answer is in terms of probabilities rather than certainties. The problem is this: Is the difference between the means of the two groups large enough so that it is unlikely that it could have occurred by chance?

Applying statistical techniques to the data from the experimental and control groups, we can calculate a probability value for the difference between the means. This figure represents the probability that this difference could have occurred by chance. Psychologists have arbitrarily established two levels of significance: a probability (p) of 0.05 and a p of 0.01.

Achieving a p value of 0.01 means that a difference as large as that obtained in the experiment would occur by chance only one time out of every hundred. A difference of this level of significance can be attributed to the new training method used with the experimental group and not merely to chance. If the difference had reached a p value of 0.05, we would have a little less confidence in our results, since this would indicate that there was one probability in twenty that the difference could have occurred by chance.

We can have greater confidence in findings that reach the 0.01 level of significance, but whatever level of significance is reached, this statistical tool gives the psychologist a firm basis on which to make the decision about the new training program. Note that the researcher must still exercise judgment. The use of statistics does not eliminate the need for decision making; it helps to guide the researcher in that task. Statistical tools are means to an end, not the end in themselves.

SUMMARY

Knowledge of the **research methods** used by industrial psychologists is important to you in your working career. As a manager in an organization you will be working with the findings of psychologists and perhaps deciding whether a specific psychological research program should be supported. You can better understand the contributions of psychologists if you first understand how they work.

There are several requirements of psychological research: observations must be **objective, well controlled** and systematic, and capable of duplication and **verifiability.** These requirements are difficult to satisfy in psychological research but their achievement is vital.

There are certain limitations to psychological research: not every problem in human behavior can be investigated by psychological research (some are too complex or potentially dangerous); the act of observing some behaviors may interfere with or change them; and some research must be conducted in artificial settings (this may limit the generalizability of the findings).

There are three methods of conducting psychological research in industry: the experimental method, the naturalistic observation method, and survey methods.

The essence of the **experimental method** is to investigate one influencing variable at a time while holding the other variables constant. The variable being investigated is called the **independent variable** and the resulting behavior is called the **dependent variable.** To properly conduct an experiment, the subjects must be divided into two groups: the **experimental group** and the **control group.** The groups must be as similar as possible. This similarity is brought about by random group design (subjects are assigned at random to the two groups) or by matched group design (subjects in the two groups are evenly matched on personal characteristics).

The method of **naturalistic observation** involves observing behavior in the real world. The experimenter has control over the independent variables but cannot manipulate them as can be done under laboratory conditions. Although not as desirable as the experimental method, naturalistic observation does offer the advantage of studying behavior under realistic conditions.

Survey methods of research focus on our attitudes and opinions. Three survey techniques are personal interviews, telephone surveys, and mail surveys. The personal interview is the most expensive and time-consuming method but it offers the possibility of securing the most useful information.

Two styles of question are used in surveys: **open-end** and **fixed-alternative.** The latter restricts the respondents to a few choices rather than allowing them to answer the questions fully in their own words.

Representative samples of people to be questioned may be selected by **probability sampling** (each person in the population has a known probability of being included in the sample) or by **quota sampling** (constructing a duplicate, in miniature, of the larger population).

Once data have been collected, they must be analyzed and interpreted by means of statistical techniques. Large amounts of raw data can be summarized and described by **descriptive statistics.** Data can be presented in graphic form or reduced to a single number that adequately describes them. Three ways of measuring the central tendency of a distribution of data are the **mean, median,** and **mode.**

When sufficient data are collected from a representative sample of the population, they form a bell-shaped distribution called a **normal curve,** in which most of the scores fall in the center or average range.

To measure the **variability** of a distribution, researchers use the **standard deviation,** a distance along the baseline of a distribution. The standard deviation provides information on the percentage of scores that lie above and below any raw score.

The **correlation coefficient** is a means of determining the direction and strength of the relationship between two variables. Correlation coefficients range from −1.00 (a perfect negative relationship) through zero to +1.00 (a perfect positive relationship), and enable us to predict performance on one variable from performance on another variable.

Inferential statistics are used to determine the level of **statistical significance** of the difference between the means of two groups by indicating whether the difference is large enough such that it is unlikely that it occurred by chance. Psychologists use two levels of significance: a probability of 0.05 (one chance in twenty that the difference occurred by chance) and a probability of 0.01 (one chance in one hundred that the difference occurred by chance).

SUGGESTED READINGS

Anderson, B. F. *The Psychology Experiment: An Introduction to the Scientific Method,* 2nd ed. Belmont, Calif.: Wadsworth Publishing Co., 1971.

Bachrach, A. *Psychological Research: An Introduction,* 3rd ed. New York: Random House, 1972.

Bouchard, T. Field research methods: Interviewing, questionnaires, participant observation, systematic observation, unobtrusive measures. In M. Dunnette, Ed., *Handbook of Industrial and Organizational Psychology.* Chicago: Rand McNally, 1976. Pp. 363–413.

Erdos, P., and Morgan, A. *Professional Mail Surveys.* New York: McGraw-Hill, 1970.

Fromkin, H., and Streufert, S. Laboratory experimentation. In M. Dunnette, Ed., *Handbook of Industrial and Organizational Psychology.* Chicago: Rand McNally, 1976. Pp. 415–465.

Hardyck, C., and Petrinovich, L. *Understanding Research in the Social Sciences: A Practical Guide to Understanding Social and Behavioral Research.* Philadelphia: W. B. Saunders, 1975.

Kanuk, L., and Berenson, C. Mail surveys and response rates: A literature review. *Journal of Marketing Research,* 1975, **12,** 440–453.

Runyon, D., and Haber, A. *Fundamentals of Behavioral Statistics,* 3rd ed. Reading, Mass.: Addison-Wesley, 1976.

Siegel, M. H., and Ziegler, H. P. *Psychological Research: The Inside Story.* New York: Harper & Row, 1976.

Warwick, D., and Lininger, C. *The Sample Survey: Theory and Practice.* New York: McGraw-Hill, 1975.

Wheeler, M. *Lies, Damn Lies, and Statistics: The Manipulation of Public Opinion in America.* New York: Liveright, 1976; Dell, 1977.

Wright, R. *Understanding Statistics: An Informal Introduction for the Behavioral Sciences.* New York: Harcourt Brace Jovanovich, 1976.

PERSONNEL PSYCHOLOGY

The areas of application that are generally called *personnel psychology* include the many activities involved in selecting, training, and evaluating new and current employees. Persons applying for a job undergo an extensive selection process; an organization may use techniques ranging from application blanks to sophisticated psychological tests. Once hired, new employees must be trained to perform their jobs efficiently.

Selection and training principles are also used when persons are being considered for promotion within the organization for which they work. The same process of matching employees' abilities and skills with the job's requirements and demands must be undertaken, and employees who are promoted to more responsible jobs must be trained for their new roles.

The performance of all employees—the newly hired and those who have been on the job for some time—must be objectively and fairly evaluated periodically. These evaluations serve three purposes:

1. Performance evaluations provide information to the organization about the effectiveness of their selection and training procedures. In other words, the evaluations will indicate if the right kind of person is being hired and if he or she is being trained in the most appropriate way.
2. Performance evaluations provide information about how well an employee is doing the job. This information helps the organization make the difficult decisions about salary increases, promotions, demotions, and terminations.
3. Performance evaluations can be of value to the employee by providing feedback about progress on the job. By becoming aware of personal strengths and weaknesses, the employee can be guided in his or her growth and development as an individual and as an employee.

You can see how important selection, training, and evaluation activities are and how they can determine the kind of work we do and the way in which we do it. These are among the original activities of industrial psychologists and still form a substantial part of the field.

Chapters 3 and 4 are devoted to problems of selection. Chapter 3 discusses the general principles, processes, and problems of selection and basic selection techniques (application blanks, interviews, letters of recommendation, and assessment centers). Chapter 4 is concerned with the use of psychological tests for selection purposes. Problems and methods of evaluating work performance are discussed in Chapter 5, and principles and techniques of training are considered in Chapter 6.

3

Employee Selection I: Principles and Techniques

INTRODUCTION

When you leave college and begin your first job, there is almost a 50 per cent chance that you will quit that job within five years. However pessimistic that may sound, it does reflect the reality of the employment situation. For a variety of reasons, nearly half of the students in your college graduating class will not find enough satisfaction in their work to stay with the first organization they join. They may find the job to be quite different from what they were told by a company recruiter, in a fancy brochure, or by a personnel department. Or they may find that their own abilities and characteristics are not what they had thought them to be, or that they are temperamentally, intellectually, or socially unsuited to a particular kind of work.

Whatever the reasons may be for dissatisfaction with the job, and irrespective of where the fault may lie, it is an unfortunate and disheartening situation in which both the individual and the organization are losers. And this situation emphasizes the importance of employee selection principles and practices. Improper matching of the person and the job, of the person's abilities and characteristics and the job's demands and requirements, leads to disharmony and unhappiness in the work situation. Much of this discontent may be unnecessary. Selection techniques are available that are capable of closely matching the person and the job, but these techniques must be used wisely and well by both participants in the selection process—the employing organizations and those who apply for work.

Selection is not limited to the world of work. Throughout our lives, from infancy to old age, we are constantly involved in the process of selection. Sometimes we are the ones being selected; other times we do the selecting. We are selected as playmates, friends, teammates, lovers, and club members, and, at the same time, we select those with whom we choose to socialize or work or play.

In these everyday situations, selection is usually based on subjective factors—the way a person looks, acts, or dresses—without any attempt to make a systematic and thorough evaluation of the qualifications and abilities of the person being selected. Unfortunately, this kind of careless and haphazard selection process still occurs in some employing organizations. Some business leaders believe that they can "size up" candidates for a job by the strength of a handshake, the length of the candidates' hair, their manner of dress, or some other equally subjective and worthless criterion.

Because improper selection is so costly, management must make better use of all available psychological tools and techniques so as to ensure that the majority of those who are hired will work to the ultimate advantage of themselves and their organization.

AN OVERVIEW OF THE SELECTION PROCESS

There is more to proper selection methodology than simply putting an advertisement in the newspaper, having those who appear in the personnel office fill out an application blank, and questioning them in a ten-minute interview. A proper selection program involves a number of additional steps between company and applicant.

Suppose a personnel manager finds that as a result of a new product the company will shortly begin to produce, two hundred new employees must be hired to operate highly complex machinery. How can these new workers be found?

First, the nature of the job for which employees are being sought must be thoroughly investigated. The company will not know what abilities to look for in potential employees unless it is known in detail what they will be expected to do to perform the job successfully. A process known as *job analysis is* undertaken to determine the specific skills and abilities necessary to the job. Then, from an analysis of the job, it is possible to develop an analysis of the potential worker.

Once the personnel manager knows the qualifications that must be sought in the applicants, the most effective means of identifying these characteristics must be determined. Does the job require the ability to read blueprints? Does it require experience with a particular type of machinery? Must the worker be a high school graduate? Does the work require excellent vision or a high level of intelligence or mechanical ability? What are the most efficient ways of finding out this information?

The necessary skill and background characteristics, determined from the job and worker analyses, must be assessed in each applicant. Cut-off scores or levels for the various abilities are established; that is, a minimal score on a test, or a fixed number of years of experience is proposed, and no one is hired who falls below this level. It may be necessary to determine cut-off scores by conducting a research program to study current workers in the same or a similar job.

Recruitment decisions follow. Where should the company advertise for new employees? In a newspaper, a trade journal, or through an employment agency?

How many potential employees are obtained by the recruiting program? This affects the caliber of those who are finally hired. For example, if there are only two hundred and fifty applicants for the two hundred jobs, the personnel manager must be less discriminating in hiring than if there are four hundred applicants to choose from. Psychologists speak of this as the *selection ratio,* the relationship between the number of people to be hired and the number of people who are available to be hired. The available labor supply directly influences the stringency of the requirements established for the job. If there is a shortage of applicants and the jobs must be filled in a few weeks, some requirements (perhaps the cut-off score on an intelligence test or the level of education) will have to be lowered.

The actual selection from among the job applicants—classifying them as suitable or unsuitable—can be accomplished by a variety of techniques. This chapter considers interviews, application blanks, letters of recommendation, and the increasingly popular assessment centers. As a rule, hiring decisions are not based on a single technique, but on a combination of methods. For example, a large computer firm uses the following sequence of six steps to determine if an applicant should be offered a position.

1. *Preliminary interview.* This initial look at an applicant is a rough screening device that provides a general impression of the individual. From this, a decision is made as to whether the applicant has the general characteristics and qualifications to warrant further consideration.
2. *Application blank.* Those who pass the general screening complete a formal application blank providing detailed background information on personal characteristics, employment history, and education.
3. *Employment tests.* Psychological tests are administered to those who appear from their application blanks to be qualified. The

    tests determine specific abilities, attitudes, and characteristics and range from tests of typing ability for secretaries to personality tests for managers.

4. *Final interview.* Based on the considerable information now available on the applicant, detailed and insightful questions are prepared for an intensive interview. The applicant may be questioned by more than one member of the company so that several impressions can be obtained and compared.

5. *References.* If the person has successfully completed all the steps thus far, the personal and business references named by the applicant are contacted. The purpose is to determine the level of performance in past jobs.

6. *Physical examination.* Since some jobs have demanding physical requirements, the applicant may be examined by a physician. Most companies have minimum medical standards for all jobs in their organization.

These selection procedures are complex and costly but in the long run, they are less complex and costly than selecting the wrong person for the job. It is better to find out before hiring who is not suitable for a position than to find out after that person has been hired, trained, and become an unhappy and unsatisfactory employee.

There is more to the selection process: the testing of the selection procedures themselves. After the initial two hundred workers in our example have been hired, the personnel manager must find out how many of them succeed on the job. Successful job performance is the ultimate test of the worth of a selection program.

Every new selection program must be investigated to determine its predictive accuracy or validity. This can be done only by evaluating the performance of the employees selected by the new procedures. For example, we can ask the supervisors of our two hundred new workers to rate them after six months on how well they do their job. We compare these ratings with their performance on the selection procedures to see how well the two measures correlate. Were the selection procedures capable of predicting who among the applicants would be the better workers?

Suppose we learn that all those who received high ratings from their supervisors had performed very well on the psychological tests used for selection, and that they all possessed similar background factors such as level of education. If those who received low supervisor ratings had performed poorly on the selection measures, we than have evidence that our selection methods discriminate between potentially good employees and potentially poor ones. The selection techniques can be used in the future with confidence to find the right kind of person for this job. To evaluate the selection process, however, we must have some criterion of job performance to compare with performance in the selection situation. The ways of determining such criteria—methods of performance or work evaluation—are discussed in Chapter 5.

If the correlation between selection and job performance is very low, new selection procedures will be required and the entire process must be begun again. The development of a sound selection system requires a great deal of skill on the part of the industrial psychologist, and money and patience on the part of management.

THE CHALLENGE OF FAIR EMPLOYMENT

Successful selection has been rendered even more difficult in recent years by the requirements of the Equal Employment Opportunity Commission (EEOC). All job applicants, regardless of race, religion, sex, or national origin, must be given equal opportunities for employment. This problem has special relevance for members of minority groups. It has been alleged that some of the selection procedures used by employing organizations discriminate against educationally and culturally deprived individuals. Not only is such discrimination unethical and immoral but it is also illegal. The Civil Rights Act of 1964 and the enforced guidelines of the EEOC (established in 1972) have declared it against the law to discriminate against job applicants.

Title VII, Section 703, of the Civil Rights Act states that "It shall be an unlawful employment practice for an employer to fail or refuse to hire or to discharge any individual, or otherwise to discriminate against any individual with respect to his compensation, terms, conditions, or privileges of employment, because of such individual's race, color, religion, sex, or national origin." The EEOC is empowered to bring legal action against any organization employing fifteen or more persons that violates the provisions of Title VII.

As a result, employing organizations must try to ensure that all persons have access to job and training opportunities. Because of this legislation and the increased social awareness, personnel departments have had to examine their screening procedures to ensure that a job applicant is not discriminated against simply because he or she is black, Mexican-American, or Puerto Rican, and may have had less opportunity to develop personal skills than a middle-class white person.

Suppose, for example, that a personnel department has established specific levels of arithmetic ability and verbal skill, plus a high school diploma, as requirements for a particular job. These requirements may disqualify certain minority group members who may not have been able to complete high school for reasons having nothing to do with their mental ability. Similarly, many psychological tests place a minority group member at a disadvantage because he or she may have experienced cultural and educational deprivation.

Until recently, persons of minority status did not have an equal chance of passing selection standards; this resulted in their underemployment in North American industry. Where they were able to secure a job, it was usually a low-level, unskilled laboring position that offered little opportunity for advancement.

To further equalize employment possibilities of minority groups, industry has been actively seeking job applicants. Recruiters are sent to predominantly black high schools and colleges, for example, instead of waiting for interested individuals to come to the personnel office.

The law requiring equal opportunity of employment has placed specific limitations on virtually all selection devices. (We see in Chapter 4 the impact of this legislation on the use of psychological tests.) Interviews and application blanks are particularly affected. Psychologists and personnel departments are highly sensitive to what can and cannot be asked of a job applicant. Questions that might discriminate against minority group members or women can result in lawsuits. Also, what is considered discriminatory varies among states depending on the wording of each state's human rights laws.

To give you some idea of the kinds of questions that can no longer be asked of job applicants, and to test your own knowledge in this sensitive area, consider the following pre-employment inquiry quiz. Try to answer each question and compare your responses with the correct answers at the end of the quiz.[1]

Only three of these nineteen inquiries, numbers (6), (10), and (12), are considered to be lawful questions to ask a job applicant. A prospective employer can ask applicants if they are citizens of the United States (according to Title VII they *must* ask this question), about their knowledge of foreign languages, and details of prior work experience. It is unlawful, at least in some states, to ask any of the other questions.

Let us examine some of these items to learn why they could be considered discriminatory. Items (2), (3), (4), and (5) could easily identify the national origin, race, creed, or color of an applicant, as could items (7), (8), (13), (14), (15), and (16). Also, much of the information asked in these items has no bearing on the applicant's ability to perform the job for which he or she is being considered. Therefore, in

---

[1] Adapted from Robert L. Minter, "Human rights laws and pre-employment inquiries," *Personnel Journal,* **51** (1972), 432.

Pre-employment Inquiry	Lawful	Unlawful
1. Asking applicants if they have ever worked under another name.	_____	_____
2. Asking applicants to name their birthplace.	_____	_____
3. Asking for the birthplace of applicants' parents, spouse, or other close relatives.	_____	_____
4. Asking applicants to submit proof of age by supplying birth certificate or baptismal record.	_____	_____
5. Asking applicants for religious affiliation, name of church, parish, or religious holidays observed.	_____	_____
6. Asking applicants if they are citizens of the United States.	_____	_____
7. Asking applicants if they are naturalized citizens.	_____	_____
8. Asking applicants for the date their citizenship was acquired.	_____	_____
9. Asking applicants if they have ever been arrested for any crime, and to indicate when and where.	_____	_____
10. Asking applicants to indicate what foreign languages they can read, write, or speak fluently.	_____	_____
11. Asking applicants how they acquired the ability to read, write, or speak a foreign language.	_____	_____
12. Asking applicants about their past work experience.	_____	_____
13. Requesting applicants to provide names of three relatives other than parents, spouse, or minor-age dependent children.	_____	_____
14. Asking male applicants for their wives' maiden names.	_____	_____
15. Asking applicants for their mothers' maiden names.	_____	_____
16. Asking for the full names of the applicants' brothers and sisters.	_____	_____
17. Asking applicants for a list of names of all clubs, societies, and lodges to which they belong.	_____	_____
18. Asking applicants to include photographs with their applications for employment.	_____	_____
19. Asking applicants to supply addresses of relatives such as cousins, uncles, aunts, nephews, nieces, or grandparents who can be contacted for references.	_____	_____

addition to being possibly discriminatory, these questions serve no useful purpose in predicting the applicant's potential for success on the job.

It is considered unlawful to ask applicants if they have ever been arrested (9); minority group members are much more likely to be arrested on suspicion, owing to the possible prejudices of arresting officers, and this should not be held against them. It *is* lawful, however, to ask applicants if they have ever been *convicted* of crimes. This could be relevant to job performance; for example, in the case of a person convicted of embezzlement who is applying for a job in a bank.

Great progress has been made in recent years in meeting the legal requirements of equal employment opportunity, but the problem remains a serious one. The social injustices committed by discrimination in hiring have not yet been fully eliminated, and they present moral, legal, and technical challenges for personnel psychologists.

JOB ANALYSIS: PURPOSE AND METHODS

We have noted the steps involved in setting up a selection program. Let us now examine some of these steps more closely, particularly the preliminary ones of job analysis and recruitment.

The purpose of job analysis is to describe, in specific terms, the precise nature of the component tasks performed by the workers on a particular job. Job analysis includes information on the kind of equipment or tools used, the operations performed, unique aspects of the job such as safety hazards, education or training required, pay scale, and so on. The value of job analysis in personnel selection has already been mentioned. Unless the company knows exactly what is required for the successful performance of a job, it will have no way of knowing what qualities to seek in applicants for that job.

Job analysis has other important uses in organizational life. In order to establish a training program for a particular job, for example, the nature of the job must be known; a company can't expect to train a person to perform a job unless the specific tasks, steps, and operations necessary for job success are known. Job analysis can aid in efforts to restructure a job so that it can be performed more efficiently. An analysis might reveal, for example, that a lathe operator has to walk twenty-five feet from the machine each time he or she needs to replenish the supply of raw material. This wasted time and effort can be easily eliminated but it might never have been noticed by management had the job not been analyzed. Job analysis can also reveal safety hazards in equipment or operating procedures and suggest equipment design changes for greater efficiency.

To begin a job analysis, an investigator might look for *published analyses of similar jobs*. There are limitations to this approach, however, since the other jobs, no matter how similar, will most likely not be identical to the one in question. A standard and comprehensive list of jobs is found in the *Dictionary of Occupational Titles* (DOT), produced by the U.S. Employment Service. This periodically revised compendium defines briefly some twenty-two thousand jobs. The definitions are concise and not as detailed or comprehensive as a job analysis must be, but they do serve to familiarize researchers with the general form of any job.

As an example of the scope of jobs covered by the DOT and the manner in which they are described, two job definitions are presented: coppersmith and egg breaker.

Coppersmith—Lays out, cuts, bends, and assembles pipe sections, pipefittings, and other parts from copper, brass, and other nonferrous metals: Lays out full-scale floor drawings or makes templates, following blueprints of pipe assemblies. Builds framework on bending slab to use as guide for bending, shaping, and joining assemblies. Cuts pipe, using handtools or shop machinery, and packs it with sand, rosin, or other material to prevent flattening during bending. Heats bend area with gas torch to soften metal and bends pipe, allowing for stretch at outside radius and compression at inside radius, using pipe-bending machines. Rebeats and hammers pipe to eliminate wrinkles resulting from bending. Solders or brazes flanges on end of pipe. Flares or bells pipe mouths, using belling and flaring tools and mallet. Bends tubing to form coils for parts, such as feed water or oil heater. Lays out patterns and templates on sheet stock, using knowledge of geometry. Bends, hammers, bumps, razes, and planishes sheet stock to fabricate such parts as expansion joints, tanks, heads, cowls, and air chambers, using handtools, gas torches, and shop machinery. Sweats, rivets, solders, or brazes seams to finish part. Coats parts by dipping them in mixture of molten tin and lead to prevent erosion, and galvanic and electrolytic action. Conducts hydrostatic tests to detect leaks in fabricated pipe. May install piping aboard ship.

Egg Breaker—Separates yolk and glair (white) of eggs for use in food products: Strikes eggs against bar, allows contents to fall into bowl, and throws empty shells into receptacle. Smells broken eggs to detect spoiled ones and dumps them into waste container. Pours broken eggs from bowl over egg separating device. Pulls lever to retain yolk and to allow white to fall into cup below. May be designated according to specific task performed as *Egg Smeller*.

There are usually additional job analyses on which investigators can draw. In a large organization it is likely that the same or similar jobs have been analyzed in the past. Although such investigations cannot be applied directly to the current analysis, they can provide useful information.

A more commonly used technique of job analysis involves extensive *interviewing* of those directly connected with the job—the workers currently performing the job, their foremen, and the instructors who trained the workers for the job. This can involve face-to-face interviewing of individuals or of a group of workers, or the use of questionnaires.

Full cooperation and understanding on the part of those being questioned are required. The U.S. Employment Service suggests the following guidelines.

1. The person being questioned must be fully briefed as to who the interviewer is, why he or she is asking so many questions, and why it is important for the worker to answer fully and honestly. The workers, in short, must know what is required and why.
2. The questions must be thoroughly planned and worded in advance. This is where information from published job analyses is helpful. It gives the analyst some idea of what to look for.
3. The interviewer must secure the information as quickly as possible, recognize that the worker knows more about the job than the interviewer does, and express appreciation to the person being interviewed.

The interview approach has several advantages. Those who are directly concerned with the job are in the best position to know the details of the work. The face-to-face interaction between the worker and the job analyst provides the former with an understanding of what the latter is trying to accomplish. As a rule, workers who are fully informed of the importance of the project and of their vital role in it will be more helpful and cooperative than those who are not so informed.

Questionnaires may take less time than interviews but they have two disadvantages. Workers may not be as motivated to answer an impersonal questionnaire with the same degree of thoroughness and accuracy as they might bring to the more personal interview situation. Also, unless the questionnaire is excessively long (which might discourage careful responses), the answers will not be sufficiently detailed to provide a comprehensive analysis of the job. When conditions of the job permit, the interview approach is usually more useful.

A third approach to job analysis is direct *observation* of the worker on the job. Sometimes this involves simply watching the workers perform their various tasks, but occasionally sophisticated methods of observation, such as filming, are used. It is well known from psychological research that persons may behave differently when they know they are being observed, so it is necessary for the analyst to remain as unobtrusive as possible. Also, the analyst must observe a sample of the workers (not just one) and must make the observations at various times during the workday to take account of changes caused by factors such as fatigue. (A worker may be more productive in the morning than in late afternoon, for example.)

A fourth technique of job analysis involves having the workers maintain a *systematic activity log* of everything they do in a given period of time. If these records are made with care, they frequently reveal details of the job not otherwise obtainable or observable.

Another approach is the *critical incidents* technique, which records those behaviors (incidents) that are vital to the successful performance of the job. The goal is to identify from supervisors, co-workers, and others familiar with the job, behaviors that differentiate successful from unsuccessful workers. The critical incidents technique focuses on the specific acts that lead to desirable or undesirable consequences on the job. A single critical incident is of little value, but hundreds of them can effectively describe a job task sequence in terms of the unique behaviors required for successful performance.

Whatever technique is used to undertake a job analysis, the facts must be presented in a concise and easily understood format. Figure 3–1 shows the form used by the U.S. Employment Service. The full job description is used as a source of information to prepare a *job specification* that is then used to delimit the characteristics sought in workers applying for the job. The value of job analysis for selection, then, is to identify the kinds of workers, in terms of their abilities, background, training, and experience, to be selected for a particular job.

From the information obtained through job analysis and job specification, it is possible to develop a *worker analysis* and *worker specification*. For example, in selecting workers for a physically demanding job in a steel company, a personnel psychologist wants to know the relative importance of the following worker characteristics:

1. General health and physical strength.
2. Manual dexterity.
3. Eye-hand coordination.
4. Visual acuity and color discrimination.
5. Keenness of hearing.
6. Numerical facility.
7. Mechanical ability.
8. Oral and written expression.
9. Decision-making ability.
10. Planning ability.

U.S. DEPARTMENT OF LABOR
BUREAU OF EMPLOYMENT SECURITY
UNITED STATES EMPLOYMENT SERVICE

JOB ANALYSIS SCHEDULE

1. Job title _____

2. Number _____

3. Number employed M _____ F _____

4. Establishment No. _____

6. Alternate titles _____

5. Date _____

_____

Number of sheets _____

_____

8. Industry _____

_____

9. Branch _____

7. Dictionary title and code _____

10. Department _____

11. WORK PERFORMED:

(CONTINUE ON SUPPLEMENTARY SHEETS)

Analyst _____

Reviewer _____

Figure 3–1. Job analysis schedule.

11. Initiative.
12. Emotional stability.
13. Behavior under stress.

Once the psychologist has this information, it is possible to determine the most useful selection procedures for identifying applicants who possess these qualifications.

SOURCES OF WORKERS

12. Experience: None — — — — — — — — Acceptable —
— —
— —

13. Training data: Minimum training time — — (a) Inexperienced workers.
　　　　　　　　　　　　　　　　　　 (b) Experienced workers.

TRAINING	SPECIFIC JOB SKILLS ACQUIRED THROUGH TRAINING
In-plant (on job) training	
Vocational training	
Technical training	
SRW Eng. General education	
Activities and hobbies	

14. Apprenticeship: Formal — — — — — Informal — — — — — Length required — — — — — — — — — — — — —

15. Relation to other jobs:

(a) Promotions from and to, transfers, etc.: —
— —
— —

(b) Supervision received: General — — — — — — Close — — — — — By — — — — — — — — — — — — — —
　　　　　　　　　　　　　　　　　　　　　　　　　　　　　　　　　(Title)

(c) Supervision given: None — — — — — — Number supervised — — — — — — — Titles — — — — — — — —
— —

The following items must be covered on supplementary sheets.

PERFORMANCE REQUIREMENTS

16. Responsibility (consider material or product, safety of others, equipment or process, cooperation with others, instruction of others, public contacts, and the like).

17. Job knowledge (consider pre-employment and on–the–job knowledge of equipment, materials, working procedures, techniques, and processes).

18. Mental application (consider initiative, adaptability, independent judgment, and mental alertness).

19. Dexterity and accuracy (consider speed and degree of precision, dexterity, accuracy, coordination, expertness, care, and deftness of manipulation, operation, or processing of materials, tools, instruments, or gauges used).

COMMENTS

20. Equipment, materials, and supplies.
21. Definition of terms.
22. General comments.

Figure 3–1. (cont'd.)

RECRUITMENT

Since recruiting methods influence the number of applicants for a particular position, they also determine the minimum requirements sought in the selection procedure. The recruiting process will directly affect the predictive accuracy of selection devices. For example, if the cut-off scores on a battery of psychological tests must be lowered because there are only a few more applicants than there are vacancies, the predictive value of the test will be reduced.

Despite its importance, the recruiting process has received relatively little attention from personnel psychologists, many of whom regard it as an adjunct to, but not really a part of, the selection process. Most companies do not even know how effective their recruiting practices are. Research to compare various recruiting techniques is possible. It would not be difficult to compare the number and quality of job candidates lured to a company by various recruiting methods. As with all personnel research, it would be expensive, but the results could, in the long run, save much more money than would be spent on the research.

For lower-level jobs, most companies rely on persons visiting their personnel office, referrals by current employees, or, if the need is great, newspaper advertisements or employment agencies. At higher levels—executives, scientists, engineers, and other professionals—industry resorts to more sophisticated and costly recruitment techniques.

The higher the job rank in industry, the more intense is the recruiting or selling effort. This is particularly apparent on college campuses where corporate personnel officers interview students in a search for new managerial talent. There is some evidence, however, that this recruiting is not producing the most desirable results. As we noted, half of all college graduates leave their first job within five years.

Part of the reason for dissatisfaction on the part of new graduates can be traced to their initial contact with the company: the campus recruitment interview. Many students obtain a false picture of the company during this interview and of their possible role in it. This is sometimes because of the students' naiveté—they don't really know what questions to ask the recruiter since they have had no experience in corporate life. Also, students want to present the best possible image of themselves and may tend to hide weaknesses, attitudes, or ideals they think the recruiter may not like. Another reason for the misleading view, however, is the fault of the recruiters. Their job is to find people with promise for their company and to accomplish this they all too often paint an idealized picture of the organization and of the graduate's first job in it.

Both sides, then, are guilty of presenting false images of what each has to offer, and the result is likely to be disaffection when each side turns out to be less than perfect. The obvious solution is greater frankness and honesty, with each party presenting both good and bad points. Some organizations have realized this problem and are striving to present to applicants a realistic preview of what a job is like.

Job Previews

One of the first companies to offer realistic job previews was Sears, Roebuck, which enlightens recruits about disadvantages as well as advantages of working for the company. Candidates are told bluntly about long and erratic hours, frequent transfers, and the hectic pace— nothing is hidden from potential employees. As a result, fewer of those recruited and offered jobs will accept them, but Sears' management feels that they are hiring better people than before. Recruits who do accept these positions know what to expect on their first job; the less desirable aspects will come as no surprise. Further, applicants who would not like working under such conditions can turn down the job offer instead of accepting it and quitting after a year or two. This is certainly to the advantage of both the employee and the organization. The college students recruited by Sears, Roebuck report that they liked this procedure. One said: "They treat us with respect. That's a lot more than you get at most companies."

Other organizations are now providing more realistic job previews. These include Southern New England Telephone, Prudential Insurance, Texas Instruments, and the U.S. Military Academy at West Point. Wherever realistic job previewing has been used, the results have been very favorable.

One of the most thoroughly researched instances is at the Southern New England Telephone Company.[2] Prospective telephone operators are shown a film in which current operators describe the positive and negative aspects of their jobs as truthfully as possible. (There are twice as many negative comments as positive ones!) What impact does this have on potential employees? Very few who were offered a job turned it down (only two out of more than eighty). When a job was accepted it was with a full awareness of what the work would be like. No one began work with a false or idealized picture of the nature of the job. Three months after being hired, 62 per cent of the employees who had seen the film were still on the job; of a group of employees who had not seen the film, only 50 per cent were still on the job three months later. The group that was given the realistic job preview also showed a higher level of job satisfaction after three months on the job and said that they thought less about quitting.

Using another approach, Prudential Insurance Company and the U.S. Military Academy give brochures to applicants that describe realistically what life is like in their organizations. In both cases, the survival rate has been higher for those who have received this job preview than for those who have not.

[2] J. Wanous, "Tell it like it is at realistic job previews," *Personnel*, **52**(4) (1975), 50–60.

Another way of providing more realistic job expectations is to let applicants actually perform a sample of the work. In this job sample approach, applicants not only get a chance to see if they like the work but they (and the organization) also have the opportunity to see if they can perform the work. Thus, the job sample can also serve as a selection device.

A great deal of research on job samples for recruiting and selecting insurance agents has been conducted by the Life Insurance Agency Management Association.[3] Providing a sample of exactly what applicants would be doing as insurance agents increased both the survival rate and the sales figures for their first year on the job when compared with a group of applicants who had not been given the job sample.

A shirt manufacturing company gave a two-hour job sample to sewing machine operator applicants and found that it led to a much higher survival rate during the first six weeks on the job, as compared with those hired without a job sample.

Providing some form of realistic job preview is certainly advantageous to both recruits and employers. Applicants know what they are getting into, their expectations about the job will more closely match reality, and they are much less likely to experience the disappointment and frustration that often result when people begin a job and find it quite different from what they were told. In recruiting, honesty is indeed the best policy.

Research on Recruiter Characteristics

Another important aspect of recruiting is the nature of the recruiters themselves. The recruiter is the first representative of an organization whom potential employees meet. In a very real sense, the recruiter *is* the organization; applicants will judge the nature of the organization by their image of, and reaction to, the recruiter.

A study conducted at the University of Texas investigated the reactions of a group of college seniors to the recruiters who had interviewed them.[4] What did the students like or dislike about the recruiters? Such information can be valuable to an organization; it should directly influence the kind of person sent as a college recruiter, and this, in turn, will influence the number and quality of applicants that the organization gets. Most of the students in this study refused to consider a job with a particular company if they did not like the recruiter.

[3] M. A. Raphael, "Work previews can reduce turnover and improve performance," *Personnel Journal*, **54**(1975), 97–98.
[4] W. F. Glueck, "How recruiters influence job choices on campus," *Personnel*, **48**(2) (1971), 46–52.

The students preferred the following recruiter characteristics: knowledgeable, enthusiastic, dedicated to the company, likable, convincing, interested in each student, honest, and straightforward about the job and the organization. The students also preferred recruiters to be in the thirty-five to fifty-five age range, graduates of their own university, and experienced in the students' own specialty areas.

The most common complaint the college seniors had about recruiters was their lack of personal interest in the students. Some recruiters were judged to be interested only in filling their quota of job applicants. They were impersonal with the students, and treated them as though they were numbers instead of human beings. Another common complaint of the students was a lack of enthusiasm on the part of the recruiters, some of whom seemed bored and conducted the interviews in a perfunctory, mechanical way. The students also resented recruiters' attempts to analyze them by asking intimate questions such as their relationship with their parents. Some students who were questioned in this manner simply walked out in the middle of the interview; others informed other students, with the result that these recruiters found a number of subsequent interviews canceled. Finally, students resented recruiters who took up a lot of time with a prepared talk about the company, offering information that the students could have read in a brochure at another time. The students wanted more time to ask questions themselves.

Research on Job Characteristics

Another way in which personnel psychologists aid in the recruiting process is through research aimed at identifying the aspects of a job that are appealing to various types of applicant. If an organization knows what potential employees are looking for in their work, it can design a recruiting campaign accordingly. Two representative studies indicate how valuable this kind of research can be.

One study dealt with the recruiting of unskilled workers, a social responsibility of which industry has recently become aware.[5] Conducted with three hundred and fifty underemployed and unemployed in rural South Carolina, this research attempted to determine the kinds of appeals that would attract these people to apply for jobs in industry.

The low level of literacy and education among this target population was a major consideration in constructing a questionnaire that would attract their interest and be easy to understand and complete. The instructions were worded as simply as possible and the questions were in the form of cartoons, as shown in Figure 3–2.

[5] J. E. Champagne, "Job recruitment of the unskilled," *Personnel Journal*, **48**(1969), 259–268.

Figure 3–2. Reprinted with permission from J. E. Champagne, "Job recruitment of the unskilled," *Personnel Journal,* **48**(1969), p. 262. Copyright April 1969.

The questionnaire dealt with twelve job factors that were thought to be significant in recruiting. The unskilled workers ranked these factors as follows.

1. Steady job.
2. Fair pay.
3. Fair boss.
4. Job extras—pensions, sick pay.
5. Job close to home.
6. Interesting work.
7. Good working conditions.
8. Nice people to work with.
9. Chance for promotion.
10. Vacations and holidays with pay.
11. Praise for good work.
12. Working with friends and neighbors.

The most important factor was the security offered by the job. It was rated as being of much greater importance than the second factor, fair pay. It is noteworthy that the factors of interesting work (6) and chance for promotion (9) were not considered to be very important. Perhaps to persons accustomed to deprivation and low-level employment, such rewards are relatively unknown and difficult to even consider as possibilities.

Research findings of this sort can be of considerable importance to a personnel manager of a southern textile plant, for example, in a campaign to recruit unskilled workers. The recruiter would know exactly which factors to emphasize in an attempt to sell the idea of working for the company.

A second study dealt with recruitment of college graduates.[6] What aspects of a job can successfully be used to lure a college senior to a specific company?

Two groups of students were questioned: seniors with average grades, and seniors in an honors program with at least a *B* average. Not surprisingly, the two groups were concerned with different job factors, as shown in Table 3–1. The importance of the study is not in terms of the specific job factors listed by the students, but rather the demonstration that different kinds of students may be looking for different satisfactions in their work. Both groups of students agreed that they disliked close supervision, limited freedom, and being forced to join a union.

From these research results, it is clear that recruiters must offer

[6] F. T. Paine, "What do better college students want from their jobs?" *Personnel Administration*, **32**(1969), 26–29.

TABLE 3–1

IMPORTANT JOB FACTORS FOR AVERAGE AND HONORS STUDENTS

Rank	Average Student	Honors Student
1	Salary increases	Interesting work
2	Interesting work	Self-development
3	Promotion	Quality work
4	Steady employment	Respect
5	Respect	Freedom on the job

Data from F. T. Paine, "What do better college students want from their jobs," *Personnel Administration*, **32** (1969), 28.

different inducements for different people. A student with a C average, for example, would be interested primarily in learning about opportunities for salary increases; an A student would be more concerned with the inherent interest of the work itself. Of course, promising people exactly what they want may recruit them for the company, but unless the job lives up to that promise, they will not be motivated to stay. The A student promised an interesting and challenging job will react with frustration and anger (and soon quit) if the job turns out to be routine and boring. Again, honesty is the best and only policy for job recruiting.

Personnel psychologists have a great deal to contribute to the crucial initial meeting of job applicant and organization, a contribution that works to the advantage of both partners in the relationship.

METHODS OF SELECTION: APPLICATION BLANKS

Rarely is anyone hired by an organization at any level of employment without being asked to complete an application blank. Indeed, this is probably the most frequently used technique in personnel selection and hiring. Even when other methods of assessment are used, the application blank is usually the initial step for the applicant to take. Not only does it provide useful information but it can also provide leads for subsequent interview questions.

The information solicited on an application blank ranges from routine biographical data such as name, address, sex, marital status, education, work and military experience, or dependents, to more personal items such as financial situation, criminal conviction record, or hobbies.

The most crucial problem in constructing an application blank involves deciding what information to ask of an applicant. What information does the employer need to know in order to find out if the applicant is suitable for the job in question? Beyond the routine biographical data, it is important that the company ascertain those facts about the candidate that may correlate with subsequent success on the job.

In one company, for example, research had demonstrated that successful executives were all college graduates who had achieved or exceeded a specific gradepoint average, and had engaged in certain extracurricular activities while in college. Obviously, then, this is the kind of information the personnel department wants to know about an applicant as quickly as possible. If the application blank indicated that a candidate did not possess these qualifications, then the company would not have to go to the time and expense of further selection procedures such as administering a battery of tests or flying the job applicant to the home plant.

Much valuable predictive information can be obtained from application forms. Knowledge of a candidate's financial or marital situations may provide an indication of emotional stability and responsibility. Extracurricular activities may tell something of leadership ability or provide a clue to personality characteristics that can be investigated in an interview.

One company asks applicants how much life insurance they carry. The organization, a life insurance company, has found that the amount of insurance a person has is a valid predictor of how successful he or she will be in selling life insurance to others.

Such predictive information can be obtained only through careful research. Each relevant item on an application form must be correlated with a later measure of job success. If a high positive correlation is found, that item can be used with confidence in selecting new employees.

An application form should be limited to questions that provide useful guides for selection. Some companies use excessively long application blanks in an attempt to gather information on every conceivable facet of an applicant's life, whether or not the data are known to be useful. Surely this is a wasted effort for the applicant (who may lose interest by the fifth page) and for the personnel manager (who may be so overwhelmed with data that the nature of the applicant is lost).

The fair employment legislation discussed earlier has caused a significant change in application forms: Questions about race or religion, for example, are no longer asked. Most companies now boldly state at the top of the form that they are "An Equal Opportunity Employer."

Weighted Application Blank

Once the correlation between each item of information and subsequent job success has been determined, it is possible to score an application blank with specific weights for each item.

For example, a psychologist analyzed and weighted an application blank for the company and found the relationships shown in Table 3–2. Research shows that 80 per cent of all married workers were rated by their supervisors as successful in their jobs; a new job applicant checking "married" on an application blank will therefore be given a score of 8. A single candidate will get a score of 6 because only 60 per cent of the company's single workers were rated as successful. The job applicant who would obtain the highest score is a married high school graduate who owns a home. The person least likely to be hired, then, is a divorced nongraduate who rents a home.

Research on each item of an application blank must be repeated periodically to check on the continuing predictive value of the information, particularly if there has been a change in job procedure or the overall labor supply. Assuming careful research and periodic follow-ups, the weighted application blank can be as useful a predictive device as some psychological tests. Further, they can be graded or scored as objectively as a test, thus eliminating any personal bias in the selection procedure.

Application blanks can be more than a formality in the selection process if proper attention is paid to their development. For maximum effectiveness, application blanks must be geared to the specific needs of an organization and to the different job levels within that organization. Most large companies have one form for managerial and professional employees and another for lower-level employees. The application blank is a vital part of any selection program and each

TABLE 3–2

SAMPLE RESULTS FROM WEIGHTED APPLICATION BLANK

Item	Successful Workers	Weight Assigned
Married	80%	8
Single	60%	6
Divorced	10%	1
High School Graduate	70%	7
Nongraduate	20%	2
Owns Home	80%	8
Rents Home	30%	3

organization must ensure that its form reflects those characteristics that psychological research has found to be related to job success.

Biographical Inventories

Closely related to the weighted application blank is the biographical inventory or biographical information blank, a technique that has become popular in recent years. The approach has been shown to be a valid predictor of success in a variety of jobs: scientist, office worker, middle manager, military officer, production worker, and salesperson.

Biographical inventories are usually much longer than application blanks and cover information on the applicant's life history in greater detail. The rationale for this extensive probing is that on-the-job behavior is related to past behavior in a variety of situations, as well as to attitudes, preferences, and values. Examples of the kind of information asked on biographical inventories are contained in Table 3–3. Such an inventory is very much like a psychological test in terms of the type of question asked and the multiple-choice format of the responses.

Biographical inventories usually are developed for a specific job and considerable research is necessary in order to determine the background experiences that correlate with success on the job. The process of item validation is essentially the same as for the weighted application blank; each item is correlated with some measure of job performance.

A pharmaceutical company used this approach with great success to select research personnel. They found that the more creative scientists checked out on the inventory to be independent, overinvolved in their work, desirous of challenge, and had permissive parents, among other characteristics. Of course, this same cluster of characteristics could be identified through a combination of interviews and psychological tests, but it is more efficient and less costly to elicit this information with one procedure.

The Exxon Corporation employs this technique in its continuing search for future managers and executives. Through the use of a 292-item biographical inventory, developed on the basis of extremely thorough research, Exxon looks for certain characteristics and actual behaviors that correlate with later success in management positions. The questions cover a wide range of behavior, including the educational level and work experience of the applicant's parents, early family relationships, friendships outside the family, and extracurricular interests in such areas as community organizations and sports.

Many of the questions are highly personal, such as, "How many close friends did you have in your last year in high school?" Other

TABLE 3–3

SAMPLE BIOGRAPHICAL INVENTORY ITEMS

Classification Data

What is your present marital status?
1. Single.
2. Married, no children.
3. Married, one or more children.
4. Widowed.
5. Separated or divorced.

Habits and Attitudes

How often do you tell jokes?
1. Very frequently.
2. Frequently.
3. Occasionally.
4. Seldom.
5. Can't remember jokes.

Health

What is your usual state of health?
1. Never ill.
2. Never seriously ill.
3. About average.
4. Feel poorly from time to time.
5. Often feel "under the weather."

Human Relations

How do you regard your neighbors?
1. Not interested in your neighbors.
2. Like them but seldom see them.
3. Visit in each others' homes occasionally.
4. Spend a lot of time together.

Money

How much of your yearly income would you plan to save as head of a family under normal conditions?
1. 5% or less.
2. 6% to 10%.
3. 11% to 15%.
4. 16% to 20%.
5. 21% or more.

Parental Home, Childhood, Teens

During most of the time before you were 18, with whom did you live?
1. Both parents.
2. One parent.
3. A relative.
4. Foster parents or nonrelatives.
5. In a home or institution.

TABLE 3–3 (cont'd.)

Personal Attributes

How creative do you feel you are?
1. Highly creative.
2. Somewhat more creative than most in your field.
3. Moderately creative.
4. Somewhat less creative than most in your field.
5. Not creative.

Present Home, Spouse, and Children

Regarding moving from location to location, my spouse:
1. Would go willingly wherever my job takes me.
2. Would not move under any circumstances.
3. Would move only if it were absolutely necessary.
4. I don't know how he or she feels about moving.
5. Not married.

Recreation, Hobbies, and Interests

About how many fiction books have you read in the past year?
1. None.
2. 1 or 2.
3. 3 or 4.
4. 5 to 9.
5. 10 or more.

School and Education

How old were you when you graduated from high school?
1. Younger than 15.
2. 15 to 16.
3. 17 to 18.
4. 19 or older.
5. Did not graduate from high school.

Self-Impressions

Do you generally do your best:
1. At whatever job you are doing.
2. Only in what you are interested.
3. Only when it is demanded of you.

Values, Opinions, and Preferences

Which one of the following seems most important to you?
1. A pleasant home and family life.
2. A challenging and exciting job.
3. Getting ahead in the world.
4. Being active and accepted in community affairs.
5. Making the most of your particular ability.

TABLE 3–3 (cont'd.)

Work

How fast do you usually work?
1. Much faster than most people.
2. Somewhat faster than most people.
3. At about the same pace as most people.
4. Somewhat slower than most people.
5. Much slower than most people.
6. Unable to tell.

From J. R. Glennon, L. E. Albright, and W. A. Owens, *A Catalog of Life History Items*. Reproduced by the Richardson Foundation for the Scientific Affairs Committee, American Psychological Association, Division 14, 1966.

items probe the candidates' opinions or evaluations of themselves, asking, for example, how high in management they thought they had the ability to go.

The Exxon biographical inventory was developed by testing the predictive value of the items with its current executives, each of whom was rated in terms of effectiveness on the basis of salary, rank, and the judgment of peers. The responses of job applicants were then compared with the responses of already successful executives. The inventory is now being used not only for selection but also for promotion of current employees to higher levels of responsibility. Beginning in 1966, all of Exxon's professional and technical employees were given the opportunity of taking the test after two years with the company. When they reach age thirty, employees are invited to take a follow-up series of tests. The company reports that only a small number of employees have refused to take the test and management has been careful not to penalize them in any way.

One important point about Exxon's use of the biographical inventory is that they do not allow a person's score or performance on the test to take precedence over actual job performance, in cases where an employee is being considered for promotion. The test performance is used as only one part of the total evaluation procedure.

Also, the company reports that the test results are of value primarily in the early years of employment, where high scores are given considerable importance in gauging the progress to be expected (and encouraged) of a person. Those who score well on the inventory are given greater responsibility early in their careers and, if their performance matches the predicted potential, promotion thereafter will be more rapid than usual.

As noted, biographical inventories have become very popular although the amount of published research on them has decreased, perhaps indicating a concern with some of the problems inherent in this technique. First, there is the obvious problem of invasion of privacy. Some items on biographical inventories are of a very personal nature and some people (reasonably) object to being asked to reveal intimacies. Of course, not all people are bothered by being asked to reveal personal information. There are great individual differences in the questions people find objectionable. In one study of a large group of job applicants, it was found that they were most offended by questions dealing with finances and family background.[7] They were less disturbed when asked about their interests and values, social adjustment, and personal background.

But various segments of the group reacted in different ways to these personal questions. Older job applicants were less bothered by items involving interests, values, and social adjustment than were younger applicants. Women objected more than men to being asked about personal background, interests, values, and social adjustment, but were less bothered by questions about financial matters. Level of education, rural or urban background, and level of income also affected what topics the applicants considered to be private.

Invasion of privacy is a sensitive and important issue and has an obvious bearing on the selection process wherein an organization is trying to learn as much as possible about an individual. How much personal information should we have to reveal in order to get a job? There is no easy answer but it is a matter to which personnel psychologists, who design and administer biographical inventories and psychological tests, must be sympathetic.

Another problem with biographical inventories relates to equal employment opportunities. Many biographical inventory items deal with social and economic variables—homeowner versus renter, for example —and members of minority groups may be excluded from consideration because they have not had the economic advantages that are available to some others.

There is also the problem of face validity. Applicants may justifiably wonder what relationship there is between the ability to perform a certain job and their fathers' occupation, marital status, or tendency to tell jokes.

Despite these problems, however, biographical inventories have been successful as a selection device and are being used frequently and with enthusiasm.

[7] B. L. Rosenbaum, "Attitude toward invasion of privacy in the personnel selection process and job applicant demographic and personality correlates," *Journal of Applied Psychology,* **58**(1973), 333–338.

INTERVIEWS

It is extremely unlikely that anyone is hired nowadays without being subjected to a personal interview. Regardless of what other selection techniques are used, every prospective employer seems to want the chance to meet a job candidate in person. Interviews range in length from cursory meetings of five to ten minutes to elaborate affairs lasting two full days, even including questioning over dinner. Those who have been on both sides of the interview situation can attest to their grueling and tiring nature. In a university, for example, an applicant for a faculty position must talk with every member of a department, the department head, at least two deans, and the chancellor. No wonder many people consider the interview to be a stressful situation.

The primary purpose of the interview is to provide a face-to-face meeting for evaluating an applicant's suitability for employment. A frequently overlooked point about the interview is that it can provide a two-way flow of information, allowing each party to assess the other. Not only do employers gain additional information about the candidates, but applicants can learn about the organization and the job under consideration. If applicants ask the right questions, the interview situation can be used to determine if the job and company are right for them. Some candidates do this so well that the interviewers feel *they* are being interviewed!

Personnel departments and managers rely heavily on the interview as a selection tool and are extremely reluctant to hire persons without the chance to meet and question them. Personnel psychologists, on the other hand, are considerably less enthusiastic and optimistic about the value of the interview for selection; the evidence shows consistently that the interview is not a good predictor of job success. The predictive validity of the interview remains embarrassingly low, a conclusion first demonstrated in 1915 by Walter Dill Scott [8] (a founder of industrial psychology discussed in Chapter 1). Scott's conclusion is corroborated in the psychological research literature as psychologists periodically write articles summarizing the negative findings on the utility of interviews.

Experience has demonstrated, however, that no matter how many validity studies personnel psychologists conduct, the interview continues to be used for selection purposes. As a result, personnel psychologists are focusing on the mechanics and dynamics of this complex face-to-face meeting in the hope of understanding its processes and

---

[8] W. D. Scott, "The scientific selection of salesmen," *Advertising and Selling*, **25** (1915), 5–6, 94–96.

problems. The more we learn about what actually happens during an interview, the better chance there is of improving its usefulness.

Two basic kinds of interview are the standard or unstructured interview and the patterned or structured interview.

The *unstructured* interview is characterized by a lack of structure or advance planning. So loose is this method that it is sometimes considered to be haphazard. The format and approach to questioning, as well as the questions asked, are left entirely to the discretion of the individual interviewer. Thus, it is possible that five interviewers conducting separate unstructured interviews with the same applicant could receive five different impressions of the person.

A basic weakness of the unstructured interview is its lack of consistency in assessing candidates. Interviewers may be interested in different aspects of a candidate's background, experience, or attitudes, and so the results of the interviews may reflect more of the characteristics, biases, and prejudices of the interviewers than objective abilities of the applicant. This lack of consistency among interviews causes this method to be extremely low in predictive accuracy. Despite its recognized limitations, however, the unstructured interview is heavily relied upon in many organizations. Some companies use this approach as a preliminary, get-acquainted technique and follow it up in the selection process by a more structured interview.

Following an unstructured interview, some organizations require interviewers to note their impressions of a candidate on an evaluation form. Figures 3–3 and 3–4 show portions of two forms designed to be filled out immediately upon completion of the interview. Note the scope of the judgments called for in areas ranging from physical appearance and education to ability to work with others, maturity, drive, and potential. These are extremely difficult characteristics to assess on the basis of a limited interview and it is not surprising that such assessments are often deficient.

The opposite of the loose and haphazard unstructured interview is the patterned or *structured* interview. This approach uses a predetermined list of interview questions that are asked of every applicant in a particular job category. Thus, the entire interview procedure is standardized so that the resulting assessment of candidates is less open to interviewer bias. Although subjective and personal factors can still influence the interviewer's judgment (no procedure can eliminate this factor entirely in an interpersonal situation), this is less of a problem in the structured interview.

In conducting a structured interview, the interviewer uses a printed form containing the questions to be asked of each applicant. The candidate's responses are recorded on the same form. So formalized is this approach that it has been characterized as an application blank

EMPLOYMENT EVALUATION

CIRCLE ONE		COMMENTS
ABOVE AVERAGE / OUTSTANDING BELOW AVERAGE / AVERAGE		Appearance; physical characteristics; dress; grooming as required by the position applied for.
BELOW AVERAGE / AVERAGE ABOVE AVERAGE / OUTSTANDING		General education; total academic record at high school and college in relation to the requirements of the job.
AVERAGE / OUTSTANDING ABOVE AVERAGE / BELOW AVERAGE		Other education; achievement at technical, trade, military, business, secretarial and similar schools.
OUTSTANDING / AVERAGE BELOW AVERAGE / ABOVE AVERAGE		Work history; demonstrated work performance; type of previous positions held, length of employment with each employer; reasons for leaving and work gaps in employment record.
ABOVE AVERAGE / OUTSTANDING BELOW AVERAGE / AVERAGE		Specific skills, type of skills possessed, and the applicant's ability to perform these skills, as required by the position applied for.
BELOW AVERAGE / AVERAGE ABOVE AVERAGE / OUTSTANDING		Ability to deal with others, work well with supervisors and fellow workers; sense of public relations; communications skills.
AVERAGE / OUTSTANDING ABOVE AVERAGE / BELOW AVERAGE		Financial responsibility, obligations handled promptly; total debts and cost of living are consistent with current and past earnings.
OUTSTANDING / AVERAGE BELOW AVERAGE / ABOVE AVERAGE		Intelligence, problem-solving ability and alert thinking.
ABOVE AVERAGE / OUTSTANDING BELOW AVERAGE / AVERAGE		Maturity; practical individual; ambitions and goals in relation to capabilities; responsible person; record free of law violations.
BELOW AVERAGE / AVERAGE ABOVE AVERAGE / OUTSTANDING		Over-all evaluation; a summary of your judgments on the above items as they relate in importance to the position applied for.

DIRECTIONS

PLEASE READ CAREFULLY BEFORE COMPLETING THE EVALUATION

In considering applicants, (including employees requesting promotions/transfers) remember our policy *not* to discriminate on the basis of race, creed, color, national origin, sex, or age.

Based on your interview discussion, evaluate the applicant on each of the specific items to the (left). *Complete this evaluation immediately after the interview in order to preserve all of the pertinent details.*

For each item, decide how the applicant compares with employees successfully performing the responsibilities of the position applied for. Is the applicant:

Outstanding—Ranking among the top 10% on this factor.

Above Average—Ranking among the top 25%, but not the top 10% on this factor.

Average—Ranking among the middle 50% on this factor.

Below Average—Ranking among the bottom 25% on this factor.

Exercise careful judgment in interpreting facts and records. Have available the specific requirements of the position for which the applicant is being considered. Avoid the tendency to rate leniently or always average. Circle the one category which best expresses your judgment for each item.

Figure 3–3. Postinterview applicant evaluation form. Reprinted by permission of Eastern Airlines Inc.

that the interviewer fills out on the basis of what the applicant says.

Sample structured interview questions are listed as follows. These are used by a company to select college graduates for management positions. The first set of questions deals with prior work experience and is intended for applicants who have had at least one job since graduation.

1. What was your first job after leaving college?
2. What would you say your major accomplishments were on that job?
3. What were some of the things you might have done less well, things that perhaps pointed to the opportunity for further development?
4. What did you learn about yourself on that job?
5. What aspects of the job did you find most stimulating and satisfying?
6. What are some of the things you look for in any job?
7. What are your thoughts about the future? What sort of work would you like to be doing five or ten years from now?
8. Looking back over the past ten years, what would you say were the most important ways in which you have changed in that time?

The following set of questions involves the applicant's early home-life. (Recall the earlier discussion of invasion of privacy.)

1. How would you describe your father in terms of his temperament or personality?
2. What influence would you say he had on your development?
3. How would you describe your mother?
4. What influence would you say she had on your development?
5. Was discipline at home strict, lenient, or what?
6. What traits or characteristics would you say you picked up from your parents—it is only natural that, after living with people for a number of years, some of these characteristics should be shared.
7. What parent would you say you resemble the most? In what way?
8. What, if anything, about your early home background, do you wish might have been different?

Since all applicants are asked the same questions in sequence, there is a firmer basis for the comparison of candidates than there is using the random questioning procedures of the unstructured interview.

PERSONAL PRESENTATION AND COMMUNICATIONS SKILLS—Consider the candidate's ability to communicate with others in relation to the requirements of the position applied for.

CIRCLE ONE

Appearance	Superior	Above Average	Average	Below Average	Unable to Rate
Poise/Polish	Unable to Rate	Below Average	Average	Above Average	Superior
Written Communication (clear, concise, logical, etc.)	Superior	Above Average	Average	Below Average	Unable to Rate
Oral Communication (clear, concise, logical, etc.)	Unable to Rate	Below Average	Average	Above Average	Superior

SKILLS IN PERSONAL RELATIONSHIPS—Consider the candidate's ability to deal effectively with subordinates, peers and superiors in relation to the requirements of the position applied for.

CIRCLE ONE

Tact	Superior	Above Average	Average	Below Average	Unable to Rate
Consideration for Others	Unable to Rate	Below Average	Average	Above Average	Superior
Ability to Get Work Done *With* Others	Superior	Above Average	Average	Below Average	Unable to Rate
Ability to Get Work Done *Through* Others	Unable to Rate	Below Average	Average	Above Average	Superior
Leadership	Superior	Above Average	Average	Below Average	Unable to Rate

DRIVE—Consider the candidate's ability in "getting on with the job" in relation to the requirements of the position applied for.

CIRCLE ONE

Initiative/Self-starter	Superior	Above Average	Average	Below Average	Unable to Rate
Enthusiasm	Unable to Rate	Below Average	Average	Above Average	Superior
Capacity for Work	Superior	Above Average	Average	Below Average	Unable to Rate

PERSONAL GOALS—Consider the degree to which the candidate has thought through goals and objectives.

CIRCLE ONE

Goals/Objectives (definite, well thought out)	Superior	Above Average	Average	Below Average	Unable to Rate
Career Plans (definite, well thought out)	Unable to Rate	Below Average	Average	Above Average	Superior
Consistency of Goals and Objectives with Capabilities (reasonable, realistic)	Superior	Above Average	Average	Below Average	Unable to Rate

POTENTIAL—Consider the degree to which the candidate is capable of assuming future responsibilities.

CIRCLE ONE

Growth—Can assume increasingly more responsible positions similar or related to the position applied for	Superior	Above Average	Average	Below Average	Unable to Rate
Flexibility—Can assume increasingly more responsible positions not necessarily similar or related to the position applied for	Unable to Rate	Below Average	Average	Above Average	Superior
Level Capable of Reaching— Supervisor	Superior	Above Average	Average	Below Average	Unable to Rate
Manager	Unable to Rate	Below Average	Average	Above Average	Superior
Director	Superior	Above Average	Average	Below Average	Unable to Rate
Officer	Unable to Rate	Below Average	Average	Above Average	Superior

OVERALL EVALUATION—Considering all of the preceding factors, assess the degree to which the candidate meets the total requirements of the position applied for.

CIRCLE ONE

Superior	Above Average	Average	Below Average

Structured interviews represent a considerable improvement over unstructured interviews and have the potential for higher predictive validity. A number of studies verify this. In one investigation,[9] three interviewing strategies were compared: (1) a structured interview in which the interviewer followed explicitly the questions on an interview guide, (2) a semistructured interview in which the guide was followed but the interviewer was free to interject additional questions, and (3) an unstructured interview in which no guide was used. The results strongly favored the fully structured interview; there was considerably greater agreement among interviewers as compared to the less structured approaches. Under the structured interview condition, interviewers were able to apply a consistent frame of reference to all applicants since the identical questions were asked in the same order. The interviewers using the semistructured and unstructured approaches were able to get more information from the applicants (since interviewers could diverge from the interview guide), but this information was not systematic or organized (or necessarily relevant) and served only to make the evaluation of the applicants more difficult.

Thus, the interview can be made a more useful selection device if it is formalized and structured. Unfortunately, the structured interview is not universally used; many organizations still rely on the freewheeling, undependable, unstructured approach.

A relatively recent innovation in interviewing is the use of videotape. This does not involve a traditional, face-to-face, question-and-answer interview. Rather, it is the applicant's side of an interview that the personnel manager can see and hear, but not respond to. Nevertheless, videotape can save time and money for both employers and applicants.

Employers may obtain much useful information by watching a tape of applicants describing themselves—their interests, abilities, values, and backgrounds. Clearly unsuitable candidates can be eliminated before undertaking the effort and expense of other selection procedures. An employment agency with a file of interview tapes can greatly speed up the initial screening process for a large organization.

Videotapes can work in the other direction as well. Some employment agencies maintain tape files of personnel managers describing the requirements and advantages of available jobs with their organizations. Applicants can quickly weed out jobs that are obviously unsuitable for them, saving them the time and expense of a personal visit to each company.

[9] R. Carlson, D. Schwab, and H. Heneman III, "Agreement among selection interview styles," *Journal of Industrial Psychology*, **1** (1970), 8–17.

Figure 3–4 (opposite). Postinterview professional employment candidate evaluation form. Reprinted by permission of Eastern Airlines Inc.

The use of the videotape interview seems to offer definite advantages in the selection process and is rapidly gaining in popularity.

It is fortunate that in at least some organizations the interview is not the sole selection technique, since it is so notoriously inaccurate by itself. There are a number of additional problems with its use that must be overcome.

(1) Failure of Interviewers to Agree

A major problem with the interview is the difficulty of getting several interviewers to agree in their assessments of the same applicant, particularly with the unstructured interview technique. A classic study in the area [10] involved having twelve interviewers rate fifty-seven applicants on their suitability for a sales job. The interviewers were experienced sales managers who, throughout their careers, had conducted many interviews with job applicants. There was a total lack of agreement among the interviewers. Some applicants ranked first by one interviewer in order of suitability for the job were ranked last by another. Figure 3–5 shows the rankings of one applicant by the twelve interviewers.

If the person responsible for making the final decision about hiring this individual were given this interview information, it would surely be of little help. It offers no firm basis on which to make the decision. Remember that these assorted ratings were all assigned to the same applicant; the differences are because of the interviewer, not the interviewee.

It is possible to partially overcome this lack of consistency. If interviewers are trained to follow standard patterns in their questioning (as in the structured interview technique), and to make their evaluations in standard objective terms, then consistency can be increased. The more highly formalized or structured is the interview procedure, the greater will be the agreement among interviewers. Although this is feasible in principle, it is not widely practiced.

(2) Failure to Predict Job Success

Even if the problem of interviewer consistency were solved, there remain the difficulties with the predictive accuracy or validity of the interview technique. Research has demonstrated a disappointingly low correlation between interview judgments and subsequent job success.

[10] H. L. Hollingworth, *Vocational Psychology and Character Analysis* (New York: Appleton, 1929), pp. 115–119.

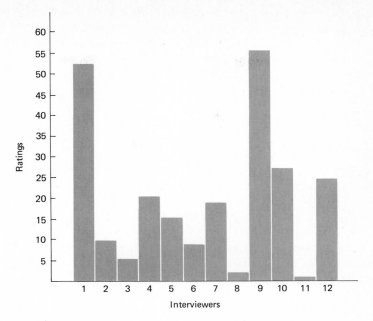

Figure 3–5. Ratings of one applicant by twelve interviewers. Data from H. L. Hollingworth, *Vocational Psychology and Character Analysis* (New York: Appleton, 1929).

However, the highly structured interview has been shown to be a more valid predictive device than the unstructured interview.

As noted, the major cause for the lack of predictive utility is that the interview is a subjective interpersonal process. The interviewer's assessment of a candidate can be distorted by personal prejudices as well as by the nature of the interview situation.

(3) Stress of the Interview Situation

In an interview, it is natural to expect a certain amount of nervousness on the part of the applicants. They know that the impression they make on the interviewer will determine, at least in part, whether or not they will be offered the job. As a result, normally calm and composed persons may appear tense and unable to express themselves well. They may behave in a manner totally uncharacteristic of their subsequent behavior on the job, and this atypical behavior may mislead the interviewer.

A trained and experienced interviewer can do much to prevent or reduce applicants' nervousness by trying to establish a rapport early in the interview. How sympathetic, understanding, and friendly the interviewer appears can influence the applicants' behavior which, in turn, influences the interviewer's assessment.

Stress in the interview situation can also operate on interviewers, particularly if they are behind in their quotas and are being pressured by the home office. In one study, three groups of managers evaluated descriptions of the same applicants: one group of managers was behind in its quota, another group was ahead, and the third group had no quota. The managers under the quota pressure perceived the applicants as having greater potential and said that they would hire more of them than did the other two groups of managers who were evaluating the same applicants.

(4) Interviewers' Standards of Comparison

Many interviewers see many job applicants, often one after another, and how they evaluate a particular applicant depends on the characteristics of those persons whom they had interviewed previously. For example, after having interviewed three very undesirable candidates, an interviewer will tend to see an average candidate in a more favorable light than that candidate's qualifications actually merit. That average candidate would be viewed less favorably by the interviewer if the previous applicants had all been highly qualified for the job.

In addition to pointing up the importance of your place in an interviewer's schedule, this situation means that interviewers often do not have any standard for the kind of person who is considered a suitable employee. Applicants are not evaluated on an absolute basis but rather are judged relative to the other applicants on a particular day or week. How favorable an applicant appears depends on how good or poor the others are; in other words, the standard for the suitable employee is constantly changing.

(5) Interviewers' Prejudices

Another characteristic of interviewers that can influence their judgment is their own likes and dislikes. An interviewer may dislike people who smoke, have foreign-sounding names, red hair, and do not meet the interviewer's gaze. This short, white-haired, fastidious, conservative interviewer will not be kindly disposed toward a tall, shy, red-haired, chain-smoking job applicant whose name has five syllables.

Biases can operate both ways. Just as interviewers may dislike people with certain characteristics and disqualify them for a job regardless of their qualifications, they may also hire others simply because they exhibit some characteristic the interviewer likes. For example, in the human factors department of one aerospace company, no employee was taller than the rather short department head. A short person had a definite advantage in being favorably assessed.

This phenomenon of generalizing from one trait or characteristic to the entire person, in either a positive or negative direction, is called the *halo effect,* and it is present whenever we fallible human beings make personal judgments about others.

As difficult, limited, and error-prone as the interview is, it continues to be part of virtually every selection program in industry and government. The danger lies in placing too much emphasis on it. If used sparingly and wisely as an adjunct to more objective methods of selection, the interview can be of help to both the company and the applicant. (At least it may not do much harm.)

REFERENCES AND LETTERS OF RECOMMENDATION

A frequently used technique in the total selection process involves obtaining information about applicants from those who have known them, for example, former teachers, co-workers, employers, and perhaps friends. The purpose of this is to explore other people's impressions of the applicants and to verify the nature of the work experience the applicants report. It is not unreasonable to expect that the workers' performance, attitude, and general behavior in a past job will provide some indication of how they may behave in the job for which they are applying.

The major limitation to the use of letters of recommendation is that they may present a misleading picture of the applicant. The person writing the reference may deliberately lie about a candidate's abilities, for several reasons. A past employer may simply wish to be kind and so will not say anything unfavorable about a former employee. Or, an applicant's present employer may give an undesirable employee a glowing letter of recommendation in hopes that another company will hire the employee.

There are less sinister reasons for inaccurate letters of recommendation. A former employer may not have known the employee well enough to offer an evaluation and will therefore send a general form letter signifying little. Further, even if the worker was known to the employer, the latter may not possess the ability to describe and assess the worker accurately. In general, most letters of recommendation tend to be overly lenient; most employers are reluctant to give a negative reference to former employees.

Traditionally, there are four approaches to securing letters of recommendation. Usually, the former employer is asked to write a *letter* describing various aspects of the candidate. Sometimes a *questionnaire* is used and the former employer is asked to provide detailed information where known.

The U.S. Civil Service Commission uses the questionnaire approach, sending the Employment Recommendation Questionnaire (ERQ) to an applicant's list of references. Extensive research on the ERQ has demonstrated that even this objective questionnaire approach has limited predictive validity.

When success on the job was compared with the source of the ERQ recommendations (whether the reference was provided by a friend, co-worker, or relative), one study showed that former supervisors and friends supplied the most valid recommendation information. The recommendations of personnel workers were totally lacking in validity and the recommendations of relatives were negatively related to job success.

An interesting and potentially useful way of checking references involves the *forced-choice questionnaire*. In this situation, the person giving the reference is forced to choose the one item in each of a number of pairs of items that best describes the former employee. What makes this unique is that the items in each pair appear to be equally favorable to the employee.[11] For example:

(1)	(2)
Has many worthwhile ideas ———	Always works fast ———
Completes all assignments ———	Requires little supervision ———

Neither of the alternatives in pair (1) or pair (2) seems unfavorable and so the person giving the reference may still feel that he or she is giving a positive recommendation. However, one item in each pair is more highly predictive of success; it has a higher correlation with actual job performance.

This seems to be a promising technique although it is expensive and time-consuming to conduct the necessary research relating the individual questionnaire items to job performance. For that reason, the force-choice reference check is usually limited to selection for clerical or other types of jobs that an organization fills in large numbers. Assuming that the research is soundly conducted, this technique may be the most valid way a prospective employer has of finding out what past employers think of one of their former employees.

[11] S. J. Carroll, Jr., and A. N. Nash, "Effectiveness of a forced-choice reference check," *Personnel Administration*, **35**(2) (1972), 42–46.

Another way of checking references is to interview the persons over the *telephone*. A skillful interviewer can obtain a more accurate and thorough evaluation of a candidate in this manner than with a questionnaire or letter. People are often more willing to speak frankly when they are not committing their views to paper. Also, more specific as well as follow-up questions can be asked in a telephone conversation because it is a more flexible interview situation.

A costly and time-consuming approach is the *field investigation* in which references are interviewed in person. Research with this technique has shown that it can elicit a great deal of information not obtainable through letters. For example, in comparing the results of the ERQ with field interviews on the same applicants it was found that damaging information such as job incompetence, homosexuality, and alcoholism uncovered in the field interviews with references had not been mentioned in the written recommendations.

Obviously, the amount of effort a prospective employer is willing to expend on checking an applicant's references depends on the level and importance of the job, a point equally applicable to all selection techniques. The more effort put into a selection technique, the greater the chance of securing meaningful and helpful information about the candidate.

ASSESSMENT CENTERS: SELECTION BY SIMULATION

The assessment center is a popular method of selection that places applicants in a simulated job situation so that their behavior under stress can be observed and assessed. This approach, also called situational testing, was initially developed and used during World War II by the Office of Strategic Services (OSS).

The mission of the OSS was to send secret agents behind enemy lines; their selection procedures were designed to induce a high level of stress. How candidates reacted to these conditions, it was thought, would be predictive of how they would react to the stress of behind-the-lines operations.

One test required the candidate to build a bridge across a stream in a fixed period of time. No plans were given but the candidate was assigned a group of workers. In this way, the candidate's ingenuity, ability to improvise, and leadership skills could be appraised in a real-life setting. Further, to see how the candidate reacted to frustration, some of the workers assigned were stooges, instructed to do everything possible to prevent the building of the bridge. Many candidates broke down in tears when faced with such maddening frustration.

The simulation techniques used by business organizations today are not quite as stressful as those of the OSS, but they are realistic enough so that it is possible to see how candidates work under pressure, or how flexible they are in adapting to rapidly changing situations.

The use of situational testing in industry was pioneered by the American Telephone and Telegraph Company (AT&T) in the mid-1950s and has since been adopted by many organizations including IBM, Standard Oil of Ohio, the U.S. Department of Agriculture, Ford Motor Company, and Kodak. More than one hundred thousand people have already participated in assessment centers, at least seventy thousand from AT&T alone. For the most part, assessment centers are used to select managers and executives.

Assessment centers usually involve six to twelve candidates at a time who are evaluated as they work through a series of exercises over several days. Candidates may be given psychological tests (particularly intelligence and personality tests), and they are interviewed extensively, but most of the time is devoted to exercises designed to simulate the problems of high-level jobs. The candidates perform these work samples using the in-basket technique or the leaderless group discussion. Both exercises are faithful reproductions of managerial-level work.

The *in-basket* test presents each applicant with an in-basket such as that found on virtually every managerial or executive desk. The in-basket contains the typical problems, questions, and directives that managers would find when they returned to work from vacation. The applicants must process this material in a fixed period of time; that is, they must demonstrate how they would handle such questions and problems on the job. After the exercise, the applicants may be required to justify their decisions in personal interviews with the assessors.

In the *leaderless group discussion,* the applicants meet as a group to discuss an actual business problem. For example, they might be given information about a group of subordinates from among whom they must select one for promotion. As the meeting proceeds, their behavior is observed to see how each participant interacts with the others and what leadership and persuasive skills each displays.

The most widespread campaign to assess future managers by the assessment center technique has been undertaken by AT&T. Using sixty assessment centers located throughout the Bell Telephone System, the company assigns six or seven managers for six months of duty at the centers, and they are given three weeks of training by company psychologists before evaluating candidates.

AT&T's program relies heavily on the in-basket exercise. The candidate, acting as a supervisor, must process twenty-five items—memos, orders, and correspondence—in three hours. The assessors observe the candidates to see if they are systematic and establish priorities, delegate authority to subordinates, or become enmeshed in trivialities. For most candidates, this is their first taste of managerial responsibility; some don't like it and refuse any forthcoming promotion. It certainly seems better for the employee and the company to come to this realization at this point, rather than later, after the employee has spent an unsatisfactory and frustrating period on the job as a manager.

AT&T also uses the leaderless group discussion. In one example, a group of five or six candidates were told that they were managers of a company directed to increase profits in a fixed period of time. They were given information about the company and the market, but no one was appointed leader and no rules were set forth as to how they would accomplish their goal. Usually, one candidate will assume leadership and his or her ability to fulfill leadership responsibilities can be evaluated. The other group members are assessed on their cooperation in performing the tasks assigned by the leader.

To induce additional pressure, the group is notified of a change in price or costs every twenty minutes, sometimes immediately after the total problem has been solved! The new information must be considered, however, and the discussion renewed. All the while the candidates are being watched by the assessors and the clock is ticking away. The situation is extremely stressful for the participants. Some become tense, nervous, and angry, disrupting the group and being obstructive. As the exercise progresses, the contrast between those who can function well under this kind of pressure and those who cannot becomes obvious.

In another example of the use of assessment centers, Sears, Roebuck sends all of its college graduate applicants to an assessment center where they participate in two simulated management exercises as part of the selection process. The graduates who are hired as management trainees are exposed to a second round of simulation exercises thirty-two weeks after they are hired. Those who do well on these exercises and have shown promise on other selection tests are designated for faster promotion to middle and upper management. The Sears management believes that the simulation exercises are an extremely valuable supplement to the standard techniques of selection.

Assessment centers can be a target of resentment and complaint, particularly from those who perform poorly in the exercises. Many persons believe that being evaluated unfavorably in an assessment center marks the end of their career, no matter how brilliant a record they may have compiled in their years on the job. Some candidates believe that success in an assessment center depends more on being outgoing, glib, or having a sparkling personality than on competence at managerial tasks.

There may be some truth to these charges. Several studies have demonstrated that interpersonal skills play a major role in the assessments given. Active and aggressive participation becomes an important criterion in the evaluations, perhaps to the point where quantity rather than quality of participation is rewarded. Of course, interpersonal skills are an undeniable part of executive functioning. Research does confirm, however, that the second criterion on which ratings are based is organizing and decision-making ability. This provides a more direct reflection of managerial competence.

Organizations using the assessment center technique believe that it is well worth the estimated $500 to $600 it costs to evaluate each candidate. Studies have shown that those persons selected for managerial jobs by means of assessment centers, or promoted from within the organization to higher-level jobs, perform as much as 50 per cent better than those selected by traditional techniques. Other studies have shown that job candidates who received favorable assessments were much more likely to be promoted in the organization (even when their superiors did not have access to their assessment center evaluations) than were those who were assessed unfavorably. The latter were also much more likely to fail as managers.

An unintended but valuable advantage of the assessment center technique is the development of behavioral observation, group dynamics, and problem-solving skills in the assessors. Assessors are typically managers from the organization who are sent to a center for a short period of time. Initially, their role was just to evaluate candidates, but the experience also provided them with extensive management development training.

The assessment center experience is also a training exercise for the candidates. Their management and interpersonal skills (in addition to being assessed) are refined by the feedback they receive from the assessors.

Another advantage of assessment centers is that they do not conflict with legal requirements for equal employment opportunities. The exercises present realistic samples of the job for which a candidate is applying. Therefore, they are not open to the charge of irrelevance, as is the case with some psychological test or application blank information. The exercises are clearly job related.

STANDARD SUCCESS PREDICTORS FOR MANAGERS

When a company is choosing from among a group of college graduates, it almost always considers the applicant's performance on several background success predictors such as college grades, quality of the college attended, and extracurricular activity participation. Regardless of the selection techniques used by a company, these standard factors will be determined early in the selection process. Often, a candidate with a poor showing on these items will be eliminated.

On the surface, this approach seems to make sense. It is reasonable to suppose that an applicant who graduated with top grades from a prestigious Ivy League university will make a better manager than one with average or lower grades from a lesser known university.

Research has shown, however, that these alleged success predictors do not always predict subsequent successful job performance. Surveys were conducted at Dartmouth College and Purdue University. In both cases, grades were indeed found to be positively related to later job success, but a significant number of graduates who received low grades also went on to become successful in management. In the Purdue study, 25 per cent of the graduates who had received high grades advanced to high salary levels; 9 per cent of those with low grades also advanced to high salary levels.

These and other studies suggest two things about the background success predictors: (1) not all those who are high in these characteristics are later successful on the job; and (2) some of those who are low in these characteristics are successful on the job. Although common sense seems to favor choosing those high on standard predictor variables, it is a waste of talent to automatically reject persons low on these variables, without giving them a chance to demonstrate their abilities on additional selection procedures.

No matter which selection technique or criterion is preferred, it should not be relied upon exclusively. No technique is infallible. A selection program should include a combination of techniques in order to maximize the chances of matching the right person with the right job.

SUMMARY

The proper selection of employees—matching the right person with the right job—is a vital and complex process. A selection program requires a sequence of specific operations including (1) job analysis, (2) worker analysis, (3) establishment of minimal requirements and cut-off scores for the selection techniques, (4) recruitment of applicants, (5) administration of the chosen selection techniques, and (6) validation of the techniques (finding out how well they correlate with some measure of subsequent performance on the job).

The selection process has been greatly affected by federal and state legislation designed to guarantee equal employment opportunities for all persons regardless of race, color, religion, sex, or national origin. Every method of selection must be shown to be nondiscriminatory.

The first step in the selection process, **job analysis,** involves a highly detailed description of the component tasks performed on a job. The results are used not only for selection but also to set up training programs, to redesign jobs, and to reveal safety hazards in equipment design or work procedures. Job analysis can be undertaken by (1) referring to published job analyses such as the *Dictionary of Occupational Titles,* (2) interviewing those who are directly connected with the job in person or through questionnaires, (3) directly observing the workers performing the job, (4) having the workers keep a systematic log of daily job activities, and (5) recording critical incidents that are vital to successful performance of the job. On the basis of the information collected in the job analysis, a **job specification** is written, which defines the characteristics to be sought in those persons who apply for the job.

Recruitment procedures influence the **selection ratio,** which, in turn, influences the standards of employment. For example, if not enough people are recruited, there will be fewer job applicants to choose among. Some requirements, therefore (a certain score on an intelligence test, perhaps), will have to be lowered.

A major problem in recruiting is honesty, presenting an accurate description of the job. This can be accomplished through a realistic **job preview** that presents—on film, in a brochure, or in an actual job sample—the good and bad points of the job so that applicants do not have unrealistic expectations about what the work will be like.

Psychologists have conducted much research on the characteristics of recruiters to identify those aspects of recruiter behavior that are appealing or repulsive to job candidates. Also, the recruitment process is aided by psychological research on what satisfactions job seekers desire in their work.

Specific techniques of selection that have been discussed are application blanks (and derivatives such as weighted application blanks and biographical inventories), interviews, letters of recommendation, and assessment centers.

Application blanks can provide much useful information about job candidates that can be directly related to the probability of success on the job. As an instrument of selection, the application blank first requires research to correlate each item of information with some subsequent objective measure of job performance. Weighted application blanks and biographical inventories have been successful in predicting success on the job and are not unlike some psychological tests in objectivity of scoring and the types of questions that are used.

The **interview** as a selection device, despite consistently unfavorable research findings, continues to be relied upon by employing organizations. The weakest interview is the **unstructured** approach; the **structured** interview is a potentially more valid predictive device. Basic weaknesses of interviews are (1) failure of interviewers to agree, (2) failure of interviews to predict job success, (3) pressure of the interview situation, (4) interviewers' subjective standards of comparison, and (5) interviewers' prejudices.

Letters of recommendation, despite the recognized tendency of letter writers to be overly kind, are part of most selection programs. There are four ways for an employer to secure recommendations on a job applicant: (1) ask the person's former employer to write a letter or (2) fill out a questionnaire, (3) telephone the former employer, and (4) interview the former employer in person. A promising technique is the forced-choice questionnaire, which is designed to eliminate the tendency of the reference to be lenient.

A selection technique that is used primarily for selecting managers and executives is the **assessment center,** in which job candidates perform a series of exercises that realistically simulate problems found on the job. Using mainly the **in-basket technique** and the **leaderless group discussion,** applicants are assessed by trained managers on their interpersonal skills and leadership and decision-making abilities. Although the assessment center approach has some problems, these seem to be far outweighed by advantages that include high predictive validity, compatibility with equal employment opportunity legislation, and management development training for both the candidates and the assessors.

No matter which selection technique or criterion is preferred, it should not be relied upon exclusively. No technique is infallible. A selection program should include a combination of techniques in order to maximize the chances of matching the right person with the right job.

SUGGESTED READINGS

General

Asch, P., and Kroeker, L. Personnel selection, classification, and placement. *Annual Review of Psychology,* 1975, **26,** 481–507.

Bray, D., and Moses, J. Personnel selection. *Annual Review of Psychology,* 1972, **23**, 545–576.

Guion, R. Recruiting, selection, and job placement. In M. Dunnette, Ed., *Handbook of Industrial and Organizational Psychology.* Chicago: Rand McNally, 1976. Pp. 777–828.

Oliva, M. Selection techniques and the black hard–core male. *Personnel Journal,* 1970, **49,** 424–430.

Application Blanks and References

Asher, J. J. The biographical item: Can it be improved? *Personnel Psychology,* 1972, **25,** 251–269.

Carroll, S., and Nash, A. Effectiveness of a forced–choice reference check. *Personnel Administration,* 1972, **35**(2), 42–46.

Hershey, R. The application form. *Personnel,* 1971, **48**(1), 36–39.

McKillip, R., and Clark, C. *Biographical Data and Job Performance.* Washington, D.C.: U.S. Civil Service Commission, Personnel Research and Development Center, 1974. TM 74–1.

Novack, S. Developing an effective application blank. *Personnel Journal,* 1970, **49,** 419–423.

Owens, W. Background data. In M. Dunnette, Ed., *Handbook of Industrial and Organizational Psychology.* Chicago: Rand McNally, 1976. Pp. 609–644.

Assessment Centers

Baker, D., and Martin, C. *Evaluation of the Federal Executive Development Program Assessment Center.* Washington, D.C.: U.S. Civil Service Commission, Personnel Research and Development Center, 1974. TM 74–4.

Bender, J. What is "typical" of assessment centers? *Personnel,* 1973, **50**(4), 50–57.

Finkle, R. Managerial assessment centers. In M. Dunnette, Ed., *Handbook of Industrial and Organizational Psychology.* Chicago: Rand McNally, 1976. Pp. 861–888.

Huck, J. Assessment centers: A review of external and internal validities. *Personnel Psychology,* 1973, **26,** 191–212.

Kraut, A. A hard look at management assessment centers and their future. *Personnel Journal,* 1972, **51,** 317–326.

Moses, J. The development of an assessment center for the early identification of supervisory potential. *Personnel Psychology,* 1973, **26,** 569–580.

Wilson, J., and Tatge, W. Assessment centers—further assessment needed? *Personnel Journal,* 1973, **52,** 172–179.

Fair Employment

Bem, S., and Bem, D. Does sex-biased job advertising "aid and abet" sex discrimination? *Journal of Applied Social Psychology,* 1973, **3,** 6–18.

Foxley, C. *Locating, Recruiting, and Employing Women: An Equal Opportunity Approach.* Garrett Park, Md.: Garrett Park Press, 1976.

Minter, R. Human rights laws and pre–employment inquiries. *Personnel Journal,* 1972, **51,** 431–433.

Mitchell, E. *The Employer's Guide to the Law on Employment Protection, Sex and Race Discrimination.* Boston: Cahners, 1976.

Petersen, G., and Bryant, L. Eliminating sex discrimination: Who must act? *Personnel Journal,* 1973, **52,** 587–591.

Ruch, F. The impact on employment procedures of the Supreme Court decision in the Duke Power case. *Personnel Journal,* 1971, **50,** 777–783.

Seligman, D. How equal opportunity turned into employment quotas. *Fortune,* 1973, **87**(March), 160–163.

Interviews

As you were saying: Innovation in personnel recruitment. *Personnel Journal,* 1973, **52,** 913–914. (about videotape interviewing)

Carlson, R., Thayer, P., Mayfield, E., and Peterson, D. Improvements in the selection interview. *Personnel Journal,* 1971, **50,** 268–275.

Hollman, T. Employment interviewers' errors in processing positive and negative information. *Journal of Applied Psychology,* 1972, **56,** 130–134.

Lopez, F. *Personnel Interviewing,* rev. ed. New York: McGraw-Hill, 1975.

O'Leary, L. *Interviewing for the Decisionmaker.* Chicago: Nelson–Hall, 1976.

Rogers, J., and Fortson, W. *Fair Employment Interviewing.* Reading, Mass.: Addison–Wesley, 1976.

Valenzi, E., and Andrews, E. Individual differences in the decision process of employment interviewers. *Journal of Applied Psychology,* 1973, **58,** 49–53.

Job Analysis

McCormick, E. Job and task analysis. In M. Dunnette, Ed., *Handbook of Industrial and Organizational Psychology.* Chicago: Rand McNally, 1976. Pp. 651–696.

Prien, E., and Ronan, W. Job analysis: A review of research findings. *Personnel Psychology,* 1973, **24,** 371–396.

Recruiting

Alderfer, C., and McCord, C. Personal and situational factors in the recruitment interview. *Journal of Applied Psychology,* 1970, **54,** 377–385.

Brecher, R. Ten common mistakes in college recruiting—or how to try without really succeeding. *Personnel,* 1975, **52**(2), 19–28.

Glueck, W. How recruiters influence job choices on campus. *Personnel,* 1971, **48**(2), 46–52.

Raphael, M. Work previews can reduce turnover and improve performance. *Personnel Journal,* 1975, **54,** 97–98.

Schmitt, N., and Coyle, B. Applicant decisions in the employment interview. *Journal of Applied Psychology,* 1976, **61,** 184–192.

Wanous, J. Effects of a realistic job preview on job acceptance, job attitudes, and job survival. *Journal of Applied Psychology,* 1973, **58,** 327–331.

Wanous, J. Tell it like it is at realistic job previews. *Personnel,* 1975, **52**(4), 50–60.

Ward, L., and Athos, A. *Student Expectations of Corporate Life: Implications for Management Recruiting.* Boston: Harvard University Graduate School of Business Administration, 1972.

4

Employee Selection II: Psychological Testing

INTRODUCTION

An important personnel selection technique used by a great many employing organizations is the psychological test. As virtually everyone can attest, the use of psychological tests is widespread at all levels and periods of life.

Most public school systems give intelligence, aptitude, and interest tests to pupils at various stages in their education. If students are experiencing academic or social difficulties in school, they are likely to be referred to a school psychologist who will administer additional psychological tests to help diagnose the problem.

Nearly all those who attend college are admitted partly on the basis of their performance on an entrance examination. Those who want to pursue their education in professional or graduate schools must take competitive examinations. In addition, persons headed for military service find that there is a test for almost every job and rank in the military. Indeed, one of their first few days in the service will be spent taking a comprehensive battery of tests.

In industry, tests are used to select employees for all levels of corporate responsibility, from apprentice to president. Many organizations administer tests not only to applicants but also to current workers to determine which ones have the ability to be promoted.

Some people believe that organizations rely too heavily upon psychological tests. Others suggest, with good reason, that many of the tests in daily use are worthless. Still other critics, including the U.S. Congress, argue that testing constitutes an unwelcome and unwarranted invasion of privacy. And finally, the problem of providing equal employment opportunities offers a massive challenge to the use of tests as selection devices, a challenge so severe that the use of testing in industry is experiencing a slight decline for the first time in its long history.

However, in spite of these growing criticisms, it is still true that in most walks of life it is impossible to progress without being asked to take some kind of psychological test. In your working career, your performance on psychological tests can determine not only if you will be hired for a job but also what level you will reach by the time of retirement.

The technical and ethical questions involved in emphasizing test performance are constantly argued by psychologists in universities, government, and business. But as long as tests continue to play such a prominent role in your life, it is vital that you have some understanding of what they are, what they can and cannot do, and what their dangers and limitations may be.

WHAT IS A PSYCHOLOGICAL TEST?

A psychological test is a measuring device, a yardstick applied in consistent and systematic fashion to measure a sample of behavior. Of course, the basic idea of a test is nothing new to you at this stage of your career—you have been accustomed to taking them for many years.

The kinds of tests used to measure level of comprehension of the material in a college course are similar, in principle, to the psychological tests used to assess more complex abilities or characteristics. (Your next quiz in this class represents a measuring device used by your professor to gauge your ability to learn this information.) Each test in a course measures a sample of knowledge or behavior. For example, if your first test in a course in industrial psychology covers Chapters 1–4 of this book, you will be expected to know all of that material. The examination, however, will not question you on every item of information contained in the four chapters. Such a test would have to be almost as long as the chapters themselves. It is sufficient to question you on only a portion of the material in order to sample your knowledge. The same is true for psychological tests. On an intelligence test it is impractical to question persons on everything they know in order to measure their level of intelligence, nor is it necessary. Useful measures of intelligence (or of personality, interest, or mechanical aptitude) can be obtained by asking only a sample of what persons know.

Thus, both a classroom test and a psychological test measure a sample of behavior, but here the resemblance ends. The psychological test is a more sophisticated and rigorous measuring device that has been developed through patient, thorough, and careful research.

PURPOSES OF PSYCHOLOGICAL TESTS

Two purposes are served by psychological tests: selection and placement. Both functions involve making a prediction about an individual's future behavior. The same kinds of tests are used for both purposes; the difference lies in how the results are applied.

For *selection*, the emphasis is on finding a person with the right qualifications for a particular job; the stress is on the job itself and on trying to select from among many applicants the ones who will succeed on that job. Selection is not limited to the initial hiring of an individual. The process is used at all levels, wherever an organization has a vacancy to fill. For example, if a sales manager quits, the company may have to decide who among their current sales force has the ability to be promoted. Selection at this level is more important than at the level of initial employment; the wrong person in a higher-level job can do more harm.

For *placement*, the emphasis is on the individual. The problem is to find the right kind of job for a particular person. This process is usually aided by a vocational or guidance counselor who attempts to diagnose an individual's capabilities in order to suggest the work in which he or she is most likely to succeed. Psychological tests are rarely used for placement in industry, but are usually given in schools and colleges.

CHARACTERISTICS OF PSYCHOLOGICAL TESTS

Well-developed and soundly researched psychological tests have several characteristics that set them apart from the "tests" printed in the Sunday newspaper (the "Are You a Good Spouse?" or "What Is Your Sex Quotient?" variety). A good test involves much more than a list of questions that may sound relevant to the variable being measured. A proper psychological test is standardized, objective, based upon sound norms, reliable, and valid.

Standardization

Standardization refers to the consistency or uniformity of the conditions and procedures for administering a test. If we expect to compare the performance of several persons on the same test, it is imperative that they all take that test under identical circumstances.

Each test must have its own standardized procedure that must be followed precisely each time the test is given. This means that every person taking the test reads or listens to the same set of instructions (with no variation), is allowed the same amount of time in which to respond, and is situated in a similar physical setting.

Any change in testing procedure may produce a change in individual performance on the test. For example, if the air-conditioning system breaks down in a plant on an extremely hot day, those persons who are unlucky enough to be taking a test may not do as well as those who took the test the day before at a more comfortable temperature. Or, if an inexperienced tester fails, out of carelessness, to read the complete instructions to a group of applicants, that group is not taking the test under the same conditions as had others.

The appropriate testing procedures can be designed into a test by its developers, but maintaining standardized conditions is the task of the persons actually giving the test. This is why it is so important that test administrators be properly trained. An excellent test can be rendered useless in the hands of an inexperienced or careless tester.

Objectivity

Objectivity, as a characteristic of psychological tests, refers primarily to the scoring of the test results. In order for a test to be scored objectively, it is necessary that anyone scoring the test be able to obtain the same results. In this way the scoring process is free of subjective judgment or bias on the part of the scorer.

In the discussion of interviewing we noted that a weakness of the interview was the subjective nature of the interviewer's judgments about an applicant's qualifications. Similarly, a subjective test is liable to misinterpretation because of a scorer's attitudes, prejudices, or momentary mood.

In your college career, you have no doubt taken objective and subjective examinations. With objective tests (such as multiple-choice or true-false), scoring is a mechanical process that requires no special training or knowledge. A clerk in a company's personnel department or an undergraduate grader in college can score an objective test as long as a scoring key with the correct answers has been provided. Scoring a subjective test (such as an essay exam) is more difficult and is liable to be influenced by personal characteristics of the grader, including a like or dislike of the person who took the test.

In order to make fair assessments of job applicants, as well as equitable comparisons among them, objective tests are clearly the more desirable. Industry does use a few subjective tests for selection purposes, but their results are questionable.

Norms

In order to interpret the results of a psychological test, a frame of reference or point of comparison must exist so that the performance of one individual can be compared with the performance of other, similar individuals. This is accomplished by means of test norms, the distribution of scores of a large group of people similar in nature to the job applicants being tested.

The scores of this group—the standardization sample—serve as the yardstick against which the applicants' scores are compared to determine their relative standing on the ability being tested. For example, if a high school graduate who applies for a job that requires mechanical skill achieves a score of 82 on a test of mechanical ability, the score alone reveals nothing about the degree of mechanical ability the person possesses. But if we can compare that score of 82 with a distribution of scores from a large group of high school graduates— the test norms—then we can ascribe meaning to the individual score. If the mean of the test norms is 80 and the standard deviation 10, we know immediately that an applicant who scored 82 possesses only an average or moderate amount of mechanical ability. With this comparative information, we are in a much better position to evaluate objectively this applicant's chances of succeeding on the job relative to the other applicants tested.

Some widely used psychological tests have sets of norms for different age groups, sexes, and levels of education. The adequacy of a test's norms can determine its usefulness as an aid to employee selection.

Reliability

Reliability refers to the consistency of response on a test. If a group takes an intelligence test one week and achieves a mean score of 100, but repeats the test a week later and achieves a mean score of 72, we would have to describe the test as unreliable; it yields inconsistent measurements. It is common to find slight variation in test scores when a test is retaken at a later date, but if the fluctuation is great, it suggests that something is basically wrong with the test or the scoring method.

Before a test can be administered to the public, it is necessary to have a precise indication of how reliable the test is. There are several methods for determining reliability.

The *test-retest* method involves administering a test twice, to the same group of people, and correlating the two sets of scores. The closer the correlation coefficient (called the reliability coefficient, in this case) approaches a perfect positive correlation (+1.00), the more reliable is the test. There are several limitations to this approach. It is uneconomical to require workers to be away from their jobs to take the test twice; learning and other experiences between the two testing sessions may cause the group to score higher the second time, and the workers may recall some of the questions and therefore score higher on the retest.

The *equivalent forms* method uses a test-retest approach but instead of taking the same test a second time, a similar form of the test is given and the two sets of scores are correlated. The disadvantage of this approach is the difficulty and expense of developing two separate, equivalent tests. It is often costly enough to develop one good version of a test.

A third approach to the determination of the reliability of a test is the *split-halves* method. The test is taken once, divided in half, and the two sets of items are correlated with each other. This is less time-consuming than the other approaches since only one administration of the test is required. Also, there is no opportunity for learning or memory to influence the second score.

Whatever method is used, the investigation of reliability is necessary in the development of a useful test. In choosing a test to be used for selection or other purposes, the reliability coefficient ideally should exceed +0.80.

Validity

One of the most important requirements of any psychological test is that it actually measure what it purports to measure. The technical term for this is validity. As with reliability, validity is a simple concept to understand, but more difficult to attain.

Suppose that a psychologist working for the U.S. Air Force develops a test of radar operator proficiency. The test can be considered valid if it measures those skills needed for competence in this task. One way to determine this is to correlate the test scores with subsequent job performance. If persons who score high on the radar operator proficiency test also perform well on the job (and those who score low on the test perform poorly on the job), then the correlation between test score and performance will be high and the test will be considered a valid predictor of job success. (When the correlation coefficient is used to determine validity, it is called a validity coefficient.)

This definition of validity is not concerned with the inherent nature or properties of the test but only with the correlation between the score on the test and some subsequent measure of job performance. This approach to defining and establishing validity, which is called *empirical validity,* is the most frequently used approach. However, in recent years psychologists have become interested in another aspect of validity, that which relates to the nature or content of the test, independent of its correlation with some external criterion. This kind of validity is called *rational validity.*

Personnel psychologists are concerned with two approaches to empirical validity. *Predictive validity* involves giving the test to all job applicants in a specific time period and then hiring them all, regardless of their performance on the test. At a later time, when some measure of job performance has been obtained on each worker, the test scores and job ratings are correlated to determine how well the test actually predicted job success. Most managements are not in favor of this expensive practice because some of those hired will turn out to be poor workers. However, when the personnel psychologist can persuade management of the wisdom of this approach, it does provide the best data obtainable on test validity.

The usual approach in industry to establishing the empirical validity of a test is *concurrent validity.* This procedure involves giving the test to employees already on the job and then correlating test scores with job performance measures. The major disadvantage of this method is that by using workers already on the job, the validation sample contains only the better employees. Poorer workers will have already been fired, demoted, transferred, or have quit. It is impossible, therefore, to determine with concurrent validity if a test can truly discriminate between good and poor workers.

The best available psychological tests include in their manuals the results of validation studies. It is expensive and time-consuming to establish a test's validity coefficient, but without this information a personnel department can have little confidence that the test is actually measuring the qualities and abilities being sought.

Rational validity, as noted, focuses on the nature of the test itself rather than on the correlation between the test and job performance. In certain situations, it is not feasible to use empirical validation, perhaps because an organization is too small to support these expensive procedures or because the job in question is new. Consider the original selection of the U.S. astronauts, for example. For some years, until the first space flights, there was no measure of job performance that could be correlated with test scores.

Two approaches to establishing the rational validity of a test are content validity and construct validity. *Content validity* involves an attempt to assess the content of a test to assure that it includes a representative sample of all the questions that could be asked. This is accomplished by analyzing the requirements for the job and determining if the test is sampling the skills and abilities that are needed to perform that job. For example, in hiring secretaries, typing and shorthand tests are certainly related to job performance; tests or test questions pertaining to mechanical skills, however, might not be related. Content validity cannot be established by statistical means. There is no number to tell us if the test is sufficiently valid for selection purposes. Instead, content validity is based on the judgments of experts who must determine how appropriate the tests and test items are for the job.

Construct validity is an attempt to determine the psychological characteristics measured by a test. How do we know, for example, that a new test that purports to measure intelligence does, in fact, do so? One way to statistically determine this is to correlate scores from the new test with scores on well-established intelligence tests. If the correlation is high, we can have some confidence that the new test is actually measuring the trait or ability it claims to measure.

Another type of validity is *face validity*. This has nothing to do with the statistical nature of a test and cannot itself be measured. Face validity is concerned with how well the test questions appear to be related to the job for which the person is being tested. In other words, does the test appear to be valid or relevant to the testee?

Experienced commercial airline pilots would not think it unusual to take tests dealing with the mechanics of flight or of navigation; these questions are directly related to the job they expect to perform. These pilots might balk, however, at being asked if they loved their parents, or when they had their first date, because they might not understand what such questions had to do with flying an airplane. Such tests lack face validity and may well cause the applicants to take them less seriously than they should. This, in turn, could lower their motivation to perform well on the tests. If their test performance is affected, it is certainly not in the best interests of the applicants or the company.

FAIR EMPLOYMENT LEGISLATION AND TESTING

Validity has always been a requirement of psychological tests used for selection purposes. The passage of the equal employment opportunity legislation, however, has dramatically increased the attention that psychologists must pay to test validation. Psychological testing has come under close scrutiny to ensure that its use does not violate the 1964 Civil Rights Act. Section 703(h) of the Civil Rights Act dealing with testing states that, "It shall not be . . . an unlawful employment practice for an employer to give and act upon the results of any professionally developed test provided that such test . . . is not . . . used to discriminate because of race, color, religion, sex, or national origin."

This federal legislation and the growing number of similar state laws have resulted in many investigations by the Equal Employment Opportunity Commission of organizational hiring and testing practices. In 1971 the Supreme Court ruled that tests used by employers must be directly related to the work to be performed.

Suppose, for example, that a company uses an intelligence test to select applicants for a training program for skilled workers. If the records show that most blacks failed this test and most whites passed it, this may suggest that the test discriminates against blacks, not necessarily in terms of their ability to learn the skills, but rather because their educational background may put them at a disadvantage with respect to whites in passing the test. Intelligence tests are heavily weighted with verbal items. White applicants from better schools or home environments that encouraged learning may have an advantage over blacks from poorer schools or disadvantaged home environments. The test may not be measuring native intelligence as much as the available educational and cultural opportunities. Further, white applicants may fare better on selection tests because they may have had more experience in test taking and so do not react to it with as much anxiety.

Civil rights and equal employment opportunity legislation are directed against this kind of discrimination. What must be determined in this example is whether blacks' lower scores on the intelligence test have any relation to performance on the job. It could be the case that the applicants have ample ability to learn the skills necessary for the job but simply lack the background and preparation to pass the test. The burden of proof in demonstrating that a psychological test is job-related is on the employing organization.

Of course, this is not a problem with all tests. Tests of specific skills such as typing are free of potential bias with regard to race, or any factor other than typing ability.

One result of these legislative and judicial decisions is an increase in validity research. If studies clearly show, for example, that applicants of all races who score below a certain level on a test perform unsuccessfully on the job, then the test is not discriminatory by race. Validity research should be conducted anyway. If a test cannot choose among applicants in terms of ability to perform the job, it is worthless as a selection device. Nowadays, however, validity studies are required by law to show that a test is not being used as an illegal discriminatory device.

Empirical validation procedures (correlating test scores with actual job performance) are required by Equal Employment Opportunity Commission guidelines where feasible. Alternatively, rational validation procedures (content validity and construct validity) may be used. Employers must demonstrate the validity of all psychological tests that they use for selection. Tests that cannot be shown to be valid can no longer be used. As a result, some smaller companies no longer use psychological tests. A survey of twenty-five hundred companies in 1975 showed that 75 per cent of them have cut back on their use of tests in selection.

Another result of fair employment practices is the increasing importance of industrial psychologists in employing organizations. Industrial psychologists are needed more than ever before for their expertise in conducting validation studies and for their service as expert witnesses in the many court cases that have arisen out of alleged violations of equal employment opportunity legislation.

ESTABLISHING A TESTING PROGRAM

The basic steps in setting up a testing program are essentially the same as those necessary for any kind of selection program. The first requirement is to investigate the nature of the job for which testing is to be used as a selection device. Once job and worker analyses have been performed, the proper test or tests to measure the behaviors and abilities necessary for success on the job must be carefully chosen or developed. This is a crucial point: no matter how exhaustively a job has been investigated, if a poor test is subsequently used, the selection program is doomed.

Where do psychologists find suitable tests? They can use tests already on the market or can develop new tests specifically for the needs of the job and the company.

There are several thousand commercially available tests. No matter what kind of job is under study, there is probably a test that purports to measure abilities and predict success on that job. Unfortunately, testing is one area of industrial psychology in which the charlatan has been at work. Some prepared tests are little more than dozens of items (often borrowed from other tests) thrown together, given a professional-sounding title, and promoted as "sure fire" ways to hire the right people. Such "tests" are worth little more than those that appear in popular magazines. Most of these test makers publish no information regarding reliability or validity studies for a very good reason: they did no research on their tests to determine these requirements. For the same reason, no norms are provided.

Trained personnel psychologists, who know what is important in selection devices, would never consider using these phony tests, but untrained personnel managers (having little, if any, background in psychology) might well be persuaded of the value of such tests by an impressive title or a glib sales representative. The tragedy of this situation is that it takes months or years before the company discovers that the test was worthless, before the poor quality of the workers selected on the basis of the bogus test becomes known to the management. In addition, well-qualified applicants might have been turned down by the company because of their score on the fraudulent test.

This unfortunate experience, which occurs all too often in industry, is not only expensive to the companies involved but also acts to undermine confidence in psychologists and in legitimate psychological testing programs. Personnel managers stuck with a useless test that caused them to hire some poor employees are likely to conclude that all psychological tests are worthless and never consider using them again.

Only properly trained and qualified psychologists can set up worthwhile selection programs, especially ones that include the use of psychological tests. The personnel manager who would not think of having an amateur diagnose chest pains, all too often calls on amateurs to diagnose selection problems.

Psychologists can choose or develop the most appropriate selection tests and conduct the exacting research necessary to ensure the success of the complete selection program.

When psychologists are searching for a published test to use, they know precisely what to look for and where to find it. The best tests include information on reliability and validity, and make test norms available for public evaluation. In addition, there are several sources of information on the nature and statistical characteristics of psychological tests. The major source of information is the comprehensive and periodically revised *Mental Measurements Yearbook,* edited by Oscar K. Buros. This reliable handbook contains critical reviews and evaluations of over eleven hundred tests. The seventh edition was published in 1972.

A leading journal in the field, *Personnel Psychology,* also publishes information on the validity of tests available for use in industrial selection. In addition, the general psychological research literature contains published reports of validity studies conducted on various tests. These can be found through the *Psychological Abstracts.*

Psychologists know how to evaluate the information obtained, and thus can learn much about the tests being considered for selection purposes. An intelligent choice among tests can only be made on the basis of full knowledge of the pertinent material.

There are several important factors to be considered in deciding whether to develop a new test or to use one already published. Cost is always important; it is considerably less expensive to purchase an existing test than to construct a new one, especially if only a small number of workers are to be selected.

Time is also important. The company needs qualified workers as soon as possible and may be unwilling or unable to wait for a useful test to be developed. A large-scale testing program may require months of research before the test can be used for actual selection purposes, whereas a published test can be used almost at once, assuming it meets the specific needs of the job in question. Some research may be necessary to determine the adequacy of an existing test, but usually far less research than is required when developing a new test.

There are sound economic reasons, therefore, why management prefers to use an existing test, but there are also disadvantages to this approach. The fact that a test for selecting aircraft mechanics, for example, has proven to be valid for one company, does not automatically guarantee that it will work equally well for another company. There may be subtle differences in the job from one plant to another, or a company located in one part of the country may attract applicants with different characteristics and motivations than the same kind of company located elsewhere. If the job is entirely new, it may require new skills, such as those needed to operate advanced and complex equipment. It is unlikely that an existing test will be able to measure the abilities needed for success in a new kind of work.

If, for these reasons, a company decides to develop its own tests for particular jobs, the personnel psychologist must write or compile a list of suitable items or questions. Then the psychologist proceeds to "test the test"; that is, to find out if it really measures what it is supposed to measure. In other words, the test's validity must be determined.

The psychologist critically examines and evaluates each item in the test. An *item analysis* is conducted to determine how effectively each item discriminates between those who scored high on the total test and those who scored low. In essence, this involves correlating a person's response on each item with the response on the test as a whole. A perfectly valid test question, then, is one that was answered correctly by everyone who scored high on the complete test and was answered incorrectly by everyone who scored low on the complete test. Only items with a high correlation coefficient are retained for the final form of the test.

The level of difficulty of each question must also be determined. If the majority of the test questions are too easy, then most people will obtain high scores. The resulting small range of scores makes it difficult to discriminate effectively between those who are very high on the characteristic or ability being tested and those who are moderately high. A test on which most of the items are too difficult presents the opposite problem. It would be difficult to distinguish between those who possess extremely low ability and those who possess only moderately low ability.

Much of the research necessary to test a test involves the determination of reliability and validity by the methods discussed previously. Recall that the investigation of the test's validity usually requires the determination of some measure of job performance—a criterion with which the test scores can be correlated. Ideally, this assessment of a test's predictive validity is carried out by administering the test to a large group of applicants. All applicants will be hired without reference to their test scores. (At this point in the research, the value of the test is unknown so it makes little sense to base hiring decisions on level of test performance.) Each worker's level of job success is later measured, after being on the job long enough to develop some job competence, and these ratings are compared with the test scores.

Unfortunately (as usual, for reasons of economy), this approach remains more of an ideal than a reality. By far the most common approach in use to establish a test's validity involves testing those already on the job (concurrent validity).

Even less ideal than testing current workers to validate a test is the unfortunate management practice of testing only the most superior workers. One industrial psychologist described a company that had identified its best salespersons and planned to test only these and to use the results as the basis for selecting salespersons in the future. The rationale in this approach is that the characteristics of the top workers are the standard with which job applicants will be compared. The psychologist was able to convince the company's management of both the fallacy of this approach and the wisdom of testing all the salespersons, both good and bad. The reason for doing so when using a new test is simple: It could be the case that both good and poor workers would score alike on the test. This means that the test is not capable of discriminating between levels of competence—that it is not a valid test—perhaps because it did not measure the specific behaviors necessary for job success.

When the psychologist was able to administer the test to all of the company's salespersons, he found, as suspected, that both poor and good salespersons perform at the same level on the test. Had the company tested only its best workers, and then hired applicants who scored at the same level, there would have been no improvement in the quality of employees hired by the company. The test could not distinguish between good and poor salespersons.

The importance of this point cannot be stressed too heavily. Psychological tests used for employee selection programs yield meaningful data only if they can discriminate between good and poor workers who have been rated on some criterion of job performance. A personnel manager who believes that we need only look at the good people and use them as a standard is making a serious mistake. This admonition applies equally to existing tests and to those newly developed for a specific company. Both must be shown to correlate with success on the actual job in question.

One other point must be mentioned in our discussion of the problems of establishing the validity of a psychological test. It must not only discriminate between good and poor candidates, but it must also deal with abilities directly related to the job in question; that is, it must have high content validity. A test of spelling would probably be a good device for discriminating between company presidents and janitors, but it does not follow that a psychologist can select company presidents by testing their level of spelling ability.

Why? Because all those eligible for the position of company president would most likely score high on this ability. Such a test would be worthless for choosing from among the applicants. The test would not be valid for the specific purpose needed.

There are, then, many facets to the problem of test validity. The more effort expended on this crucial phase of test development, the greater the value of the test, and, of course, the better the workers selected. There are money-saving shortcuts, but in the long run they are self-defeating. A cheap testing program is a false economy.

Once validity and reliability of a test have been found to be satisfactory, the problem of setting a cut-off score (the score below which an applicant will not be hired) must be resolved. This depends partly on the available labor supply—the greater the number of applicants, the more selective a company can be.

In setting cut-off scores, we cannot assume that the better workers will always be those with the higher scores. For example, it has been found that very intelligent people often do not work well in routine assembly line jobs. It is necessary, therefore, that both minimum and maximum cut-off scores be determined for an intelligence test that is part of this kind of company's selection program. The applicants must be intelligent enough to be able to learn the job, but not so intelligent that they will be bored with it.

When the research has been completed and the test pronounced satisfactory as a predictive device, potential difficulties arise in the actual administration of the test to job applicants, problems that may reduce the test's validity. Many people, particularly older ones who have been out of school for years, become anxious about the prospect of taking a psychological test. It is in their best interest that the examiner attempt to establish rapport with all applicants and try to put them at ease as much as possible. The testing conditions must be standardized so that every applicant takes the test under identical circumstances. Also, the testing conditions must be as agreeable and comfortable as possible so that applicants are in the best personal condition to do well on the test.

In basic training in military service, for example, when just two days after induction, feeling tired, confused, sick of inoculations and sergeants, and generally unhappy, one must spend half a day in an extremely hot room taking a lengthy battery of psychological tests, the conditions are not likely to induce a high level of performance. An army research study has shown that test performance of a group of trainees improved considerably when they were given the test again at a later time, when they were better adjusted to army life. Of course, a portion of the increase in scores might be attributed to greater familiarity with the test during the second testing session, but the primary reason for the better performance was the more agreeable conditions under which the test was taken.

This experience points up the need for well-trained test administrators. The task requires considerable technical skill plus sympathetic understanding of and interest in those being tested.

A Sample Testing Program

In this section we discuss the program developed by Sears, Roebuck to identify executive potential,[1] in order to give you some idea of the

---

[1] T. Guyton, "The identification of executive potential," *Personnel Journal*, **48**(1969), 866–872.

effort involved in developing a sound program of psychological testing. The program dates from 1942 when an internationally known leader in psychological testing, Dr. L. L. Thurstone, was hired as a consultant by Sears to develop a testing program for executive personnel.

A test series—called the Sears Executive Battery of Psychological Tests (SEBPT)—was constructed to measure the factor of general executive competence. The research program had two aims: (1) to determine the characteristics of Sears's executives, and (2) to predict executive potential in those persons eligible for promotion.

To investigate the characteristics of the company's executives, the SEBPT was given to a random sample of more than two thousand executives. The tests were given not only to superior executives but to a sample of all executives, in order to include some at every level of competence. The resulting profile showed that executives differed substantially from the general population. In brief, executives were found to possess the following characteristics:

1. A high level of intelligence, superior to the average college student.
2. A high level of social leadership and social composure.
3. A high level of self-confidence.
4. Objectivity in their perceptions of self and of others.
5. A high tolerance of others.
6. A great concern with recognition and economic matters.
7. A strong goal-orientation.

To extend the research on the characteristics of executives, Sears gave a questionnaire dealing with work-related values to fifteen hundred executives. A clear-cut pattern of values emerged: a concern with opportunity for advancement, a strong identification with the company, and a concern with salary, status, and recognition.

The second phase, predicting executive potential, took much longer to accomplish. Using a shortened version of the SEBPT, more than two thousand sales personnel and low-level supervisors were tested. Five years later, the level of progress of each of those tested was analyzed. The correlation between SEBPT test scores and job performance ratings showed that the test battery efficiently discriminated between those who had been promoted within the five-year period and those who had not (or who had left the company). The predictive accuracy of the test is shown in Figure 4–1, which demonstrates that those who scored highest on the test were the most likely to have been promoted. Thus, the Sears psychologists could conclude that the test battery could be used with great confidence to predict executive potential in current employees and in new job applicants.

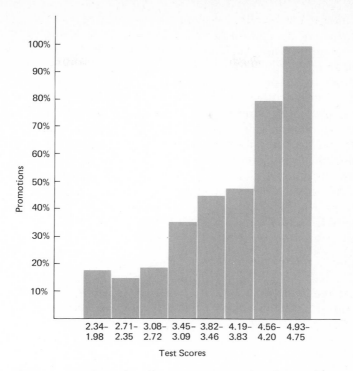

Figure 4–1. Relationship between test scores and promotion. Data from T. Guyton, "The identification of executive potential," *Personnel Journal,* **48**(1969), p. 870.

The next step in Sears's comprehensive program was to determine the specific psychological factors or characteristics capable of distinguishing between the successful and the unsuccessful executive. In one study, the SEBPT was given to (1) a group of executives who had been dismissed for incompetence and (2) a group of young successful executives. As expected, the test results clearly differentiated between these two extreme groups.

The specific traits shown to be capable of differentiating between the two groups included intelligence, sociability, optimism, social leadership, self-confidence, dominance, drive, and objectivity.

The continuing selection research being conducted by Sears is a model of thoroughness and sophistication. The program has enjoyed the support of top management throughout its development and implementation, and the company has been willing to spend considerable money and time on it.

Such extensive management support is, unfortunately, the exception rather than the rule. The investment has paid considerable dividends for Sears, and the company is so convinced of the efficiency and validity of its testing program that for twenty-five years, no one has been allowed to advance to the upper ranks of management without first taking the SEBPT. The company also uses other procedures in appraisals of executive candidates, but the testing program remains a central part of the selection process. Sears is generally considered to have one of the brightest and most alert management groups in industry today. Thus, if conducted properly, a psychological testing program can be a sound investment for any organization.

TYPES OF PSYCHOLOGICAL TESTS: ADMINISTRATION

There are a number of ways to categorize psychological tests. They can be discussed in terms of how they are scored, constructed, and administered or in terms of the kinds of behavior they are designed to measure. There are many styles, types, and purposes of psychological tests.

Individual and Group Tests

Some tests are designed so that they can be administered to a large number of people at the same time. These *group tests* are advantageous in a situation that requires the testing of many people. The military, for example, tests thousands of people each year; it would be extremely expensive and time-consuming if each recruit had to be tested individually. Many large-scale testing programs in industry and government involve a similar situation. A test designed for group administration can be given to 20, 200, or 2,000 applicants; the only limit is the size of the testing facility.

Individual tests, administered to one person at a time, are more costly and, therefore, are used to a lesser degree in industry than are group tests. For vocational guidance and counseling, and for clinical and diagnostic work with emotionally disturbed persons, however, individual tests are preferred. It is easier to establish rapport with the person being tested in the individual testing situation. Also, it is usually possible to delve more deeply into the behavior being measured by using an individual test. One limitation is that the behavior of the individual is more dependent upon the skill, sensitivity, and friendliness of the test administrator.

Computer-Assisted Testing

A dramatic innovation, computer-assisted testing, is currently being developed at the Personnel Research and Development Center of the U.S. Civil Service Commission.[2] Designed for large-scale group testing, computer-assisted testing is nevertheless an individual testing situation in which the person taking the test interacts with a computer. The questions appear one at a time on a television screen and the person presses a key corresponding to the answer selected.

The advantage to computer-assisted testing is greater than just the mechanical presentation of questions. If you take, for example, an intelligence test in the usual paper-and-pencil format, you are presented with many questions that are designed to cover the full range of intelligence. Some questions will be ridiculously easy for you (since your intelligence is higher than the level at which these questions are aimed), whereas other questions will be more difficult (since they are at or above your level of intelligence). In order to obtain a score on the test, however, you must take the time to answer all of the questions, even the very easy ones.

In the computer-assisted testing situation you do not have to waste your time answering questions that are below your level of intelligence. The computer begins the test by presenting a question of average difficulty, one that people of average IQ can answer. If you answer the question correctly, the computer proceeds to a question of greater difficulty because you have already demonstrated that your level of ability is at least average. Had you answered the question incorrectly, the computer would have given you a less difficult question.

Let us assume that a particular ability being measured ranges from 0 to 100. The first question is at the 50 level. If you answer this question correctly, the computer asks you a question at the 60 level. If you also answer this question correctly, the next question is at level 70, and if you answer this question incorrectly, the computer backtracks and asks you a question at level 65. And so the process continues, progressively focusing on your precise level of ability.

Remember that on a traditional test you would have been required to answer all questions covering the full range of ability from 0 to 100. Computer-assisted testing thus considerably reduces the time needed to take a test. The Personnel Research and Development Center has demonstrated that a precise measurement of a trait or ability provided by a one hundred-item conventional test can be provided by only twelve questions using the computer.

[2] C. Clark. *The Personnel Research and Development Center of the U.S. Civil Service Commission* (Washington, D.C.: U.S. Civil Service Commission, 1975), pp. 9–10.

There are other advantages to computer-assisted testing. Testing can occur at any time a candidate applies for a job, not just when a qualified test administrator is available. Moreover, a wide range of abilities can be measured in a short period of time, thus ensuring that the motivation and interest of the test taker will not wane (as sometimes happens when taking a conventional test). Also, immediate feedback is available to the personnel department; the computer provides the applicant's scores in a matter of seconds.

This is, however, an expensive and sophisticated procedure that is appropriate only for large organizations that regularly test great numbers of people. The program is scheduled to be operational in the federal government by 1980.

Speed and Power Tests

The difference between speed and power tests is in terms of the time allotted for completion of the test. A *speed test* has a fixed time limit, at which point everyone taking the test must stop. A *power test* has no time limit—the examinees are allowed as much time as they feel they need in order to finish the test. Often, a power test will contain more difficult items than a speed test.

A large-scale testing program is facilitated by the use of speed tests since all test forms can be collected at the same time. Also, there are cases in which working speed is a vital part of the behavior being measured. Tests of clerical ability, for example, contain relatively easy items and most people, given enough time, would be able to respond correctly. The important predictive factor in clerical jobs such as typist or factory jobs such as mail sorter is the quality of work that can be performed in a fixed period of time. A power test would not be able to properly evaluate this ability.

Paper-and-Pencil and Performance Tests

Paper-and-pencil tests are the kind with which you are most familiar. The questions are in printed form and the answers are recorded on an answer sheet. Most of the standard group tests of intelligence, interest, and personality are paper-and-pencil tests.

Some behaviors or characteristics do not lend themselves to evaluation by paper-and-pencil means. Mechanical ability, for example, is tested better by having the applicants *perform* a series of mechanical operations than by having them answer questions about the nature of these operations. Consider again the evaluation of typing ability. The best way to assess this skill is to observe the typist in operation. For the evaluation of more complex skills, expensive equipment may be required. Performance tests may take longer to administer than paper-and-pencil tests and also may require an individual testing situation.

Objective and Subjective Scoring

We have discussed the importance of *objectivity* in testing. For the reasons noted, the majority of the tests used for industrial selection purposes are objective.

Subjectivity in test scoring, as in interviewing, allows personal prejudices and attitudes to enter into the testing situation. This can lead to distortion of the evaluation. The use of subjectively scored personality tests for selection purposes is discussed later in the chapter.

TYPES OF PSYCHOLOGICAL TESTS: BEHAVIOR MEASURED

Perhaps the most useful distinction among psychological tests for selection purposes is in terms of the characteristics or behaviors they are designed to measure. The basic types are tests of mental ability, interest, aptitude, motor ability, and personality.

Mental Ability

Several tests of mental ability (better known as intelligence tests) are used in industrial selection. Group intelligence tests, the kind used most often, are primarily a rough screening device. The tests are short, take little time to complete, and can be administered to large groups. They can be rapidly and easily scored by a clerk or a machine.

Intelligence test items relate mostly to educational material such as spelling, reading, or mathematics. They do not measure native intelligence as much as what a person has formally learned in the classroom. (It is assumed that those high in native intelligence have learned more from their educational experience.) In general, intelligence tests have been shown to be better predictors of success in training programs than of success in actual job performance. Some of the intelligence tests commonly used in industry are the following.

The *Otis Self-Administering Tests of Mental Ability* is one of the most frequently used selection tests. It has proven to be useful for screening applicants for a wide variety of jobs including office clerks, assembly line workers, calculating and tabulating machine operators, and lower-level foremen and supervisors—jobs not requiring an extremely high level of intelligence.

The test is group-administered and takes little time to complete. It is less useful for professional or high-level supervisory positions because it does not discriminate well at the upper ranges of intelligence.

The *Wonderlic Personnel Test,* a shortened version of one of the Otis series of tests, is particularly popular in industrial selection because it takes a mere twelve minutes to complete, making it a very economical screening device. Despite its brevity, this group test has been useful in predicting success in certain lower-level jobs, particularly of the clerical variety. Both the Otis and Wonderlic tests, though valid for certain jobs, have been vigorous targets of the EEOC because they have frequently been misused for the purpose of discrimination.

The *Wesman Personnel Classification Test* is another group test requiring about thirty minutes to complete. This test provides separate Verbal and Numerical scores, as well as a general or total score. Norms are available for salesclerks, production supervisors, and executive trainees.

The Verbal part of the test is in the form of analogies (for example: ———— is to night, as light is to ————). A number of alternatives are provided from which the person chooses the proper words to fill the blanks. The Numerical part is made up of items requiring computation and the understanding of numerical relationships.

The *Wesman* test seems better suited to somewhat higher level personnel than either the *Otis* or the *Wonderlic.*

The *Wechsler Adult Intelligence Scale* (WAIS) is a lengthy, individually administered test, not widely used for selection purposes. Its use is generally restricted to very high-level management personnel. The administration, scoring, and interpretation of the WAIS require much training and experience on the part of the examiner.

There are eleven subtests of the WAIS in two sections—Verbal and Performance. The Verbal portion consists of the following subtests: Information, Comprehension, Arithmetic, Similarities, Digit Span, and Vocabulary. The Performance subtests consist of Digit Symbol, Picture Completion, Block Design, Picture Arrangement, and Object Assembly. Two separate measures of intelligence, therefore, can be obtained, as well as a total score combining verbal and performance portions.

Interest

Interest inventories are of greater value in vocational guidance and counseling than in industrial personnel selection. Nevertheless, some companies do include measures of interest as part of their total testing program. (You are probably familiar with interest inventories— many high schools routinely administer them to help students choose the kind of work for which they seem best suited.) Basically, interest tests include items about many daily activities and objects from among which the test takers select their preferences. The rationale is that if a person exhibits the same pattern of interests and preferences as those who are successful in a given occupation, the chances are good that the individual will find satisfaction in that occupation.

It is important to note that just because a person possesses a high degree of interest in a particular occupation, it is no guarantee that he or she has the ability to succeed in that job. All it suggests is that the individual's interests are compatible with the interests of people who are successful in that career. Of course, if the test shows that a person has absolutely no interest in an occupation, his or her chances of succeeding in it are limited.

Two widely used interest inventories are the *Strong–Campbell Interest Inventory* (SCII) and the *Kuder Occupational Interest Survey.*

The SCII is a group-administered test composed of more than three hundred questions that deal with occupations, school subjects, activities, and amusements, some of which are to be ranked in order of preference and others rated as "like," "dislike," or "indifferent."

The SCII replaces the *Strong Vocational Interest Blank* (in use for more than forty years), which had separate forms for men's and women's occupations. The SCII groups occupations in six areas: realistic, investigative, artistic, social, enterprising, and conventional.

The *Kuder Occupational Interest Survey* consists of a large number of items arranged in groups of three. Within each triad examinees must indicate which activity they most prefer and which they least prefer. They are not allowed to skip any group (if they don't like any of the alternatives) or to check more than one as the most preferred activity.

Two sample sets of items are presented.[3]

Visit an art gallery.	Collect autographs.
Browse in a library.	Collect coins.
Visit a museum.	Collect butterflies.

The *Kuder Occupational Interest Survey* can be scored for 77 occupations for men and 57 occupations for women.

Both of these interest inventories are primarily for use in vocational counseling, where the focus is on trying to select the right kind of

[3] G. F. Kuder, *Manual* (Chicago: Science Research Associates, 1953).

work for an individual. One difficulty with their use as a selection tool is the problem of faking responses; the success of any such inventory rests largely on the honesty of a person's answers. Presumably, when taking an interest inventory for vocational counseling, a person will answer honestly (since the results are used to help the person find a suitable area of employment). In a selection situation, however, the person's answers may determine whether he or she is hired for a particular job, and the motivation to falsify answers may be great.

Aptitude

For many jobs, aptitude tests must be created especially to measure the skills required by that job, but there are published tests that measure general aptitudes for mechanical and clerical skills. Often, as part of the testing for skilled jobs, the applicant's keenness of vision and hearing will be tested, primarily by mechanical means. These are sometimes called aptitude tests and in a very general sense they are. We limit the discussion, however, to the measurement of more complex abilities by means of psychological tests. Several tests measure *clerical aptitude* and are useful in the prediction of success for clerical workers. These tests are concerned primarily with speed and accuracy of perception.

The *Minnesota Clerical Test* is a group test consisting of two parts, number comparison and name comparison, examples of which are given in Figure 4–2.

The test is a speed test to determine the individual's accuracy when working in a limited time period. The test instructions urge the examinees to work as fast as they can without errors. The tasks involved are similar to work actually performed in clerical jobs.

The *General Clerical Test* is a group speed test published in two booklets: A—Speed and Number and B—Verbal. Booklet A contains items on checking, alphabetizing, numerical computation, error location, and arithmetic reasoning, and is suitable for testing job applicants for accounting or payroll clerk positions. Booklet B contains

When the two numbers or names in a pair are *exactly the same*, make a check mark on the line between them.

66273894 _____ 66273984
527384578_____527384578
New York World _____ New York World
Cargill Grain Co. _____ Cargil Grain Co.

Figure 4–2. Sample items from Minnesota Clerical Test. Reproduced by permission. Copyright 1933, renewed 1961 by The Psychological Corporation, New York, N.Y. All rights reserved.

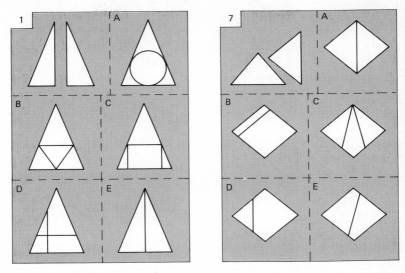

Figure 4–3. Sample items from Revised Minnesota Paper Form Board Test. The subject must pick the figure (from A to E) that shows how the parts will look when assembled. Reproduced by permission. Copyright 1941, renewed 1969 by The Psychological Corporation, New York, N.Y. All rights reserved.

items on spelling, reading comprehension, vocabulary, and grammar, and is suitable for applicants for secretarial jobs.

Tests to measure *mechanical aptitude* focus on the abilities of mechanical comprehension and spatial visualization.

The *Revised Minnesota Paper Form Board Test* is a measure of spatial relations or visualization, a necessary ability for occupations such as drafting. The applicant is presented with drawings of figures cut into two or more segments and must be able to picture how the total figure would appear if the pieces were put together. Sample items from this test are shown in Figure 4–3.

Research conducted with this test has demonstrated some degree of validity in predicting successful performance in mechanical work, engineering shopwork, and power sewing machine operation, as well as classroom performance of art and dental students.

Another widely used test of mechanical aptitude, in both the military and private industry, is the *Bennett Mechanical Comprehension Test*. This test employs pictures, with questions about the mechanical principles involved in them, and provides norms for various levels of training and background. Sample items are shown in Figure 4–4.

141

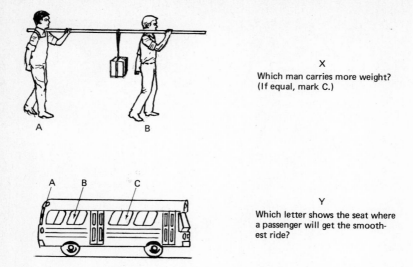

X
Which man carries more weight?
(If equal, mark C.)

Y
Which letter shows the seat where
a passenger will get the smooth-
est ride?

Figure 4–4. Sample items from Bennett Mechanical Comprehension Test. Reproduced by permission. Copyright 1940, renewed 1967; 1941, renewed 1969; 1942, renewed 1969; © 1967, 1968 by The Psychological Corporation, New York, N.Y. All rights reserved.

Motor Ability

Many jobs in industry require a high degree of motor skill involving muscular coordination, finger dexterity, or precise eye-hand coordination.

The *MacQuarrie Test of Mechanical Ability* is one of the few tests of motor ability in paper-and-pencil form. The seven subtests include the following tasks:

1. *Tracing*—a line is drawn through very small openings in a number of vertical lines.
2. *Tapping*—dots are made on paper as quickly as possible.
3. *Dotting*—dots are made in circles as quickly as possible.
4. *Copying*—simple designs are copied.
5. *Location*—specific points must be located in a smaller size version of a stimulus figure.
6. *Blocks*—the number of blocks in a drawing must be determined.
7. *Pursuit*—the visual tracing of assorted lines in a maze.

Some of these tasks are pictured in Figure 4–5.
The *Purdue Pegboard* is a performance test that simulates conditions on an assembly line and measures finger dexterity as well as

142

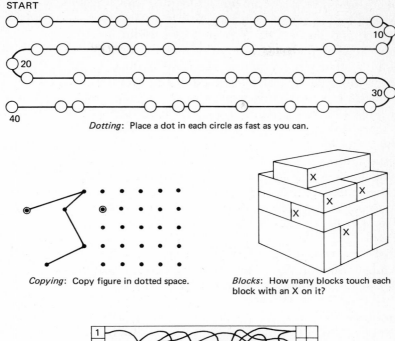

START

Dotting: Place a dot in each circle as fast as you can.

Copying: Copy figure in dotted space.

Blocks: How many blocks touch each block with an X on it?

Pursuit: Follow each line by eye and show where it ends, by putting the number in the correct square at the right.

Figure 4–5. From MacQuarrie Test of Mechanical Ability by T. W. MacQuarrie. Reproducted with permission of the publisher, CTB/McGraw-Hill Monterery, Calif. 93940. Copyright © 1925, 1953 by T. W. MacQuarrie. All rights reserved. Printed in the U.S.A.

larger movement skills of fingers, hands, and arms. The task is to place pins in a series of holes as rapidly as possible, first with one hand and then the other. Each of these tasks takes thirty seconds.

The *Purdue Pegboard* also includes a one-minute test involving the simultaneous use of both hands to assemble pins, collars, and washers in each hole.

The *O'Connor Finger Dexterity Test* and *Tweezer Dexterity Test*

143

measure how fast a person can insert pins into small holes, both by hand and by the use of tweezers. This is a standard measure of finger dexterity, and the test has proven to be useful in predicting success among sewing machine operator trainees, dental students, and a variety of other tasks requiring precise manipulative skills.

The *Minnesota Rate of Manipulation Test* consists of two parts. The examinee's task in the first part is to place sixty cylindrical blocks in sixty wells in a board. The second task is to turn all the blocks over. The score is the amount of time taken to complete each task.

The *Crawford Small Parts Dexterity Test,* using a somewhat more realistic task, is a measure of precise eye-hand coordination. In the first of the two tasks, examinees use tweezers to place pins in holes and then slip collars over the pins. In the second task, a screwdriver is used to place small screws in their holes. Norms are provided for several employee groups, including electrical and electronic assembly workers.

There are other tests of motor ability that measure coordination. The most common ones utilize the pursuit rotor, in which the testee uses a stylus to follow a dot on a revolving disk.

One variation of this procedure is the *Purdue Hand Precision Test.* As an upper disk with a hole revolves, the person being tested must touch target holes in a plate underneath the disk by using a stylus. The score is kept electronically as the stylus activates a counter.

Occasionally, special apparatus is developed to measure motor skills—sophisticated machines on which the examinee performs highly complex motor activities in response to visual signals. Such equipment is considerably more costly than the standard motor ability tests.

Personality

Personality tests, the most controversial type of test, are used extensively for selection purposes, despite evidence casting doubt on their predictive validity. Some personality tests are successful, although the continuing attack on them from many directions may be responsible for the decline in their popularity.

Two approaches to the measurement of personality are self-report inventories and projective techniques. The *self-report inventory* presents examinees with a variety of items that deal with specific situations, symptoms, or feelings, and they are asked to indicate how well each item describes themselves or how much they agree with each item.

A major problem with the self-report personality test is the honesty of those taking the test. People who wish to appear in a certain manner, or who may want to hide some bothersome facet of their personality, can do so quite easily on most of these tests. The questions are frequently transparent and reasonably intelligent applicants (say salespersons who wish to appear extraverted) can make themselves seem qualified with little difficulty. Fortunately, some inventories are designed to detect such faking. Since most of these tests can be easily distorted, however, their predictive efficiency is less than desirable. They do offer the advantage of being easy and economical to administer and score.

The *projective technique* approach to personality testing presents the individual with an ambiguous stimulus such as an inkblot. The task is to give some structure and meaning to this stimulus; in other words, to tell what is seen in the figure. The theory behind this approach is that an individual will project personal thoughts, desires, wishes, and feelings onto this amorphous structure in an effort to give it some meaning.

These tests cannot be faked because there are no right or wrong answers. They are time-consuming and must be administered individually. Extensive training and experience are required to interpret them properly. Since there are usually no objective scoring keys, there is ample opportunity for the examiner's subjective feelings to influence the interpretation. Some psychologists have said that the examinee's responses become a projective technique to the examiner who then projects his or her own thoughts and fears onto the responses of the person being tested! Although projective techniques are used in personnel selection, particularly at the executive level, the evidence against their use is overwhelming.

Self-report Inventories

The *Guilford-Zimmerman Temperament Survey* [4] is one of the more widely used paper-and-pencil personality inventories. The items are in the form of statements rather than questions, and the examinee responds by checking "yes," "no," or "?". Three sample items from this test are the following:

1. You start work in a new project with a great deal of enthusiasm .... YES ? NO
2. You are often low in spirits .... YES ? NO
3. Most people use politeness to cover up what is really "cutthroat" competition .... YES ? NO

The test yields separate scores for ten independent personality traits: General Activity, Restraint, Ascendance, Sociability, Emotional

[4] Beverly Hills, Calif.: Sheridan Psychological Services, Inc.

145

Stability, Objectivity, Friendliness, Thoughtfulness, Personal Relations, and Masculinity. As a check against deliberate faking or carelessness in responding, the test has three falsification scales based on the answers to selected test items.

The *Minnesota Multiphasic Personality Inventory* (MMPI), probably the best known and most influential of all the self-report inventories, contains 566 items classified by the respondent as "true," "false," or "cannot say." Its excessive length limits its usefulness for selection purposes; a high level of motivation is required to respond to each item with care. One advantage of the MMPI is the use of four validity scales that can be scored to determine if the examinee was faking, careless, or misunderstood the directions.

The clinical scales or personality traits including the following symptoms or conditions: Hypochondriasis, Depression, Hysteria, Psychopathic Deviate, Masculinity-Femininity, Paranoia, Psychasthenia, Schizophrenia, Hypomania, and Social.

There are additional self-report inventories that measure a variety of traits, and there are also tests that measure specific personality traits such as introversion-extraversion, sociability, ascendance-submission, emotional maturity, or emotional security.

Self-report inventories are usually used for selection at the executive or managerial level. As to the question of their usefulness, the record is largely a poor one (with some notable exceptions). However, these tests continue to be used enthusiastically by many personnel departments.

The moral, ethical, and legal implications of probing an individual's personality as a requisite for hiring have caused considerable debate in recent years (and are discussed later).

Projective Techniques

Projective tests of personality were developed primarily for use in clinical psychology for work with emotionally disturbed individuals. However, they are also used, to a limited degree, to assess candidates for high-level executive positions. Since the tests were originally intended to distinguish between psychotic and normal persons, it is not surprising that they usually fail to discriminate among normal persons in a selection situation.

The best known projective technique is the *Rorschach*, popularly called the "inkblot" test. Examinees are shown, individually, ten standardized inkblots and asked to report what they see in the figures. Some of the inkblots are in colors and others are in shades of black and gray. After all ten cards have been seen, the examiner reviews each card and asks the applicants specific questions about what they said they saw in the inkblots. The process of interpreting the responses is complicated and is based on whether the applicants reported seeing movement, human figures, inanimate or animate objects, and so on. The scoring is subjective and depends upon the training, skill, and personality of the examiner.

Research conducted on the value of the *Rorschach* for personnel selection consistently indicates low predictive validities.

Another well-known projective test is the *Thematic Apperception Test* (TAT) in which twenty ambiguous pictures showing two or more persons in different situations are presented. Applicants are asked to make up a story about each picture. The stories are analyzed by a subjective, unstandardized process that is open to the biases of the analyst. The TAT is used primarily in clinical psychology and research, but occasionally in the industrial selection situation.

Several other commercially available projective tests use various kinds of pictures to be interpreted or arranged sequentially by applicants. Some tests also use the incomplete sentence method; the beginning of a sentence is presented (such as, "I like . . .") and the person is requested to complete it.

ADVANTAGES OF PSYCHOLOGICAL TESTING

The primary advantage of psychological tests as a selection technique—indeed the only valid reason for using them—is that they can improve the selection process. A testing program such as the one developed by Sears, Roebuck can be of great value to any organization. The cost of hiring and training inexperienced workers approaches several hundred dollars per person. For higher-level professional or managerial personnel, this cost can increase to several thousand dollars per person. In view of this expense, a company must try to hire the best people available if it expects to realize any return on its initial hiring investment. Newly hired sales managers who quit or are fired after a year on the job are expensive wastes to themselves and to their companies. Any procedure that can reduce this waste more than pays for itself in the long run.

Psychological tests offer specific advantages over the other selection devices discussed. One advantage (excluding, of course, projective tests) is their objectivity. Compared to interviews or letters of recommendation, tests are less susceptible to biased interpretations on the part of the examiner. Also, it is somewhat easier to conduct evaluative research on psychological tests than on some other methods of selection. In part, this is because of the precise quantification of test results, something that is more difficult to achieve with, say, interview results. Psychological tests also offer the advantage of providing a great amount of information about an individual in a short period of time.

As noted, tests are only as good as the quantity and quality of the research preceding and accompanying their use. Continuous supporting research is required if psychological testing is to be a positive addition to a selection program.

In terms of predictive value, it is generally true that tests have been more useful in predicting success in training programs than in predicting successful job performance. This is less the fault of the tests than that the characteristics necessary for learning a job may be different from those that ensure success on the job. For example, applicants may be bright enough to learn the skills of a particular job very rapidly, but if the job itself does not satisfy their personal needs, they may not perform well.

In terms of the predictive efficiency of tests for various kinds of jobs, the following general conclusions can be drawn.

1. For clerical jobs, tests of speed and accuracy (measured by clerical aptitude tests) have been very successful in predicting job performance. Tests of intelligence and arithmetic are also useful.

2. Tests for jobs such as assembly line operator and general factory worker have proven valuable for prediction of job performance. The primary kinds of tests used measure dexterity, spatial abilities, and mechanical comprehension. For some highly skilled jobs, general intelligence tests are also useful.

3. Tests predicting performance in sales work have not been generally successful, although there are some reported instances of strikingly successful prediction. The characteristics and abilities required for a successful sales career are complex. Apparently, personality factors are very important, but this is one area in which testing seems to be least efficient.

4. The prediction of potential managers and executives has been a major focus of personnel psychologists, and many tests have been developed and applied with mixed results. As with sales jobs, the work in question and the skills necessary for success are complex and not completely understood. The kinds of tests used include projective and objective personality tests and tests of mental ability; the latter are among the more valid predictors of executive success.

The higher the level of the job, the more difficult it has been to predict performance by means of psychological tests. It is precisely these high-level jobs, however, that are the most important in industry and that demand better and more efficient means of selection.

As is the case with the other selection techniques, the usefulness of a psychological testing program to an organization depends on the amount of time and money the management is willing to invest in the necessary psychological research.

LIMITATIONS AND DANGERS OF PSYCHOLOGICAL TESTING

Overacceptance of Tests

A continual danger with psychological tests is their excessive and uncritical use by gullible personnel managers who lack the ability to discriminate between good and poor tests. Tests may have been over-sold to those in a position to use and abuse them. Because there is such broad acceptance and (alleged) need for various kinds of psychological tests, there are many test developers—professional and charlatan—who are willing to satisfy this need by producing more tests. There is no lack of tests advertised as "exciting," "the latest thing," or "just what your company needs." Each year, scores of new tests are marketed. Apparently, it is more profitable to bring out a new test than to refine or modify an existing one. Obviously, if personnel managers were not buying them, they would not be produced and promoted at such a rapid rate.

Part of the reason for this overacceptance is that personnel managers are taken in by slick promises of instant success in solving their personnel selection problems. All too frequently, a personnel manager will choose a test just because it is new, without making any attempt to investigate the research conducted on the test or the test's reliability and validity. Sometimes a test will continue to be used even when information about it is negative, usually because the personnel manager is unaware of the evidence. Often, there is no research evidence to investigate because no research was ever conducted on the test. What is needed is more and better research on the tests already in existence. In general, the more long-term data available on a test, the more effective that test will be.

Given a trusting and naïve personnel manager, and a greedy or fraudulent test developer, we can begin to understand the reasons for the overacceptance of tests (at least of the wrong kinds of tests). The harm generated by improper testing affects not only the personnel manager and the company but also you, the applicant, when an ineffective test disqualifies you unfairly from a job.

Unfair Rejection of Applicants

Even the best psychological tests are not completely valid. There is always a margin of error in the prediction of job success. Sometimes unqualified people will be hired, but the reverse situation is also true; sometimes otherwise qualified persons are rejected on the basis of their test performance. (It should be pointed out, in fairness to psychological tests, that this error of prediction also exists with the other methods of selection.)

Chiefly for this reason, a selection program should not be based on a single device. The use of several techniques allows for the gathering and evaluating of as much information as possible on an applicant.

A study that demonstrated the margin of error that can exist with psychological tests involved the administration of several standard personality inventories to a group of corporation presidents, board chairmen, and promising middle management executives. The people being tested had proven records of success. How did they perform on the tests used to evaluate candidates for their positions? The researcher concluded that "if the tests were rigorously applied across the board today, half of the most dynamic [leaders] in business would be out walking the streets for a job." [5] They did not perform well enough to be hired!

Of course, this is an extreme example and does not represent the thoroughly researched and sound testing programs developed by Sears and some other companies. On the other hand, the Sears program does not represent the majority approach to testing.

Human behavior is so complex that it is difficult, if not impossible, to predict success with complete accuracy. There will always be unfair rejections, but they can be minimized when a competent person uses a competent test. The more carefully researched the testing program, the smaller is the number of applicants rejected unfairly.

The overacceptance of tests and the problem of unfair rejections point again to the need for qualified psychologists to be actively involved in developing and running a selection testing program. The pitfalls in administering such a program are magnified when it is run by someone untrained in the proper use of psychological tests.

[5] W. H. Whyte, "The fallacies of 'personality' testing," *Fortune*, **50** (September 1954), 118.

Faking Test Responses

We mentioned the problem of deliberately distorting responses on a psychological test in such a way as to maximize the possibility of appearing in a favorable light. This is a crucial problem with some tests used for personnel selection. If the applicant does not answer honestly, any prediction of future job performance is likely to be inaccurate.

With certain kinds of tests, faking is not a problem. It is not possible, for example, to improve your score on an intelligence test or a test of mechanical comprehension by deliberate faking. However, with objective personality tests and interest inventories, it is easy to distort the answers. Faking may be the greatest single liability in the use of personality and interest tests—the motivation to lie is frequently very strong.

Suppose you are in desperate need of a job and apply for a sales position. The company's test includes questions such as:

I enjoy meeting new people.	YES_____	NO_____
I get along well with most people.	YES_____	NO_____
I find it easy to talk to people.	YES_____	NO_____

If you really want the job, you can easily answer in the way you think the company expects salespersons to answer, indicating that you enjoy meeting people, get along well with them, and find them easy to talk to. Unless these characteristics truly apply to you, however, your answers will provide the company with a false picture. You may be hired, but you probably will not succeed or be happy in the job because it requires characteristics you do not, in truth, possess.

In the long run, therefore, faking test responses may work to your disadvantage—but it is hard to convince an avid job-seeker of this in advance.

Faking may be so widespread in selection situations that it cannot be assumed that most applicants will answer personality and interest tests honestly. The best we can do is to detect faking when it occurs and discard the test results of those found to be deliberately dishonest. A few tests (including the MMPI and the *Kuder Occupational Interest Survey)* have lie detection scales built into their design.

There is an interesting moral dilemma here in that applicants willing to lie may be rewarded with a job. They may later find themselves unsuited for the job but most likely they won't blame themselves for having misrepresented their abilities in the first place.

On the other hand, persons who respond honestly, admitting perhaps to low-level neurotic behaviors (which most of us possess), may be punished by not getting the job. Everyone—the honest and the dishonest applicants, the psychologist who sets up the testing program, and the company—may lose in the long run. The company may be hiring skilled and practiced liars and losing the honest and perhaps better qualified applicant.

Conformity

One frequent criticism of the use of psychological tests for selection is that they lead to the hiring of the same type of person—not inclined to rock the boat, unimaginative, interested in preserving the status quo. The argument is that the truly exceptional and questioning individual is penalized, particularly by personality tests, which gauge everyone by a standard of normalcy.

Companies using personality tests do establish a profile of personality patterns to define the kind of individual they are seeking. Those whose test results match the profile are hired; those who show extreme deviations are not. As a result, after several years of selecting people on the basis of their test results, they will all exhibit similar personality patterns.

Two points can be made against the argument that testing leads to conformity. First, some conformity may not be negative. A company could, for example, establish a profile that identifies the creative, imaginative, and innovative individual. In this case, the unimaginative person would not match the profile and would not be hired. Thus, the company would be looking for those who conform to a norm, but it is a norm of dynamic, creative talent. Second, even if the company's profile does reward the person whose test results show him or her to be unimaginative and conventional, there is always the expectation that creative people may be hired anyway (perhaps because they faked the test results in the direction in which they felt the company was looking).

At any rate, most organizations need both kinds of people, the conservative and the exceptional—some to perform the routine work (even at the executive level) and others to lead and challenge. We should not minimize the negative aspects of conformity that can be brought about by personality testing. Where the situation exists, however, it is more a fault of the organization and less of the tests it uses.

Quality of Psychological Testing Programs

Another weakness and danger of testing, independent of the quality of the tests themselves, is the lack of care paid to the everyday business of giving the tests in an employment situation. We are not talking about the quality of the research in setting up the program, or of faking or unfair rejection practices but, simply, sloppy test administration.

One study investigated the testing practices of twenty-eight government and industrial organizations that used psychological tests. The results were not encouraging. Although most organizations provided sufficiently large testing facilities, two thirds of them failed to keep the testing room free of interruptions while testing was underway. Any interruption of the testing procedure violates the condition of standardization that is vital to the reliability and validity of the test results. Most organizations lacked sufficient concern for this important condition of proper testing.

Only 13 per cent of the organizations surveyed required any kind of training for the persons who administered the tests. Further, only 15 per cent of the companies had conducted any research to find out if the tests they used were really of any value to them in selecting the right people for the jobs. In terms of overall quality of the testing program, only 9 per cent were judged good, 46 per cent moderate, and a large 30 per cent poor. None were rated excellent or superior.

This is a major indictment of the testing programs of these organizations. Such shoddy administrative procedures can negate the years of sound research devoted to developing the program. One untrained or careless clerk can virtually destroy the effectiveness of the most expensive and thorough selection system.

ATTITUDES TOWARD PSYCHOLOGICAL TESTING PROGRAMS

In recent years the general attitude toward psychological testing has become increasingly critical. Popular books and articles have attacked the use of tests, particularly in the public school systems, but also their widespread use in industry and government for selection purposes.

It is probably true that psychological tests (indeed, any kind of test) have never been popular with those who are required to take them and who find their future dependent upon the outcome. But most people have little choice about taking tests, either in school or in industry. True, we can refuse to take the tests a company wants to give us as a selection device, but this almost invariably means that we won't be considered for the job.

Many people react with uneasiness, anxiety, or even fear to test taking, and this reaction may be mixed with suspicion and hostility. Labor unions also view tests with suspicion. They have rarely encouraged the establishment of testing programs in industry. They seem to believe that testing serves only the company, never the employee. (We have seen, however, that a soundly researched testing program can be of tremendous value to the employees by guiding them into the kind of work for which they are best suited.) Whether or not their attitude is well founded, unions remain distrustful of testing programs and any company developing such a program must consider this factor.

The American Psychological Association is justifiably concerned about the ethical practices of all psychologists, whether engaged in research in a university or selecting persons for jobs in business. Principles for proper conduct have been published with the following preamble: "The psychologist believes in the dignity and worth of the individual human being. He is committed to increasing man's understanding of himself and others. While pursuing this endeavor, he protects the welfare of any person who may seek his service. . . ."

Unfortunately, the spirit of this credo is sometimes violated and many of these violations occur with the use of psychological tests for selection purposes. Some tests have been used for selection in the absence of adequate validity data. This is harmful to the applicants and surely does not represent a concern for their dignity and worth.

The ethics code of the American Psychological Association discusses proper safeguards for the distribution and use of psychological tests.

1. Test users. Those who administer and interpret tests should be aware of the principles of psychological measurement, of validation, and of the limitations of test interpretation. They must avoid any discrimination and bias in their work and should always consider more than one means of assessment. They must adhere strictly to the standardized procedures for administering a test and make every effort to achieve accuracy in the scoring and recording of test results.

2. Test security. Actual questions from tests should never be reprinted in any public medium such as a newspaper or magazine. It is permissible to publish sample questions—those resembling the real questions—but not items used in the actual scoring of a test. (The test items reproduced in this chapter are sample questions.) Tests should be sold only to professionals who will safeguard their use. The specific test in question will

determine the qualifications necessary for proper use of the test.

3. Test interpretation. Test scores should be given only to those qualified to interpret them. For example, the scores should not be given to anyone outside of the personnel department, such as the applicant's potential supervisor, unless he or she has the training necessary to interpret the scores. However, the person being tested has the right to know his or her score and what it means.

4. Test publication. Tests should not be released for use without adequate background research to support the claims of the test. Fully informative and current test manuals, containing data on reliability, validity, and norms, should be made available with all tests. Advertisements should describe the tests accurately and not use emotional or persuasive claims.

One aspect of psychological testing that has come under attack in recent years is the use of personal or intimate questions. Critics charge that such personal probing is an unwarranted and unnecessary invasion of privacy, and that individual freedom is violated by requesting information not directly relevant to the specific job for which the person is applying. The primary target of this criticism is the personality test questions that range from sex life to the condition of one's digestive tract.

The U.S. Congress held hearings in 1965 on the privacy aspects of personality tests. The major concern was with the practice of forcing employees to answer test questions that deal with personal factors such as sexual behavior, religious beliefs, family relationships, and political attitudes. Partly as a result of these hearings, the MMPI was barred from use by federal government personnel offices.

Few people question the right of an organization to investigate job applicants. The company must know something of an applicant's background, training, and abilities in order to determine whether to hire the individual. The issue is the relevance of the information sought by the employer to the job. Critics of personality testing argue that the generally low validities of personality tests in terms of predicting job performance, as well as the ease of faking responses, suggest that such information is of little value in selection. Certainly, personal characteristics that have been shown to be directly related to job performance must be investigated, but personal questions that have no known relevance constitute an unnecessary invasion of privacy and must be avoided. Even if such questions could be used to predict job performance, however, there remains the issue of how much of themselves people have to reveal to a potential employer.

SUMMARY

Psychological tests are measuring devices that are used to consistently and systematically assess a sample of behavior. Tests serve two purposes: placement and selection. **Placement** is concerned with determining what kind of job is suitable for a particular person; **selection** is concerned with determining what kind of person is suitable for a particular job.

Psychological tests must meet and satisfy the following characteristics. **Standardization** refers to the consistency of procedures and conditions under which people take a test. **Objectivity** involves the accurate and consistent scoring of a test, unbiased by the personal characteristics of the scorer. All tests must have one or more sets of **test norms,** scores of a group of people who are similar to those taking the test, which serve as a point of comparison for individual scores. **Reliability** refers to the consistency of responses on a test and can be determined in three ways: the **test-retest method,** the **equivalent forms method,** and the **split-halves method. Validity** of a test is concerned with how well it measures what it intends to measure.

Validity is of two types: empirical or rational. **Empirical validity** is determined by the methods of **predictive validity** or **concurrent validity. Rational validity** is established by either **content validity** or **construct validity.** There is also the concept of **face validity**—how valid or relevant the test appears to the person taking it.

Fair employment legislation has had a strong impact on the use of psychological tests in selection, making it illegal to use any test that discriminates against applicants because of their race, color, religion, sex, or national origin. The Equal Employment Opportunity Commission has prescribed the kinds of validation studies that must be conducted on all tests used for selection to ensure that they are measuring characteristics that are clearly related to the job in question.

A number of steps are required to establish a testing program: (1) conducting a job and worker analysis, (2) finding or developing a suitable test, (3) conducting an item analysis of each question on the test, (4) determining the level of difficulty of each question, (5) establishing the reliability and validity of the test, and (6) setting the cut-off scores.

The testing program conducted by the Sears, Roebuck organization illustrates the time and effort necessary to develop a truly worthwhile testing program.

Psychological tests can be categorized by the ways in which they are **constructed, scored,** and **administered,** or in terms of the **behavior**

they measure. Categories of tests include individual or group tests, speed or power tests, paper-and-pencil or performance tests, and objectively or subjectively scored tests.

The kinds of behavior measured include mental ability, interest, aptitude, motor ability, and personality. Examples of specific tests for each kind of behavior are presented.

Personality testing is particularly controversial. Personality characteristics are measured by self-report inventories or projective techniques.

There are advantages to the use of psychological tests for selection purposes. Tests can aid the selection process (assuming thorough developmental research), they are objective measures, and their effectiveness is easier to evaluate than some other selection devices. Psychological tests are better able to predict success in training programs than in predicting actual job performance. In general, tests are more useful in predicting success in lower-level jobs such as clerk, assembly line operator, and general factory worker than in predicting success in higher-level positions such as manager or executive.

The limitations and dangers of psychological testing include over-acceptance, unfair rejection of applicants, faking of test responses, conformity, and poor quality of test administration.

In recent years, the general public has become more critical of psychological tests and there are serious ethical issues involved in their use as selection devices, including the matter of invasion of privacy.

SUGGESTED READINGS

Abrahams, N., Neumann, I., and Gilthens, W. Faking vocational interests: Simulated versus real life motivation. *Personnel Psychology,* 1971, **24**(1), 5–12.

American Psychological Association. Psychological assessment and public policy. *American Psychologist,* 1970, **25,** 264–266.

Anastasi, A. *Psychological Testing,* 4th ed. New York: Macmillan Publishing Co., 1976.

Buros, O. K., Ed. *The Seventh Mental Measurements Yearbook.* Highland Park, N.J.: Gryphon Press, 1972.

Byham, W. C., and Spitzer, M. E. *The Law and Personnel Testing.* New York: American Management Association, 1971.

Clarke, W. Who gains when you cheat on a personality test? *Personnel Journal,* 1974, **53,** 302–303.

Cronbach, L. *Essentials of Psychological Testing,* 3rd ed. New York: Harper & Row, 1970.

Einhorn, H., and Bass, A. Methodological considerations relevant to discrimination in employment testing. *Psychological Bulletin,* 1971, **75,** 261–269.

Fincher, C. Personnel testing and public policy. *American Psychologist,* 1973, **28,** 489–497.

Ghiselli, E. The validity of aptitude tests in personnel selection. *Personnel Psychology,* 1973, **26,** 461–477.

Gough, H. Personality and personality assessment. In M. Dunnette, Ed., *Handbook of Industrial and Organizational Psychology.* Chicago: Rand McNally, 1976. Pp. 571–607.

Jones, A., and Whittaker, P. A. *Testing Industrial Skills.* New York: Halsted Press, 1975.

Lipsett, L. Selecting personnel without tests. *Personnel Journal,* 1972, **51,** 648–654.

Miller, K. M., Ed. *Psychological Tests in Personnel Assessment.* New York: Halsted Press, 1975.

Samuda, R. J. *Psychological Testing of American Minorities: Issues and Consequences.* New York: Harper & Row, 1975.

Sparks, C. Validity of personnel tests. *Personnel Psychology,* 1970, **23,** 39–46.

Tenopyr, M. L. *Selected References on Employee Selection With Emphasis on Testing the Disadvantaged.* Washington, D.C.: U.S. Civil Service Commission, 1972.

5

The Evaluation
of Performance

INTRODUCTION

The frequent, continuous, and impartial evaluation by an organization of the performance of its employees is vital not only for the growth of the organization but also for the growth of the individual employees. A company must know who are its outstanding workers, who needs additional training, and who is not contributing to the efficiency and welfare of the company.

At all levels of employment, personnel decisions relating to promoting, retaining, or firing workers are made daily and, ideally, such decisions are based solely on the merit or ability of the employees. The quality of a worker's performance on the job must be assessed in some way, and such assessments will be more fair and useful if they are based on objective and systematic criteria. These criteria must involve factors relevant to the person's ability to perform the job.

In your own organizational career, your performance will be monitored and evaluated periodically and your level of salary, rank, and responsibility will depend on how well you satisfy the established criteria of job performance.

Performance evaluation is not practiced only in business. Indeed, it has been taking place throughout your academic career. Classroom examinations, term papers, and special reports are all techniques of performance evaluation used by educational institutions. In principle, they are similar to the techniques used in the world of work; that is, they are methods of gauging or assessing the quality of your work. And, as in industry, the results of these evaluations have an important bearing on your future—they determine whether or not you will be promoted to the next grade level or will graduate.

Although you may not take formal examinations in your working career, performance evaluations in industry are just as difficult and important. Whether or not you are considered qualified for a pay raise or promotion will have an obvious and direct bearing not only on your income and standard of living but also on your self-esteem, emotional security, and general satisfaction with life. In a sense, then, you are never finished passing tests of one kind or another. Once you have passed the various selection criteria used by a company and been hired, you will continue to be tested (although in a different manner).

It is important to remember that performance evaluation is as beneficial to you as to your company. Just as classroom examinations tell where you stand and show where you need improvement, so the well-run performance evaluation program will enable you to gauge your rate of development on the job. Performance evaluation will point up strengths and weaknesses and, if you act wisely on this information, you may improve your ability to perform the job.

Performance evaluations, like psychological tests and other selection devices, serve you by enabling you to find the right job and perform successfully in it. It is important, therefore, that you understand the principles and procedures of performance evaluation. Also, it is vital that the procedures used by your company be as objective and systematic as possible; that is another task of the personnel psychologist.

PURPOSES OF PERFORMANCE EVALUATION

The overall purpose of performance evaluation is to provide an accurate measure of how well a person is performing the job. On the basis of this information, decisions will be made affecting the future of the individual employee.

Performance evaluation can fulfill a number of functions for management.[1]

1. Top management wants a system that will motivate high performers to do even better and low performers to improve.
2. Managers want a system that will identify those with high potential for advancement and those who are consistently low performers so that the latter may be encouraged to leave.
3. Managers and personnel people want accurate and complete information for making decisions on salary increases, promotions, transfers, and terminations.

[1] P. Thompson and G. Dalton, "Performance appraisal: Managers beware," *Harvard Business Review*, **48** (January–February 1970), 151.

4. Supervisors want an objective rating system to justify salary increases and to motivate subordinates.
5. Subordinates want to know how they are viewed by their supervisors and what the future holds for them in the organization.

As this list indicates, performance evaluation can provide something for everyone, from the employee to the immediate supervisor to the highest level of management.

Let us consider the functions of performance evaluation in greater detail.

Validation of Selection Criteria

As noted in Chapters 3 and 4, selection devices must be correlated with some measure of job success in order to establish their validity. Whether we are dealing with psychological tests, application blanks, or interviews, we cannot determine the usefulness of a technique until we examine the subsequent performance of the workers who were hired on the basis of that technique. We can have no confidence in a selection technique until we can compare a measure of the performance of successful and unsuccessful workers on the job with scores on a test or on other selection techniques. Thus, performance evaluation is vital to the success of employee selection programs.

Training Requirements

A careful evaluation of an employee's performance may uncover weaknesses or deficiencies in a specific job skill, knowledge, or psychological attitude that, once identified, may be remedied through additional formal training. Assuming that the employee's service has been otherwise satisfactory, it may be worth the cost to the company to enable the employee to improve on a weakness.

Occasionally, an entire work crew or section is found deficient in some aspect of job performance. Information of this sort can lead to the redesigning of the training program for new employees and the retraining of current workers to correct the shortcomings in job performance.

Performance evaluation can also be used as a means of measuring the worth of a training program by determining how much job performance may have improved after the training has been completed.

161

Employee Improvement

Performance evaluations are important to employees because it tells them how they are doing. This factor—knowledge of personal progress or performance—appears to be crucial to maintaining high morale. It is not sufficient for a supervisor to be made aware of the strengths and weaknesses of individual workers—the employees must be apprised of them also.

The results of a performance evaluation, communicated tactfully and constructively to employees, can indicate to them how they might alter behaviors or attitudes to improve their job efficiency and value to the company. This purpose of performance evaluation is similar to that of improving training requirements except that in this case a worker's deficiencies can be changed through self-improvement, rather than through a formal training program.

Promotions, Wages, and Transfers

Most people feel, justifiably, that they should be rewarded for above average or superior performance. Surely in your college work, fairness dictates that if your performance on examinations or term papers is superior to that of someone else, you should receive a higher grade. If differential recognition and reward were not practiced—if, for example, everyone in a class received a C regardless of his or her academic performance—there would be little motivation or incentive for hard work.

In industry, the rewards are in the tangible form of salary increases, promotions in rank, or transfers to a more desirable opportunity. To maintain initiative and morale, these changes in status must not be based on personal bias or prejudice, but on objective evaluation of an employee's merit. Performance evaluations are the basis for these career decisions.

It must be noted that many labor unions require that seniority, not performance evaluation, be used as the basis for promotion. However, length of employment alone is no indication of ability to perform a higher-level job. An assembly line worker with twelve years' experience may know everything about that job, but without a more formal and objective evaluation of the worker's competence, there is no basis for concluding that he or she would be a good foreman. Senior people should be given the first opportunity for promotion, but they should be qualified for that promotion on the basis of ability, not just length of service.

Reductions in Force

An unfortunate but seemingly ingrained aspect of our economic system is the periodic recession, sometimes in a single industry and sometimes over the entire economy. During these times it often becomes necessary to lay off a portion of the working force—a *rif*, or reduction in force, as it is euphemistically described.

In these critical times, a company will benefit by dismissing the least competent of its employees and retaining, as long as possible, those who have proven themselves to be better workers. Such decisions should be made in terms of objective analyses of actual job performance.

However, union requirements again may dictate that seniority determine any such dismissals; that is, those who have been with the company the shortest period of time should be the first dismissed. As with promotion, seniority does deserve consideration, but many argue that it should be weighed against the worker's job performance, as measured by objective techniques of performance evaluation.

Thus, there is no single aspect of a working career that cannot be influenced directly by performance evaluation. Despite its recognized importance, however, there are still those who actively resist the installation and implementation of work evaluation programs.

OPPOSITION TO PERFORMANCE EVALUATION

As noted, labor unions are not overly enthusiastic in supporting performance evaluation programs. As a rule, they have been the greatest source of opposition to such programs. The source of their resistance stems from their understandable motivation to provide the greatest degree of job security possible for their members. Unions traditionally have been committed to the principle of seniority as the determining factor in welfare and status decisions of the worker (for example, promotions and pay increases).

Of course, if all such decisions were made on the basis of seniority alone, there would be little need (and even less hope) for a system of merit or ability rating, such as is provided by performance evaluation. Fortunately, it is only in a minority of cases that union contracts dictate seniority as the determining factor in personnel decisions.

Most unions do recognize the need for considering the ability of the worker, but even then seniority remains the ultimate context within which personnel decisions must be made. In practice this means that even where ability is evaluated, it remains secondary. Workers who have been at their jobs the longest time are given the advantage over short-term employees, even though the latter might be better qualified.

Union opposition affects only those jobs covered by union contracts. This does not include the majority of job holders in the United States; one in four U.S. workers belongs to a labor union. Bowing to reality, many companies concentrate their performance evaluation programs on nonunion job categories.

Another source of opposition to performance evaluation can be the individual employee. Few of us enjoy being tested or evaluated, particularly if we feel we might not receive a favorable rating. Few of us are so confident of our abilities that we consistently expect to receive glowing comments from our superiors. Further, few of us suffer criticism gladly, regardless of its objectivity, truth, or the tact with which it is presented to us. And so, since many people would rather not be assessed and told of their weaknesses or deficiencies, they often react with suspicion and hostility to the idea of performance evaluation.

Sometimes, particularly when a performance evaluation program is being introduced, an entire section or department of employees will band together to protest to their supervisor. Front-line supervisors, who must work closely with employees and maintain their loyalty, are placed in a difficult situation when faced with such opposition. They are under pressure from superiors to implement the program and under equally strong pressure from subordinates not to implement it. Sometimes the result is that supervisors merely go through the motions of the program without giving anyone a bad rating, in order to maintain peace and harmony among the employees.

When individual opposition is combined with resistance from a labor union, the company is usually on the losing side of the battle, but so are the employees in the long run.

Another source of resistance to programs of performance evaluation is members of management who may oppose such appraisals because of unfavorable experiences with them. As with psychological tests or other selection methods, a poorly designed and inadequate performance evaluation system can do more harm than good. Unfortunately, industry has all too often introduced these programs without adequate preparation and care, and many managers feel that performance evaluation has a bad reputation.

The concept of performance evaluation is highly complex and its application requires the services of professional psychologists. When companies introduce programs in the absence of skilled psychological advice and recommendations, they are usually disappointed. Just as some executives disdain the use of psychological tests because of unfavorable experiences in using poor ones, so do some managers consider performance evaluation programs worthless. And, it should be noted, even sound performance evaluation programs have sometimes been less than satisfactory.

In addition, some managers dislike performance evaluation systems because they are required to assume the role of judge. Managers may look upon worker evaluation as "playing God" and are unwilling or unable to accept the burden of directly affecting the future of their subordinates.

Despite the resistance to performance evaluation, it remains a vital activity of organizational life. Its critics often overlook the point that some form of performance appraisal is inevitable. Some basis must be established for deciding on pay raises, transfers, promotions, or training requirements. These determinations cannot be made haphazardly or by the toss of a coin, and neither should they be based on subjective factors such as a supervisor's likes and dislikes. Evaluations of performance must be made, and they can be either objective and accurate or subjective and error filled. Surely employer and employee alike would prefer, even insist, that ability be appraised in a manner that reflects, as objectively as possible, the qualifications and abilities to do the job.

TECHNIQUES OF PERFORMANCE EVALUATION

Several techniques to measure job performance have been developed. In general, the specific technique chosen varies with the type of work. The work performed in a routine, repetitive assembly line job differs from sales work or the duties of an advertising account executive, and the performance measure used must reflect the nature and complexity of the job. Assembly line job performance can be assessed more easily and objectively than the daily activities of the executive.

There are two categories of performance measure: those for production jobs and those for nonproduction jobs. Some sample performance measures for both kinds of work are listed below.

Production jobs:

1. Quantity of output—the number of units assembled or produced in a given period of time.
2. Quality of output—assessed by inspection standards or the number of faulty units produced.
3. Accidents—accident record of the worker.

4. Salary—earnings history of the worker, rate and frequency of increases.
5. Absenteeism—number of days lost from work.
6. Rate of advancement—record of promotion.

Accidents, salary, absenteeism, and advancement may also be used in assessing performance on nonproduction jobs.

Nonproduction jobs:

1. Assessment by supervisors—appraisal of level of proficiency.
2. Assessment by peers—co-workers' judgments of performance level.
3. Self-assessment—appraisal of one's own performance level.

As you can see from these sample performance measures, the criteria used differ greatly for the two job categories. Production jobs readily lend themselves to more objective measures of performance and output (although subjective factors do enter into the assessment), whereas nonproduction jobs require more judgmental and qualitative assessments.

Production Jobs

The measurement of performance on production jobs is relatively easy in principle and usually involves a simple recording of the number of units produced in a given period of time. This measure of quantity is widely used in industry, partly because records of production are readily available.

In practice, however, performance evaluation of production jobs is not so simple. The quality of the work produced must also be assessed. Consider the example of two secretaries: one types seventy words per minute and the other types fifty-five words per minute. If we use quantity as the sole measure of job performance, the first secretary receives the higher evaluation. However, if we appraise quality of performance, we find that the first secretary averages twenty mistakes per minute and the second makes none. The performance ratings reflecting these quality considerations should now be reversed—the second secretary receives the higher evaluation.

There are additional complications in measuring performance on production jobs. Even when the quantity of output data have been corrected for quality, there is still the possibility that other factors may contaminate or distort the resulting performance measure.

In the case of the two secretaries, perhaps the one who made so many typing errors works in a noisy office filled with distractions and the other works in quiet and peaceful surroundings. The quantity and quality of the work produced by each may be seriously influenced by the office environment. This factor also must be considered in the fair assessment of the typing ability of both secretaries. Note that this contaminating factor is extraneous to the task itself—a condition not a part of the actual job but that nonetheless affects job performance.

Another contaminating factor may be found in differences in the nature of the same job from one worker to another. For example, one secretary types only short business letters and the other types complex technical engineering reports in quadruplicate. It would be unfair to determine the level of performance without in some way correcting for the difference in level of difficulty of the work.

A final contaminating factor is length of job experience. Studies have shown that usually the longer employees are on a job, the greater is their productivity. Hence, the performance evaluations of two otherwise identical workers on the same job—one with twenty years' experience and the other with two years' experience—may be expected to differ. It does not necessarily follow, however, that the lower performance evaluation of newer workers indicates that they are not good employees. They may be quite efficient considering their amount of job experience.

Thus, several factors must be recognized in order to evaluate the performance of a production job. The more contaminating factors are taken into account, the less objective is the final appraisal. Personal judgments must be made on the nature and extent of extraneous influences and some modification applied to the measure of production. Therefore, even with production jobs in which there is a tangible product that can be counted, performance evaluation may not be completely objective. Whenever any judgment is required, an opportunity is provided for personal factors to bias the evaluation.

Job-related Personal Data

Items of personal data—absenteeism, earnings history, accidents, rate of advancement—are also used in assessing performance. These factors are considered primarily for production jobs but are also used for some nonproduction jobs.

It is usually simpler to acquire job-related personal information than it is to measure production. Companies maintain complete records so this information can be easily obtained from personnel office

167

files. This availability is, of course, an advantage, but what do personal data tell us about an employee's actual job performance?

The evidence shows that such factors may tell very little about a worker's ability on the job but they can be used to distinguish good from poor employees if we make the semantic distinction between "employees" and "workers." Consider a highly skilled and experienced machine operator who is prone to excessive absenteeism and tardiness. This person could be considered an excellent "worker" (when actually on the job) but a very poor "employee" in that the company cannot rely on the person to contribute consistently to the efficiency of the organization.

Job-related personal data have a definite use in assessing the relative worth of employees to the organization, but they do not substitute for measures of performance evaluation.

Nonproduction Jobs

A nonproduction job is one in which competence or efficiency is measured in qualitative terms because these employees do not produce a countable product, or not one that it makes any sense to count. How would you evaluate the performance of firefighters? Should we count the number of fires they put out in a day? How would you judge brain surgeons? Should we count the number of brains they operate on each week? Or in evaluating business executives, do we count the number of decisions they make each month?

In each of these cases, we must find some way to assess and judge the merit or ability of the person's work, not by counting, but by observing work behavior over a period of time and rendering an opinion as to its quality. Thus, to determine how good or effective a nonproduction worker is, we have to ask someone who is familiar with the person and his or her work—usually the supervisor, but occasionally co-workers as well.

Merit Rating Approach

A worker's performance level is usually judged through the procedure known as merit rating.

Throughout our lives, we make judgments about the people with whom we come in contact. We assess them in terms of their intelligence, personality, humor, agreeableness, and the like. Based on these informal judgments, we decide whether to like or dislike these people, invite them to join our club, or marry them. Of course, while we are busy judging others they are likewise judging us and making the same kinds of decisions. Our judgments are sometimes incorrect—the would-be friend becomes an enemy or the spouse becomes an adversary in divorce court. The reason for errors in judgment lies in the fact that the process is subjective and unstandardized; we judge on the basis of false and misleading criteria, on superficial and meaningless factors.

The process of judgment used in merit rating is more formal and specific; relevant criteria are established to serve as standards for comparison. The fallible human beings who are the raters can inject their own biases or prejudices into the judgment process, but that is not the fault of the technique. The merit rating is designed to be an objective evaluation of work performance compared with established standards.

Several merit rating techniques are rating, ranking, paired comparison, forced distribution, forced choice, and critical incidents.

Rating Technique

The most frequently used method of performance evaluation is the rating technique. The supervisor's task is simply to specify how, or to what degree, each relevant characteristic is possessed by the worker. In rating the quality of work, based on observations of the worker's performance, the supervisor might express a judgment in terms of the following scale and decide at what point the work quality falls. The worker in this example has been judged as producing at slightly above average quality.

		X		
1	2	3	4	5
Poor		Average		Excellent

Not all firms use this numerical scale format, but the principle is the same: The individual receives a rating or score at some point along a dimension ranging from low to high, or poor to excellent.

Figure 5–1 shows part of a performance evaluation rating scale form used by a large textile company. Instead of a numerical rating scale for each characteristic, this company uses verbal designations to describe the range from exceptional to poor. In the column at the right of the form the rater is asked to compare the current evaluation with the worker's last appraisal and to indicate whether the worker has shown improvement, slipped back, or shown no change on each characteristic. Space is provided for additional comments on each characteristic, an opportunity to explain extenuating circumstances

PERFORMANCE REVIEW

NAME	POSITION
COMPANY	DEPARTMENT
DATE	DATE OF LAST REVIEW

INSTRUCTIONS

Evaluate the employee on the job now being performed. Circle the dot in the space above the horizontal line which most nearly expresses your over-all judgment on each quality. The care and accuracy with which this appraisal is made will determine its value to you, to the employee and to the organization.

Consider the employee's performance since the last appraisal and show by a check (√) whether he/she has gone back, remained stationary or gone ahead in each of the qualities listed to the left.

						HAS IM-PROVED	LITTLE OR NO CHANGE	HAS GONE BACK
KNOWLEDGE OF WORK: Consider knowledge of job gained through experience; general education; specialized training.	Well informed on all phases of work.	Knowledge thorough enough to perform without assistance.	Adequate grasp of essentials. Some assistance.	Requires considerable assistance.	Inadequate knowledge.	COMMENTS		
QUANTITY OF WORK: Consider the volume of work produced under normal conditions. Disregard errors.	Rapid worker. Unusually big producer.	Turns out good volume.	Average.	Volume below average.	Very slow worker.	COMMENTS		
QUALITY OF WORK: Consider neatness, accuracy and dependability of results regardless of volume.	Exceptionally accurate, practically no mistakes.	Acceptable, usually neat, occasional errors or rejections.	Seldom necessary to check work.	Often unacceptable, frequent errors or rejections.	Too many errors or rejections.	COMMENTS		
ABILITY TO LEARN NEW DUTIES: Consider the speed with which he/she masters new routine and grasps explanations. Consider also ability to retain this knowledge.	Exceptionally fast to learn and adjust to changed conditions.	Learns rapidly. Retains instructions.	Average instruction required.	Requires a great deal of instruction.	Very slow to absorb. Poor memory.	COMMENTS		
INITIATIVE: Consider the tendency to contribute, develop and/or carry out new ideas or methods.	Initiative resulting in frequent saving in time and money.	Very resourceful.	Shows initiative occasionally.	Rarely shows any initiative.	Needs constant prodding.	COMMENTS		
COOPERATION: Consider manner of handling business relationships.	Goes out of the way to cooperate.	Gets along well with associates.	Acceptable.	Shows reluctance to cooperate.	Very poor cooperation.	COMMENTS		
JUDGMENT AND COMMON SENSE: Does he/she think intelligently and make decisions logically.	Thinks quickly, logically. Outstanding.	Judgment usually logical.	Fairly reliable.	Inclined to be illogical.	Poor. Unreliable.	COMMENTS		

Figure 5–1. Performance review form.

that may have adversely affected a worker's performance, or to add praise beyond that indicated in the formal rating.

Once supervisors have carefully judged a worker on the seven characteristics noted, this company then asks them to answer general questions about the employee in their own words (Figure 5–2).

The questions noted on the performance review form in Figure 5–2 require written answers, the content of which exceeds the relatively simple ratings required in Figure 5–1. Of course, supervisors' comments are expected to be based on their ratings, but should be more elaborate.

Ratings are a popular way of evaluating performance for two rea-

INSTRUCTIONS: Based on the appraisal you have made on the reverse side please answer the following questions in your own words.

IS EMPLOYEE WELL SUITED FOR TYPE OF WORK HE/SHE IS NOW DOING?	☐ YES ☐ NO	(If "no" indicate type of work for which he/she is suited)

WHAT CONTRIBUTION HAS EMPLOYEE MADE TO COMPANY, DEPARTMENT OR DIVISION BEYOND NORMAL REQUIREMENTS OF POSITION?

ALONG WHAT LINES DO YOU FEEL THAT HE/SHE NEEDS TO IMPROVE SELF?

WRITE HERE ANY ADDITIONAL COMMENTS GOOD OR BAD, WHICH YOU FEEL HAVE NOT BEEN COVERED.

WHAT WOULD BE YOUR OVERALL EVALUATION OF EMPLOYEE? (Place check (√) above horizontal line)

1	2	3	4	5
EXCELLENT	GOOD	SATISFACTORY	FAIR	POOR

	REVIEWED BY	DATE

Figure 5–2. Performance review form.

sons: (1) they are relatively easy to construct, and (2) they attempt to be as objective as possible. We know by now that no procedure that depends upon one person judging, assessing, or forming an opinion of another can be totally objective or free of personal bias, but well-designed rating scales attempt to keep biasing factors to a minimum.

Ranking Systems

In the ranking technique, supervisors list or rank their workers in order from highest to lowest or best to worst on specific characteristics or in terms of overall job effectiveness. There is a major conceptual difference between ranking and rating. In ranking, each employee is compared with all the others in the unit or section; rating compares the individual with his or her own past performance or a company standard. Ranking is not as direct as rating (although raters may unconsciously compare one individual with another in their judgments).

One advantage of the ranking technique is its simplicity. No elaborate forms or complicated instructions are required. Ranking can be accomplished quickly and is usually accepted by supervisors as a routine sort of task to perform. Further, supervisors are not being asked to judge workers on a variety of traits, some of which they may not be competent to judge.

The ranking method has limitations when working with a large

171

number of employees, however. A supervisor would be expected to know all the employees in the unit quite well in order to make comparative judgments of their efficiency. With a group of fifty or one hundred subordinates, it is difficult and tedious to rank them in order of merit from best to worst.

Another limitation is that because of its simplicity, ranking supplies much less evaluative information on each employee than does rating. For example, specific strengths and weaknesses of workers cannot be readily determined. Hence, the ranking method may provide less useful feedback to employees about how well they are doing or what they might do to improve performance.

The use of the ranking method to evaluate employees makes it difficult to indicate similarities in efficiency among workers. For example, in ranking ten workers, a foreman may feel that three of them are equally outstanding and two others equally poor, but there is no way to specify this. The workers must be ranked in order from highest to lowest. Only one of the three outstanding workers can receive the highest performance evaluation, but all three deserve it.

Another problem concerns the magnitude of the differences between the ranks. These differences may appear equal but may not be so in practice. For example, is the difference between the workers ranked fourth and fifth the same as the difference between the workers ranked fifth and sixth? Since they are only one number apart, the tendency is to think that the differences are equal, but there is no way of being certain because the estimate is subjective.

These limitations make the ranking method a crude measure of performance evaluation at best. It should be applied where only a small number of workers are involved and where little information is desired beyond an indication of the relative standing of the workers as a unit.

Paired Comparison Systems

The paired comparison technique requires that each worker be compared with every other worker in the work unit. It is similar to the ranking technique, and the result is a rank ordering of workers but the comparative judgments are more rigorously controlled and systematic.

Comparisons are made between two people at a time and a judgment made as to which person within the pair is superior. If specific traits or characteristics are judged, the comparisons must be repeated for each item. When all possible comparisons have been made, an objective rank ordering is obtained, based on the person's score in each comparison. For example, suppose that a supervisor is asked to evaluate six workers by the paired comparison technique. This means that fifteen paired comparisons must be made, since there are fifteen possible pairs obtainable with six people, based on the formula

$$\frac{N(N-1)}{2}$$

where N is the number of persons to be evaluated.

A major advantage of the paired comparison approach over the ranking procedure is that the judgmental process is simpler. The supervisor only has to judge one pair of workers at a time instead of an entire section or department. Another advantage is that it is possible to give the same rank to those of equal ability.

The major disadvantage lies in the large number of comparisons required when dealing with many employees. If a supervisor has 60 employees in a department, he or she would be required to make 1,770 comparisons—a task that would not only be monotonous but which would leave the supervisor little time to supervise! Further, if the performance evaluation calls for the ranking of workers on, say, five separate traits, each of the 1,770 comparisons would have to be made five times. The use of this technique, therefore, is restricted to small groups and usually to a single ranking in terms of overall effectiveness.

Forced Distribution Technique

The forced distribution technique, useful with somewhat larger groups, rates employees in terms of a predetermined distribution of ratings. The supervisor must rate the workers in certain proportions. In other words, a fixed percentage of the workers must be placed in each of several categories. The standard distribution used is as follows:

Superior	10%
Better than average	20%
Average	40%
Below average	20%
Poor	10%

Employees must be assigned in accordance with this distribution on whatever characteristics or abilities are being evaluated. If, for example, 100 persons are being rated, 10 must be assigned to the superior category, 20 to the better than average category, and so on.

The judgments of ability are made on a relative rather than an absolute basis; that is, workers are assessed as poor, for example, relative to their performance in the particular group in which they work. On an absolute standard of performance, these employees may not be the least effective workers, but relative to their particular work group, they are so rated.

A disadvantage of the forced distribution approach is that it forces a supervisor to use predetermined rating categories that might not represent a particular group of workers. Suppose, for example, that all the workers in a department are well above average in job performance. They all deserve good ratings. The forced distribution technique, however, would dictate that 30 per cent of these workers receive below average or poor ratings; this is obviously unfair.

Forced Choice Technique

A major difficulty with the rating techniques discussed previously is that raters are fully aware of whether they are giving good or poor ratings to the employees. This awareness may allow personal bias or favoritism to influence the ratings. To eliminate this knowledge on the part of the supervisor, the forced choice technique was developed; this approach prevents raters from knowing how favorable or unfavorable a rating they are giving an employee.

With the forced choice method, raters are presented with a series of descriptive statements (in pairs, or groups of three or four) and asked to select the phrase that best describes an employee and/or the phrase that least describes the same employee. The phrases within each group are designed to appear equally favorable or equally unfavorable.

For example, raters are asked to choose one statement in each of the following pairs of statements that best describes a worker.

1. Is reliable.	1. Is careful.
2. Is agreeable.	2. Is diligent.

Next, raters pick one statement in each of the following pairs that is least descriptive of that worker.

1. Is arrogant.	1. Is uncooperative.
2. Is not interested in the job.	2. Is sloppy on the job.

Given a number of these sets of statements, it becomes difficult for supervisors to deliberately give good or poor ratings to a worker. How would they determine which of each pair of statements represents a desirable or an undesirable characteristic? The pairs appear to be equally favorable or equally unfavorable.

In the development of statements for the forced choice technique, each phrase is evaluated to determine how well it correlates with a measure of job success. Thus, although the statements seem equal in terms of their favorable or unfavorable nature, they are not equal in fact. One statement in each pair has been found to discriminate between more efficient and less efficient workers.

An advantage of this technique is the prevention of the possible influence of personal bias on the performance evaluations. However, this is more than offset by several disadvantages so that the forced choice technique is not very popular in industry.

A considerable amount of research is necessary to determine the predictive validity of each item. Thus, the forced choice technique is considerably more costly to develop than other methods of performance evaluation. Also, it is a difficult technique for many raters to understand and perform. The task of choosing one of a pair of equally favorable or unfavorable statements is tedious. Raters often experience difficulty in making their choices. Another disadvantage is that despite the useful information provided to the organization, the technique yields little information on the strengths and weaknesses of the employees.

Critical Incidents Technique

This approach, discussed in Chapter 3 as a method of job analysis, is sometimes used in performance evaluation. Since the method stresses description rather than evaluation of behavior on the job, it is perhaps less susceptible to bias on the part of the rater than some other techniques, although it does not completely eliminate bias.

Supervisors are asked to observe the performance of their workers and to record those behaviors that are critical to success on the job. Through these observations, a series of critical incident behaviors are established—some associated with superior performance and others with poor or unsatisfactory performance. These behaviors can then be used as standards for judging the efficiency of individual workers—standards developed on the basis of actual job performance. Actual behavior incidents are being rated, then, not vague, general characteristics or traits. This focus on job behavior also makes the critical incidents technique valuable for counseling individual employees because specific ineffective or undesirable behaviors can be pointed out.

Much of the success of this approach depends upon the observational skill of the supervisors in determining the kinds of behavior that are truly critical to successful or unsuccessful performance on the

175

job. If the list of critical incidents is inadequate, any performance evaluation based on these behaviors may be misleading.

The effective compilation of a list of critical incidents requires a great deal of time and effort. Supervisors must be continually alert to the specific behaviors of their subordinates and must record each instance. It is not sufficient to wait until a performance evaluation is required and then to try to remember specific behaviors. Supervisors should be prepared to meet with each subordinate and point out examples of desirable and undesirable job behaviors that have occurred since the previous evaluation. This requires supervisors to keep what may have to be a daily log of the critical events they have observed.

SOURCES OF ERROR IN PERFORMANCE EVALUATION

Regardless of the sophistication of the techniques, performance evaluation remains basically a subjective procedure. No matter how much control is exerted over rating or ranking procedures, the process still involves one human being judging, assessing, or estimating the characteristics of another. This means that human frailties and prejudices will affect the evaluations. All of us tend to judge people and things in our life in terms of our own preferences or fears. One person's assessment of another's abilities can be influenced by the other person's religion, race, mode of dress, or attractiveness, as well as by more objective characteristics and abilities. Also, it has been shown that the competence of supervisors can influence their perceptiveness in assessing others. Supervisors who are very effective in their own jobs have been shown to be more capable of discriminating between good and poor workers. Poor supervisors seem less capable of judging the performance abilities of their subordinates.

In addition, raters differ in terms of a characteristic known as *social differentiation,* which refers to the ability to make discriminative judgments among people. Those who are low in social differentiation are poor at a task such as performance evaluation because they believe that people are more uniform than they really are. Thus, they tend to give similar ratings to all their subordinates. Those who are high in social differentiation, on the other hand, are much better able to perceive fine degrees of difference among people, and so tend to give those whom they are evaluating a wider range of ratings.

Other sources of error can distort performance evaluations. These include the halo effect, constant bias, most-recent-performance error, inadequate information error, and average rating error.

The Halo Effect

The halo effect involves the familiar tendency to judge all aspects of a person's behavior on the basis of a single attribute or characteristic. If we find a person to be extremely likable, friendly, and easy to get along with, we tend to evaluate that person favorably on all other personality characteristics.

A supervisor who finds an employee high on one factor of a rating scale may tend to rate that person high on all other factors. This distorting effect is particularly likely to occur when a high rating is given on one or two traits and the other traits to be rated are difficult to observe or define, are unfamiliar, or involve vague or ambiguous personality characteristics.

One method of attempting to control the halo effect is to have more than one person rate a worker on the assumption that the biases and prejudices of different raters will tend to cancel each other out. This method can only be used when the raters have had experience with and opportunity to observe the worker being evaluated.

Another way of counteracting the halo effect is to have supervisors rate all subordinates on one trait or characteristic at a time, instead of rating each person on all traits at the same time. When workers are compared on only one characteristic, there is somewhat less opportunity for an individual's rating on this trait to be carried over to another trait.

Constant or Systematic Bias

This source of performance evaluation error has its basis in the standards or criteria used by the raters. Some supervisors may expect more than others from their employees. A similar phenomenon exists in college; some professors have reputations as easy graders and others are known to be hard graders. The systematic biasing error means that a top rating given by one supervisor may not be equivalent to a top rating given by another supervisor—just as an *A* in one course may not mean the same (as an evaluation of merit or ability) as an *A* in another course.

One possible means of correcting this constant bias is to require supervisors to distribute their ratings in accordance with the normal curve of distribution. This introduces another potential problem, however, in that some workers will receive low ratings that may be undeserved. The method is unfair to a group of outstanding workers who all happen to be employed in the same unit and, consequently,

are evaluated together. Similarly, in a class where all students performed well on an examination, the forcing of the distribution (grad-
ing on a curve) dictates that some students would have to receive
lower grades than their ability warranted.

Most-Recent-Performance Error

Performance evaluations are usually made periodically, every six or
twelve months. As a result, there is an understandable tendency to
base the rating on the most recent behavior of the workers, not taking
into account or being able to remember their performance throughout the period since the last evaluation.

It is natural for memory to be clearer about that which occurred
more recently, but recent behavior may be atypical or distorted by
extraneous factors. A worker could, because of illness or marital
problems, for example, fall down on an otherwise exemplary performance in the weeks prior to the evaluation. Or, if a worker is
aware that an evaluation is forthcoming, he or she may substantially
improve job efficiency just prior to the rating. In either case, the
performance being evaluated is not typical of overall job performance
and a falsely high or low rating would result.

One way of reducing this problem is to require more frequent
evaluations. By shortening the time between evaluations, there might
be less tendency to forget a worker's typical behavior. Training supervisors to be aware of the potential error induced by most recent
performance has also been found to be useful.

Inadequate Information Error

When it is time for performance evaluation, supervisors are required
to rate employees whether or not they know enough about them to
do so fairly. To admit to their superiors that they lack adequate
knowledge of their employees might be construed as a personal failing, so supervisors rate the workers anyway.

The resulting evaluations are worthless to the organization since
they cannot reflect accurately the abilities and characteristics of the
employees. Further, considerable harm can be done to the workers
in terms of the false picture presented of them.

The best solution to this problem is a program of education for
supervisors on the value of performance evaluations, the harm committed by ratings based on inadequate knowledge, the opportunity
for supervisors to refuse to rate employees about whom they have

little information, and the assurance that such refusal will not be met with disapproval.

Average Rating Error

Some people, when placed in the position of judging others, are reluctant to give extreme scores in either direction—very good or very poor. The result is the tendency to assign average ratings to all workers. When examining the ratings of a small number of workers, it is not unusual to find them clustered around the middle of the scale with no more than one or two points separating them.

Thus, the range of abilities indicated is restricted and the ratings so close together that it becomes difficult to distinguish between good and poor workers. This error in performance evaluation does not result in a true reflection of the range of differences among the workers and such ratings provide no useful information to the company or to the employees.

The fact that performance evaluations can be so easily biased by the raters is no reason to abandon hope of achieving objective evaluations. It is possible to train raters so as to minimize sources of error. Training can involve two steps: (1) creating an awareness of the fact that abilities and skills are usually distributed in accordance with the normal curve, so that it is perfectly acceptable to find large differences among a group of workers, and (2) developing the ability to define appropriate criteria for the behaviors being evaluated, a standard or average performance against which employees may be compared. The time and effort devoted to rater training will be repaid in objective, fair, and useful performance evaluations.

PERFORMANCE APPRAISAL OF EXECUTIVES

The performance evaluation of executive personnel presents problems not faced in the assessment of lower-level workers. Although the traditional rating and ranking systems discussed previously are often used in the evaluation of low-level supervisory personnel, executives usually require other methods of appraisal.

One difficulty in assessing the performance of executives is the diversity of responsibilities, tasks, and skills found among them. An assembly line crew supervisor has a fairly homogeneous group of workers to rate—the job each performs and the skills required are similar. A company vice-president faced with the task of assessing several department heads, however, may find no common job requirements or responsibilities among them. The head of the research department, for example, is subject to demands and duties quite different from those of the head of the shipping department. This means that it is virtually impossible to define standards or criteria of behavior on the job against which all executives at the same level may be compared. Further, this heterogeneity makes comparison of one executive with another very difficult.

Performance evaluation of executive personnel is thus extraordinarily complex and it can have important implications for the continued success of an organization. Just as the effects of a poor selection or training program are more harmful to an organization at the executive level, so too is a poor appraisal system of executive performance on the job. For this reason, great stress is placed on assessing how well executives perform. Approximately 85 per cent of the organizations in the United States use some form of management appraisal.

Several ways of undertaking executive assessment are the in-basket technique, assessment centers, and evaluation by superiors, by colleagues, and by the executives themselves.

The In-basket Technique

We discussed the in-basket technique in Chapter 3 as a selection device. It is used in essentially the same manner for executive performance evaluation. The persons being evaluated are instructed to imagine themselves to be functioning at a particular level of executive responsibility for a hypothetical company. In the in-basket are memos, telegrams, letters, or directives, each of which requires some decision or action. The executives behave as if they were actually performing the job—not merely saying what they would do, but taking appropriate action (writing letters, ordering materials, setting up meetings, for example).

This approach to executive evaluation does not yet enjoy widespread usage but research is being conducted to determine how effective an appraisal technique it may become. One disadvantage is that it does not provide an assessment of actual behavior on the job, but rather tests behavior in a simulated situation. The basic question still unanswered is how well performance on the in-basket technique reflects performance on the job.

The Assessment Center Technique

The assessment center was discussed in Chapter 3 as a selection device. It is used in the same way as a means of performance evaluation. Managers are put through a variety of simulated tasks such as management games, group problem solving, tests, and interviews. The staff of the assessment center evaluates each person on how well these tasks are performed, and the evaluation is sent to each person's superior. Like the in-basket technique, assessment centers do not assess actual behavior on the job. The correlation between behavior in simulated and actual job situations must still be determined.

Evaluation by Superiors

The most frequently used means of executive appraisal is assessment by the person's superior in the organization. In actuality, an assessment by the immediate superior is often supplemented by the judgments of higher-level superiors. The latter step of evaluation presents a problem. The greater the distance between the executive and superiors in the hierarchy of the organization, the less intimate and detailed will be the latters' knowledge of the former. To provide an example from the academic community, a department head is able to give a better evaluation of a professor in the department than is the dean or chancellor. The chairman works closely with the professor and is in a better position to assess personal strengths and weaknesses.

It is rare for an executive evaluation to be carried out using a standardized rating sheet. Usually, the executive's superior writes a description of the individual's level of job performance.

Peer Rating

This technique, developed during World War II (and known as "buddy rating"), requires that all executives or managers at the same level rate or assess each other in terms of general ability to perform the jobs or on specific traits or characteristics. This approach is still used extensively for the evaluation of officers in the military and is also on the increase in industry and business where it seems especially valuable in identifying those with the potential for promotion to higher levels. Although peer ratings tend, on the average, to be somewhat higher than ratings given by superiors, it has been found that there is a high correlation between high ratings from one's peers and subsequent promotion.

Of course, there is the potential for bias whenever a person is asked to express judgments on colleagues who may be close friends or intense rivals for the next promotion. The situation offers the temptation to slant the evaluation favorably or unfavorably. It is also possible for colleagues to get together and agree to assign only good ratings, or at least not to give bad ones!

Self-evaluation

An unusual approach to executive evaluation is to ask individuals to assess their own performance and abilities. The information thus obtained seems to be more useful for the diagnostic function of performance evaluation than for personnel decisions.

The usual procedure is for executives and their superiors to establish mutually a set of objectives, such as new skills to be developed or weaknesses to be improved upon. After a period of time, the executives meet with their superiors and discuss how well they feel they have attained the objectives.

It is not surprising to learn that the results of self-evaluations tend to be higher or more favorable than those given by superiors. Self-ratings also tend to stress different aspects of job performance than ratings given by superiors. Whereas ratings by superiors stress initiative and job skills, self-ratings focus more on interpersonal skills.

Combined Ratings

Since ratings by superiors, colleagues, and the executives themselves are relatively easy to obtain, it seems logical to combine the three viewpoints on each person into one overall appraisal. This may also reduce potential bias from self-ratings and peer ratings. If all parties know that their ratings will be compared with those given by others, they may be more inclined toward objectivity in their assessments.

In cases in which all three ratings are consistent, decisions about · the executive's future can be made with confidence. Further, the executive may be more willing to accept critical evaluations when they come from a source other than the immediate supervisor. If the ratings greatly disagree, however, the individual may be reluctant to accept a negative assessment and recommendations for improvement.

In general, the combined approach to executive assessment promises to provide useful information to both the organization and the individual.

THE POSTEVALUATION INTERVIEW

As noted at the beginning of the chapter, performance evaluation serves two purposes—supplying information to management for personnel decisions, and diagnosing specific strengths and weaknesses of employees. The latter function is not fulfilled by conducting the evaluation alone. The results, interpretations, and recommendations of the appraisal must be communicated to the employees if the assessments are to be of any value. This is usually accomplished through an interview between the worker and the supervisor, a situation that can easily become antagonistic. When an appraisal contains criticism, the stage is set for the interview to be trying, frustrating, or even hostile. It has been shown that as the amount of criticism in a postevaluation interview increases, defensiveness on the part of the subordinate increases along with the tendency to reject the criticism.

Perhaps the primary purpose of telling employees how they fared in a performance evaluation is the hope that they will improve their behavior on the job. For example, if an employee is told that he or she asks the supervisor too frequently how a task should be performed, it is hoped that in the future the employee will take the initiative to find the answer.

The expectation of behavioral improvement may be naïve on the part of management. Some workers when criticized react by behaving in a contradictory manner as an imagined means of revenge. A worker may never again ask a supervisor for assistance, for example, and may make many more mistakes on the job as a result. Far from helping subordinates, criticism often leads to a deterioration in job performance.

Perhaps it is also naïve to expect that a brief meeting every six months or so will be sufficient impetus for employees to want to change their behavior. Habits of behavior and attitude are deeply ingrained by adulthood, and a postevaluation interview may not produce behavioral change lasting more than several days.

Finally, it may be unrealistic to expect that supervisors, in the absence of special training, have the insight necessary to properly diagnose the reason for a worker's below average job performance, and to prescribe means of improvement. Lacking these abilities, many supervisors may be reluctant to make the judgments necessary to the success of a performance evaluation program.

If feedback on employee performance were provided more skill-fully and frequently, the motivation to alter job behavior, and to per-sist in the new behavior, might be enhanced.

Another purpose of the postappraisal interview is to reward or praise workers for better than average job performance in the hope that such praise will spur them to even more efficient behavior. Un-fortunately, this goal too remains more ideal than real. In cases in which there is criticism as well as praise, many workers focus unduly on the criticisms and minimize or ignore the praise. A study con-ducted at a large international organization showed that praise for a job well done had almost no effect on future behavior when the feed-back also included criticism.

We might legitimately ask, then, if there is any diagnostic value in the postappraisal interview. The answer is yes, but only under certain conditions. Criticizing a subordinate must be undertaken with the ut-most tact and understanding. To most of us, the job we perform is vital, not only in terms of financial security but also in psychological terms—a job provides us with much of the basis of our sense of self-worth, esteem, and pride. Criticizing the way we do our jobs goes much deeper than just criticizing our work behavior. It can influence our whole self-image.

One supervisor wrote: "If you give a man a rating of 35, he can't look himself in the eye. If you give him a 30, he goes numb; it's a terrible jolt to his pride. When a man's rating is lowered two points, his performance goes to pot. A few men will work harder if you lower their ratings but most will give up." [2]

More frequent and informal interviews may make the postevalua-tion meeting more constructive. Apprising workers of their job progress and general level of effectiveness should be done more than once or twice a year. Frequent feedback weekly or even daily pro-vides a more continuous record of development and achievement.

Even more important is the desirability of setting specific goals in each feedback session for employee improvement, goals reached by mutual agreement between worker and supervisor. The goals should relate to actual behavior rather than to general characteristics, and mutually agreed-upon deadlines should be set. This approach to the postappraisal interview has been very well received by workers and supervisors, and has led to improvement of performance in the ma-jority of cases in which it has been used. Rather than focusing on past behavior, this type of interview is oriented toward the future and maximizes the participation of the employee.

Informality in meetings between worker and supervisor could also aid in performance diagnosis. In a formal postappraisal interview sit-

[2] P. Thompson and G. Dalton, op. cit., p. 152.

uation, workers usually see the printed rating or evaluation sheet the supervisor has filled out. They know that the information will be part of the official record and this may cause them to attack the criticisms more intensively. An informal, conversational approach, without displaying the formal rating scale, could serve to reduce the potential defensiveness of the workers.

The relationship between superiors and subordinates is tenuous at best, and filled with possibilities for misunderstanding and animosity. Postappraisal interviews, improperly conducted, can easily turn workers and supervisors into adversaries.

A Model Diagnostic Appraisal Program

On the basis of extensive research on performance appraisal systems, General Electric instituted an approach that it calls Work Planning and Review (WP&R). This program incorporates some of the findings discussed previously and involves frequent meetings between worker and supervisor, sometimes as often as weekly, but not at fixed intervals. Their frequency is determined mutually by worker and supervisor. The discussions focus solely on actual job behavior and do not delve into the worker's attitudes or personality.

Each meeting is concerned with solutions for specific work problems, achievement of past goals, and the establishment of future work goals. They do not involve discussions of salary or promotion so supervisors are free to concentrate on their role as helper rather than judge. Since workers realize they are not being assessed in these sessions, a climate of confidence can be established.

The WP&R system was used with half the employees for a year, whereas the others continued under the more traditional performance evaluation program. Through questionnaires and personal interviews, both groups of employees were studied and the differences found were dramatic.

One criterion of success of such a program is the extent to which employees follow the suggestions of their supervisors. The group evaluated by WP&R abided by 70 per cent of their supervisor's suggestions; the traditional group followed only 40 per cent of their manager's suggestions. An explanation for the difference is that the suggestions under the WP&R program were more specific and related directly to the job.

The WP&R group also showed the following changes after one year.[3]

[3] E. Huse, "Performance appraisal: A new look," *Personnel Administration*, **30**(March–April 1967), 3–5, 16–18.

1. Employees believed that their supervisor was giving them much more help in improving performance on their present job and in developing their potential for higher-level jobs.
2. There was more mutual agreement on job goals.
3. Employees believed that they had greater participation in job-related decisions.
4. Employees believed that their supervisors improved in their own decision-making and planning skills.
5. Considerably greater opportunities for employees to discuss job problems in an open exchange of views and to obtain mutual understanding were noted.

As a means of improving performance on the job, the WP&R approach has been a great success. It is clearly superior to the standard methods and enlists the enthusiastic cooperation of worker and supervisor—an enthusiasm sorely lacking in traditional approaches to employee diagnostic appraisal. Overall, perhaps the basic reason for the success of the WP&R approach is that it is designed to help employees, not solely to judge them.

PERFORMANCE EVALUATION: A POOR RATING

It is possible to develop effective and worthwhile programs of performance evaluation that will benefit both employees and management. Unfortunately, innovative programs such as WP&R are rare. Most organizations evaluate their workers by traditional methods that, as we have seen, have disadvantages and limited success. As a result, both parties to the appraisal may view it with suspicion, and the gap between worker and supervisor often widens. Performance evaluations may be one of the least popular programs that are currently in use in the world of work. Few people like them in spite of the recognition that appraising performance in some fashion is necessary.

Why do performance evaluation programs get such a poor rating? We have already discussed the many opportunities for error with these evaluation techniques. There are other reasons as well. Consider the supervisor, the person responsible for making periodic evaluations. Work appraisal systems demand much time and conscientious effort from supervisors who, in many cases, are already subject to stresses and strains. A supervisor with thirty subordinates can devote many hours to observing them in order to develop sufficient knowledge of their capabilities to be able to assess them fairly, and additional hours to filling out the performance evaluation forms. In practice, supervisors resist performance evaluation programs to the point of filling out the forms only when pressured to do so by their superiors. Also, evaluations are often hastily completed, a situation that is not conducive to thorough and systematic appraisals. Many supervisors do not like the idea of judging employees, of being in a position to adversely affect their future, and so they may be reluctant to give their subordinates low ratings, even for poor performance.

Employees also do not seem to like the idea of performance evaluations. They fear the effect of the assessment on their future, they are apprehensive that their supervisor will use the opportunity for evaluation against them for misunderstandings or personality clashes unrelated to their work ability, and they often do not know the criteria by which they are being judged, or even precisely what is expected of them on the job.

In many organizations that go through the confrontation of a performance evaluation, the results of the assessment are filed in the personnel department and are never used for the intended purpose: to help make decisions about promotions and pay increases or to counsel employees. And this simply increases the negative attitudes toward the whole idea of performance evaluation.

In sum, the system of performance evaluation, as generally practiced in industry today, is unsatisfactory. New approaches and techniques must be developed because performance evaluation, in some fashion, must be carried out. Judgments and appraisals of job ability at all levels of employment are necessary. The question is not whether to use an employee appraisal system, rather it is which is the most effective approach to take. This can be determined only through additional research.

SUMMARY

Performance evaluation programs are vital to employer and employee for several reasons. They are used to validate selection criteria; to determine the need for and success of training programs; to improve individual employee behavior; to determine promotions, wages, transfers, and reductions in force; and to identify workers with promotion potential.

Despite the importance of performance evaluation programs, there are several sources of opposition. Labor unions do not favor performance evaluation because of their commitment to seniority as the basis for personnel decisions. Employees (the persons being evaluated) dislike performance evaluation because few of us like being judged or criticized. Supervisors (the persons doing the evaluations) don't like to make appraisals that directly affect the future of their subordinates.

However, evaluations of performance on the job are necessary in some fashion—informally or formally, subjectively or objectively, carelessly or systematically. It will surely benefit all concerned if performance evaluation is conducted in the most objective and systematic way possible.

There are two approaches to performance evaluation: that designed for **production jobs** in which a tangible product can be counted, and that designed for **nonproduction jobs,** which do not result in a tangible product. In general, production jobs lend themselves more readily to objective measures of performance than do nonproduction jobs, although, in both cases, objectivity in evaluation is the goal.

Production jobs can be evaluated by considering the quantity and quality of output, accidents, salary, advancement history, and absenteeism. Nonproduction jobs are more difficult to evaluate and must be done in more qualitative terms by having supervisors assess the workers' ability to perform on the job. These assessments are usually made through the process of **merit rating** that includes several specific techniques: rating, ranking, paired comparisons, forced distribution, forced choice, and critical incidents. These techniques are subjective in that they involve one person judging the ability or characteristics of another.

Raters differ in their prejudices, competence, and ability to discriminate among people (social differentiation), and are a potential source of error. Other sources of error in merit rating include the halo effect, systematic bias, most-recent-performance error, inadequate information error, and average rating error.

The evaluation of **executive** performance is extremely difficult but may be accomplished through the in-basket technique; assessment centers; or evaluation by supervisors, by colleagues, or by the executives themselves. Of particular value may be the integration or combination of superior, colleague, and self-ratings into one overall appraisal.

Once a performance evaluation has been completed, it must be communicated to the employee in order to provide him or her with an evaluation of job strengths or weaknesses. This **feedback** must be given with tact and sensitivity, particularly when criticism is involved, for it can cause defensiveness on the part of the employee and might even lead to a decline in job performance. To be maximally effective, feedback sessions should be frequent, informal, focus on setting specific goals, and allow for the subordinate's participation. A model performance evaluation program conducted by General Electric was discussed, which stressed helping employees develop rather than judging them.

In practice, performance evaluation is not very popular with those who have to do the rating as well as with those who are rated. However, the fact remains that, in some way, performance must be assessed.

SUGGESTED READINGS

Cherry, R. Performance reviews: A note on failure. *Personnel Journal,* 1970, **49,** 398–403.

Cowan, J. A human-factored approach to appraisals. *Personnel,* 1975, **52**(6), 49–56.

Cummings, L. L., and Schwab, D. P. *Performance in Organizations: Determinants and Appraisal.* New York: Scott Foresman, 1973.

Haynes, M. Do appraisal reviews improve performance? *Public Personnel Management,* 1973, **2,** 128-132.

Kellogg, M. S. *What to Do About Performance Appraisal,* rev. ed. New York: American Management Association, 1976.

Lasher, H. The employee performance syndrome: Is improvement possible? *Personnel Journal,* 1974, **53,** 897–901.

Macoy, W. Conducting a performance appraisal interview. *Supervisory Management,* 1970, **15**(February), 13–16.

Maier, N. R. *The Appraisal Interview: Three Basic Approaches.* San Diego, Calif.: University Associates, 1976.

Massey, D. Narrowing the gap between intended and existing results of appraisal systems. *Personnel Journal,* 1975, **54,** 522-524.

Patz, A. Performance appraisal: Useful but still resisted. *Harvard Business Review,* 1975, **53**(May), 74–80.

Pizam, A. Social differentiation—a new psychological barrier to performance appraisal. *Public Personnel Management,* 1975, **4,** 244–247.

Rieder, G. Performance review—a mixed bag. *Harvard Business Review,* 1973, **51**(July), 61–67.

Schowengerdt, R. How reliable are merit rating techniques? *Personnel Journal,* 1975, **54,** 496–498.

Scott, R. Taking subjectivity out of performance appraisal. *Personnel,* 1973, **50**(4), 45–49.

6

Training in Organizations

INTRODUCTION

Regardless of the sophistication and predictive validity of a selection program, it is almost always necessary to expose newly hired employees to some kind of training before they can be maximally effective on a new job. Even if the company is fortunate enough to find employees who are experienced with the machinery or equipment they will be operating, it may still be necessary to inform them of operating procedures or company policies that may be unique to the organization. However informally such information may be presented, it does constitute a kind of training, the purpose of which is to increase the employees' productive efficiency.

Training requirements are made more complicated when the workers have had little actual job experience or are being hired for a type of work they have never performed. The organization's selection procedures ideally ensure that new employees have sufficient intelligence, aptitude, and attitude to learn the job, but once hired, the organization must then properly train these employees in the specific skills required for successful performance of the job.

Thus, proper training is certainly as important as proper selection in the delicate relationship of placing the right person in the right job. The two activities are complementary; as a rule, one cannot succeed fully without the other. The best *potential* lathe operators, for example—those who possess the proper degree of mechanical aptitude and spatial relations—will not be able to realize their potential without adequate formal training. On the other hand, the most sophisticated training program is of limited value if used to train persons who possess little ability to be lathe operators.

Some form of training seems always to have existed in the world of work. Historical records tell of formalized apprentice programs in which a young man became indentured to a skilled craftsman for a number of years, during which time he learned the skills of the trade.

In modern, complex work environments, ironically, we often find much less systematic training methods. A new employee may be assigned to a more experienced worker and told to "watch Joe" or "do what Jane does." Fortunately, this informal, and often unsatisfactory, kind of training differs sharply from other organizational programs in which new employees attend lectures, watch movies, and practice the job under the watchful eyes of skilled instructors—people who have been trained to train.

Industrial psychologists have devoted considerable effort to exploring ways of imparting information and skills to new employees. Since the nineteenth century, much research on human learning has been conducted by psychologists. Applying what is known about the learning process to the world of work, however—where questions of money and management support are paramount—has not always been easy or successful. In cases in which learning principles have been applied with the support of management, organizations have realized great returns on the time and money invested. It is not unusual for overall job efficiency or production to increase as much as 40 per cent as a result of proper training. Also, training can lead to greater job satisfaction and morale, reduced accident rate, and decreased employee turnover, all factors that make for a more efficient organization.

Training does more than serve the organization—it serves you, the employee, and society as a whole. Employees are recognizing that training can increase their feeling of job security, provide greater opportunities for advancement, and enhance their sense of status, self-worth, and prestige. Indeed, the provision of a good training program is regarded by many workers as an important fringe benefit—an inducement to work for a company.

With the growth of a social consciousness in modern organizations, an obligation to underprivileged persons is being recognized. Many companies are placing special emphasis on training programs for minority group members to assure them a responsible place in the economy. When former "unemployables" can be trained to become contributing members of society, the entire social and economic system benefits.

Training needs in industry have always been important and it is expected that even greater demands will be placed on them in the future. Methods of manufacturing are undergoing drastic and rapid changes. Wholly automated machinery is being designed, much of which requires little in the way of human work. Huge oil refineries can be staffed by a handful of workers. New procedures for galvanizing steel require only three or four highly skilled employees per shift, replacing methods that employed thirty to forty semiskilled operators. Many jobs are being phased out completely. It is society's responsibility to provide retraining opportunities so that those whose skills are obsolete can find new employment. These changes also place new demands on the human relations abilities of managers and supervisors, and, in addition, expanding industry means that more people must be trained to assume these leadership roles.

Your training and growth as an employee will continue throughout your working career with, in many cases, formal instruction at least as difficult as college-level courses. And both you and your employer will benefit from the opportunities offered for training in organizations. Through training programs, you will be able to advance as far as your ability and motivation carry you.

THE SCOPE OF ORGANIZATIONAL TRAINING

From high school dropout to college graduate, from hard-core unemployed to seasoned executive—in industry today, all of these people are involved in some form of training program. So extensive is organizational training that a chemical company executive exclaimed, "When I look at the money we spend on education and training, I wonder whether we're running a chemical business or a damned college!" An official with a large automobile company asked, "At what point do you cease being a manufacturer and become a school?" In this section we briefly examine how several organizations are becoming schools.

Companies located in major cities, such as New York, are increasingly pressed to train new employees, not only in specific job skills but also in the more basic area of how to work. Many underprivileged ghetto youngsters have never been taught the sense of responsibility necessary for reliable work habits—the importance of coming to work regularly and on time, for example. Wholly new attitudes (indeed, a new way of life) must be learned. Further, many employers must offer high school (or lower) level training in remedial reading and basic mathematics. These deficiencies must be corrected before training for a specific job can begin.

The First National City Bank of New York has found it necessary to give remedial reading courses and has established a school system larger than those found in many small towns. With a teaching staff of sixty-five, and the latest in closed-circuit television and videotape recorders, the school has more than six thousand employees as students each year. The purpose of the training is to bring employees to the level at which they may begin to learn their jobs.

Is it worth it? The bank thinks so, and it has reported that several dozen formerly unemployable ghetto youths had advanced to teller positions and become motivated and loyal employees. Without remedial training, these persons would have had little, if any, opportunity to find secure or meaningful jobs. The program represents a considerable investment on the part of the bank but in addition to improving the quality of its employees, the bank is making an undeniable contribution to society.

A greater investment in training is Western Electric Company's Corporate Education Center—a company college devoted to instruction in engineering and business management. With more modern and elaborate instructional equipment than many traditional colleges, this facility offers more than 300 courses on its 190-acre campus. A dormitory is maintained where employee-students can live while taking courses. Some courses last as long as 22 weeks.

Almost all of the engineers hired by Western Electric participate in six-week orientation programs—one during the first six months of employment, and a second during the next six months. Engineers already employed by the company may attend four-week courses in their specialty areas—classes designed to keep them informed of the latest developments in their field. Engineering supervisors may choose among a variety of courses intended to update their technical knowledge in order to make them more competent as supervisors of other engineers.

A unique part of Western Electric's educational program is the opportunity for engineers to earn an advanced degree while employed full time. In conjunction with Lehigh University in Bethlehem, Pennsylvania, the Corporate Education Center offers a Master of Science degree in several fields.

If employees cannot come to the Corporate Education Center, the Center will come to them in the form of more than one hundred correspondence courses. Thus, widespread opportunities are provided for Western Electric engineers to improve their knowledge, obtain advanced degrees and, in the process, become more valuable to themselves and to the company.

The Corporate Education Center also offers management training at four levels, from first-line supervisor to manager. Attendance at these training courses is by invitation—the most promising candidates for promotion are given the opportunity to enroll. Courses range from planning and interdepartmental relationships to urban affairs and industrial psychology. The management training is not conducted by the lecture methods widely used in the engineering program, but by group techniques, role playing, and business games.

This ambitious venture of Western Electric's is not atypical in

American business. Industry seems to be assuming an ever-increasing share of the responsibility of education. Sophisticated training centers have been established by many large firms. IBM offers a four-week school for rising executives, General Electric conducts a nine-week general management course, and Avis Rent-A-Car trains one hundred employees a month at its educational center in a variety of job tasks.

In 1975, the Xerox Corporation opened a $55-million International Center for Training and Management Development on a twenty-two hundred-acre site outside of Washington, D.C. Designed to house and train as many as one thousand employees at a time, the center offers courses ranging from machine repair to sales and management. Students live in suites of private rooms in the strikingly modern buildings and study in classrooms filled with the latest audio-visual instructional equipment. When not studying, employees are free to use the gymnasium and swimming pool or relax in luxuriously appointed lounges.

So do not be surprised if your first month on the job finds you back in a classroom. Although you may not welcome that prospect now, it can provide you with the key to job advancement in the future.

SPECIFYING TRAINING OBJECTIVES

The first step in establishing a formal training program is the precise formulation of objectives. These objectives must be in terms of particular behavioral criteria—acts or operations employees must perform on the job, and the way in which they should perform them in order to maximize job efficiency. It is impossible to determine what the training should involve without knowing what it is intended to accomplish. In other words, what must employees be taught in order to maximize their level of job performance?

The objectives of the training program, then, must derive from the specific needs of the organization. Unfortunately, it occasionally happens that a company subjects employees to a training program in the absence of a need to develop a particular ability or skill. For example, a company may establish a training department because a competitor has done so or because it's "the thing to do." Although a program not based on company needs may not hurt anything, its chances of success are not high.

The investigation of training objectives is usually difficult, but there are situations in which the need for a training program is obvious. A company that automates a manufacturing process, thereby eliminating a number of jobs, may—if vacancies exist elsewhere in the organization—want to retrain its employees to fill these positions. Rapid expansion creating a number of new jobs requires a training program to fill the vacancies. A high accident rate in a department or operation may call for training in safe job performance skills.

In the absence of a clear indication that training is needed, the responsibility falls upon an enlightened management to periodically analyze its entire operation in order to determine if any part might benefit from additional training. This is where the difficulty occurs: A deficiency or poorly performed operation must first be noticed and then analyzed in order to determine if the problem can be corrected by training. (It may be, for example, that substandard performance is caused by faulty equipment, not by faulty work habits.)

This kind of general organizational analysis can suggest broad training needs that can be translated into the specific needs of the individual employees, a task accomplished by job analysis, critical incidents, or performance appraisal techniques.

Job analysis, which was discussed in Chapter 3, is the most frequently used technique for determining training needs and objectives. The job analysis yields a detailed list of the characteristics needed to successfully perform a job, plus the precise sequence of operations that are required. From this analysis it is possible to determine how performance might be improved by new training procedures.

The *critical incidents* technique, which focuses on particularly desirable or undesirable behaviors on the job, can provide valuable information on how employees are equipped to cope with critical events that occur from time to time. For example, how well do assembly line workers cope with jammed machinery, or supervisors with personal disputes among their subordinates? An examination of such critical incidents can tell a training director where instruction is needed.

The third source of information on training needs is the periodic *performance evaluation* that most workers receive. These point up an employee's weaknesses and strengths and often lead to a recommendation for training to correct a specific deficiency.

By whatever method, the determination of a training program's needs and objectives is important and can decide if the entire training program will be worth the effort.

THE TRAINING STAFF

The quality of an instructor in college can have a tremendous influence on your performance as a student. Some teachers are able to bring the subject matter to life, to organize and present it with enthusiasm, and to inspire interest in the class. Other instructors teaching the same material can make the classroom experience frustrating, tiring, and boring. The important factor in teaching anything at any level seems not to be the level of competence or expertise in the subject matter. Competence is a necessary but not sufficient condition for success. You have observed that some professors possess a comprehensive knowledge of their subject but lack the ability to communicate it to others. Success in instruction depends on something more. It is for the purpose of teaching that "something more"—the ability to teach—that colleges of education were established. And this is true for organizational training also—the trainers must be trained. A program designed to teach job skills may never achieve the desired success if the teachers are not capable of communicating the material to their students and motivating them to learn. Consequently, a crucial task in establishing an organizational training program is the education of those who will be instructors.

Research has been conducted on groups of job trainees who were learning a skill under instructors trained in teaching methods and under instructors with no such training. The evidence consistently shows that the trained instructors induced a higher rate of learning. Unfortunately, despite this clear evidence, training in organizations is too often conducted by persons widely experienced in the task or skill to be taught, but who have had no formal instruction in how to teach that task effectively to others.

It is also customary in industry to use foremen or front-line supervisors to instruct new employees in their jobs. Like experienced workers as instructors, supervisors may know a great deal about the job, but without preparation to teach, they may well provide inadequate training.

The solution is to use professional teachers—people trained both in the skills to be taught and in methods of teaching. Some large companies have full-time teaching staffs—persons equipped to teach a number of subjects, as in the public schools. Not only does this provide maximally effective instruction but it also prevents interference with the ongoing operations of the plant (as is the case when supervisors or co-workers must take time from their jobs to instruct new employees).

Of course, the matter of a professional training staff rests on the familiar problem of the willingness of management to pay the price necessary to develop a truly effective training program. As we saw with selection programs, a company gets what it is willing to pay for. If it wants a cheap program it will get just that—a shoddy, second-class effort that may not even be worth the low price paid for it.

PSYCHOLOGICAL PRINCIPLES OF LEARNING

Psychologists have devoted considerable effort to the experimental study of learning. The literature contains thousands of human and animal research studies on a variety of factors and conditions that are capable of influencing the learning process. This should not suggest that psychologists know all the answers about this complex activity, but certain factors that can facilitate or hinder learning have been uncovered, some concerned with characteristics of the learner (motivation and ability to learn) and others with how the training program and material to be taught should be organized and presented.

Despite the years of research on learning, it is still difficult to apply the findings to specific organizational training problems. Most of the research is artificial—conducted on rats running mazes or college sophomores memorizing nonsense syllables. These experiences do not directly relate to most jobs. Therefore, any generalization of research findings and principles must be made with caution. The principles of learning can serve as general guidelines, but not as specific rules.

Individual Differences in Ability

People differ in their ability to profit from instruction. Those with higher levels of mental ability may be capable of learning to perform a job task in a very short time while others are still struggling with the fundamentals. Some may drop out (or be pushed out) because of failure to grasp the basics. The rate of instruction, then, must be geared to the ability levels of the trainees, some of whom will be capable of learning faster than others. Ideally, the training staff will have some indication of the individual differences in ability, perhaps from the trainees' psychological test results or past performance evaluations.

Instruction should be individualized as much as possible so that the fast learner in a class is not held back, or the slow learner is not expected to improve too rapidly. Either situation can lead to the trainee's frustration and disappointment. Some training methods provide for differential rates of learning.

Education or training will often benefit the brighter person more than the less bright one. If two individuals are far apart in ability before entering a training program, this gap may increase by the end of the program. The slower learner will learn to perform the task, but the brighter one will learn to perform it at a more efficient level.

197

Training does not always equalize differences in ability; it may well magnify them.

Motivation

The motivation or desire to learn is of utmost importance in training. Learning will not take place unless the person really wants to learn, and this is true regardless of ability. To some degree, a high level of motivation can compensate for a lower level of ability. Every profession or trade includes people who have attained their position with less than superior levels of intelligence but who possess great drive and motivation to succeed.

Some people are driven to achieve in whatever they attempt to do. The attainment of success satisfies a basic need in their personality. They seem to have a built-in motivation and need no other impetus to do well in a training program. Others need to be inspired in order to do well in any training endeavor, and this is where the skill of the trainer is vital. If the trainees can be persuaded that the training program will have a definite influence on their future, and if the material presented is meaningful to them and to the job, then the chances are good that they will be sufficiently motivated to learn.

In addition to presenting material, a good trainer is aware of individual differences in motivation among the trainees and gears the level of instruction accordingly. The trainer must be able to create adequate motivation in the trainees so that they desire to learn the material.

Several principles of learning are concerned with the arrangement or manipulation of the methods of learning and the materials to be learned.

Active Practice of the Material

Practice may not always make perfect, as the saying goes, but it is a great help. In order for learning to be maximally effective, trainees must be actively involved in the learning process, not merely passive recipients of information. It is not sufficient to read about the operation of a machine or to watch someone else—on film or in person—operate it. These presentations can provide basic principles of operation but they cannot train persons to become proficient at a task. The training program must provide sufficient opportunity to actively practice the skills required on the job.

Imagine trying to learn to drive an automobile by listening to a lecture, memorizing highway regulations, or watching a film of someone driving. This can help make you a better driver, but you cannot learn how to drive the car until you actually start practicing it.

This principle holds for learning academic material. Actively taking notes in class, outlining the material from the textbook, or discussing it with friends facilitates learning much more than simply sitting in the classroom, soaking up lectures like a sponge. (Fully soaked sponges, you may have noticed, get soggy, heavy, and useless.)

It is not desirable for workers to start to practice a complex task without prior instruction. They could easily learn incorrect or unsafe work procedures. The practice must be guided so that trainees perform the task in the most efficient and safe manner. Until they have achieved a certain degree of proficiency, they must operate under close supervision.

Massed Versus Distributed Practice

What is the best way of scheduling practice sessions? How long should they be? Should there be a few relatively long sessions (massed practice), or a large number of shorter sessions (distributed practice)? The distributed practice method is usually, but not always, the better approach to learning. It depends on the nature and complexity of the task or material to be learned.

Short, simple material can be learned quite well by massed practice since the sessions will not have to be excessively long in order for trainees to learn this type of material. Difficult, lengthy material often must be broken up into shorter units and is learned better by distributed practice.

The optimal practice schedule for the particular material or task to be learned must be determined. If massed practice periods are too long, trainees may become tired or bored. If the breaks between distributed practice sessions are too long, trainees may forget too much information from one session to the next. If practice periods are too short, they may not hold the trainees' interest and their motivation may wane.

Deciding on the better approach to training sessions requires careful evaluation of the material to be learned. (This should be undertaken in training programs anyway.)

Whole Versus Part Learning

Whole versus part learning refers to the relative size of the unit of material to be learned. Should the material be divided into small parts, each of which is learned individually, or should it be learned as a whole? The better approach depends upon the nature and complexity of the material and the levels of ability of the trainees. Neither method is superior in all situations, and each offers advantages and disadvantages.

More intelligent trainees are capable of learning larger units of material that might confuse or frustrate slower learners. The latter, presented the material in smaller doses, may be able to learn it better and faster than if dealing with it as a whole.

Some tasks and skills adapt themselves well to whole learning; indeed, some require it for efficient learning. Recall the example of learning to drive a car. It serves no useful purpose to break down driving skill into component parts (for example, turn on the ignition, shift from neutral to first gear), and to practice each part separately. Driving is an interdependent flow of movements and actions (take one foot off the gas pedal and simultaneously apply the other to the brake, for example), and can more efficiently be learned as a whole.

Where a task does require the initial learning of several subskills, the part method is the more efficient. The various parts are mastered at a certain level before being integrated into the total behavior pattern or operation.

The trainer must decide on the basis of the trainees' abilities and the nature of the material whether whole or part learning is more efficient.

Transfer of Training

Organizational training often takes place in an artificial setting—a training facility that may use similar equipment as the job, but that differs from the actual job environment in several ways. Even in cases where training does occur on the job, differences between the training situation and the actual work situation may still exist. For example, a supervisor may be more friendly and helpful during the training sessions than after training.

The discrepancy between the training and job environments must be bridged. The training program must ensure that there will be a transfer or carry-over of the skills learned during training to the job itself. The question is one of relevance: Is everything taught during training relevant and meaningful to job performance? How accurate is the correspondence between behaviors and attitudes taught during the training sessions and those required on the job? Will everything the employee learns in a training situation be used on the job? Will the information be used in the same way?

If there is a close correspondence between the requirements of the two situations, *positive transfer* is likely to develop. This means that information learned during training aids or facilitates actual job performance. The opposite may also occur. If there is little similarity between job and training situations, or if a behavior or attitude stressed during training is downgraded by co-workers on the job, *negative transfer* will occur. In this case, the learned behavior hampers or interferes with performance of the job. In negative transfer situations, learned behaviors must often be unlearned or changed, in order to perform successfully the work in question.

Psychologists and managers who design training programs must ensure that the conditions of training accurately reproduce the conditions of the job, in order to avoid negative transfer and maximize positive transfer.

Knowledge of Results

People learn more readily when they are given a clear idea of how well they are doing. Feedback or knowledge of results indicates to learners the level of progress being made and can be very important in terms of maintaining motivation.

Knowledge of results contributes directly to proper training in that it tells trainees what they are doing wrong. If they were not provided with this information, they might continue throughout the entire training session to learn and practice inadequate or inappropriate behaviors and methods of job performance.

Classroom examinations in college are aimed at providing you with a means of gauging your progress. The knowledge of your results, given periodically throughout a semester, may enable you to correct faulty study habits or to improve your understanding of the material.

To be maximally effective, feedback must occur as soon as possible after the behavior. If a behavioral operation is incorrect and must be performed another way, the desired change is more likely to be brought about if trainees are told immediately, rather than, say, a week later. Training proceeds most rapidly where provision is made for fast and frequent knowledge of results.

Also, learning is facilitated by the specificity of this feedback. The more detailed the knowledge of results, the more useful it will be to trainees in correcting or changing their behavior.

Reinforcement

Reinforcement refers to the consequences of behavior. Those behaviors that lead to or result in a reward of some kind tend to be learned; behaviors that do not lead to a reward (or that lead to punishment) usually are not repeated and hence not learned.

The greater the reward or successful consequence that follows a behavior, the more readily and rapidly that behavior will be learned. The reward can take many forms—a good examination grade, a gold star for good conduct, a pat on the back and a smile from the foreman or training supervisor, or a promotion for successful completion of the training program. The reward, whatever its nature, is controlled and manipulated by the trainer. By introducing a series of reinforcements or rewards, a trainer can establish and maintain high morale and motivation and can effectively shape the trainees' behavior by rewarding only those acts that are intended to be learned.

In order to be maximally effective, reinforcement should be given immediately after the desired behavior has occurred. The longer the delay between behavior and reinforcement, the less effective the reinforcement will be, primarily because the connection between displaying a particular behavior and being reinforced for that behavior will be less clear.

Reinforcement should be given every time the desired behavior is displayed in the early stages of training, but it is not necessary to continue constant reinforcement once some level of learning has taken place. The behavior can be maintained and strengthened by providing only partial reinforcement. For example, trainees could be reinforced every third or every tenth time they display the desired behavior. That schedule of reinforcement, called a *fixed ratio schedule,* is an effective means of facilitating learning. (Most of what is known about reinforcement derives from the work of the eminent behavioristic psychologist B. F. Skinner.)

Reinforcement as a means of changing behavior—known as *behavior modification*—has been used with great success in prisons, mental hospitals, and schools, and with individuals who have behavior problems such as stuttering or bedwetting. Recently behavior modification has begun to be applied to organizational problems with equal success.

The use of punishment as an aid to learning has little to recommend it. Punishment may eliminate an undesirable behavior, but it may leave in its place anxiety, hostility, or anger on the part of the trainee. The use of reward or reinforcement is a much more positive aid to learning.

TRAINING METHODS: I. NONSUPERVISORY EMPLOYEES

Now that we have seen how general psychological principles can be used to facilitate learning, let us consider specific techniques used in organizational training today. Each technique offers unique advantages, and the training psychologist must determine the best method for a particular training program.

There are two types of training methods, each having different goals and designed for different levels of employee. In this section, we discuss methods appropriate for training nonsupervisory and nonmanagement personnel. The next section discusses techniques used for training managers and executives.

On-the-Job Training

One of the oldest and most widely used training methods in industry takes place directly on the job for which the worker is being trained. Under the guidance of an experienced operator, supervisor, or, occasionally, a trained instructor, trainees learn while working. For example, they operate the machine or assembly process in the actual production facility and develop proficiency while they work.

This approach offers certain advantages, not the least of which, it is argued, is economy. The company does not have to establish a separate training facility with duplicate or simulated equipment. If workers or foremen can serve as trainers, then not even the cost of a professional instructor is necessary. However, this technique may be expensive in the long run. Workers or supervisors must take time from their regular jobs to train new employees. Some reduction in their productivity is inevitable. An additional cost is in the form of slower production, or damage to the equipment or product, because of the new and inexperienced operators.

These costs are hidden and not easily determined by management; the cost of establishing a separate training facility is not only visible but also formidable. Since on-the-job training appears economical to many organizations, it is generally considered to be a cheaper training method than other approaches.

Another advantage (and this is more real than apparent) is the provision for positive transfer of training. The workers do not have to carry over their performance in a training situation to the actual work situation since the training and the job are conducted at the same place.

On-the-job training implements several other psychological learning principles. Active practice on the task is provided from the outset. The learning situation is obviously relevant to the job, and this should ensure a high degree of motivation. Knowledge of results is immediate and visible—an error can lead to the production of a faulty unit.

The disadvantages of on-the-job training can outweigh the benefits, however. In practice, it is often carelessly planned and poorly implemented. There is the danger that production facilities can be damaged, that production rates can be slowed, or that finished products fail to pass inspection. In certain jobs, allowing untrained persons to operate machinery may be hazardous not only to the trainees but also to others working nearby. Accident rates among trainees on the job are usually higher than among experienced workers. Another disadvantage is in the use of current workers as trainers. Just because a person performs a job competently does not mean that he or she has the ability to teach that job to someone else. Unless closely and professionally supervised, this kind of training can be haphazard, erratic, and generally inadequate. Often, such training amounts to no more than the foreman saying to the trainees, "Go ahead and start. If you have any questions, come see me."

Another potential problem is that when skilled workers are told to "break in" the new workers, they may look upon the assignment as a chance to get away from their own job for a while and goof off. As a result, the trainees are neglected and do not receive the attention and guidance they need and deserve. Also, skilled workers may resent new employees, feeling that the latter are being trained to take over their job. This insecurity can have obvious and detrimental effects on the kind of instruction the workers give to newly hired trainees.

The problems with using current workers as trainers can be overcome by training them in proper techniques of instruction, emphasizing the importance of their role as trainers, and trying to change their attitudes toward the new employees. Unfortunately, this effort is rarely made in industry.

Despite these difficulties, on-the-job training sometimes works quite well if proper care is taken in the development of the training program. With the necessary safeguards, on-the-job training can be effective, particularly in teaching relatively simple skills such as those required for clerical, production, or retail sales positions.

Vestibule Training

As noted, on-the-job training can interfere with the production process. Partly for this reason, many companies prefer the vestibule training method in which a simulated work space is set up in a separate training facility. Using the same kind of equipment and operating procedures as in the actual work situation, trainees learn to perform the job under the guidance of skilled instructors, not experienced workers. The research evidence suggests that vestibule training can be very effective in reducing the time required for training and in the resulting level of job proficiency.

There are several advantages to vestibule training. Since its purpose is solely to train workers, there is no emphasis or pressure on production. This, plus the use of professional trainers, means that more personalized attention can be given individual trainees. Also, trainees do not have to worry about making costly or embarrassing errors in front of future co-workers. Nor do they have to be concerned about damaging equipment or slowing down the production process. They are free to concentrate on learning the skills necessary for successful performance of the job.

The greatest disadvantage of vestibule training is the expense. The organization must equip a facility and maintain a staff of instructors. The cost may seem particularly burdensome when there are not enough new employees to make full use of the training facility.

If the training situation does not closely match the actual working situation, there will be the problem of transfer of training. Without a close correspondence between the two situations, trainees may need informal on-the-job training when they actually begin work.

The problem of transfer can be aggravated by the common practice of using obsolete equipment, retired from the production floor, in the training program. This false economy could result in negative transfer if the equipment in actual use is sufficiently different from the training equipment.

Apprenticeship

Probably the earliest recorded training method still in existence is the apprenticeship program for skilled crafts and trades. Conducted today both on the job and in the classroom, apprenticeship involves extensive background preparation in the craft and actual work experience under the guidance of experts.

Apprenticeships average four years, although in some skills they last as long as seven years. The standard procedure is for trainees to agree to work for a company for a fixed period of time in return for a specified period of training and a salary, usually about half that earned by skilled craftsmen.

Trainees usually must complete their apprenticeship successfully before they are allowed to join a trade union, in which membership is vital to securing employment. Apprenticeship programs thus represent a joint effort by industry and labor to maintain an adequate supply of thoroughly trained workers.

This combination of classroom instruction and actual work experience can provide excellent training in highly complex skills. If it is sometimes unsuccessful, that is not the fault of apprenticeship itself, but of those who misuse it. Sometimes a company provides inadequate formal training, exploiting apprentices as a cheap supply of labor, expecting them to learn a job quickly by providing a slapdash version of on-the-job training. Such a company is not truly concerned with training, but only with increased production.

Labor unions can also be criticized for the conduct of apprentice programs. Some apprenticeships seem much longer than necessary to learn the job. Unions may have a vested interest in maintaining lengthy programs. If there are too many craftsmen in a particular job category, there might not be enough jobs or sufficient scarcity of qualified personnel to maintain high wage rates.

The rapidly changing nature of manufacturing techniques sometimes renders a job obsolete by the time apprentices have finished the required period of training. For example, automation has completely altered the printing industry in recent years and has totally revised the skill requirements. Also, there is pressure on the housing industry for factory-produced homes as an alternative to on-site construction. The skills required of a carpenter working on an assembly line to build one part of a house are different from those required of the on-site carpenter.

Apprenticeship programs must be flexible and capable of modifying their requirements and procedures in line with changes in modern industry. Apprenticeship is generally a very effective training method and is likely to remain useful for many years.

Programmed Instruction

An exciting development in training, and in education in general, is the widespread use of programmed instruction. This method is popular in the military, industry, the U.S. Civil Service, schools, and universities.

There are several techniques for carrying out programmed instruction, ranging from paper-and-pencil book-type formats to costly computer-assisted electronic equipment. All means of programmed instruction involve self-instruction: trainees proceed at their own pace.

In essence, detailed (programmed) information is presented to the trainees who must make frequent and precise responses to the material. The instructional material begins at a very easy level and gradually becomes more complex. The steps of increasing difficulty are designed to be small so that slower learners can progress with relative ease. On the other hand, faster learners are allowed to proceed more rapidly through the material. The trainees' rates of learning are determined solely by their own motivation and mental ability.

Two approaches to programmed instruction are *linear programming* and *branching programming*. In the linear program, all trainees follow the identical program in the same sequence. The learning steps are so small and simple that trainees rarely make incorrect responses. Therefore, they receive frequent positive reinforcement.

Branching programs are designed to conform more to individual differences in level of ability. Trainees are allowed to skip steps if they are learning the material well, or to go back for remedial work if they are not learning it well. If trainees respond incorrectly to a set of questions at any point, they are directed to a new set of questions dealing with the same material. If trainees are proceeding well, they are directed to move on to the next section. If they are doing extremely well, they may be directed to skip intervening sections, and to move on to more difficult material.

Figure 6–1 portrays a sample linear program. A card is used to cover the answers on the right-hand side. As soon as the trainees record their answers in the blanks provided, they shift the card to compare their response with the correct one.

In terms of the general psychological learning principles, there are certain advantages to programmed instruction.

1. Programmed instruction provides for continuous active participation on the part of the trainees who must record their answer to one item before proceeding to the next. In machine-assisted programmed instruction, it may be impossible to move on to the next item until the current one is answered.
2. Programmed instruction provides constant and immediate feedback or knowledge of results. After each item, the trainees are informed of the adequacy of their response.
3. Positive reinforcement is provided. The items are purposely constructed to increase the probability that the trainees will be able to learn the correct response.

Proponents of programmed instruction suggest additional advantages.

Frame 1

    Transfer of training exists when information learned during training affects actual job performance. Therefore, how efficiently we perform on the job depends upon_____ of training.

TRANSFER

Frame 2

    Transfer may be positive or negative. If information learned in the training program facilitates job performance, the transfer is positive. If training takes place on equipment similar to that used on the job, transfer is likely to be_____ .

POSITIVE

Frame 3

    If information learned in the training program interferes with job performance, the transfer is negative. If training takes place on obsolete equipment, transfer is likely to be_____ .

NEGATIVE

Figure 6–1. Sample programmed material.

1. Programmed instruction eliminates the need for an instructor. Especially with the book form, trainees may learn where and when they choose. They do not have to be assembled at one time and place.

2. Because programmed instruction caters to individual differences, brighter trainees may complete a course of instruction more quickly than in a group teaching situation, which would have to be geared to the average level of the class. (This is particularly true with branching programs.)

3. The course of instruction is standardized. All trainees are exposed to the same material. This may not be the case if groups of employees are taught by several instructors, each of whom may emphasize, change, or omit different areas of the material to be learned.

4. A complete record is provided of the progress of each trainee that could aid in the future counseling of those who might experience difficulties.

This method may seem ideal for organizational training but certain disadvantages must be considered. The kind of material that can be taught by programmed instruction is limited. It is not effective in teaching complex job skills, but it is capable of teaching items of knowledge, particularly those requiring rote memorization. In general, it is more useful for training blue-collar workers than managers and executives.

Programmed instruction techniques can be very costly to develop and operate. Even when expensive equipment is not involved, the cost of writing the program is still high. Therefore, programmed instruction in organizations is usually restricted to training programs that involve very large numbers of trainees. Some persons report boredom and restlessness using programmed instruction. Initial acceptance is usually enthusiastic but as the small steps continue in robotlike fashion, a number of trainees develop a dislike for the experience.

Most of the research comparing the learning effectiveness of programmed instruction with traditional training methods has shown that programmed instruction is a very effective approach, although this statement must be qualified. Programmed instruction has been shown to be a faster method of training but the level of learning is no higher than with traditional teaching methods. Thus, programmed instruction does not seem to improve the quality of learning but it does provide for faster learning; this could be an asset to an organization that needs trained workers within a short period of time.

Programmed instruction is an important and widely used organizational training tool. Whether it becomes the revolution in training that some have predicted is still undetermined, but at the very least it is a standard training technique.

Computer-Assisted Instruction

An innovation in training, which is a logical derivative of programmed instruction, is computer-assisted instruction (CAI). Although still in the developmental stage, CAI is being used by military, government, and business organizations with initial reports of great success.

A computer, which stores an entire program of instruction, becomes the teacher and interacts with each trainee on an individual basis. Each answer provided by the trainee is instantly recorded and analyzed by the computer. The next item that is presented to the trainee is based on this continuing analysis of the trainee's progress. In a variation of this form of instruction, CAI can be used in conjunction with a training instructor who introduces the material and then directs the trainee to the computer for specific topics.

The major advantage of CAI is the greater amount of individualized instruction it offers as compared to programmed instruction. Using

CAI is similar to being privately tutored by an excellent teacher who has full command of the subject matter and who never becomes tired or irritated. The computer instantly responds to the progress of each trainee without sarcasm or prejudice or error. Because CAI also assumes complete record-keeping functions and always has an up-to-date performance analysis of each trainee, instructors have more time to devote to individual problems.

CAI allows the trainee to actively participate in the learning process, and it provides positive reinforcement and immediate knowledge of results.

Research indicates that CAI-trained students performed at the same level or higher than those who were trained by traditional methods or even by programmed instruction, and that learning took place in a much shorter period of time. Whether faster learning is worth the extremely high cost of CAI systems is the question that most organizations must answer for themselves.

Behavior Modification

In the discussion of reinforcement as a learning principle, we mentioned behavior modification and its recent introduction to the world of work. The idea behind the use of behavior modification in industry is simple. A performance audit is conducted periodically in an organization to determine the existence of specific problems or employee behaviors that should be changed. Then, a program of positive reinforcement is introduced whereby employees are reinforced when they display the desired behavior. Punishment is not used; instead of being punished for displaying undesirable behaviors, trainees are rewarded for displaying desirable behaviors.

In one case, a hardware company, plagued by the absenteeism and tardiness of its employees, began a six-month plan to reward good attendance.[1] The company organized a monthly drawing—the prize was some type of home appliance. In order to be eligible for the drawing, employees must have come to work each day, and been on time, for the preceding month. At the end of six months, there was an additional drawing for a color television set. Eligibility for the additional drawing required perfect attendance and punctuality for the entire six months.

The program was very successful. After it had been in effect for a year, payments for sick leave had fallen by 62 per cent and absenteeism and tardiness had decreased by 75 per cent. Employees were

[1] W. Nord, "Improving attendance through rewards," *Personnel Administration,* **33**(November–December 1970), 37–41.

much more likely to come to work with mild colds, whereas before the program was in effect they would have stayed home. Even severe snowstorms did not keep the employees away from work.

A more impressive demonstration of behavior modification in organizations took place at Emery Air Freight, where the behavioral changes induced were directly connected with job performance.[2] A performance audit revealed two problem areas: (1) despite the employees' belief that they were responding within ninety minutes to 90 per cent of the customer telephone inquiries, they were actually so responding to only 30 per cent of customer inquiries; (2) employees were combining packages into containers for shipment only 45 per cent of the time, whereas the company's executives thought that containers were being used almost 90 per cent of the time. The goals in the behavior modification training program were to get the employees to respond faster to customer inquiries and to use containers for shipment whenever possible.

All managers at Emery were given instruction (through programmed instruction techniques) on positive reinforcement and the importance of feedback, and on how to put these into practice. One workbook for managers discussed one hundred and fifty different recognitions and rewards to bestow on employees, ranging from a smile and a nod to highly specific praise for a job well done. (The latter turned out to be the most effective.) Managers were taught to reinforce desirable behaviors as soon as possible after they had occurred and to shift gradually from constant to partial reinforcement.

In terms of feedback, Emery required employees to keep a detailed record of what they had accomplished each day so that they could compare their performance with the desired standard of performance (for example, the standard of responding to customer requests within ninety minutes). In this program of reinforcement and feedback, money (bonuses or increased pay) was not used to try to change behavior. The company found that praise and recognition were sufficient incentives to improve job performance.

And the job performance at Emery did improve; the company saved $3 million in three years, considerably more than the cost of instituting the program. Emery has since expanded the program into other areas, and both employees and management are delighted with the results.

The behavior modification technique seems to have a great deal of potential for changing job behavior. Its record of success in other areas has been impressive; there seems no reason why it cannot be applied to performance on the job.

[2] E. J. Feeney, "Performance audit, feedback, and positive reinforcement," *Training and Development Journal,* **26**(1972), 8–13.

TRAINING METHODS: II. MANAGEMENT

The need for training does not diminish when we move up the organizational ladder to the level of supervisor or manager. If anything, it is more critical at these higher levels; the cost to a company of an incompetent department head can be far greater than that of an incompetent assembly line operator. Industry devotes considerably more money, time, and effort to management training than to the training of nonsupervisory employees.

It is generally recognized that few people are born leaders. Many may possess good leadership characteristics (certain levels of intelligence, personality, aptitudes), but they still must be trained in the development and exercise of their capacities before they can function as effective managers and executives. Assuming that an organization's selection procedures find good potential managers, they will remain only potential until they are trained in specific leadership skills and abilities.

Interest in management training began during the early 1940s. Since then, management training has become a major focus for personnel psychologists.

It is estimated that more than 75 per cent of businesses and government agencies operate some form of management training program. An indication of the scope and variety of training programs, and executive interest in them, is provided by a recent survey of sixteen hundred high-level government managers. The managers were asked several questions about management training programs including (1) how beneficial did they feel management training was, (2) how valuable several different types of training were, and (3) how committed the top management of their organization was to such training. The answers received to these questions provide a good indication of how executives who are in a position to implement management training programs feel about them.

A majority (86 per cent) of those surveyed believed that management training was beneficial; only 14 per cent disagreed. A moderate to strong commitment to management training was reported by 92 per cent of the respondents. The relative value of several kinds of training is shown in Table 6–1. The kinds of training inquired about ranged from specific and directly applicable to the job to broad and attitudinal. The greatest percentage of respondents favored training in human and interpersonal relations (2). Second was training devoted to a broad range of managerial science (3). These types of training were favored by more than two thirds of the respondents, which

TABLE 6–1

OBJECTIVES OF MANAGEMENT TRAINING PROGRAM

	Rank (in percentages)				
	1	**2**	**3**	**4**	**5**
1. Technical training in methods and procedures of operations.	11	14	20	18	33
2. Training in human and inter-personal relations.	38	29	16	9	4
3. Training in a broad range of managerial science principles and techniques.	30	28	15	16	8
4. Training in agency objectives, goals, and strategies.	15	18	26	29	9
5. Training in broad governmental principles and objectives.	5	10	20	22	29

From M. J. Gannon, "Attitudes of government executives toward management training," *Public Personnel Management,* **4**(1) (1975), 64. Reprinted by permission of the International Personnel Management Association, 1313 East 60th Street, Chicago, Illinois 60637. Copyright 1975 by the International Personnel Management Association.

indicates that they preferred more general training to that involving specific job skills. Specific job training (1) was ranked first in importance by only 11 per cent of the executives polled.

Before discussing specific management training techniques, let us briefly examine the training provided by the Western Electric Company in its Corporate Education Center (described earlier). One part of Western Electric's ambitious training program is designed for low-level managers who have exhibited strong potential for promotion to top management. Approximately thirty candidates each year are selected to attend a twenty-two-week program that uses a variety of instructional techniques. For example, trainees are assigned a program of independent reading, ranging from management practices to Plato.

In addition, trainees attend lectures and discussions. Frequently, they are formed into groups of four to six for intensive discussions called buzz sessions. Role-playing techniques are also used in which actual job situations are presented to the trainees and they must assume various managerial roles in attempting to solve the problems. Most of the discussions and role-playing exercises are recorded on videotape so that trainees and instructors can later watch and criticize. Many trainees consider this experience more demanding and challenging than their college work.

There are two goals in management training today. First, there is training in the general skills required for leadership roles: decision making, problem solving, delegation of responsibility, and other abilities necessary for managerial success. Second, there is human relations or sensitivity training directed toward optimizing the interpersonal relations vital to manager-employee harmony. Today's executives must possess more than the technical skills of leadership. In order to carry out their leadership roles, they must learn to effectively interact with subordinates as well as colleagues and superiors. Simply stated, managers must be able to get along with people if they are to become successful leaders.

There are a number of specific techniques useful for one or both of these training goals. Some approaches for nonsupervisory employee training are also useful for management training. On-the-job training and programmed instruction, for example, are used at the managerial level, as are traditional lecture, classroom, and discussion methods. Some techniques, however, are used exclusively for management training.

Case Study Method

The case study method, developed by the Harvard School of Business, is frequently used in executive training programs. In this approach, a complex problem, of the kind faced daily by managers and executives, is presented to the trainees prior to their general meeting. The trainees are expected to thoroughly familiarize themselves with the case and to find, on their own, additional relevant information.

When the trainees meet as a group, each member must be prepared to advance and discuss an interpretation of and solution to the problem. Through the presentation of diverse viewpoints, the trainees ideally come to appreciate the fact that there are different ways of looking at a problem and, consequently, different ways of attempting to resolve it.

Usually, the case studies chosen have no one correct solution. The leader of the group discussion does not suggest a solution; the group as a whole must resolve the issue.

The purpose of the case study method is to teach trainees the skills of group problem solving and decision making, the ability to analyze and criticize their own assumptions and interpretations, and the ability to be amenable to points of view other than their own.

A modification of the case study method involves the presentation of a brief incident in a management situation rather than a complex problem. This approach—the *incident process*—is a more formalized training procedure in that the instructor takes an active role in the discussion. The incident is investigated by the trainees in question-and-answer fashion; the instructor supplies the answers. Then the trainees record and debate their solutions to the incident. Finally, the instructor tells the group how the incident was actually handled on the job and what the outcome was. Such definitive solutions are not supplied in the case study method.

Business Games

Another popular approach to executive training involves the gaming process in which a complex, real-life situation is simulated. Like the case study method, this approach is intended primarily to develop problem-solving and decision-making skills, and to provide practice in exercising these skills in a situation in which mistakes will not harm the organization.

Teams of trainees compete against one another, each team representing a separate business organization. The team companies are given detailed information on all aspects of the operation of their organization, such as data on finances, sales, advertising, production, personnel, and inventories. Each group must organize itself; that is, assign various responsibilities and tasks to its members and proceed to handle the problems that face the company. As decisions are made, instructors (often aided by computers) evaluate their results. The group may be required to make additional decisions on the basis of these results.

The problems presented to the trainee teams are realistic and most trainees become emotionally involved with their company and its problems. The trainees gain experience in making decisions on a variety of real problems under the pressures of time and competing organizations.

At the end of the game (or sometimes at intervals throughout the game), instructors conduct critiques of the decisions made. Discussion is encouraged about other approaches to the problem that might have been taken.

Several hundred business games are available. They differ in terms of their complexity and how realistically they simulate the operation of a business organization. Basically there are two types: (1) *top management games,* dealing with the decision-making problems faced by high-level corporate officers, and (2) *functional games,* dealing with the operation of a single aspect of a company, such as production control or marketing.

In-basket Training

The in-basket technique was discussed in Chapter 3 as a method of selection. The same procedure is used to train prospective managers in the principles of executive leadership. When used for training, the in-basket technique is conceptually a business game in that it simulates the job of a manager. Unlike the business game, however, the trainee usually operates alone in the in-basket technique, rather than as part of a group. (There is a variation of the in-basket technique in which trainees operate in groups of four.)

Trainees are given a stack of letters, memoranda, customer complaints, requests for advice from subordinates, and other similar items, presenting them with the problems faced by managers on the job. The trainees must take action on each item, indicating exactly how they would handle it, within a certain period of time. After completing the tasks, each trainee reports on the decisions to a small group of other trainees and the trainer, and individual actions are discussed and criticized. This kind of training focuses on decision-making skills rather than on interpersonal skills or the learning of factual material.

Role Playing

In role playing, management trainees project themselves into a particular role and act out the behavior they believe is appropriate in that situation. For example, trainees may be asked to imagine themselves to be a supervisor who must discuss with an employee a poor performance evaluation. This role playing is often conducted in front of other trainees and instructors. Also, the trainees may play a variety of roles. In the previous example, one trainee plays the supervisor and another the employee. Then they may be asked to reverse roles and replay the situation. Usually, a critique is offered by other trainees or the trainer, and trainees may be shown a videotape of their role-playing performance.

Many people feel awkward or foolish about acting out a role in front of others but, once begun, most trainees develop a feeling for the role and try to become the person they are pretending to be.

At this point, the procedure can be a valuable learning device. It enables trainees to get a feel for the various roles they will be expected to play on the job. Not only do they gain practical experience in the role but also, through the analyses of other trainees and instructors, they learn how to improve their behavior. Further, they are able to practice these job-related behaviors in a situation in which mistakes will not interfere with production or jeopardize on-the-job interpersonal relations.

Role playing can provide the trainees with a greater sensitivity to others, particularly subordinates. Many management trainees, assuming the role of a worker in relation to a supervisor, gain an appreciation of the worker's viewpoint, which they would otherwise never experience.

University and Special Institute Courses

A growing number of universities and institutes are offering special liberal arts programs for executives that are designed to improve their management skills and broaden their general outlook. The executives chosen to attend these programs live on university campuses for the duration of the course. Here, executives have an opportunity to meet and work with others—from a variety of organizations or from branches of their own company—who are at approximately their own level of experience.

One program that concentrates on liberal arts is conducted by the University of Pennsylvania for executives of the Bell Telephone System. The program is longer than most—ten months—and includes an array of subjects (art, history, music, literature, ethics, history of science, and logic).

More pragmatic course offerings for executives are given by schools of business administration. Universities such as Harvard, Stanford, and Columbia offer summer programs that deal with specific job-related topics such as marketing management, computer resources management, public policy, and product planning.

The Aspen Institute of Humanistic Studies in Colorado offers popular two-week summer sessions for executives from many organizations including IBM, Chase Manhattan, Atlantic Richfield, and John Hancock. For a fee of approximately $2,000, participants study works such as Plato's *Republic,* Sophocles' *Antigone,* Rousseau's *Social Contract,* and Marx and Engels' *Communist Manifesto.* Williams College in Massachusetts offers a six-week, $3,000 program that combines the study of foreign policy, art, architecture, literature, and philosophy with visits to cultural attractions such as operas, ballets, and concerts.

Of what value are history, art, or music to practical business executives? How will these areas be of help to the executive on the job? There is no precise answer; it may take many years before any impact on executive skills or corporate profits is felt. Many corporate leaders, however, believe that such programs are valuable. A vice president of one large company said that the summer institute "won't help the financial state of a company as much as it will help a company's moral state. We came away seeing that corporations must stop being myopic and learn to cope with long-term problems that might well destroy us." [3] This kind of awareness alone could represent a handsome return on the cost of such programs.

Sensitivity Training

A popular development in management training is sensitivity or T-group training (also known as laboratory training, encounter groups, or action groups) designed to develop an understanding of interpersonal communication and interaction. Originating in the late 1940s at the National Training Laboratories in Maine, the technique shows individuals how others react to or perceive them, and what effect their behavior has on others. In this way, it is hoped that the trainees will develop a clearer and more accurate picture of themselves.

Trainees usually meet in groups of twelve, a few hours a day, for a number of weeks, although some sessions are marathons lasting eight to ten hours a day over a weekend. Often, the training course takes place at a comfortable retreat, far removed from the pressures, strains, (and securities) of everyday life and work. Before the sessions begin, trainees are given lectures on the sensitivity process and on the elements of learning and growth in social situations.

After these introductory lectures, the trainers assume a passive role in the T-group process, stressing that the responsibility for discussion and growth lies with the individual group members. There is no agenda or format for the discussion; in the beginning, it tends to be vague and formless. The topic of discussion also seems immaterial. The important thing is that something be discussed and that everyone be actively involved in the discussion. Ideally (although sometimes prodding by the trainer is necessary), the members begin to discuss themselves and each other, pointing out weaknesses and strengths. The conversations become frank and open, highly emotional, and often hostile, and it is these feelings of anger or hostility that become the main focus of discussion.

"Why did Jim get so mad when I said he was still emotionally dependent on his parents?" "Why does Susan accuse Mary of being wishy-washy?" "Why does Harold let his wife dominate him?" These probing personal questions are flung back and forth in a charged atmosphere of emotional involvement. Participants shout and scream at each other one moment, then break into tears and embrace. Often, an emotional intimacy will develop among the group members.

[3] S. Greenhouse, "Broader horizons for executives," New York Times, July 7, 1974.

What do the trainees gain from such an experience? Supposedly, they learn about themselves and emerge with a more effectively integrated personality and a greater sensitivity to the needs of others. Proponents of sensitivity training argue that participants come to realize the effects of their behavior on others, why others behave as they do, and how groups of people develop and operate. In addition, trainees have an opportunity to try different ways of behaving to see how appropriate they may be.

Sensitivity training is being offered throughout the United States by consulting organizations, religious groups, universities, and, unfortunately, a large number of poorly trained persons. There is increasing fear that the intimate frankness and personal attacks may hurt people more than they help. Studies of the aftereffects of participation in sensitivity training show psychological casualty rates ranging from less than 1 per cent to almost 50 per cent. Whatever the incidence of harmful effects, it is clear that some people are damaged emotionally by sensitivity sessions.

On the positive side, there is evidence (although it is mostly anecdotal) that many managers develop greater tolerance and acceptance of others, increased self-insight, greater self-control, and a more cooperative and tactful attitude toward others. There is little sound research support for these conclusions, however.

Whether these possible changes make any real difference in the trainees' productive capacities and decision-making leadership abilities (their worth to the company) has yet to be demonstrated. In any case, many organizations are sending their executives to T-group sessions. Some companies require executives to attend, and this raises an important ethical question. Does an organization have the right to compel employees to participate in such an emotionally revealing and potentially harmful process? If managers perform well at their jobs, isn't that sufficient? How much more should the company ask? Must it demand that they bare the innermost secrets of their emotional lives in order to keep their jobs? Even if there were indisputable evidence that sensitivity training produced greater leadership skills, this ethical question would still be paramount. In the absence of such evidence, this issue must be considered by every organization using this training technique.

TRAINING THE HARD-CORE UNEMPLOYED

In Chapters 3 and 4 we noted that organizations are making efforts to recruit and hire members of minority groups, including persons labeled hard-core unemployed. Hiring these people, however, is not enough; because of their impoverished background, they require a heavy investment in training opportunities before being able to fully realize their potential. As a result of this need, business and government organizations are devoting much time and effort to training those who had once been considered unemployable.

Who are the hard-core unemployed? On the average, they are almost always members of minority groups (usually blacks), have no more than a sixth-grade education (with a third-grade reading level and a fourth-grade mathematics level), have no transportation of their own to get to work, have been unemployed for one and one-half years, have no marketable skills, and are married with three children.

One of the earliest programs to train the hard-core unemployed was conducted by Boeing Aircraft in 1968. It still serves as a model of thoroughness. Many problems never before encountered by trainers were discovered when the program began. There were serious problems in communication, not just in communicating ideas or concepts, but the more basic problem of understanding spoken words. If the trainers were white, there was hostility and fear on the part of the trainees. Many trainees had mannerisms, habits, and dress styles that trainers found unorthodox and even offensive. A rapport had to be established before the actual job training could begin. The trainees needed to be convinced that the program was genuine and that the training was geared directly to a job and to correcting their deficient abilities. Only in this way did trainees develop any real motivation to learn.

Boeing found that the training must contain five elements: (1) basic education and remedial work in areas such as English and mathematics and communications skills; (2) prevocational training involving the establishment of the relevance and meaning of vocabulary, arithmetic, and other skills basic to the actual job, as well as proper attitudes toward work, such as punctuality, reliability, and mode of dress; (3) characteristics of the job itself (preassignment training) involving a simulated work environment in which specific job skills were taught; (4) on-the-job training under the supervision of a working foreman; (5) supportive services such as personal and job counseling, medical help, aid with transportation and finances (these elements were present throughout the training program).

Experience from other hard-core unemployed training programs has demonstrated the necessity of dealing with motivational and attitudinal factors as well as with actual job skills. In addition, these programs have pointed up the importance of the first-line supervisors to whom trainees are assigned after completing their training. The supervisors may also require training in order to understand the backgrounds, fears, and anxieties of the new employees. One of the most important factors affecting the job behavior of hard-core unemployed persons is the support, tolerance, and understanding they receive from their supervisors once they undertake the job. In fact, supervisor support may be more influential than job-skill training in determining how well these employees perform and how long they stay on the job.

Behavior modification was applied in at least one job skill training program. A manufacturer of bed frames was having great difficulty teaching disadvantaged workers to package the finished product and place it on a skid. On-the-job training was unsuccessful and the company decided to try a behavior modification program.[4] The overall job was broken down into a number of individual, simple operations. Trainees were awarded points (which could later be converted into money) for successfully learning each operation and again for successfully performing the entire sequence of operations. The points received were tallied on a chart mounted next to each trainee's machine so that feedback was immediately visible to the trainee. In addition, verbal praise was used as a positive reinforcement. Trainees were able to learn the job in two or three days under this system. Then they were put on a regular pay schedule but the verbal praise from their supervisor was continued.

In this example, behavior modification was used only for teaching a particular skill, but it could also be applied to attitudinal training. For example, trainees could be given positive reinforcement for punctuality, for displaying nonhostile behavior, or for maintaining a certain level of competence.

Training is a complex task with all levels of employee, but it is much more difficult when dealing with disadvantaged persons. Business and government organizations are making major efforts to bring the hard-core unemployed into the economic mainstream.

EVALUATING TRAINING PROGRAMS

Regardless of how impressive and sophisticated a training program or facility may appear, it is necessary that the effects or results of the training be evaluated in systematic and quantitative fashion. Unless evaluative research is conducted, an organization that has devoted large amounts of money and time to the program will have no idea of how worthwhile the effort has been. Are employees learning the

---

[4] C. E. Schneier, "Behavior modification: Training the hard-core unemployed," *Personnel,* **50**(1973), 65–69.

skills needed for their jobs? Does production increase after training? Are accidents and wastage declining? Have interpersonal skills and leadership abilities improved? To answer these questions adequately, the psychologist must compare the performance of trained with untrained workers in the same job, or compare the same workers before and after training with a comparable control group that was not exposed to training. In this way, the organization can determine if a training program should be modified, eliminated, or extended for use throughout the plant.

With such a large investment at stake, one expects executives and training directors to be eagerly and constantly examining the utility of their training programs. This is not the case, however. Most programs are evaluated, if at all, on subjective or intuitive terms.

A survey of forty-seven firms that used some form of human relations training found that fewer than half of the organizations made any effort to evaluate their programs in terms of behavior changes on the part of the trainees. Only one fourth of the companies attempted to measure behavior before and after training, and only one company compared a group exposed to the training with a group that was not.

A survey of three hundred firms reported that the majority of the companies said that training was valuable to their organization, yet more than half of these companies reported that training concepts needed additional research in order to improve their utility to management. There seems to be much talk about the evaluation of training, but little done about it.

Aside from the cost of such research, other factors contribute to the lack of training evaluation. Many nonpsychologists involved in corporate training do not themselves have the proper training to conduct this research. Also, a number of organizations are involved in training, not because they are convinced of its worth, but because their competitors are doing it. Given that motivation to institute a training program, it is easy to see why the firm would be reluctant to spend even more money to test the effectiveness of its program.

Another reason for the scarcity of evaluative research has to do with the nature of the behavioral changes that result from training; some are more easily evaluated than others. It is simple, for example, to determine the effectiveness of training to operate a machine or assemble a part. The training goal and the measure of the behavioral change are straightforward. The number of units produced per unit time by trained and untrained workers (or workers trained by a different technique) can be determined objectively and compared. At this work level, training programs have been shown to be quite effective.

But in dealing with the more nebulous behaviors involved in human relations or sensitivity training, and in other aspects of management training, it is difficult to evaluate the effects of these programs. Management training is definitely favored by many top executives in North American industry, but is it truly worthwhile?

The only way to answer this question is with considerable and thorough research. In general, the conviction that management training is accomplishing its objectives seems to be a matter of faith, and is more of an emotional, gut-level reaction than a belief based on rational, experimentally based proof. The face validity of management training is high; everybody says it is good and it looks good for an organization to have such a program. Many training directors defend management training by pointing out that a large number of the graduates of management training programs are promoted to higher levels of responsibility. This in itself is not a valid measure of the worth of the training since only the most capable and promising individuals were chosen to participate in management training programs initially; in other words, the trainees are the most promotable candidates even without the training programs. Training directors also defend the worth of their program by indicating how much the participants liked the training. Though it is nice when trainees enjoy a training session, that is no indication that the experience will result in better performance on the job.

A major challenge faces psychology and industry today. Organizations must be encouraged to expend the resources necessary to appraise their elaborate training programs. It makes little sense to continue to support an activity in the absence of firm knowledge about its value. Psychologists, both industrial and academic, must focus research attention on the specific behaviors involved at the various levels of training (particularly management training) so that they can determine the best means of modifying those behaviors effectively for job success.

SUMMARY

Training takes place at all levels of employment, from unskilled ghetto youngsters to seasoned corporate vice presidents, from the first day on a job to the final months before retirement. Training is a continuing organizational activity, particularly at the management level, on which a great deal of money and effort are expended. Training is not restricted to specific job skills. Much training activity is directed toward changing attitudes, motivations, and interpersonal skills. At any level of employment or type of training, the goal is to improve performance on the job and, in the process, to increase the value of individual employees to themselves and to their organization.

The first step in establishing a training program is to specify the training objectives; in other words, to determine specifically the objectives that the training is intended to accomplish. These can be determined by several techniques: **job analysis, critical incidents,** and **performance evaluation.**

Also of importance in a training program is the selection and training of the **training staff,** those persons who will conduct the formal teaching. Those who are knowledgeable in the subject matter, in communicating effectively, and in interpersonal skills have been shown to be the best instructors.

Psychological principles of learning relate to training in organizations. These derive from the vast amount of psychological research that has been conducted on the human learning process. Two principles—**individual differences in ability** and **motivation**—deal with characteristics of the learner. Other principles deal with various ways in which the subject matter can be organized and presented: **active practice of the material, massed versus distributed practice, whole versus part learning, transfer of training, knowledge of results,** and **reinforcement.**

Specific training techniques used for nonsupervisory employees and for managers are presented. Techniques used for nonsupervisory employees include (1) **on-the-job training,** in which trainees learn while actually working at the job, (2) **vestibule training,** in which training takes place in a simulated work space away from the actual job, (3) **apprenticeship,** in which trainees undergo both classroom experience and work experience under the guidance of skilled craftsmen, (4) **programmed instruction,** in which the material is presented in easy steps, for each of which the trainees must indicate if they are comprehending the material, (5) **computer-assisted instruction,** in which trainees interact with a computer that contains the course content, and (6) **behavior modification,** in which trainees are reinforced or rewarded for displaying the desired behaviors. Advantages and disadvantages of these techniques are presented, along with examples of actual use.

Some of the techniques used for training nonsupervisory employees are also used for training managers. In addition, the following techniques are used for management training: (1) the **case study method,** in which trainees analyze, interpret, and discuss a complex problem faced by managers on the job; (2) **business games,** in which a group of trainees interact in a simulated business situation; (3) **in-basket training,** another simulated business situation in which trainees respond individually; (4) **role playing,** in which trainees play the roles of workers or managers; (5) **university and special institute courses,** in which instruction is provided in specific management skills as well as in the liberal and fine arts, to broaden the managers' backgrounds; and (6) **sensitivity training,** in which groups of individuals develop skills in relating to one another.

Special training for the hard-core unemployed is offered by a number of organizations. It is necessary to focus on motivational and attitudinal training as well as on specific job-related skills with these persons. Behavior modification has also been used to train the hard-core unemployed.

Perhaps the weakest point in the overall training process is the evaluation of training. This has rarely been carried out on a systematic and quantitative basis. Many training programs remain in use because of subjective judgments about their worth. It is important to evaluate the actual behavior changes that result from training.

SUGGESTED READINGS

Back, K. Beyond Words: The Story of Sensitivity Training and the Encounter Movement. New York: Russell Sage Foundation, 1972.

Broadwell, M. Supervisor and On the Job Training, 2nd ed. Reading, Mass.: Addison-Wesley, 1975.

Campbell, J. P. Personnel training and development. Annual Review of Psychology, 1971, **22,** 565–602.

Campbell, J. P., Dunnette, M., Lawler, E. E., and Weich, K. Training and development: Methods and techniques. In J. P. Campbell et al., Managerial Behavior, Performance, and Effectiveness. New York: McGraw-Hill, 1970.

Carroll, S. J., Paine, F. T., and Ivancevich, J. J. The relative effectiveness of training methods—expert opinion and research. Personnel Psychology, 1972, **25,** 495–509.

Feeney, E. Performance audit, feedback, and positive reinforcement. Training and Development Journal, 1972, **26,** 8–13.

Gannon, M. Attitudes of government executives toward management training. Public Personnel Management, 1975, **4**(1), 63–68.

Goldstein, I. Training: Program Development and Evaluation. Monterey, Calif.: Brooks/Cole, 1974.

Goodman, P., Salipante, P., and Paransky, H. Hiring, training, and retraining the hard-core unemployed: A selected review. Journal of Applied Psychology, 1973, **58,** 23–33.

Hague, H. Executive Self-Development. New York: Halsted Press, 1974.

Hamblin, A. *Evaluation and Control of Training.* New York: McGraw-Hill, 1974.

Hartley, D., Roback, H., and Abramowitz, S. Deterioration effects in encounter groups. *American Psychologist,* 1976, **31,** 247–255.

Hinrichs, J. R. Personnel training. In M. Dunnette, Ed., *Handbook of Industrial and Organizational Psychology.* Chicago: Rand McNally, 1976. Pp. 829–860.

Howell, D. Supervisory development for small business firms. *Personnel Journal,* 1970, **49,** 570–576.

Humble, J. *Improving the Performance of the Experienced Manager.* New York: McGraw-Hill, 1973.

In-company college: New era in training. *Modern Manufacturing,* 1970, **3,** 78–79.

Kirchner, W., and Lucas, J. The hard-core in training—who makes it? *Training and Development Journal,* 1972, **26,** 34–38.

Lieberman, M., Yalom, I., and Miles, M. *Encounter Groups: First Facts.* New York: Basic Books, 1973.

Newell, G. How to plan a training program. *Personnel Journal,* 1976, **55,** 220–225.

Nord, W. Improving attendance through rewards. *Personnel Administration,* 1970, **33**(November–December), 37–41.

Posthuma, A., and Posthuma, B. Some observations on encounter group casualties. *Journal of Applied Behavioral Science,* 1973, **9,** 595–608.

Recknagel, K. Why management training fails and how to make it succeed. *Personnel Journal,* 1974, **53,** 589–597.

Schneier, C. Behavior modification: Training the hard–core unemployed. *Personnel,* 1973, **50,** 65–69.

Schneier, C. Training and development programs: What learning theory and research have to offer. *Personnel Journal,* 1974, **53,** 288–293.

Stein, C. Group-grope: The latest development bromide. *Personnel Journal,* 1973, **52,** 19–26.

Swedmark, D. *Developing the Company Training Program.* New York: Davlin, 1975.

Taylor, J. Ten serious mistakes in management training development. *Personnel Journal,* 1974, **53,** 357–362.

Tracey, W. *Managing Training and Development Systems.* New York: American Management Association, 1974.

Wessman, F. Determining the training needs of managers. *Personnel Journal,* 1975, **54,** 109–113, 125.

ORGANIZATIONAL PSYCHOLOGY

Organizational psychology includes those functions and processes that define the social and psychological climate within which we work. Few people work alone. Most of us work in small groups, such as a crew on one unit of an assembly line or a department in a corporate office, and here we form cliques—influential informal groups that generate their own values and attitudes (which may not be compatible with those of the organization).

We are also affected by the formal structure of the organization for which we work—the company, government agency, or university that employs us. Like the informal groups, formal groups generate a psychological climate of ideals and attitudes that influences our feelings about our job and the way in which we perform it.

Formal organizations range from rigid and hierarchical bureaucracies to loosely structured and flexible companies in which employees participate in decision making at all levels. The participative organization is the modern approach; it is distinguished by a focus on the intellectual, emotional, and motivational characteristics of the individual employees. The older bureaucratic style focuses solely on the form of the organization, with no regard for the psychological characteristics of employees.

Employee attitudes and work behavior are affected by both the social factors of the organization and the psychological factors of the individual members of the organization. Organizational psychology (Chapters 7–9) is concerned with the relationships between these two sets of factors.

Leadership (Chapter 7) is a major source of influence on worker attitudes and behavior. Various styles of leadership—from dictatorial to democratic—create different social climates. Organizational psychologists are concerned with the influence of leadership styles and the psychological characteristics of the leaders—their motivations, stresses, and job duties.

Chapter 8 deals with the motivations that employees bring to their work and the ways in which organizations can satisfy (or fail to satisfy) these needs. The chapter also discusses the quality of working life today—the satisfactions and frustrations that characterize our lives at work.

Chapter 9 is devoted to formal and informal organizations and the psychological climate fostered by each. The movement to humanize work through participatory democracy is discussed along with ways in which organizations can adapt to social and technological innovations.

Organizational psychology is directly related to your working career. Your motivations, the style of leadership under which you function, the style you may exercise yourself, and the form of organization for which you work determine the quality of your working life. This, in turn, influences your satisfaction with life in general.

7

Leadership in Organizations

We know that organizations today place great stress on finding and training leaders at all levels—from supervisor to president. Indeed, a major portion of all selection and training activity is devoted to leadership; the success or failure of any organization depends, in large measure, upon the quality of its leaders. Some analysts believe that the basic difference between a successful and an unsuccessful organization is its leadership. All types of organization—business and industry, government and military agencies, universities and hospitals— recognize the importance of the leadership function.

Research has shown that half of all new businesses fail within their first two years and only one third survive five years. In most cases, the business failures are caused by poor leadership. The chairman of the board of General Electric stated the problem forcefully:

Of all the considerations affecting the future success of business, leadership is now *the* most critical factor, and it might turn out to be the *only* critical factor. Neither machines nor money are going to be enough to solve the business problems of the future. . . . We are headed for a world that technology and financial resources will make possible, but it will be a world that only [people] will make sensible. [People] who plan, [people] who create, [people] who decide, [people] who manage.[1]

It is not surprising, then, that organizations engage in extensive searches for new methods of selecting and developing their managers and executives, and for making the best use of their leadership abilities once they are on the job. Because executives are so highly valued, they are offered inducements to join and remain with a com-

[1] R. C. Miljus, "Effective leadership and the motivation of human resources," *Personnel Journal,* **49** (January 1970), 36.

229

pany—stock options and other lucrative fringe benefits, comfortable expense accounts, and lavishly decorated offices.

Psychologists play an important role in leadership. In addition to direct efforts in selection and training, they have conducted considerable research on aspects of leadership such as characteristics of successful and unsuccessful leaders, effects of different styles of leadership behavior, and techniques for maximizing decision making. The quality of organizational leadership today reflects the research activities and practical applications of psychologists.

Anything that affects the fortunes and future of the organization for which you work also affects you, the employee; leadership is no exception. Regardless of the level of your job, the quality of leadership in your place of employment will influence you daily. Unless (or until) you are the company president, you will take orders from someone else. Much of your motivation, enthusiasm, hope for the future, and even ability to perform your job, will depend on how well your leader performs his or her duties.

Also, as college graduates, most of you will fill positions of leadership. Most organizations are developing their leaders from among the ranks of the college-educated. How well you perform your job as a leader will influence your salary, rank, and sense of self-worth.

CHANGING VIEWS OF LEADERSHIP

The ways in which leaders behave, the specific acts by which they play out their leadership roles, are based on certain assumptions about human nature. Consciously or unconsciously, leaders function on the basis of some theory of human behavior, a view of what their subordinates are like as people. Managers who closely watch subordinates to make sure they are performing the job exactly as told hold a different view of human nature than managers who allow subordinates to accomplish their work in whatever way they think best.

These concepts have been changing throughout the twentieth century, partly because of the growth in the size of business organizations since 1900, changing social forces such as the rise to power of the labor unions, and widespread psychological research and theory on the nature and motivation of people at work.

In the early years of the twentieth century, foremen—the most immediate supervisors of the workers—were promoted from the ranks of the workers and had little formal training for a leadership role. These turn-of-the-century foremen exercised virtually complete control over subordinates. Foremen hired and fired, controlled production levels, and set pay scales. Obviously, this approach left much room for abuse. All too often foremen were dictators, and not truly "leaders," in the modern sense of the term. There were few reins on their authority—no labor union, no personnel or industrial relations department, no one to whom a worker could complain.

The philosophy of management at that time was *scientific management*. This approach, established by an engineer, Frederick W. Taylor, was concerned solely with ways to maintain or increase production levels. Through the use of time and motion studies, representatives of scientific management were interested in standardizing the production process—getting the machines, and the workers who ran them to work faster and faster.

Indeed, scientific management regarded workers as extensions of the machines, and thus the relationship between workers and the organization was highly impersonal. No consideration was given to employees as human beings—people with needs, fears, and values. The organizational goal was to increase production and efficiency, and the only way to accomplish this was for workers to submit to the needs of the machinery.

Nowadays, it is difficult to imagine people working under such an extreme system. Instead of a lack of concern for their workers, some modern organizations, under several sources of pressure, view the needs of their employees as a goal. This is the *human relations* approach to management which began in the 1920s and 1930s under the impact of the Hawthorne and other studies that focused on the workers instead of on production. Since that time, the human relations style of leadership has influenced the management practices of a number of organizations.

The human relations movement brought about a recognition of workers as human beings, no longer interchangeable cogs in a giant production machine. It has made organizations alert and responsive to the personal and social needs of employees and to the interpersonal relations that develop within the organization. The task of leaders should not be solely to maintain or increase production but rather to also facilitate cooperative goal achievement among subordinates and enhance their personal growth and development.

These two approaches to management behavior were given formal theoretical expression by psychologist Douglas McGregor as *Theory X* and *Theory Y*.[2] McGregor's views have become influential in the world of work and encompass divergent images of workers and the ways in which they can be managed.

[2] D. McGregor, *The Human Side of Enterprise* (New York: McGraw-Hill, 1960), pp. 33–34, 47–48.

Underlying the Theory X approach to management are three assumptions about human nature:

1. Most people have an innate dislike of work and will avoid it if they can.
2. Therefore, most people must be "coerced, controlled, directed, threatened with punishment" in order to get them to work hard enough to satisfy the organization's goals.
3. Most people prefer "to be directed," wish "to avoid responsibility," have "relatively little ambition," and want "security above all."

Theory X provides a very unflattering image of human nature. According to this view, people would not work at all at their jobs without a dictating and demanding leader. Like children, workers must be led, scolded, threatened, and punished for they are basically irresponsible and lazy.

Theory X still represents the view of human nature held by the majority of managers. It is compatible with scientific management and with the classic form of organization called *bureaucracy*. However, Theory X is incompatible with current views of human motivation, particularly the influential work of psychologist Abraham Maslow. Maslow argues that the ultimate and overall goal of human beings is to self-actualize; that is, to realize all of our distinctly human capabilities. This conception of human nature is reflected in McGregor's Theory Y, which assumes that:

1. "The expenditure of physical and mental effort in work is as natural as play or rest." Most people do not have an innate dislike of work. Indeed, work may be a "source of satisfaction."
2. "External control and the threat of punishment are not the only means for bringing about effort toward organizational objectives." Most people will display self-discipline in working for goals to which they are committed.
3. "Commitment to objectives is a function of the rewards associated with their achievement." If self-actualization needs can be satisfied through work, employees will be highly motivated.
4. Most people, under proper conditions, are capable not only of accepting responsibility but of seeking it.
5. "The capacity to exercise a relatively high degree of imagination, ingenuity, and creativity in the solution of organizational problems is widely . . . distributed in the population."
6. "Under the conditions of modern industrial life, the intel-

lectual potentialities of the average human being are only partially utilized."

In the radically different image of human nature that Theory Y presents, people are industrious, creative, need and seek challenge and responsibility, and are not at all averse to work. These persons need and function best under a different type of leader than do Theory X persons. Rather than a dictatorial leader, Theory Y persons need a leader who will allow them to participate in the achievement of personal and organizational goals. The Theory Y view of leadership applies to the human relations movement and to modern organization theory that calls for worker participation in management decisions.

APPROACHES TO THE STUDY OF LEADERSHIP

Academic and organizational psychologists have been studying the nature of leadership for decades. Their goal is to determine the nature of leadership and the factors that cause some people to be effective leaders and others to be ineffective leaders.

Initially, the problem of delimiting leadership characteristics seemed to be simple. After all, in most situations it is not difficult to determine which persons are good leaders and which are poor. All that appeared necessary was for researchers to measure the traits of good leaders and poor leaders and see how they differed.

This *trait approach* sought those characteristics that good leaders possessed in much greater degree than did poor leaders. For example, if it was found that good leaders consistently scored high on a scale that measured extraversion and poor leaders consistently scored low (the introverted end of the scale), it might be concluded that effective leaders are persons who are extraverted. It would then be possible to predict leadership potential on the basis of a person's score on the extraversion scale, in combination with scores on scales that measured additional traits, which differentiated good from poor leaders.

Thus, the emphasis in the trait approach is on the personal characteristics of leaders. No consideration is given to the circumstances or the situation in which leadership occurs. It follows that there is no need to consider the leadership situation; if leadership ability is a function of personal traits, the person possessing the right combination of traits will be a good leader in all situations.

The trait approach to leadership has a common-sense appeal because it agrees with a popular notion that some people are "born" leaders; they possess unique characteristics that induce others to want to follow them. However, psychological research does not support the trait approach. In general, the most consistent finding from more than fifty years of studies on the trait approach is that there does not seem to be a universal set of traits that distinguishes good from poor leaders. Not even one characteristic has been shown to discriminate between effective and ineffective leaders in all situations. Why? Because the person who is a good leader in one situation may fail dismally as a leader in another situation. Leadership ability, it seems, is not a predictable set of abilities, characteristics, or behaviors. What determines effective leadership is not so much the characteristics of individual leaders, but rather the nature of the situation in which they are expected to lead, and the characteristics and needs of the followers.

When psychologists realized this, they turned from the trait approach to the *situational approach* in their investigation of the nature of leadership. This conception of leadership focuses on the dynamic interactions between leaders and followers. It is concerned with the needs of followers and with the problem or task confronting the group. Viewing leadership in this way, as a function of a particular situation, means that leadership is a dynamic process. That is, the abilities, characteristics, and behaviors necessary for effective leadership may change in response to changes in the tasks and goals of the group or in the needs of the followers. For example, a newly established business may require a different kind of leadership than a long-established, smoothly running organization. The abilities required for success in one situation may not suffice in others. In some cases, these abilities might even be counterproductive.

Leadership requirements may also change in the same situation over a period of time, as new values or outlooks are needed (such as the change from the scientific management approach to the human relations approach to management from the 1900s to the 1970s and 1980s).

This necessity for flexibility is another factor that precludes the possibility of uncovering a set of characteristics with which to predict leadership performance in all situations.

In recent years, psychologists have directed research toward leadership *behavior,* investigating what leaders do, in addition to what they are. Do good leaders behave differently from poor leaders? What do they do on the job that makes them so effective?

Leadership behavior is examined in the following way. The psychologist collects, usually by means of interviews, examples of effective and ineffective leadership that actually occurred on the job. Each specific behavioral example is then judged by a panel of experts as to how good or poor it is. Based on these expert ratings, the examples are scaled in quantitative terms and a behavioral questionnaire is developed. The questionnaire is administered to subordinates who indicate those behaviors that have been exhibited by their supervisors.

One research program using this approach detailed eighteen hundred examples that were reduced to a leader behavior questionnaire of one hundred and fifty specific behaviors. Table 7–1 contains sample items from such a questionnaire.

Once the questionnaire has been developed and validated, it simplifies the evaluation of a particular leader's behavior, and allows for the comparison of the behavior of different leaders. The scale also indicates which behaviors are the most desired or effective for a particular job, department, or work group. Current and future leaders can then be trained to develop effective behaviors and to eliminate ineffective ones.

An underlying assumption of the situational approach to the study of leadership is that leaders can be trained to function well. This contrasts with the trait approach, which holds that leaders are born with traits that cause them to be effective; those who do not possess these traits are incapable of becoming good leaders.

The trait approach to the study of leadership has not been abandoned. Although psychologists no longer look for universal leadership abilities, they are continuing to investigate the personal traits of leaders in specific situations. Thus, the search for leadership traits is conducted within the context of the situation and the nature of the followers. This restricted trait approach has revealed characteristics and abilities that distinguish successful leaders from less successful ones.

TABLE 7–1

SAMPLE ITEMS FROM SUPERVISORY BEHAVIOR DESCRIPTION FORM

1. Supervisor expresses appreciation when one of us does a good job.
2. Supervisor is easy to understand.
3. Supervisor demands more than we can do.
4. Supervisor insists that everything be done his or her way.
5. Supervisor treats subordinates without considering their feelings.
6. Supervisor is friendly and can be easily approached.
7. Supervisor rules with an iron hand.
8. Supervisor offers new approaches to problems.
9. Supervisor stresses being ahead of competing work groups.
10. Supervisor emphasizes the quantity of work.

Adapted from E. A. Fleishman, "The description of supervisory behavior," Journal of Applied Psychology, **37**(1953), 3–4.

In sum, there are several separate but interacting elements in the leadership process: the characteristics and behaviors of leaders, the characteristics of followers, and the nature of the situation in which leaders and followers interact. To fully analyze and understand the nature and requirements of leadership, all these elements must be studied.

LEADERSHIP STYLES

Increasing research has been focused on what leaders do—their style of leadership and the behaviors by which it is manifested. This section describes several dimensions that distinguish various styles of leadership.

Headship Versus Leadership

A basic distinction between leadership styles is the source of the decision about who will be the leader. Are leaders appointed by sources outside the group they must lead, or are they chosen by members of the group itself? In the first situation, *headship* or nominal leadership, leaders are imposed on the group by external sources. In the second situation, *leadership* or effective leadership, the members of the group select those whom they wish to lead them.

You can find examples of both kinds of leadership in your own experience. Elected representatives at state and federal levels of government are chosen by the people. The same is true for clubs, fraternities and sororities, and other social organizations. In most large organizations, however, leaders are usually imposed on the group. Workers rarely elect their supervisors, and enlisted personnel do not elect their officers (although this did occur during the Civil War).

Persons appointed to leadership positions are automatically given the trappings, status, and authority of superiors. With sufficient authority, such as the punitive powers of an army officer or a manager, appointed heads are able to direct the activities of a group and gain compliance, but they may not be able to "lead" the group, in the larger sense of the term.

Headship usually guarantees that leaders can direct or dominate the actions of followers, and such leaders are given the power to punish followers if the latter do not obey. But followers may not willingly or loyally cooperate with imposed heads unless the heads are also leaders. Indeed, group members may only perfunctorily carry out commands for imposed heads. This marks the crucial difference between headship and leadership. True leaders are able to enlist the cooperation of a group and enhance its solidarity and cohesion so that the members willingly work with the leaders to perform the job.

Thus, although appointed heads may begin their roles armed with the perquisites of leadership—the symbols, title, and office—their ability to work with their followers determines how effectively they will be able to lead. No appointed heads truly lead their followers and receive their active cooperation without first gaining their support, confidence, and trust.

Table 7–2 presents some of the differences between headship and leadership.

Appointed heads face special problems not shared by elected leaders. Since the majority of organizational leaders are appointed, it is important to consider the limitations and difficulties these leaders face.

Appointed leaders have a dual and sometimes conflicting set of

TABLE 7–2

DIFFERENCES BETWEEN HEADSHIP AND LEADERSHIP

Personal and Situational Variables	Headship	Leadership
Power exercised by:	Appointed head	Elected or chosen leader
Source of authority:	Delegated from above	Accorded from below
Basis of authority:	Legal or official	Personal competence
Authority vested by:	Values institutionalized in formal contract	Recognition of contribution to group goals
Relationship of superior to subordinates:	Domination	Personal influence
Responsible to:	Superiors	Superiors and subordinates
Social gap with followers:	Wide	Narrow
Behavior pattern:	Authoritarian	Democratic

Adapted from C. R. Holloman, "Leadership and headship: There is a difference," *Personnel Administration,* **31** (July–August 1968), 41.

obligations and responsibilities. First, they are responsible to those who appointed them—their superiors in the organization. If they are to retain their position, they must satisfy the company's demands and goals. Foremen, for instance, must reach and maintain the production levels set by their supervisors.

Second, appointed leaders must satisfy, where possible, the needs and wishes of subordinates. Foremen must, for example, secure the support of their workers if they hope to meet established production quotas. Foremen must arrange for satisfactory physical and psychological work conditions and adequate pay scales, and they must represent the subordinates to higher management, passing along grievances and suggestions.

Elected leaders have a single set of responsibilities. They must answer only to those who put them in their position of leadership. Although they may have obligations outside the group, their responsibility is to their followers.

Another difficulty often faced by appointed heads is a limited flexibility in their own methods of leadership. In a large business or government organization, they have to operate within established guidelines about how to accomplish various aspects of the job. The rigidity of these rules varies among organizations, but appointed leaders cannot operate too innovatively without running afoul of organizational policy.

Elected leaders are not so constrained. Since they are responsible only to their followers, they are free to lead in any way they believe will satisfy the wishes of their followers.

Leadership competence of the two types of leaders varies. It can be assumed that elected leaders have already displayed qualities necessary to satisfy the group before they are chosen to lead. If not, the group would not have made them leaders. No such assumption can be made about appointed heads. We know that it is difficult to assess management potential. Promotions and leadership appointments must often be based on proficiency in a person's current job. However, the fact that a person is best in sales for the district, for example, is no guarantee that he or she will make a good sales manager.

Although there are disadvantages and limitations to leadership by appointment, it seems unlikely that industry will alter this basic management procedure. The ideal situation is where appointed leaders are able to assume the characteristics and interpersonal relations of elected leaders—where headship becomes true leadership. This can be difficult, but two factors may facilitate this change.

First, the complexity of modern production processes necessitates a close working and consulting relationship between line supervisors and various staff specialists. For example, foremen often meet with members of the personnel department before making promotion decisions. Years ago, the foremen made such decisions on their own. The dependence of managers on other high-level personnel has decreased their autonomy and caused them to be more flexible in considering the opinions of others, including subordinates. If managers begin to listen to subordinates, they are well on the way to becoming effective leaders.

Second, the emphasis on human relations skills and participatory democracy encourages managers to be concerned with developing motivation and personal and group satisfaction among subordinates.

These two factors, then, foster the positive trend toward fusing headship and leadership.

Authoritarian Versus Democratic Leadership

The words *authoritarian* and *democratic* are familiar as forms of government. An authoritarian government is dictatorial and tyrannical, and its leaders exercise absolute political, economic, and social power. A democratic government places a large measure of power in the hands of the people who are able, through the vote, to influence the major issues affecting the country. The leaders in a democracy— elected, not appointed—must be responsive to the needs and wishes of the people or they may not be returned to office at the next election.

These dimensions of leadership are found in all kinds of organization. Whether we are dealing with nations or business organizations, the democratic versus authoritarian dimension is an oversimplification. Between these two extremes are various leadership styles in daily use that combine characteristics of both.

Leadership situations involve some modification or combination of these extremes. Think of a continuum ranging from a totally autocratic situation to one of participatory democracy in which the group as a whole must agree on any decision that affects them. There is room on this continuum, then, for considerable variation in leadership style. (A parallel is often drawn between headship and authoritarianism and between leadership and democracy.)

Figure 7–1 presents the authoritarian-democratic continuum with representative leader behaviors. There is a broad latitude in leader behavior and responsibility between the two extremes.

Academic discussions of leadership include a third style of leader behavior called *laissez faire*. This is hardly a style of leadership behavior because it is characterized by the absence of leadership. The group is left to its own devices; there is no external interference.

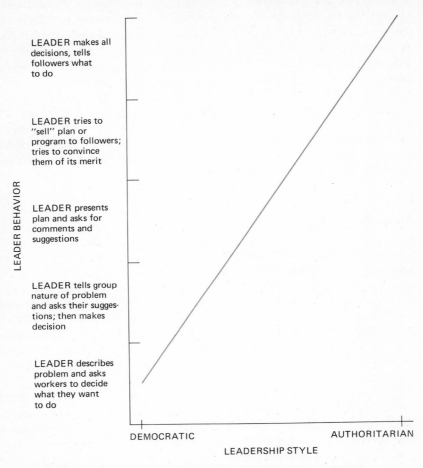

Figure 7–1. Authoritarian-democratic leadership continuum.

Usually, "leaders" make it clear that they are available to answer questions or provide information, but otherwise they remain apart from group activities. The result is often chaos, obviously of no value in any purposeful organization.

The important questions about leadership styles are as follows: Which approach is more effective? Which induces the greatest productivity and the least amount of frustration, absenteeism, turnover, or poor quality work?

The answers to these questions depend on the nature of the situation and the needs and characteristics of the followers. Some workers prefer to be told what to do and how to do it, and would find it frustrating to operate in a participatory democracy where they would be required to make frequent decisions affecting their lives. Others could not tolerate an authoritarian organization (or society) where they would have no say in the important decisions that affect them.

THE ROLE OF POWER IN LEADERSHIP

It is difficult to discuss leadership without referring to the role of power on two levels: (1) the power that leaders have over their subordinates and (2) how leaders are motivated by power.

Obviously, leaders exert varying degrees of power over their followers. Also, leaders have different kinds of power, depending on the situation, the nature of the followers, and the leader's personal characteristics (for example, how self-assured the leaders feel). Psychologists have identified five kinds of power in terms of their derivation.

1. *Reward power.* Organizational leaders possess the ability to reward their subordinates (with pay raises or promotions, for example). This gives leaders a means of tremendous control over followers and can influence employee behavior in many ways.
2. *Coercive power.* An equally strong source of power is the ability to punish subordinates by firing them, failing to give them promotions or pay raises, or keeping them in undesirable jobs.
3. *Legitimate power.* This refers to the formalization of the power structure by the rules of the organization (as in headship). The hierarchy of control in an army unit, a government agency, or a classroom legitimizes the right of the leader to control or influence followers, and the duty of the followers to accept that power.

These sources of power are derived from, and are defined by, the formal organization to which leader and subordinates belong. It is power dictated or prescribed by the organization. The next two sources of power derive from the leaders themselves. In a sense, they are earned or merited by the unique qualifications and characteristics of an individual leader as perceived by his or her followers. They may be thought of as "respect" rather than power.

4. *Referent power*. This relates to the extent to which followers identify with their leaders and the leaders' goals. It is similar to true leadership, in which followers accept the leaders' goals as their own and work with (rather than for) the leaders to achieve the goals.

5. *Expert power*. This refers to the extent to which leaders are perceived to be knowledgeable in an area that is necessary to the attainment of group goals. Followers recognize the benefits for them of their leaders' expertise and, therefore, become more willing and supportive subordinates.

The effect of these various kinds of power on variables such as productivity and job satisfaction has been the subject of little psychological research, a situation that should be remedied in the near future.

What is the role of power in motivating organizational leaders? How important is the desire to influence and control others? With high-level executives, at least, the individual need for power is great. It has been shown that effective managers demonstrate a greater need for power than do less effective managers.

The most effective managers do not seek power for personal gain. Rather, their power need is directed toward the institution for which they work and the achievement of organizational goals. As a result, they are successful in establishing and maintaining a good work climate, high morale, and team spirit among their subordinates.

Managers who are motivated by the need for personal power, on the other hand, serve themselves rather than their organization. They are capable of creating loyalty and team spirit among their subordinates, but it is a loyalty directed toward themselves and not toward the organization. They are more effective managers than those who have no motivation for power, but are not as effective as those whose power is oriented toward the organization.

The need for power does not mean that such leaders behave in an authoritarian manner. In one study, 63 per cent of the most effective managers in the company exhibited the democratic style of leadership. Among the least effective managers, only 22 per cent favored the democratic approach. All the managers studied were high in power motivation.[3]

Power plays an influential role in organizational leadership, both in leader-follower interactions and in the motivation of the leaders themselves.

[3] D. McClelland and D. Burnham, "Power is the great motivator," *Harvard Business Review*, **54**(March–April 1976), 100–110.

FUNCTIONS OF LEADERS

Let us now turn to a consideration of leadership functions, the activities and processes in which leaders engage. There are several views of the functions of leaders, determined by factors such as level of management and type of organization.

One way in which psychologists describe leadership functions is in terms of the two dimensions known as *consideration* and *initiation of structure*.[4] Considerable research has demonstrated that most management activities can be classified under one of these two headings.

The functions in the consideration dimension involve the awareness of and sensitivity to the personal feelings of subordinates. This has grown out of the human relations approach to management. In this approach, leaders must understand and accept subordinates as individuals, each of whom possesses a unique set of motivations, feelings, and needs. Leaders, if they are to be effective, must relate to each subordinate by being considerate of his or her personal characteristics. This places a great demand on the sympathy, warmth, and understanding of managers because they must, at the same time, maintain production levels and deal with the technical details of the plant's operation.

The functions in the initiation of structure dimension include the tasks traditionally associated with a leadership role—organizing, defining, and directing the work activities of subordinates. At times, this aspect of a manager's job may run counter to the demands of the consideration dimension. In order to get the job done (to initiate structure), managers must assign specific tasks to employees, direct the manner and speed at which the tasks are performed, and monitor the work to make sure it is being done properly.

These activities may call for some authoritarian behavior, and there may not always be time or opportunity for managers to consider subordinates' personal feelings about a task. A certain amount of work must be performed at a specified level of quality, in a fixed period of time, and the company's survival may depend on meeting these standards consistently. Managers are often forced to walk a thin line between the demands of the consideration and initiating structure dimensions.

How do managers balance the two often conflicting sets of demands? As we noted, because of the impact of the human relations movement on organizational life, not all managers force subordinates

[4] E. Fleishman and E. Harris, "Patterns of leadership behavior related to employee grievances and turnover," *Personnel Psychology*, **15**(1962), 43–56.

to obey orders. The manner in which growing numbers of leaders carry out their functions has changed. Successful managers must create an environment or work climate in which subordinates are able to satisfy their individual needs and attain personal goals in such a way as to contribute to the attainment of the organization's standards and goals.

Instead of issuing orders, modern managers influence or persuade subordinates by exercising appropriate managerial skills. Some techniques by which this may be accomplished are the following.[5]

1. Managers must determine realistic objectives. In all aspects of a job—production levels, safety, maintenance schedules, turn-over—managers must establish goals that are realistic in the light of the company's objectives, resources, funds, and equipment, and the workers' capabilities and level of competence. Without short-range and long-range objectives for which to strive, there is an inevitable waste of time and energy. Also, realistic goals provide the reinforcement or feedback of accomplishing an objective; this is a rewarding experience for managers and subordinates.

2. Managers must provide the necessary resources. If goals are to be reached, managers must supply the proper tools, equipment, and trained manpower to make the attainment of the objectives possible. To expect subordinates to produce at a certain level without providing the physical means to do so is stressful and frustrating for all.

3. Managers must make their expectations known. Through formal and informal communications, managers must make known to subordinates precisely what is expected of them in order to satisfy organizational goals. Subordinates must be informed about policies and procedures that affect their work, and about actual work techniques. It is unfair for managers to expect workers to proceed in the absence of clear guidelines and instructions.

4. Managers must provide an adequate reward structure. This is basic to any job, and to the needs of the employees. Rewards include salary, fringe benefits (such as company-paid insurance and retirement pension plans), good working conditions, and opportunities for promotion.

   Effective managers also provide less tangible rewards such as challenge and responsibility, praise for outstanding job performance, and intrinsically satisfying work. These rewards can satisfy individual needs and (assuming an adequate salary) bring

[5] From R. C. Miljus, op. cit., pp. 36–40.

about higher levels of motivation and production. Individuals vary greatly in their need for praise or challenge; effective managers know their subordinates well enough to be aware of their differential reward needs.

5. Managers must delegate authority and invite participation. In order to motivate and challenge subordinates, and to train them to assume greater responsibility, managers must delegate some of their functions. This can enhance subordinates' morale and ease some of the managers' burden so that they will be able to perform their job more efficiently.

   The human relations movement involves a trend toward democratic participation by all those connected with a particular work function. Studies have shown the benefits of allowing subordinates to participate in making decisions that were formerly the responsibility of the managers. For example, workers will more actively support changes in work procedures or working conditions if they have been allowed to have some say in the shaping of the new policy, rather than having the final decision announced and imposed upon them by management.

6. Managers must remove barriers to effective performance. Anyone or anything that may impede effective job performance should be removed so that the workers and the company may obtain their goals. It is the managers' responsibility to see that faulty equipment is replaced, slow delivery of materials speeded up, ineffective subordinates retrained, closed channels of communication opened, and negative attitudes overcome.

7. Managers must periodically appraise their subordinates' performance and inform them of the results. As discussed in Chapter 5, it is vital that employees know how well they are performing their jobs. Managers must evaluate each subordinate and communicate the results in an understanding and positive manner so that employees will be motivated to improve their weaknesses and will know that their strengths are appreciated.

8. Managers must show consideration for subordinates. Consideration is believed to be one of the two general leadership function dimensions. Studies have shown that considerate managers are the most effective managers.

There are additional ways of classifying the functions of leaders. For example, we could ask them what they do in the course of their daily work. One psychologist asked ninety-three executives, at a variety of levels and capacities, to describe their jobs. The resulting descriptions were analyzed and categorized in ten executive functions.[6]

1. Providing staff service in nonoperational areas. This involves providing consulting services to nonmanufacturing departments within the organization; for example, selecting new employees, gathering and dispensing information, and providing technical expertise. Executive jobs of this type include treasurers, purchasing agents, and personnel directors.

2. Direct supervision of work. Planning, organizing, and directing the work of other people characterize executives at the middle ranks of management. The higher a position in a corporation's management, the less the amount of direct supervision of the work of others.

3. Business control (including cost reduction, preparation of budgets, determination of goals, and enforcement of regulations). These activities were reported by sales executives, budget officials, and plant managers.

4. Technical concern with products and markets. This function involves considering and developing new products and empirically determining their marketing potential. Research engineering, motivation research, and sales skills are required for these activities.

5. Concern with human, community, and social affairs (including company goodwill, promotions, and the selection of managers). Executives reporting involvement with these activities were higher-level managers such as those in public relations, industrial relations, and sales departments.

6. Long-range planning. This activity is usually performed by top executives with technical, budgetary, and engineering advice from lower-level staff personnel. Long-range planning decisions (such as whether to open or close a branch office or introduce a new product) are of paramount importance to a company's future.

7. Exercise of broad power and authority. This is a general function that characterizes upper-middle and top levels of management. The higher the level of management, the more power and authority can be exerted.

8. Concern with company reputation. This manifests itself in two areas: (a) the quality of the product, and (b) the company's public image. A broad range of executive talent is devoted to this function, from middle-level supervisors who oversee pro-

[6] J. K. Hemphill, *Dimensions of Executive Positions* (Columbus, Ohio: Ohio State University Press, 1960).

duction quality standards, to vice presidents of public relations and advertising who must persuade the public that the company is a valuable member of the community. (Currently, the latter activity focuses on trying to persuade the public that the company is not polluting the environment or wasting energy.)

9. Concern with personal status. Executives who reported activities of this nature were more concerned with their own reputation than that of the company. They were engaged in behaviors designed to make them look good to superiors and to gain the friendship of important people, with the next promotion firmly in mind.

10. Preservation of company assets. This function characterizes middle- and higher-level executives concerned exclusively with the financial side of the organization's operations.

Another list of leadership functions deals with a high-level position: corporate vice president. When company presidents were asked what functions they expected their vice presidents to perform, the following activities were revealed.[7]

1. Profit performance. By far, the most important function expected of vice presidents was to develop and implement plans to increase corporate profits.

2. Developing subordinates. In order to assure the continuity of the organization, corporate vice presidents were expected to constantly seek and develop promising executive talent. In other words, vice presidents are expected to find and train their own replacements, people who can perform their job as competently as they can.

3. Enhancing the company image. This public relations function includes activities to gain and keep the esteem and respect of the employees and the community.

4. Motivating subordinates.

5. Getting along with peers.

6. Being honest and fair with others.

Several versions of specific leadership functions have been discussed. As noted, what leaders do varies among organizations and from one part of the same organization to another part. However, these specific functions can all be grouped in the two dimensions of *consideration* and *initiation of structure*. The functions deal with people or with the goals and tasks of the organization. Ideally, effective

[7] C. Reeser, "Executive performance appraisal: The view from the top," *Personnel Journal*, **54**(1975), 42–46, 66, 68.

managers are able to integrate these overall dimensions, and their ability to do so may be the most important leadership function of all.

CHARACTERISTICS OF LEADERS

We turn now to an investigation of the traits or characteristics of successful leaders, traits not possessed to the same degree by unsuccessful leaders. The trait approach to the study of leadership has proven generally unproductive, since leadership characteristics vary greatly from one situation to another. However, within one situation, it does seem possible to identify characteristics that distinguish effective from ineffective leaders. This information is vital to the continuing success of any organization. Effective leadership is required, and in order to be able to predict candidates for executive positions who are most likely to succeed, we must know the traits and abilities of executives who are already successful.

A classic study of successful executives lists the following characteristics.[8]

1. A high drive for achievement. Successful executives are hard working and possess a strong need to accomplish and achieve. The executive's greatest reward may be the sense of achievement rather than the actual result. For example, accomplishing a difficult task may be more satisfying than the promotion given for it.

2. A strong mobility drive. Successful executives need to be constantly moving upward, a drive satisfied by demonstrating competence in their work. They always need new and greater responsibilities and challenges. However, one type of successful executive demonstrates a strong mobility drive but satisfies it in a different way. He or she finds fulfillment in the prestige or status brought about by successful performance of a job and also derives satisfaction from meeting challenges and demonstrating competence. But these are means to the end of enhanced social reputation. Both types work well and hard at their jobs, but differ in terms of ultimate rewards or goals.

3. A positive attitude toward superiors. Successful executives look upon the authority figures not as forces to inhibit their progress, but rather to help in satisfying their drives. They

[8] W. Henry, "The business executive: The psychodynamics of a social role," *American Journal of Sociology*, **54**(1949), 286–291.

view superiors as people who, because of their more extensive background and experience, can guide and direct the executives' growth. Executives who have negative or hostile attitudes toward authority in general are usually unable to develop smooth working relationships with superiors. Since they resent those in authority, they are less able and willing to profit from persons with greater experience.

4. A strong ability to organize. Executives are able to take an unstructured or ambiguous situation and organize it to provide meaning and structure. They can perceive or predict, on the basis of limited information, the direction in which that information leads. They are future-oriented and find challenge in plotting the prospective course of events.

5. The ability to make decisions. Successful executives are decisive. Their jobs present problems that demand resolution, usually within a short period of time. The executives must consider alternative courses of action, select the correct one, and abide by their decision. The loss of this quality of decisiveness is the worst misfortune that can befall an executive. Superiors and subordinates quickly lose confidence in the person who vacillates and reaches a decision only with difficulty.

6. A positive self-structure. Effective executives have a strong sense of self-identity. They know clearly who they are, what their abilities are, where they are going, and how to get there. They also have confidence in their ability; they believe in themselves. This allows them to resist external influences. For example, they can continue to support their own decisions when others disagree with them.

   Of course, this strong self-structure can have negative consequences. If carried to extremes, leaders can become inflexible and unable to accept suggestions from others. If they are too firmly convinced of their own abilities, they could not admit to the possibility of someone else having a better idea or solution. In general, however, successful executives maintain sufficient flexibility and openness along with their self-confidence.

7. A high level of activity and aggressive striving. In the jargon of the business world, the executive is a "go-getter," a "dynamo," a striving, driving individual. This aggressiveness is not hostile, but rather is well-channeled, positive, and oriented toward achievement. The activity is not necessarily physical; it usually refers to a mental and emotional alertness. It is such a persistent part of the total personality that many executives

find it difficult to relax, particularly on vacation away from the job. Their relaxation typically involves as much activity as does their work. They seem to work hard even at having fun.

8. A strong apprehension and fear of failure. Behind the active striving, high drive for achievement, decisiveness, and self-confidence, lurks a strong feeling of apprehension that they will not succeed. This fear of failing seems to characterize not only work experiences but also all aspects of life. No matter how much success executives experience on the job, their apprehension goads them to undertake additional responsibilities. They must always have a goal. In a sense, they are pulled by the desire to achieve and excel while being pushed by their apprehension and fear of failure.

9. A strong orientation toward reality. Executives are highly pragmatic and oriented toward the immediate. They are concerned primarily with what is occurring at the moment. This has both advantages and disadvantages. On the positive side, executives are free to concentrate fully on the job, directing all their aggressive energy toward that task. Too great a concentration, however, may cause them to lose sight of future possibilities. They may become so engrossed in the details of the immediate situation that they are less able to plan for long-range growth.

10. A strong sense of identification with superiors and an aloofness with subordinates. Successful executives are characterized by an attachment to and identification with their superiors, who represent the higher levels of responsibility that the executives are striving for. At the same time, their relationship with their subordinates is detached and impersonal. Executives are not cold, cruel, or insensitive to subordinates, however. In general, they are sympathetic to them, particularly to those who exhibit characteristics similar to those of their superiors.

11. No emotional dependence upon parents. Executives are no longer tied to their parents, either emotionally or geographically. They are free of guilt and resentment toward parents and are able to go their own way and make their own decisions.

12. Loyalty to organizational goals. Although very much aware of self, executives depend on the organization to provide the framework, guidelines, and operating tools with which they may satisfy their needs and drives. If executives are to use the organization successfully as a vehicle for fulfillment of these needs, they must be capable of submerging, to some degree,

their total dependence upon themselves and come to depend, in part, on the organization.

Missing from this list of executive characteristics is power, which, as noted, has been shown to be an important drive of successful executives. The same study that identified the power motive also questioned the need for achievement as a characteristic of managers.[9] Whereas achievement motivation seems to typify entrepreneurs (those who independently run their own businesses), it is less characteristic of those who are managers within the structure of an organization. Indeed, motivation of this nature may run counter to some aspects of organizational life.

For example, persons who have a high need for achievement want to accomplish things by themselves, and focus on personal rather than organizational improvement. In addition, they need constant and specific feedback about their progress. Neither of these needs is well satisfied in the role of manager within an organization. Managers cannot do everything for themselves; they must delegate tasks to others. They must be concerned with organizational improvement at least as much as with self-improvement. Also, since managers are overseeing the work of others, feedback on how well their subordinates are performing may not be as immediate or frequent as if the managers were performing the tasks themselves.

Other psychologists who have studied leadership believe that the need for achievement should be included among the characteristics of successful managers. One psychologist has noted that successful managers are characterized by their needs for achievement, power, autonomy, and money, and that they tend to be intelligent, forceful, dominant, and assertive.[10]

Another psychologist described five primary traits of effective managers: intelligence, initiative, supervisory ability, self-assurance, and perceived occupational level (where they thought they belonged on the socioeconomic scale).[11]

There are similarities among these views of leader characteristics but there are also sufficient differences to demonstrate that psychologists do not know with certainty how successful managers differ from unsuccessful managers. Part of the problem is attributable to differences among organizations. Leadership in a research department of Ph.D. chemists requires a different set of characteristics than does leadership in an infantry battalion.

[9] D. McClelland and D. Burnham, op. cit.
[10] M. Dunnette, "The motives of industrial managers," *Organizational Behavior and Human Performance*, **2**(1967), 176–182.
[11] E. E. Ghiselli, "Traits differentiating management personnel," *Personnel Psychology*, **12**(1959), 535–544.

Another part of the problem is the various levels of leadership that exist in most organizations. The characteristics of a foreman who is promoted from the ranks need not be the same as those of a business school graduate hired as an assistant vice president of finance. This reinforces the importance of investigating the situation in which leadership takes place in order to understand the nature of the leadership itself.

PRESSURES AND PROBLEMS OF LEADERSHIP

Just as leader characteristics vary with the level of leadership, so do the pressures and problems. We deal with two levels of organizational leadership: the first-line supervisor and the executive. Each faces unique stresses and conflicts.

First-Line Supervisors

In most organizations, a distinction is made between first-line supervisors (usually called foremen) and higher-level managers (usually called executives). In terms of responsibilities, obligations, and background, there are many differences between these two levels. In some ways, supervisors have more difficult and demanding jobs, yet, paradoxically, they often receive less formal training in how to manage others.

In some cases, foremen have college degrees. Many company training programs place new graduates in first-line supervisory positions in one or more departments for several months to several years. The purpose is to familiarize them with various aspects of production while providing leadership experience. For college graduates, the job of supervisor is a stepping-stone to higher levels of executive responsibility.

Most foremen, however, are promoted from the ranks. The level of foreman may be their ultimate goal. At a time when business and industry stress a college education, the first-line supervisory position is about as high in management as less well-educated persons may be allowed to rise—an unfortunate and unwise utilization of talent. Many people who lack college degrees nevertheless possess the intelligence and ability to be trained for higher levels of responsibility.

Foremen promoted from the ranks are often placed in a difficult position because of conflicting demands and loyalties. Before their promotion, they were accepted as co-workers by those who shared not only the job but attitudes and values as well. They may have had many friends among their co-workers—people with whom they socialized off the job. They had an identity as a member of a particular group, a sense of belonging that provided a measure of emotional security.

What happens when they suddenly become foremen? They can no longer enjoy the same relationship with former co-workers and friends—they are no longer one of them. Even if they should try to remain "one of the gang," the others will no longer react to them in the same way—they are now "the boss." The emotional security from group affiliation and identification is lost.

New foremen become part of a new group, management, working with people whose levels of education, background, values, and lifestyles are usually vastly different. New foremen can try to emulate them, and many succeed, but it is difficult; they may have to learn new modes of dress, behavior, or conversation. They may feel the need to move to a better neighborhood, buy a bigger car, and attend symphony concerts.

New first-line supervisors are thus in an unenviable position. They may not be accepted by either world, workers or management. Some workers have been known to reject promotions to this level.

Foremen must also confront the demands of the new job. Regardless of the competence and sophistication of a company's executives, the efficiency of the plant's organization, or the quality of the management's decisions, the success or failure of any program frequently rests on the shoulders of the foremen.

Like sergeants in the army, foremen are responsible for getting things done—for implementing the department head's decision on monthly production quotas, for example. Foremen are the point of contact between management and workers, trying delicately to maintain their own balance between the often conflicting needs of both sides.

Not only do foremen present management's needs and decisions to the workers but they must also represent the workers to management if they expect to establish or retain the loyalty and cooperation of the workers. They must serve not only as a buffer between management and workers but also as a channel of communication.

What specific tasks are foremen expected to perform? They are responsible for introducing new employees to their jobs and teaching them company policies, procedures, and regulations. They may have to train or monitor the training of new workers and the retraining of current workers.

Foremen must ensure that safety procedures are being followed properly and instruct workers on new safety methods and devices,

253

be alert for unsafe practices, and explain to superiors the reasons for any accidents that may occur.

As representatives of the workers to higher management, foremen must handle any grievance on the part of their subordinates. There are many causes for complaint on a job, some legitimate and some not. In any case, how diplomatically and effectively foremen handle complaints can mean the difference between satisfied workers and a wildcat strike or work slowdown. If a grievance is not resolved in a manner that is satisfactory to the workers, they will take it to the union and it then becomes more serious in terms of morale and production.

Foremen also act as purveyors of rewards and punishments. In order for good work to continue, foremen must provide incentives in the form of verbal praise to the workers, good performance evaluation reports, and salary increases. To keep their best workers, they must convince their superiors to raise their pay. They must also act as disciplinarians in cases of sloppy work, tardiness, absenteeism, or drinking on the job. In unionized plants, they must exercise a somewhat gentle and totally impartial discipline, since the union shop steward is constantly watchful for the welfare of union members.

The more mundane and routine activities include scheduling work, arranging for equipment maintenance, answering memos from superiors, and attending meetings.

When workers become foremen, they assume a heavy responsibility that they are expected to carry out without the status and authority of higher levels of management.

Executives

The problems faced by executives change as a function of their level in the corporate hierarchy. A department or section head faces different strains and stresses than the head of the company. We can distinguish two levels of executive: middle level and top level.

Middle-level managers, despite salaries in excess of $25,000 and a host of fringe benefits, often face a great deal of discontent in their lives. Discontent always seems to have been evident at this level because of the nature of middle-management jobs. Recently, however, the idea of participatory democracy has increased this dissatisfaction.

One of the most frequent complaints voiced by middle managers is their lack of influence in the formulation of company policy, policy that they are expected to implement without question. First-line supervisors also have no say in policy making, but they seem not to expect it, perhaps because of their generally lower educational levels and aspirations.

Middle managers also complain about not having sufficient authority or resources to carry out company policy. They must constantly fight for recognition from their superiors and compete for support for their ideas and projects. As a result, there is often a great deal of frustration and tension among middle managers as they vie for position in their race for the few available slots in the hierarchy above them.

Another long-standing source of discontent is the almost universal feeling of obsolescence that characterizes middle managers when they reach their late thirties and early forties. Most employees of that age have reached their limit, the plateau from which they will rise no further in the corporate hierarchy. The realization that there will be no more promotions is part of the general midlife crisis that affects all of us; it is a time when each person takes stock of his or her life. This painful period of self-examination is especially difficult for middle-level managers. They feel threatened by younger subordinates, new managerial and cultural values, and new organizational goals (such as worker involvement in decision making). As a result, their productivity, creativity, drive, and aggressiveness often wither and die, and they retire on the job, making no further contribution to the organization.

The latest source of discontent for middle managers is the trend toward democratization of organizations. Although middle managers remain without influence in decisions affecting their own jobs, they see that assembly line workers, for example, can participate in such decisions and design their own jobs, new rights that are denied the middle managers. Sometimes, participatory democracy results in drastic changes in the ways that managers can direct their subordinates. When this occurs, middle managers must share leadership with subordinates, which results in what managers believe is a loss of their authority and status.

Democratization in some organizations has also resulted in the discarding of traditional management perquisites such as reserved parking spaces, separate dining rooms, and private offices. The more democratic an organization becomes, the fewer visible signs of class distinction are allowed. Some companies have eliminated private offices for all but top management, insisting that middle-level managers work side-by-side with their subordinates. When managers must compete with their subordinates for parking spaces, eat in the employee cafeteria instead of the executive dining room, and give up their carpeted offices for a desk on the factory floor, it is understandable that they feel that their position of superiority is threatened.

As a result of the growing discontent among middle managers, their loyalty to the organization, which was once very high, is declining. Surveys show that one out of every three middle managers expressed interest in joining a union, and growing numbers of them are leaving their jobs to seek alternate careers. (In Chapter 8 we see that those who are leaving may be those who are the better managers.)

A frequent problem facing managers (particularly high-level managers) is the intense commitment of energy and time to the organization. It is not uncommon for executives to work fifty to sixty hours a week. Most of this time is spent in the office, but many executives bring work home with them; home becomes not a haven from work but just another place to work. Many evenings are occupied with work at home or at the office, and executives often visit the plant on weekends. Companies encourage and reward this hectic involvement. One company president has said, "The willingness of a [person] 'to go the extra mile' is a quality that I very strongly consider in my appraisal of a senior manager." [12]

In addition, companies expect their executives to involve themselves actively in the community—in activities such as civic organizations and charity drives. Despite the long working hours, it is not the time that executives devote to the company that is the real problem; it is the sheer physical exhaustion of such a schedule and the limited attention they can devote to their families.

Children who grow up seeing too little of a parent are a common consequence of life in the executive suite. Also, executives often feel guilty over this neglect. Their energy and commitment are directed almost exclusively to the job, and relegating the family to a secondary status causes them great concern. Some organizations are dealing with this problem by sending executives and their spouses to counseling seminars.

The potential rewards for a management position—power, money, status, challenge, and fulfillment—are great, but so are the stresses. There is a price to be paid for success, but so is there for failure.

SUMMARY

Because of the importance of leadership in organizational life, it has long been the subject of extensive study by psychologists. How psy-

---

[12] C. Reeser, op. cit., p. 46.

chologists view leadership, and how leadership functions are carried out are based on assumptions about human nature that have changed over the last several decades.

An early view of leadership was based on **scientific management,** which was concerned solely with production. Workers were believed to be mindless adjuncts to their machines. This idea was replaced in the 1920s and 1930s by the **human relations** approach, concerned with satisfying workers' personal needs and enhancing their growth, as well as with maintaining production.

McGregor's **Theory X** and **Theory Y** give formal expression to these two extreme views of leadership. Theory X holds that people dislike work and need strong, directive, and punitive leadership. Theory Y takes a more flattering view of human nature. It holds that people are creative, industrious, and personally responsible, and function best under leaders who allow them to participate in decisions that affect their work.

There have been several approaches to the study of leadership. The **trait** approach sought traits and characteristics that distinguish leaders from followers. When it became apparent that universal leadership traits did not exist, attention turned to the **situational** approach. This focused on the nature of followers and their interactions with leaders. The **behavioral** approach investigated what leaders do rather than what they are like.

Another way of studying leadership is to investigate leadership styles such as **headship versus leadership** and **authoritarian versus democratic** leadership. They differ essentially in the degree of participation they allow subordinates to have in the leadership process.

Leaders display five kinds of **power.** These differ in terms of their base of derivation: (1) reward power, (2) coercive power, (3) legitimate power, (4) referent power, and (5) expert power. Power has been identified as an important need of leaders.

Much research has been undertaken to identify the functions of leaders, all of which can be subsumed under two general categories: **consideration** and **initiation of structure.** Consideration functions are concerned with the personal feelings of subordinates; initiation of structure functions are concerned with how the work of the organization can best be accomplished. Several lists of specific duties are presented—everyday activities by which leaders carry out their consideration and initiation of structure functions.

Several characteristics of leaders are discussed: achievement drive, mobility drive, positive attitude toward superiors, strong ability to organize, decision-making ability, positive self-structure, high level of activity and aggressive striving, strong apprehension and fear of failure, strong orientation toward reality, strong identification with superiors and aloofness toward subordinates, no emotional dependence on parents, and loyalty to the goals of the organization.

Studies have noted additional leader characteristics such as power, intelligence, initiative, supervisory ability, self-assurance, and perceived occupational level. Leader characteristics vary with the kind of organization and the level of leadership attained.

Pressures and problems of leaders also differ as a function of level. **First-line supervisors,** usually promoted from the ranks, have different problems than **middle-level managers** who may find themselves losing authority and status as a consequence of the democratization of organizational life. **High-level executives** face the problem of extremely long working hours, which can lead to guilt about their neglect of their families.

SUGGESTED READINGS

Argyris, C. *Increasing Leadership Effectiveness.* New York: John Wiley & Sons, 1976.

Basil, D. C. *Leadership Skills for Executive Action.* New York: American Management Association, 1971.

Bennis, W. *The Unconscious Conspiracy: Why Leaders Can't Lead.* New York: American Management Association, 1976.

Borgatta, E., and Bohrnstedt, G. Up. *Psychology Today,* 1971, **4**(8), 57–58, 80–81.

Bursk, E. C., and Blodgett, T. B., Eds. *Developing Executive Leaders.* Cambridge, Mass.: Harvard University Press, 1971.

Campbell, J. P., Dunnette, M., Lawler, E. E., and Weick, K. *Managerial Behavior, Performance, and Effectiveness.* New York: McGraw-Hill, 1970.

Carlisle, H. M. *Situational Management: A Contingency Approach to Leadership.* New York: American Management Association, 1973.

Drucker, P. *Management: Tasks, Responsibilities, Practices.* New York: Harper & Row, 1974.

Fiedler, F. E., and Chemers, M. M. *Leadership and Effective Management.* Glenview, Ill.: Scott, Foresman, 1974.

Goble, F. *Excellence in Leadership.* New York: American Management Association, 1972.

Greiner, L. What managers think of participative leadership. *Harvard Business Review,* 1973, **51**(March–April), 111–117.

Hill, W. Leadership style: Rigid or flexible? *Organizational Behavior and Human Performance,* 1973, **9**(1), 35–47.

Ivancevich, J. J., and Donnelly, J. Leader influence and performance. *Personnel Psychology,* 1970, **23,** 539–549.

Joyce, J. The search for leaders. *Personnel Journal,* 1970, **49,** 308–311.

McClelland, D. C. *Power: The Inner Experience.* New York: Halsted Press, 1975.

McClelland, D. C., and Burnham, D. Power is the great motivator. *Harvard Business Review,* 1976, **54**(March–April), 100–110.

Maccoby, M. *The Gamesman: The New Corporate Leaders.* New York: Simon & Schuster, 1976.

Masterson, T., and Mara, T. Leadership methods that motivate. *Supervisory Management,* 1970, **15**(January), 6–9.

Mintzberg, H. *The Nature of Managerial Work.* New York: Harper & Row, 1973.

Mintzberg, H. The manager's job: Folklore and fact. *Harvard Business Review,* 1975, **53**(July–August), 49–61.

Reeser, C. Executive performance appraisal: The view from the top. *Personnel Journal,* 1975, **54,** 42–46, 66, 68.

Stogdill, R. M. *Handbook of Leadership: A Survey of Theory and Research.* New York: The Free Press, 1974.

Tannenbaum, R., and Schmidt, W. How to choose a leadership pattern. *Harvard Business Review,* 1973, **51**(May–June), 162–180.

Vroom, V. H. Leadership. In M. Dunnette, Ed., *Handbook of Industrial and Organizational Psychology.* Chicago: Rand McNally, 1976. Pp. 1527–1551.

Vroom, V. H., and Yetton, P. W. *Leadership and Decision–Making.* Pittsburgh: University of Pittsburgh Press, 1973.

Walker, E. J. 'Til business do us part? *Harvard Business Review,* 1976, **54**(January–February), 94–101. (marital problems of executives)

Walker, J., Luthans, F., and Hodgetts, R. Who really are the promotables? *Personnel Journal,* 1970, **49,** 123–127.

8

Motivation and the Quality of Working Life

INTRODUCTION

One of the most pressing problems facing organizations today is how to motivate employees to work more productively. All around us we see examples of shoddy and imperfect work in consumer products such as new cars with faulty parts installed, or in careless mistakes made in government offices. It is a troublesome list that grows with each passing year. Department stores, manufacturers, the postal service all echo the same complaint: too many employees don't seem to care about doing a good job.

Tremendous strides have been made in recruiting, selecting, placing, and training workers. But none of these functions can improve the quality of the work being done if workers are not sufficiently motivated to do the best job possible.

Many managers believe that the answer is simple: If the workers need more motivation, pay them more. This is an old popular notion, but it no longer works.

In today's society, money no longer serves as the primary motivating force. In times of severe economic depression, such as the 1930s, when jobs were extremely difficult to find, the question of survival—of being able to provide enough food for one's family—was paramount, and money was indeed the prime mover. But in times of prosperity, such as in this country since World War II, jobs are generally plentiful and salaries high. People are not forced to remain at unsatisfying jobs, nor are they compelled to work hard at jobs they don't like. They can quit and go elsewhere. Consequently, they don't have to worry about being fired for not doing the best job possible; they can always get other jobs.

Other social forces have increased the necessity for providing adequate motivation for employees. Workers nowadays are better educated. This increases the pool of skilled and trained (or trainable) workers available to industry, but it also means they need more meaningful and challenging work. Routine, repetitive, and unstimulating jobs do not provide adequate satisfaction for workers with higher education. Thus, the number of potentially dissatisfied and frustrated workers increases every year.

Also, there have been striking changes in public attitudes toward authority since the mid-1960s. High school and college students, welfare recipients, factory workers, even soldiers, have demonstrated a growing disinclination to follow orders unquestioningly. More Americans are challenging the commands of their superiors. We know that the effective style of leader behavior has undergone a drastic change, partly as a result of the trend toward participatory democracy as people demand a say in matters that affect them. This new motivating force has produced noticeable changes in colleges, in the military, and in the world of work.

Another social change has been the decline of the Protestant Ethic, the notion that hard work, dedicated thrift, and conscientious competitive struggles are the means by which to pursue the American dream. Economic goals such as a bigger car, another television set, or color-coordinated kitchen appliances no longer motivate growing numbers of Americans who seek instead more meaning and fulfillment in their lives.

Thus, for many reasons, employees are demanding challenging jobs—work that satisfies deeper motivations than can be satisfied by money alone. Many people no longer put up with dull and boring work, no matter how high the salary. Employing organizations must provide more meaningful jobs; there is no other way to achieve productive efficiency for the organization and job satisfaction for the employees. The alternative is high turnover and absenteeism, shoddy products, and even deliberate sabotage on the job. Indeed, the survival of many companies directly depends on the motivation of their employees. No matter how well selected and trained are the workers, no matter how modern and efficient is their equipment, if workers are inadequately motivated they will not produce in sufficient quantity or quality.

The study of motivation and the quality of working life should be of great personal interest. As a consumer you are often the victim of dissatisfied workers who produce faulty products or improperly process your requests. Even more important is the fact that the research of industrial and organizational psychologists on motivation and job satisfaction can make your future work satisfying and fulfilling instead of dull and disappointing. Most of you will spend at least one third of your waking hours each week at work for forty or forty-five years of your life. That is a long time to be frustrated and unhappy, especially since unhappiness at work carries over into other aspects of life, can disrupt relationships with family and friends, and can influence physical and mental health. Also, many of you will become managers and executives and be responsible for providing the conditions of proper motivation and satisfaction for your employees.

The concepts of motivation and job satisfaction are interrelated—satisfaction can result from the fulfillment of motivations, and new sources of satisfaction can generate other motivations. From an academic and theoretical standpoint we can separate the two and discuss them individually.

MOTIVATION

Why do people behave as they do? How can we account for the workers who are always on time, exceed production quotas, and are polite to the boss, when other workers at the same plant, performing the same job under the same conditions for the same pay, behave in the opposite way?

We may say that the motivation of some workers to do a good day's job is higher than that of others, but what does this really tell us? Unfortunately, very little. It is easy to say that we must increase the motivation of employees, but unless we know precisely what factors constitute motivation in this specific instance, we will be unable to change anything.

Human motivation is very complex. We seldom behave or respond to a particular situation because of a single motive. We are driven by a variety of needs and desires, some complementary and others conflicting.

The question why people behave as they do has fascinated and frustrated seekers of knowledge for centuries, and psychologists are no exception. But although we do not fully understand our motivational structure, we do know, from psychological research, quite a bit about the forces that drive us.

This is not the place for a lengthy discussion of the psychology of motivation. We are concerned with only one aspect: human behavior at work. Most people must work in order to earn enough money to support themselves and their families, but it can no longer be assumed that this is the sole, or even the primary, reason for working. If it were, why would so many successful businessmen and entertainers, for example, continue to work at the same pace when they have more money than they could possibly spend and freely admit that they don't need any more? This is not to suggest that money has no role in motivating a person to want to work, but it has been shown that salary is of only minor importance as a motivator, once a person's income level is considered sufficient. The evidence is clear that many people work to satisfy a host of inner needs. Of course, people have different needs; the work that satisfies the needs of one may frustrate the needs of another.

It is the job of industrial and organizational psychologists to determine what these various motivations are and how jobs and working conditions can be designed to satisfy them.

Several theories of motivation have been advanced, and we consider three of them. Since they are theories, they are by definition still open to question, and cannot yet be accepted as matters of fact. Each theory has produced a body of empirical support, but each also has opponents who can offer opposing data. These motivational theories are provocative, seemingly plausible, and the research they have generated has led to new ways of thinking about why people behave as they do on their jobs.

The Need-Achievement Theory

In discussing characteristics of successful executives (Chapter 7), the need for achievement was included. This desire to accomplish something, to do a good job, to be the best, typifies many people in our society, not only successful business executives. Those who possess this need derive great satisfaction from their achievements and are motivated to excel in everything they undertake.

Since the early 1950s this motivational factor has been studied intensively by the Harvard psychologist David McClelland.[1] He and his colleagues measured the achievement need *(n Ach)* by asking people to write stories about a series of ambiguous pictures. The theory behind this projective technique is that people will project their innermost thoughts, feelings, and needs onto an ambiguous stimulus in order to give it meaning and structure. Accordingly, those with a high need to achieve will make up stories that focus on achieving or accomplishing a goal. For example, one picture shows a man at a worktable and on the table is a photograph of his family. Persons with a low *n Ach* may write a story in which the man is daydreaming about his family or reminiscing about a pleasant family experi-

[1] D. McClelland et al., *The Achievement Motive* (New York: Appleton-Century-Crofts, 1953).

ence. Such a story contains no suggestion of achievement or accomplishment.

Persons with a high need for achievement, however, would write a different kind of story. They may describe a problem on which the man is working. For example, one story told how the man solved a problem and gave the steps in his decision-making process. The focus was on work and how best to accomplish it; the family photograph was mentioned only in passing.

Business managers in the United States and other countries have been tested in this way, and all consistently show a high *n Ach*. In Poland, a Communist country, the level of concern for achievement was almost as high as in capitalist countries such as the United States. Evidence also shows that the economic growth of private companies and of whole societies is related to the level of the need for achievement among managers in the private companies and members of the societies.

Successful business managers generally score higher in need for achievement than do those who are less successful. Once high *n Ach* persons have been identified, it is possible to determine what they want and need in their work to satisfy this high achievement motivation.

The organization for which high *n Ach* persons work is not required to generate the motivation; these persons already possess the motivation. What the company must do is provide working conditions that will allow them to achieve. If they cannot satisfy their high drive for achievement, they will become frustrated and probably look for another job. If they can satisfy this drive, however, they will become happy and productive members of the organization.

McClelland's research identified three characteristics of high need achievement persons.

1. They favor a working situation in which they are able to assume personal responsibility for solving problems. If they were not solely responsible for finding the solutions to problems, they would not have any sense of achievement. They are not happy when the solution depends on chance or on external factors beyond their control. It must depend on their own efforts and ability. This is a desirable characteristic for an executive, as long as the working situation affords the opportunity for personal responsibility. The organization must provide these persons with challenging responsibility and a degree of personal autonomy.

2. They have a tendency to take calculated risks and to set moderate achievement goals. By assuming tasks of moderate diffi-

culty, high need achievement persons are able to satisfy their achievement needs. If the tasks or goals were too easy, there would be little sense of accomplishment. If they were too difficult, they might not succeed and would again have no sense of accomplishment. They must arrange the job and working conditions so as to constantly face new problems or goals of moderate difficulty.

3. High need achievement persons must have definite and continuing feedback about their progress. If they did not receive recognition for their work, they would not have a clear idea of how well they were doing. Fortunately, companies provide continuing feedback in periodic sales, cost, and production figures. High need achievement persons feel a greater sense of accomplishment if they have personal feedback from superiors in the form of congratulatory memos, pay raises, promotions, or a pat on the back.

There are unresolved questions about the need–achievement theory, and not all research supports the findings discussed. However, it seems to be a useful theory of behavior and a plausible explanation for the motivation of some people at work.

The Needs-Hierarchy Theory

The late Abraham Maslow, prominent psychologist and past president of the American Psychological Association, developed a theory of motivation in which human needs or wants are arranged in a hierarchy of importance.[2] According to Maslow, people constantly desire better circumstances; they always want what they do not yet have. Consequently, needs that have been satisfied are no longer capable of motivating behavior and a new need rises to prominence. Lower-level needs must be satisfied before attention can be paid to higher-level needs. The five categories of needs (from lowest to highest) are:

1. Physiological needs. The basic human needs including food, oxygen, water, sleep, and the sex and activity drives.
2. Safety needs. Security, stability, order, and physical safety in one's environment.
3. Belonging and love needs. Social needs involving interactions with other people such as affection, affiliation, and identification.

A. Maslow, *Motivation and Personality*, 2nd ed. (New York: Harper & Row, 1970).

4. Esteem needs. Self-respect, self-esteem, prestige, and success.
5. Self-actualization needs. The highest need level, self-fulfillment, involves achieving one's potential, realizing one's full capabilities.

The needs must be satisfied in the order presented. Persons who are hungry or fear for their safety are too busy satisfying these needs to be concerned about higher needs such as self-esteem or self-fulfillment. In times of great economic hardship, most people are so intent on survival that they cannot be concerned with esteem or self-actualization needs. But when the society or the individual has reached a sufficient level of financial security, people must move on to satisfy the next level of needs.

The social or love needs can be important motivating forces on the job—workers can find a sense of togetherness and a feeling of belonging through relations with co-workers. The human relations emphasis in organizations recognizes the sense of social security that can be provided by the work environment.

Some research studies of executive motivation provide support for Maslow's theory. For example, when a group of executives were asked why they quit their jobs to take others, half of them offered reasons that related to the need for self-actualization. Of these, 30 per cent said they quit to find greater responsibilities, and 22 per cent said greater opportunity for growth was the reason. Additional reasons included a desire for increased income (18 per cent) and disagreements with management policies (16 per cent). Thus, self-actualizing needs were behind the job changes of 52 per cent of these executives.

Other studies fail to support Maslow's hierarchy of needs concept; in general, the bulk of the evidence is against it. However, it must be recognized that the complexity of the theory makes it difficult to test adequately. Also, the theory has been immensely popular among managers and executives, who have accepted a need for self-actualization as a motivating force to be reckoned with on the job, and has influenced McGregor's Theory X/Theory Y formulation.

Most working people today are able to satisfy physiological and safety needs. Through interpersonal relationships on the job, we may also be able to satisfy belonging and love needs. The esteem needs—prestige, success, self-respect—can be satisfied in our personal life by buying a bigger house, and on the job by status indicators such as the manager's plush carpeting, a private secretary, or a reserved parking space.

That leaves only the need for self-actualization to be fulfilled. This motivation can be satisfied by providing employees with opportunities for growth and responsibility—the chance to exercise their capabilities to the utmost. A routine, boring, nonchallenging job will not satisfy this high-level need, no matter how high the salary.

The Motivator-Hygiene Theory

The motivator-hygiene theory, combining motivation and job satisfaction, was proposed by Frederick Herzberg in 1959.[8] Although controversial, the theory is a simple one and has stimulated vast amounts of research yielding important implications for the structure of many jobs. It has also had ramifications on actual job design—the way in which various jobs are performed.

Herzberg's theory is similar, in part, to Maslow's needs-hierarchy formulation. The premise of the motivator-hygiene theory is that in contemporary society, lower-level needs have generally been satisfied. Where they have not, job dissatisfaction is the result. However, the reverse is not true: the fulfillment of basic needs does not produce job satisfaction. Only higher-order needs such as self-actualization are capable of producing satisfaction. But, failure to find self-actualization in a job does not necessarily lead to dissatisfaction.

Thus, there are two sets of needs: those that produce job satisfaction and those that produce job dissatisfaction. They are separate; the presence or absence of one set of needs does not produce the opposite condition.

Herzberg calls the factors that produce job satisfaction *motivator needs*—they motivate the worker to the highest possible level of performance. These motivators are an integral part of the work itself and include the nature of the work and the person's sense of achievement, level of responsibility, and personal development and advancement. Notice the similarity between these factors and Maslow's self-actualization needs. The motivator needs can be satisfied only by stimulating, challenging, and absorbing work.

The factors that produce job dissatisfaction are the *hygiene* (or maintenance) *needs*. They have little power to produce satisfaction. They have nothing to do with the nature of the work itself, but rather involve features of the work environment such as company policy and administrative practices, type of supervision, interpersonal relations, company benefits, and working conditions.

The hygiene needs are roughly analogous to Maslow's lower-order needs (physiological, safety, and love needs). Just as Maslow's needs-hierarchy theory postulates that lower-order needs must be satisfied

[8] See F. Herzberg, *Work and the Nature of Man* (Cleveland: World, 1966).

before one is affected by higher-order needs, so in Herzberg's theory hygiene needs must be satisfied before attention is paid to motivator needs. It is important to remember, however, that satisfaction of hygiene needs will not produce job satisfaction, merely an absence of dissatisfaction.

Job Enlargement

Since so much of a person's satisfaction and motivation derive from the nature of the work, it follows that a job could be redesigned in order to maximize the motivator factors. This effort, known as *job enlargement* or job enrichment, has been a major impact of Herzberg's theory.

Herzberg suggests the following ways of enlarging a job.

1. Remove some of the controls over employees and increase their personal accountability or responsibility for their own work.
2. Provide employees with complete or natural units of work where possible. For example, instead of having them make one component of a unit, let them produce the whole unit.
3. Give employees additional authority and freedom in their work.
4. Provide reports on production on a regular basis directly to the workers instead of to their supervisors.
5. Encourage workers to take on new and more difficult tasks.
6. Assign highly specialized tasks so that workers can become expert in a particular task or operation.

All of these proposals have the goal of increasing personal growth and advancement, enhancing the sense of achievement and responsibility, and providing recognition; in other words, they all facilitate the satisfaction of the motivator needs.

Job enlargement is being implemented successfully by growing numbers of companies such as IBM, Maytag, Sears, Colonial Life Insurance, American Telephone and Telegraph, Western Electric, Chrysler, Polaroid, and Procter and Gamble. Firms that have adopted job enlargement techniques report advantages such as reduced costs of operation, increased job satisfaction, greater quantity and quality of work, and reduced monotony. The workers seem happier and more productive and corporate profits are rising.

A large subsidiary of the Bell System reported that its job enlargement program reduced turnover from 64 per cent to 38 per cent. Another company reported a 27 per cent drop in turnover as well as better productivity—a savings of $500,000 in just 18 months. In still another company, errors were reduced by 78 per cent through a job enlargement program.

As an example of how a dull job can be successfully enlarged, consider the routine task of answering correspondence in a large corporation. A group of female employees had the task of answering queries from stockholders. Under the old system, a worker would not write the reply herself, but would construct it from a supply of form paragraphs written to handle all situations. The worker would combine various paragraphs that seemed to answer the shareholder's question, add a proper salutation and closing, and submit it to the supervisor who signed it and verified its correctness.

It was an orderly system designed to ensure that no incorrect information was ever sent out. There were problems, however. Productivity was very low, turnover and absenteeism very high, and the workers made many errors that had to be corrected by the supervisor.

You can see that this job provided no satisfaction of the motivator needs—the work was not at all stimulating or challenging. To attempt to build motivation into the work, the jobs were enlarged in accordance with Herzberg's theory.

The first step involved giving the employees increased authority and responsibility. Each worker became an expert in one area of information such as transfer of stock ownership or capital gains taxes. When a letter arrived with a question in that area, the trained worker, not the supervisor, was the authority. Each worker was allowed to sign the letters with her own name. To provide greater autonomy in the work, the workers no longer had a quota of letters to answer each day. Instead, the workers set their own pace. The form paragraphs were no longer used to construct the letters. The workers wrote the letters on their own. Finally, they were given the ultimate responsibility for their letters—the letters were mailed without being checked by the supervisor. If a worker made a mistake or had given an unclear answer, the letter or complaint would come back addressed to her.

Challenge, freedom, growth, and responsibility all were added to this job. What was the result? Errors, turnover, and absenteeism fell, and production and morale markedly increased. An entirely new dimension—motivation—had been added to a dull, routine job. The employees worked much harder at their enriched jobs and they had to accept the responsibility for their own errors, but, as a result, they worked more efficiently.

There are many other examples of successful job enlargement programs. The Bell Telephone Company in Indianapolis enlarged the mechanical job of compiling telephone directories. The directories had been compiled in assembly line fashion through a series of twenty-one steps, each handled by a different employee, in much the same way an automobile is assembled. After several attempts to increase worker efficiency and cut down the extremely high employee turnover rate, management decided to try letting each employee construct an entire telephone directory. The full responsibility was shifted to the individual employees and the results were very positive.

Motorola shifted from the assembly line method to individual-worker manufacturing and found that the enlarged work required 25 per cent more workers and a longer training time. However, despite the higher cost in wages, productivity rose (which reduced production costs) and the finished products were of higher quality.

Texas Instruments enlarged the jobs of its janitorial staff by giving full responsibility and accountability to each worker. Instead of having a supervisor delegate and oversee the work, the janitors decided among themselves how the work would be divided and scheduled. They were also responsible for setting and maintaining the quality of their work. As a result of this job enlargement, the facilities were kept cleaner than ever before and the work force was reduced to 71 from 120. Also, turnover was reduced from a staggering 100 per cent to a mere 10 per cent.

St. Regis Paper Company let three hundred and fifty paper grocery bag machine operators sign their work to see if worker pride could reduce the high number of defective bags being produced in their California and Washington factories. In less than one year, rejects dropped to less than one per cent of production, a result the production manager called "amazing." Also, several quality control inspectors, no longer needed to inspect grocery bag output, were available for reassignment elsewhere in the company.

The large number of similar success stories suggests that job enlargement is more than a fad. It has been applied since the mid–1960s and shows signs of becoming a permanent technique to enhance employee motivation.

Not all attempts at job enlargement have been successful. However, in cases where job enlargement has failed, the reason for the failure can be traced to poor implementation of the idea, and not to the idea itself. One psychologist has identified six errors in planning and installing job enlargement programs that can prevent their success.[4]

1. Problems inherent in the work are not diagnosed accurately before the job is enlarged.
2. Sometimes a job only appears to have been enlarged but has not really been changed at all.

[4] J. R. Hackman, "Is job enrichment just a fad?" *Harvard Business Review*, **53** (September–October 1975), 129–138.

3. Even when the job is substantially changed, this can sometimes have adverse effects on adjacent work groups or operations if they are not similarly changed.
4. Since job enlargement programs are rarely systematically evaluated, specific sources of error are overlooked.
5. Often, managers and union officials are not taught the theory and tactics of job enlargement and, therefore, may not be fully supportive of the change.
6. The traditional bureaucratic procedures may creep into an enlarged job, thus reducing the autonomy and responsibility of the individual worker.

Through the concept of job enlargement, the motivator-hygiene theory has had considerable impact on the world of work. Though the validity of the theory remains in question, there is little doubt that its derivative—job enlargement—is quite successful in improving worker motivation.

There is at least one similarity between the need–achievement, needs-hierarchy, and motivator-hygiene theories: all focus on the importance of the work itself and the challenges, growth opportunities, and responsibilities provided for the worker. If these theories have any validity, then studies of job satisfaction should also identify the same factors as being the most rewarding to people at work.

JOB SATISFACTION: A MEASURE OF THE QUALITY OF WORKING LIFE

It is sometimes difficult to distinguish between motivation and job satisfaction because of their high degree of interrelationship. There is also such a relationship between job satisfaction and morale; many writers use these terms interchangeably. Basically, job satisfaction refers to a set of attitudes that employees have about their jobs. We may describe it as the psychological disposition of people toward their jobs—how they feel about the work—and this involves a collection of numerous attitudes or feelings. Thus, job satisfaction or dissatisfaction depends on a large number of factors ranging from where employees have to park their cars and whether the boss calls them by their first name, to the sense of achievement or fulfillment they may find in their work.

Additional factors can influence job satisfaction, factors that are not directly part of the job or work climate. For example, job satisfaction varies as a function of age, health, number of years worked,

271

emotional stability, social status, leisure and recreational activities, family relationships, and other social outlets and affiliations. Also, personal motivations and aspirations, and how well these are fulfilled, can influence the attitude we have toward our work.

Background of Job Satisfaction

Organizations today focus much attention on measuring and improving their workers' attitudes, but this was not always the case. In the scientific management era when the worker was considered to be just another machine, there was no interest in job satisfaction—after all, a machine does not have attitudes or feelings. The way in which industry tried to improve production during that time was almost exclusively through the development of more efficient selection techniques.

The human relations focus drastically changed this view. It became apparent that workers' productivity was not solely a function of their skills and abilities. During the Hawthorne studies, some twenty thousand interviews conducted with the workers convinced management that their employees did indeed have feelings and attitudes about their jobs that could affect their productivity.

As soon as industry realized this, frantic efforts were undertaken to measure attitudes and to train supervisors to be sensitive to employee feelings. It was thought that if job satisfaction and morale could be improved, job performance would improve as well. By the mid–1950s, however, it became clear that the relationship between performance and job satisfaction was much more complex than originally supposed.

Workers' attitudes must be measured, however, because they are of great value to organizations and to employees. For example, if negative attitudes toward a particular job feature are uncovered, it is possible to institute corrective procedures. Without attitude measurement, management might know something was wrong—that morale was low—but would not be able to pinpoint the problem.

Measuring Job Satisfaction

There are several techniques for measuring job satisfaction, all of which involve, in essence, asking workers how they feel about various aspects of their jobs.

The most popular technique is the questionnaire, either distributed to workers in the plant or office, or mailed to their homes. Usually, questionnaire responses are voluntary and anonymous. This means that not all workers will complete a questionnaire and there is no way of knowing which employees responded and which did not. It might make a difference, for example, if more good than poor workers responded.

A technique often used in conjunction with questionnaires is the personal interview in which employees discuss various aspects of the job with a supervisor or an interviewer from the personnel department. In Chapter 3 we discussed the low reliabilities and validities of the interview procedure; it is also time-consuming and expensive.

A newer method of measuring job attitudes is the sentence completion test. Workers are presented with a list of phrases that they are asked to complete: for example, "My job is ———," or "My job should be ———."

The critical incidents technique is also used. Employees are asked in a personal interview to describe job incidents that occurred at times when they felt extremely good or extremely bad about their jobs.

Extent of Job Satisfaction and Dissatisfaction

Every year since 1949, the Gallup poll has asked a representative sample of American workers the following question: On the whole, would you say you are satisfied or dissatisfied with the work you do? Recognizing that this question may be a simplified approach to something as complex as job satisfaction, let us examine the results. The poll shows that 10 to 13 per cent of the workers questioned each year say they are dissatisfied with their jobs. When the data are examined for the variables of sex, race, education, occupation, and age, the extent of dissatisfaction ranges from a high of 22 per cent (nonwhite workers) to a low of 7 per cent (workers over fifty years of age).

If approximately only 10 to 13 per cent of the work force is dissatisfied, why is so much attention paid to job satisfaction? Recall that the results of an opinion poll are strongly influenced by the wording of the questions. When more sophisticated and specific questions were asked about job satisfaction, different results were obtained.

For example, when blue-collar workers were asked if they would like to change jobs, substantial numbers of them said yes, even though they indicated that they were satisfied with their present jobs. Apparently, when many people say they are satisfied, they really mean that they are not dissatisfied. Although pay and external working conditions may be satisfactory, it does not follow that the jobs themselves are challenging, rewarding, or stimulating. Satisfaction is defined for many people, then, as the absence of negative factors rather than the presence of positive factors.

In another study, when workers who had said they were satisfied with their jobs were questioned in greater detail, they revealed major sources of dissatisfaction with factors such as the quality of leadership and the lack of opportunity to grow on the job.

A sensitive indicator of job satisfaction is the response to the following question: What type of work would you try to get into if you could start all over again? It is assumed that persons who were fully satisfied with their present jobs would choose the same jobs again. Only 43 per cent of the white-collar workers chose the same jobs and only 24 per cent of the blue-collar workers did so. Not surprisingly, the response to this question varied as a function of level of occupation: the higher the level, the greater was the expressed job satisfaction (see Table 8–1).

Another reliable indicator of job satisfaction is the response to the question: What would you do with the extra two hours if you had a twenty-six-hour day? Again, the answers varied with level of occupation. Among college professors, 66 per cent said they would use the extra time for their work, as did 25 per cent of the lawyers questioned. More than 80 per cent of the nonprofessional workers, however, said they would use the extra time for activities having nothing to do with their work.

There are widespread differences, then, in reported job dissatisfaction, depending on how the issue is investigated. When more sophisticated questions are used, the proportion of those sampled who express dissatisfaction with their jobs rises dramatically. When examining statistics on job satisfaction, it is thus necessary to find out

TABLE 8–1

OCCUPATIONAL GROUPS THAT WOULD CHOOSE SIMILAR WORK AGAIN (%)

White-Collar Occupations		Blue-Collar Occupations	
Urban university professors	93	Skilled printers	52
Mathematicians	91	Paper workers	42
Physicists and biologists	89	Skilled autoworkers	41
Chemists	86	Skilled steelworkers	41
Lawyers	83	Textile workers	31
Journalists (in Washington)	82	Unskilled steelworkers	21
Church university professors	77	Unskilled autoworkers	16

Adapted from *Work in America* (Cambridge, Mass.: MIT Press, 1973), p. 16.

the kinds of questions asked and the level of occupation (and other personal characteristics) of the respondents.

Job satisfaction polls also indicate specific features of the work that can lead to job dissatisfaction, such as lack of challenge, responsibility, and autonomy. Thus, much dissatisfaction can be traced to the nature of the work. However, evidence suggests that some people are chronically dissatisfied with their jobs, no matter the type or level. These workers often exhibit symptoms of emotional instability and generally tend to be discontent, introverted, not very friendly, and prone to daydream. Often, they are unable to adjust to the rigid schedule required by most jobs and to work standards set by their superiors. This is particularly true for disadvantaged and hard-core unemployed workers who have not learned responsible work habits or had opportunities to develop ambition or the satisfaction of personal achievement. Chronically dissatisfied workers also set unrealistically high personal goals. Trying to achieve above one's level of ability or opportunity easily induces frustration and dissatisfaction as the person comes to realize that he or she will not be able to reach the goal.

Of course, not all people who report unhappiness in their jobs are considered chronically dissatisfied. Many workers can find greater job satisfaction by changing to another kind of work or moving to a different company.

It is often possible to trace the source of worker dissatisfaction to specific policies or practices of an employing organization. When these sources are isolated, an alert management is in a position to institute corrective procedures in order to eliminate the causes of dissatisfaction. For example, Lockheed-Georgia (a division of Lockheed Aircraft) surveyed its employees to determine how they felt about their jobs. The company psychologist, and consultants from the Georgia Institute of Technology's Psychology Department, began by interviewing a sample of employees. From this information, a questionnaire was constructed to investigate employee feelings on sixty-six job-related items. Three forms of the questionnaire were developed, one for each level of employee at the plant: supervisory, salaried nonsupervisory, and hourly paid workers.

The questionnaire, accompanied by an explanatory letter from the company president, was mailed to each employee's home. The employees had been informed about the questionnaire by announcements in the company newspaper. Approximately 43 per cent of the employees returned the questionnaire. The return rate was higher for supervisory than for salaried nonsupervisory personnel, and higher for salaried nonsupervisory personnel than for hourly paid workers.

In analyzing the results, any item on which at least 30 per cent of

TABLE 8–2

SOURCES OF JOB DISSATISFACTION IN LOCKHEED-GEORGIA STUDY

	Employee Levels		
Items	Super-visory	Salaried Non-super-visory	Hourly
The Company and Its Management			
Company treatment of employees		X	X
Higher management appreciation of the importance of your work		X	X
Recognition for good ideas or good work		X	X
Immediate Supervision			
Prompt action on your complaints and problems by your supervisor		X	X
Information about what your supervisor expects of you		X	X
Good planning and scheduling of work by supervisor		X	X
Supervisor's concern for you as a person			X
Personnel Practices			
Promotion from within		X	X
Fairness of promotion procedures	X	X	X
Opportunity to change jobs within the company	X	X	X
Opportunity for promotion from your job	X	X	X
Job Related Personal Development			
Opportunity to use your special skills and abilities			X
Company sponsored training for your job	X	X	X
Opportunity for education or training to keep abreast of your field		X	X
Opportunity to develop new skills and knowledge in your job		X	X
Internal Communication			
Information relating to company operations	X		X
Information on company policy	X	X	X
Working Conditions			
Cooperation among departments		X	X

TABLE 8–2 (cont'd.)

| Items | Employee Levels | | |
	Super-visory	Salaried Non-super-visory	Hourly
Your work place		X	X
Opportunity to obtain good equipment and supplies			X
The Job Itself			
Chance to do different things on the job			X
Pay for work you do			X
Opportunity for contact with higher management		X	X

From R. Raskin, "Attitude survey uncovers employees' hidden discontent," *Factory*, **3**(March 1970), 86. Reprinted by special permission of *Factory*, March 1970. Copyright, Morgan-Grampian, Inc., March 1970.

the workers expressed dissatisfaction was included as a source of discontent. Table 8–2 presents the specific areas of discontent noted by the three levels of employee.

Finding sources of dissatisfaction is interesting, but it is of limited value unless accompanied by corrective action. Lockheed reasoned that the best way to determine the nature of such corrective action was to ask the employees for suggestions. Committees called "Y-groups" were formed, each consisting of a random sample of 3 to 5 per cent of the workers from each branch of the company. The groups met several times to determine why certain items on the questionnaire received unfavorable responses and what could be done to change the situation. The results of the committee meetings were presented to top management who carefully evaluated the findings before instituting any changes.

For example, engineers were dissatisfied because too much information was communicated to them orally—there were no written records to consult. By increasing the availability of manuals and data handbooks, this problem was eliminated. The employees' dissatisfaction with available information on company policy and operations was corrected by holding periodic meetings to disseminate such information. Changes were also made in the company promotion system, the nature of supervision, and in communication at all levels of the plant's operation.

This unusually thorough program is an excellent example of what can be done to correct sources of employee discontent. It requires technical expertise on the part of the psychologist, cooperation and interest on the part of the employees, and a willingness on the part of management both to listen to employees and to be flexible in bringing about changes in working conditions and procedures.

PERSONAL CHARACTERISTICS AND JOB SATISFACTION

Characteristics of the work itself, and of the context or situation in which the work is performed, strongly influence job satisfaction. By redesigning the job and the working conditions, it is possible to increase job satisfaction and worker productivity. Situational factors, then, are important in job satisfaction, but there are other notable factors as well: the personal characteristics of the workers. Satisfaction in work can be influenced by age, sex, race, level of intelligence, and length of job experience. Although these factors cannot be changed by employing organizations, they can be used to predict the relative levels of satisfaction to be expected among different groups of workers.

Age

In general, job satisfaction increases with age; the least job satisfaction is reported by the youngest workers. The high job dissatisfaction among young workers has increased in the past decade and apparently is caused by the fact that the young currently have greater expectations about their jobs than did past generations of workers.

Young workers today expect a great deal of personal fulfillment from their jobs. When asked what they want from work, students list factors such as "a chance to make a contribution," "job challenge," "self-expression," and "freedom to make my own decisions." Past generations, influenced by the Great Depression of the 1930s, listed salary, security, and promotion opportunity as their occupational goals. Their goals—external to the work—are much easier to satisfy than are the inner goals of fulfillment and satisfaction. Thus, many young people are disappointed when they begin work because they fail to find challenge and responsibility. But why does job satisfaction increase with age when the initial reaction to work is one of such great disappointment? When workers are asked how often they leave their job with a good feeling that they have done something well, the

TABLE 8–3

WORKERS EXPRESSING A GOOD
FEELING ABOUT THEIR JOBS

Age	%
20 and under	23
21–29	25
30–44	38
45–64	43
65 and over	53

Adapted from *Work in America* (Cambridge,
Mass.: MIT Press, 1973), p. 45.

percentage answering "very often" clearly increases with age (Table 8–3).

There are three possible explanations. First, the most strongly dissatisfied young workers may drop out of the labor force or change jobs so frequently in their search for fulfillment that they are no longer included in surveys. This would mean that the older the workers studied, the fewer dissatisfied people are likely to be among them. Second, a sense of reality (or resignation) sets in as workers grow older. They may give up looking for fulfillment and challenge in work and so become less dissatisfied (although not necessarily fully satisfied) with their jobs. Perhaps they are making the best of a bad situation, realizing that for family and financial reasons they must remain on the job. Third, older workers have more opportunities to find fulfillment and self-actualization in their jobs than do workers who are just starting out. Age and experience on the job usually bring greater competence, self-confidence, and esteem, and a higher level of responsibility where a person may feel a greater sense of accomplishment.

Whatever the reasons, the result is that job satisfaction does increase with age. Job dissatisfaction as a function of age is shown in Table 8–4.

Sex

Women have become an increasingly large and important segment of the American working force. Indeed, half of all women of employable age (18–64) are currently in the work force. Most women, however, work at the less desirable jobs. Most routine white-collar jobs—

TABLE 8–4

DISSATISFIED WORKERS

Age	%
Under 30	25
30–44	13
45–54	11
Over 55	6

Data from H. Sheppard and N. Herrick, *Where Have All the Robots Gone? Worker Dissatisfaction in the '70s* (New York: The Free Press, 1972), p. 5.

such as telephone operator, keypunch operator, and clerical worker —are held by women, and large numbers of women work at assembly line jobs. Since women constitute such a significant portion of the working population, it is important for employing organizations to have some understanding of their level of job satisfaction.

The evidence, however, is inconsistent and unclear. Some studies show that women are satisfied on the job, whereas other studies show the opposite. Some research shows women to be far more dissatisfied than are men with their jobs. There is some indication that women may be concerned with different aspects of the job than are men. For example, disadvantaged women evidenced a greater need to like their work and to have a fair boss; disadvantaged men were more concerned with the opportunity to prove themselves and to have a steady job. In another example, male and female workers hired by Prudential Insurance were asked what job characteristics were important to them. The results showed that long-range career objectives were much less important to women. Also, women were much more concerned with comfortable working conditions and quality of interpersonal relationships. There were no differences between men and women on the importance of internal factors such as autonomy.[5]

It is reasonable to expect different sources of job satisfaction for women who choose a career in the business world as compared to women who must work to supplement the family income. The motivations and satisfactions of career women might more closely parallel those of male executives. Working mothers, on the other hand, may not look upon outside work as the major focus in their life, deriving satisfaction from the jobs of homemaker, wife, or mother instead.

[5] P. Manhardt, "Job orientation of male and female college graduates in business," *Personnel Psychology*, **25** (1972), 361–368.

Researchers suggest that it is not a worker's sex that relates to job satisfaction, but rather a group of factors that varies with sex. For example, it is unfortunately still true that women are paid less than men for the same work, and that their opportunities for promotion are fewer than those for men. One study found that female executives felt they had to work much harder and be more outstanding in their work than male executives before they could expect to receive the same rewards and recognition.

Discrimination against female employees has been widespread in industry and business. This injustice fueled the growth of the women's rights movement in the 1970s. This, and the 1964 Civil Rights Act prohibiting sex discrimination, should bring about significant changes in the opportunities, and thus job satisfaction, for women.

Race

Nonwhite workers are twice as likely as white workers to express dissatisfaction with their jobs. Of course, one must first have a job in order to be concerned with job satisfaction. Among members of minority races, getting a job is a more basic issue. Approximately one third of the employable members of minority groups are unemployed, employed only irregularly, or too discouraged to continue to seek employment. Another one third of minority group members have full-time jobs, but these are low-level jobs offering marginal pay and little chance for advancement. Thus, the problem for most nonwhites is not finding fulfillment, achievement, and responsibility in a job, but simply finding a job that pays a decent wage.

Among the one third of the nonwhite workers who are employed in higher-level jobs offering advancement possibilities and higher pay, the rate of dissatisfaction is, as noted, twice that of white workers. Whether blue-collar, white-collar, or managerial positions, nonwhites find less satisfaction than whites in their jobs. The lowest level of satisfaction among regularly employed nonwhites was for white-collar jobs.

The high rate of dissatisfaction remains steady through age forty-four, after which dissatisfaction declines to a level below that for whites. Older nonwhite workers have about the lowest level of job dissatisfaction of any group (although their dissatisfaction with life in general remains high). It has been suggested that older nonwhite workers, having suffered years of job discrimination, have come to view job satisfaction strictly in terms of being employed versus being unemployed, and do not expect to receive any further inner reward from their work.

Intelligence

By itself, a person's level of intelligence does not appear to be of major importance in influencing job satisfaction. However, intelligence considered in relation to the kind of work being performed is a significant factor.

For many occupations and professions there is a range of intelligence associated with efficiency of performance and job satisfaction. Persons with IQs beyond this range (either too high or too low) are likely to experience boredom or frustration and dissatisfaction with the job. Much research has shown that persons who are too intelligent for the work—for example, a bright college graduate in a routine assembly line job—find insufficient challenge and become bored and dissatisfied. Likewise, those in jobs that require a higher level of intelligence than they possess will be frustrated if they are unable to handle the demands of the job. The problem of matching job level with intelligence can be eliminated by the use of adequate selection procedures.

A factor usually (but not always) related to intelligence is level of education. A number of studies have shown that persons with higher educational levels report greater general job satisfaction than those with less education.

Job Experience

The relationship between job satisfaction and number of years on the job is complex. During the early stages of employment, new workers tend to be rather well satisfied with the job. This early period on the job involves the stimulation and challenge of learning new skills and developing new abilities. Also, the work may seem attractive at first just because it is new.

Unfortunately, early satisfaction wanes unless employees receive constant evidence of their progress and growth. After a few years on the job, growing discouragement is common, brought on by the feeling that the worker is not advancing as rapidly as he or she would like. Also, in times of inflation and rapidly rising starting salaries, employees with a few years of experience find that they are making little more than beginning employees, despite the fact that they have received salary increases over the years.

Job satisfaction begins to increase again after six or seven years of employment and improves steadily thereafter.

The relationship between job satisfaction and length of experience closely parallels that with age. Perhaps they are the same phenomenon under different labels.

Utilization of Skills

A common complaint, particularly among engineering and science graduates, is that employees are not called upon to exercise the skills and knowledge developed in their college training. Studies have shown that people are happier in their work if they have the opportunity to demonstrate abilities they believe they possess. The utilization and exercise of personal abilities are part of what Maslow meant by self-actualization.

Personality

There seems to be a positive relationship between chronic job dissatisfaction and poor emotional adjustment. Although not entirely conclusive, evidence suggests that those who are more satisfied in their work are also better adjusted and more emotionally stable.

The fact of such a relationship seems clear, but the cause and effect sequence is not. Which comes first, emotional maladjustment or job dissatisfaction? Either is capable of causing the other. Emotional instability can cause discontent in every sphere of a person's life, including the job; prolonged job dissatisfaction can lead to poor emotional adjustment.

Regardless of which one might cause the other, the result is likely to be the same. Some companies have instituted personal counseling programs, particularly for managerial and executive personnel, and some maintain clinical psychologists and psychiatrists on the staff or have them available as consultants to deal with emotional disturbances of high-level personnel.

Occupational Level

The higher the occupational or status level of a job, the higher is the job satisfaction. Executives express more satisfaction with their jobs than do first-line supervisors who, in turn, are more satisfied than their subordinates. In general, the higher the level of the job, the greater is the opportunity to satisfy the motivator needs (described by Herzberg), and the greater is the autonomy, challenge, and responsibility. In a study of more than one thousand managers, satisfaction of the needs for esteem, autonomy, and self-actualization increased with each level in the organizational hierarchy.

Job satisfaction has also been found to vary with different kinds of occupation. For example, those with the highest satisfaction scores are either in business for themselves or in the construction industry. Chances of dissatisfaction in these two areas are only one in twenty. Persons in technical, professional, and managerial jobs report a one in ten chance of being dissatisfied. The least satisfying occupations are manufacturing, service occupations, and wholesale or retail business, where the chances for dissatisfaction are almost one in four.[6]

PAY AS A SOURCE OF MOTIVATION AND SATISFACTION

Salary alone no longer seems as important as a motivator and satisfier as it was at one time. In the three theories of motivation discussed, money was not an important incentive in any of them, although Herzberg did suggest that it could serve as a dissatisfier. In general, once a person's salary passes a certain point, it is not a significant determinant of job satisfaction. However, the way in which salary is determined is a potential source of job dissatisfaction.

Whatever one's theoretical point of view with regard to work motivation, then, salary is not regarded as a primary motivating force. The question of the importance of salary (none deny that it has at least some value as a motivator) is complicated and seems to vary with the individual employee.

The amount of income considered sufficient is related to the standard of living desired and to the cost of living in a given geographical location. A salary that buys a better than average living standard in a small southern town may be totally inadequate in New York City. Also, the salary that provides a comfortable standard of living for one family may be insufficient for another family in the same area. It often happens that the same salary can be a source of satisfaction to one person and a source of frustration and discontent to another person performing the same job.

Increasingly, salary is seen as a way of satisfying needs in addition to those of basic survival. With money, people can satisfy needs for status, security, recognition or affiliation. Those with a high need for status, for example, require a higher income than those who care little for status—the former will try to buy status through the acquisition of material possessions.

[6] H. Sheppard and N. Herrick, *Where Have All the Robots Gone? Worker Dissatisfaction in the '70s* (New York: The Free Press, 1972), p. 5.

At the executive level, there is evidence that salary may be more important than at lower working levels. The needs for achievement, self-actualization or recognition are greater at these levels and salary may serve as a convenient yardstick to measure how successful a person is in satisfying these higher-order needs.

Even though a higher salary at the executive level may not mean much difference in take-home pay (because of higher taxes), most executives seem motivated to gain the additional salary. Salary in this instance is not necessarily desired for the extra material possessions it will buy, but because it signifies accomplishment and achievement in one's work.

The salaries of most managers are determined on the basis of merit; those who are more competent receive larger salary increases. On the surface, this seems to be a fair approach, but it turns out that merit pay is a major source of dissatisfaction to most managers. Surveys show that as many as 80 per cent of managers are dissatisfied with this method of determining pay. There are several reasons for this dissatisfaction.

First, it has been suggested that the more that pay depends on job performance, the lower is the inherent interest of that job to the employee. In other words, when the task is focused on as a means of getting more money, then the managers' focus shifts from the task itself to the goal or reward for performing the task well.

Second, the amount of the salary increase depends solely on the judgment of the manager's superiors and their ability to discriminate among various levels of competence. And, as noted with performance evaluation, most people are not very good at making such subjective judgments. For this reason, labor unions rarely agree to merit pay plans for their members.

Third, the key role of superiors in determining salary constantly reminds managers of how directly dependent they are on their superiors for rewards. This fosters efforts by managers to please their superiors, which can be very demeaning.

Fourth, merit pay programs put managers in a situation of competing with other managers for a portion of the limited rewards. If one manager is to get a large raise, another one must get a smaller raise because a fixed amount of money is available for salary increases. By forcing this competition, managers tend to see their colleagues as enemies. This has harmful effects on working relationships.

Overall, the merit pay plan is viewed as a threat to the managers' self-esteem. Most people believe that they are above average in their abilities, and to be told that they are below average (evidenced by a small pay increase) is damaging. Instead of motivating them to work harder, such a judgment has a negative effect, causing managers to feel that their true worth is not recognized.

Thus, it is not so much the amount of the salary that can lead to dissatisfaction, but the manner in which it is determined. Ironically, when surveyed, most managers say that they want their pay to be determined by merit. In practice, however, the feeling of managers is extremely prevalent that their salaries are influenced by factors other than how well they perform their jobs. Merit pay seems to be a nice theory but it does not translate well into actual use.

There are also problems with the primary pay determination system used for blue-collar workers. Large numbers of production workers are paid on the basis of a wage incentive system, usually in terms of number of units produced in a given period of time. Through a time-and-motion analysis of the job, the average or standard time for producing a unit is determined and the wage rate incentive is established accordingly.

Theoretically, this system should provide the incentive to work hard —the more units produced, the higher the wage. But this rarely works in practice and provides yet another defeat for the notion that people are motivated primarily by money.

Most workers will not work to full capacity under a wage incentive system partly because they distrust management. They fear that the standard production rate will be set too high, forcing them to work unusually hard for a small bonus. Also, if the production rate is set too low (so that it is easy to exceed the standard and make more money), they believe that the company will then raise the rate. One survey of workers on a wage incentive system showed that 75 per cent of them felt strongly that they should not work too hard for fear of a reduction in their rate of pay per unit.

Many groups of workers establish their own standard of what constitutes a good day's work and will not produce more regardless of the wage incentive offered. They will spread out the work so that it comfortably fills the number of hours on the job. For these reasons, wage incentive systems are declining in popularity.

Another aspect of pay that can lead to job dissatisfaction is the secrecy of salaries within an organization. In most organizations, it is a standard policy to keep everyone's salary confidential, so that no one knows how much one's colleagues or superiors earn. This is particularly widespread at management levels and results in the prevalent phenomenon of managers overestimating the salaries of other managers. Studies show that managers also consistently overestimate the amount of the salary increases that their colleagues receive.

As a result, most managers tend to believe that no matter how well they are performing their job, they are getting less than average raises. Not surprisingly, this results in a lowering of their motivation. In other words, they come to believe that their salary is not based on worth. Also, when managers do not know what other managers earn, they find it difficult to judge their own worth relative to their peers. They cannot tell if their superiors perceive them to be better, worse, or the same as other managers.

One solution is to make salary information public. Only in that way is pay likely to serve as a source of motivation.

In sum, pay is intended to spur employees to higher levels of performance and to increase their job satisfaction, but it often has the opposite effect.

JOB SATISFACTION AND BEHAVIOR ON THE JOB

It is reasonable to assume that a high level of job satisfaction is directly related to positive behavior on the job, specifically to high performance, low turnover, and low absenteeism. In noting the history of job satisfaction, we mentioned that organizational leaders once thought that increasing job satisfaction would result in greater production. The relationship turned out to be neither direct nor simple. The issue of motivation and job performance is complicated and involves a wide range of job and personal characteristics. Although the relationship between satisfaction and job behavior is still recognized, it is no longer looked upon as the simple answer to production problems.

Turnover and Absenteeism

Employees who are dissatisfied with their jobs will leave them through frequent absences (sort of part-time quitting) or by finding other jobs. The research is inconclusive although the studies generally support the relationship between high satisfaction and low turnover and absenteeism. Satisfaction is only one of the variables that affects turnover and absenteeism, however. Age and mobility also enter into the relationship. Certainly, young, single, dissatisfied workers (without family or financial obligations) are more free to quit jobs if they are dissatisfied than are fifty-year-old employees with a mortgage, debts, and roots in the community. Personality characteristics and the availability of alternative jobs also confound the relationship between satisfaction and turnover.

287

Production

Level of production efficiency is certainly a major concern of any organization. If job satisfaction were not at all related to performance improvement, management would be understandably reluctant to support research in this area. Although the evidence favors a positive relationship between satisfaction and performance, it has not been demonstrated conclusively. The correlations do not tend to be high, and some studies show a lack of correlation. Part of the problem is the difficulty of conducting the research. How can successful performance be measured? Some jobs lend themselves more readily than others to objective assessments of performance level. Thus, different measures of success must be used for different jobs and this, in itself, can produce varying results.

At any rate, despite the research problems, inconclusive findings, and general lack of strong positive correlations, it still seems clear that a fairly consistent relationship exists between satisfaction and performance.

An interesting interpretation of this problem is as follows.[7] Instead of considering job satisfaction as leading to improved performance, we should think of performance as causing satisfaction. Satisfaction presumably derives from the fulfillment of our needs. If our work provides us with this fulfillment then we can, in effect, administer our own rewards by improving our levels of performance. If, for example, a job satisfies our need for achievement, by performing at a higher level we can better fulfill this need.

It has been suggested that this formulation may be more applicable to managers or executives than to lower-level workers. Managers have greater opportunities to express their needs for self-actualization, achievement, and personal growth than do workers on an assembly line. The latter have little control over their jobs and little opportunity to fulfill higher-order needs. Most of their rewards are determined by factors beyond their control; executives can operate with greater autonomy. Since most workers are unable to fulfill these needs through work, they cannot derive any satisfaction from the job. This, plus the fact that most research on satisfaction and performance has been conducted on lower-level workers, could easily explain the lack of a strong positive relationship between the two variables.

To test this theory, 148 managers in five organizations were studied.[8] It was found that high-performing managers did not receive

[7] E. E. Lawler and L. W. Porter, "The effect of performance on job satisfaction," *Industrial Relations*, **7** (1967), 20–28.
[8] L. W. Porter and E. E. Lawler, "What job attitudes tell about motivation," *Harvard Business Review*, **46**(January 1968), 118–126.

greater external rewards (such as pay) than did low-performing counterparts. However, high performers reported many more rewards from satisfying needs such as autonomy and self-realization. Further, high-performing managers reported higher levels of job satisfaction than did low performers, providing strong support for the idea that need fulfillment from a job leads to satisfaction, which, in turn, leads to higher performance.

This study also supports the theories of motivation that discuss the importance of fulfilling higher-order needs, and confirms the necessity of designing challenging and stimulating jobs that allow for growth and self-actualization.

THE SECOND CAREER: A SEARCH FOR NEW SATISFACTIONS

Growing numbers of middle-aged executives, scientists, and other professionals are attempting to switch in midlife to new and different careers. Known colloquially as "repotting," this trend is marked not by simply changing jobs, but by changing to an entirely new type of work.

For example, a forty-eight-year-old research director for a chemical company quit to become a college professor, a forty-five-year-old supervisor for Polaroid constructed and operates a golf course, and a fifty-two-year-old TWA pilot now runs a boatyard and charter boat business.

These people, and many others like them, shared a sense of disillusionment and disappointment with their previous jobs. The excitement and challenge were gone and they had nothing to look forward to or to work toward. Most of these people are bright, active, and successful in their first career. They left not out of a sense of failure but rather a sense of frustration and extreme dissatisfaction.

A forty-year-old corporation president said, "I keep feeling more and more depressed, and I can't figure out why. I've gone as high as I can go, there's nothing wrong with my life, but I just can't seem to shake this feeling of, 'so here I am, so what?'"

They have accumulated the physical trappings of success—two cars, the big house, the best country club—and found that material possessions have not brought the sense of satisfaction or accomplishment promised. Although they have achieved success in their work, it is obviously not sufficient.

Those who opt for a new career at midlife are among the most valuable employees of any organization. It has been shown that they are better adjusted, have a higher need to achieve, and a greater sense of self-esteem and ambition than those who remain in their first careers. Personal challenge and fulfillment are important factors in the lives of those who seek new careers, more so than salary. Their satisfaction apparently derives from the excitement of striving to achieve rather than from actually attaining the goal.

Repotting is a problem for growing numbers of middle-aged employees. Its seriousness is attested to by the many seminars, books, and articles on the topic. This crisis of the middle-aged professional and executive traditionally occurs around age forty-five, although, with America's obsession with youth, it can occur as young as thirty-five. It is a phenomenon, or indulgence, only possible in affluent times when alternative economic opportunities are available.

The importance of this problem for industry is that organizations are losing some of their best managers. Perhaps even more harmful to both organizations and their employees are cases in which executives are stricken with the midlife dilemma but lack the nerve or opportunity to change careers. Being forced to remain in their present positions could lead to higher levels of job and personal dissatisfaction and to retiring on the job—no longer making any contribution yet continuing to collect a salary for another twenty years. A great many middle-aged managers find themselves in this position. Not only satisfaction but also the search for satisfaction have ended.

THE LAID-OFF WORKER

It is fitting to close a chapter on the motivations and satisfactions of work by considering the state of those whose work has been taken away from them. There are many instances of workers who have been dismissed because an automated process has rendered their jobs obsolete or a company reorganization has closed a department or a plant. In periods of economic downturn, whole segments of industry can slow down or close altogether.

Thus, many workers find themselves without jobs, through no fault of their own. Studies confirm the obvious; this is a time of great stress for the individual who has been laid off. One characteristic frequently observed is the development of guilt on the part of the dismissed workers—the feeling that it is somehow their own doing. This was even observed during the Depression of the 1930s—despite massive unemployment, many people felt personally responsible for being out of work.

There is also a feeling of rootlessness or lack of connection, and a sharp increase in mental and physical illness and in suicide. There is widespread tension, understandable anxiety about the future, and strong feelings of resentment.

Higher-level employees suffer more from unemployment. They become more defensive and self-critical; lower-level workers are more adaptable. Particularly among managers and executives there is a deep and long-lasting transformation that affects life-style, expectations, goals, and values. The trauma of unemployment seems to last even when a new job has been found. In one study of unemployed men, those who found new jobs regained some level of self-esteem, but this level did not reach the level of self-esteem of a control group who had not lost their jobs.

Many jobs in our society cause feelings of dissatisfaction, but being without a job may be the most dissatisfying state of all.

SUMMARY

The problem of employee **motivation** is crucial in all kinds of organizations today and is responsible for the shoddy products we buy and the careless service we receive. It was thought that all that was necessary to produce high motivation in workers was to pay them more; this idea is no longer valid. Money is not the motivating force today that it was to past generations of workers. Modern workers demand jobs that satisfy their inner needs for fulfillment, expression, and self-actualization.

Psychologists have proposed several theories of motivation. The **need for achievement** (McClelland) posits the existence in certain people of a need to accomplish, to do a good job, and to be the best in whatever they undertake. Studies show that good executives are higher in need achievement than poor ones. High need-achievement people like working conditions in which they have responsibility and take calculated risks and set moderate achievement goals. These individuals constantly need feedback on their progress.

The **needs-hierarchy** theory (Maslow) proposes a hierarchy of five needs—physiological, safety, love, esteem, and self-actualization—each of which must be satisfied before the next one becomes prominent. Self-actualization, the highest need, involves utilizing one's capabilities to the fullest, and it can be satisfied by jobs that allow autonomy, challenge, and responsibility.

The **motivator-hygiene** theory (Herzberg) proposes two sets of needs: motivator needs (the nature of the work and its level of achievement and responsibility), and hygiene needs (aspects of the work environment such as pay and supervision). Motivator needs produce job satisfaction; hygiene needs can produce job dissatisfaction if the working conditions are inadequate. However, even if the working conditions are outstanding, hygiene needs cannot produce job satisfaction.

An outgrowth of the motivator-hygiene theory is **job enlargement,** the redesign of a job to maximize the motivator factors. Job enlargement involves (1) removing controls over employees and increasing their personal responsibility for their work, (2) providing employees with full and natural units of work, (3) giving employees more authority and freedom in their jobs, (4) providing feedback on production directly to workers, (5) encouraging workers to assume new and more difficult tasks, and (6) allowing workers to become experts or specialists in a particular task.

Examples of successful job enlargement programs are discussed, along with errors that can cause such programs to fail.

One way to determine the quality of working life is to measure the attitudes that constitute **job satisfaction.** This is usually accomplished through questionnaires and personal interviews. The extent of job dissatisfaction in the United States ranges from 7 to 22 per cent, according to the Gallup poll. However, estimates of job dissatisfaction are strongly influenced by the kinds of questions asked and by personal characteristics of the respondents. Much research has been conducted to determine the influence on job satisfaction of factors such as age, sex, race, intelligence, length of job experience, personality, and occupational level.

In general, job satisfaction increases with age, is much higher for whites than for nonwhites, for men than for women, is unaffected by intelligence (assuming the job is challenging enough or is not too challenging for a person's intelligence), bears no consistent relationship to personality, and tends to increase with length of job experience and occupational level.

The **salary** a person earns, although no longer regarded as a primary motivating force, can nevertheless influence job satisfaction. What is important about salary and job satisfaction is not the amount, but rather the way in which salary is determined. Blue-collar workers whose pay is determined by a **wage-incentive** system, and managers whose pay is determined on a **merit** basis, report dissatisfaction with salary. Merit-based pay, in particular, seems to lower motivation to work harder and is perceived by employees as inequitable in that their true abilities may not be sufficiently rewarded.

Keeping salaries confidential in an organization is also a cause of job dissatisfaction because it leads to overestimation of what employees think their peers are being paid. As a result, people feel they are being paid less than they are worth and are unable to judge their own performance relative to their peers.

The relationship between job satisfaction and behavior on the job is complex and confusing. Some studies indicate that job dissatisfaction is related to turnover and absenteeism, but other studies do not support such a relationship. The relationship between job satisfaction and production is also inconsistent. It may be that high levels of performance cause job satisfaction instead of the other way around. Perhaps high performance on a job fulfills certain inner needs, which, in turn, produces a feeling of satisfaction with the job.

A growing trend, particularly among managers and executives, is the search for new satisfactions through a **second career.** Because a job no longer provides challenge or fulfillment, many managers (especially those high in ambition, need for achievement and self-esteem) are beginning new careers to satisfy higher-level needs such as self-actualization.

Perhaps the most dissatisfied workers are those who, through no fault of their own, have been dismissed from their jobs. **Unemployment,** particularly among high-level employees, is a traumatic experience that is damaging to self-esteem and health, and that leaves emotional scars even when new employment is found.

SUGGESTED READINGS

Bradburn, N. Is the quality of work life improving? How can you tell? And who wants to know? *Studies in Personnel Psychology,* 1974, **6**(1), 19–33.

Braginsky, D., and Braginsky, B. Surplus people: Their lost faith in self and system. *Psychology Today,* 1975, **9**(3), 69–72.

Campbell, J. P., and Pritchard, R. D. Motivation theory in industrial and organizational psychology. In M. Dunnette, Ed., *Handbook of Industrial and Organizational Psychology.* Chicago: Rand McNally, 1976. Pp. 63–130.

Davis, L., and Cherns, A. *Quality of Working Life.* Vol. 1: *Problems, Prospects, and the State of the Art.* Vol. 2: *Cases and Commentary.* New York: The Free Press, 1975.

Ford, R. Job enrichment lessons from AT&T. *Harvard Business Review,* 1973, **51** (January-February), 96–106.

Ford, R., and Borgatta, E. Satisfaction with the work itself. *Journal of Applied Psychology,* 1970, **53,** 128–134.

Garson, B. *All the Livelong Day: The Meaning and Demeaning of Routine Work.* New York: Doubleday & Company, 1975.

Hackman, J. R. Is job enrichment just a fad? *Harvard Business Review,* 1975, **53** (September-October), 129–138.

Herzberg, F. Motivator-hygiene profiles: Pinpointing what ails the organization. *Organizational Dynamics,* 1974, **3**(2), 18–29.

Lawler, E. E. *Pay and Organizational Effectiveness.* New York: McGraw-Hill, 1971.

Lawler, E. E. *Motivation in Work Organizations.* Monterey, Calif.: Brooks/Cole, 1973.

Locke, E. Personnel attitudes and motivation. *Annual Review of Psychology,* 1975, **26,** 457–480.

Locke, E. The nature and causes of job satisfaction. In M. Dunnette, Ed., *Handbook of Industrial and Organizational Psychology.* Chicago: Rand McNally, 1976. Pp. 1297–1349.

Maslow, A. *Motivation and Personality,* 2nd ed. New York: Harper & Row, 1970.

Meyer, H. The pay-for-performance dilemma. *Organizational Dynamics,* 1975, **3**(3), 39–50.

Miner, M. G., and Miner, J. B., Eds. *Policy Issues in Contemporary Personnel and Industrial Relations.* New York: Macmillan, 1977.

Notz, W. Work motivation and the negative effects of extrinsic rewards: A review with implications for theory and practice. *American Psychologist,* 1975, **30,** 884–891.

Quality of Work Program: The First Eighteen Months. Washington, D.C.: National Quality of Work Center, 1975.

Ronan, W. Individual and situational variables relating to job satisfaction. *Journal of Applied Psychology,* 1970, **54,** 1–31.

Rosen, R. The world of work through the eyes of the hard core. *Personnel Administration,* 1970, **33**(May), 8–21.

Rosow, J., Ed. *The Worker and the Job.* Englewood Cliffs, N.J.: Prentice-Hall, 1974.

Sandler, B. Eclecticism at work: Approaches to job design. *American Psychologist,* 1974, **29,** 767–773.

Scanlan, B. Determinants of job satisfaction and productivity. *Personnel Journal,* 1976, **55,** 12–14.

Schultz, D. Managing the middle-aged manager. *Personnel,* 1974, **51**(6), 8–17.

Scobel, D. Doing away with the factory blues. *Harvard Business Review,* 1975, **53**(6), 132–142.

Shapiro, H. Job motivations of males and females. *Psychological Reports,* 1975, **36,** 647–654.

Shapiro, H., and Stern, L. Job satisfaction: male and female, professional and non-professional workers. *Personnel Journal,* 1975, **54,** 388–389.

Sheppard, H., and Herrick, N. *Where Have All the Robots Gone? Worker Dissatisfaction in the '70s.* New York: The Free Press, 1972.

Steers, R. Effects of need for achievement on the job performance-job attitude relationship. *Journal of Applied Psychology,* 1975, **60,** 678–682.

Tregoe, B. Job enrichment: How to avoid the pitfalls. *Personnel Journal,* 1974, **53,** 445–449.

Wahba, M., and Bridwell, L. Maslow reconsidered: A review of research on the need hierarchy theory. In K. Wexley and G. Yukl, Eds., *Organizational Behavior and Industrial Psychology.* New York: Oxford University Press. Pp. 5–11.

Walters, R. et al. *Job Enrichment for Results: Strategies for Successful Implementation.* Reading, Mass.: Addison-Wesley, 1975.

Ward, E. Elements of an employee motivation program. *Personnel Journal,* 1974, **53,** 205–208.

Warr, P., Ed. *Personal Goals and Work Design.* New York: John Wiley & Sons, 1976.

Warr, P., and Wall, T. *Work and Well-Being.* Baltimore: Penguin Books, 1975.

Work in America. Cambridge, Mass.: MIT Press, 1973.

9

The Organization of the Organization

INTRODUCTION

All of us live and work within the framework of some kind of organization, a context that provides written and unwritten, formal and informal rules and guidelines about how its members should conduct themselves. As an everyday example, recall your childhood when you were growing up in an organization called a "family." A climate was established by your parents that defined the rules of surviving in the family; acceptable attitudes and values and behaviors blended to make your family a unique organization that was different from the families of your friends. Perhaps a family up the street had a personality based on orthodox religious beliefs and strict standards of behavior whereas a family down the street was moderate in its religious beliefs and raised its children permissively. These families functioned within different styles of organization; they established their own climate, expectations, fears, and values for the family members.

Various organizational styles are also evident in your classes. One professor may be stern, even dictatorial, allowing no student participation, and another may operate an open class in which students decide how the course is to be conducted.

Differences in organizational style occur in the work place. Some companies are rigid, hierarchical bureaucracies (such as the military) in which detailed rules and regulations prescribe what workers do and how they do it, and no deviation is tolerated. In fact, virtually all businesses were once organized along these tight bureaucratic lines.

In recent years, however, a new organizational style has developed as part of the general trend toward the humanization of work. This new look in organizational life is much less rigid and hierarchical. It treats workers as integral members of the organization and allows them to participate in the planning of the work that takes place. This is a radical shift in organizational structure and it is bringing about monumental changes in the nature of work. Indeed, the movement might well be called a revolutionary one.

To investigate these trends in organizational style, and to determine their impact on individual workers (and vice versa), the field of organizational psychology was begun. We have seen that leadership and motivational factors are important aspects of the organizational influence. In this chapter, we discuss the factor that most influences leadership and motivation—the organization of the organization.

CLASSIC VERSUS MODERN ORGANIZATIONAL STYLES

The two extremes in organizational style have previously been noted: the older bureaucratic style and the newer participatory style. There are many styles that incorporate aspects of both positions but we concentrate on the extremes, because the differences between them indicate clearly the changes that are currently taking place in the quality of working life. You should be aware of the influences of both styles for a practical reason. You will be working in one climate or another or some variation of them. As noted, most organizations are bureaucratic although a rapidly growing number of companies are experimenting with worker participation (often called "participatory democracy").

The Classic Organizational Style

Nowadays we think of bureaucracies in derisive terms as bloated, inefficient, grossly overorganized, highly structured, and wrapped in miles of red tape that prevents the accomplishment of anything creative or original. These bureaucracies represent a kind of system that exists everywhere but for which no one wants to work. And there is some truth to this attitude, as we well know from our everyday experiences trying to deal with bureaucracies.

Yet, it is interesting to remember that the introduction of the bureaucratic style of organization was once just as revolutionary as today's participative approach, and it was considered just as humanistic in its intentions. Bureaucracy was devised to improve the quality of working life.

As a movement of social protest, bureaucracy was designed to correct the inequities, favoritism, and downright cruelty that marked organizations at the beginning of the industrial revolution. Companies were owned and managed by their founders, and there were a great many abuses in the lives of the workers. The owner-managers had absolute control over the work place and employees were at the mercy of the owners' whims, biases, and subjective judgments.

To attempt to correct this deplorable situation, the German sociologist Max Weber proposed a new organizational style that would operate in a manner that was free of social and personal injustice.[1] Bureaucracy was to be a rational, formal structure in which the roles of managers and workers were rigidly defined. It would operate along impersonal and legal lines rather than personal and subjective ones, an orderly, predictable system in which all members knew their roles and their rules and abided by them. Like a machine, the bureaucratic organization would operate with precision and efficiency, uninfluenced by personal prejudice. Workers would have the opportunity to rise in the organization on the basis of their ability rather than as a result of social class or favoritism. Compared with the prior situation of workers, bureaucracy was a tremendous improvement and served, in its day, to humanize the work place.

Basically, the change in organizational style involved breaking down or decentralizing the organization into its component parts and operations, each of which is linked to the others in a rigid hierarchy of control. Weber described four dimensions by which the bureaucratic organization functioned: (1) division of labor, (2) delegation of authority, (3) span of control, and (4) structure.

Recall that the essence of the bureaucratic organization is its reduction to a number of component units. This specialization characterizes the administration of the organization as well as the actual work performed. Different work units were established to manufacture different products or different parts of the same product. Thus, *division of labor* entered the world of work, a concept later fostered by scientific management and technological developments, notably the assembly line. Jobs tended to become simpler and more highly specialized. Therefore, a new system of managing or coordinating work and its administration had to be developed. With increasing specialization of functions, no individual could hope to oversee it all, so leadership and management also needed to become specialized. Authority had to be delegated to a series of interconnecting smaller units.

Delegation of authority meant that for each activity in the organization, one person had to be responsible, and this responsibility was not

[1] M. Weber, *The Theory of Social and Economic Organization* (New York: Oxford University Press, 1947).

to be shared or overlapped with anyone else's area of responsibility. Also, every member of the organization would report to only one superior. All communication would flow to, through, and from that superior, effectively cutting the worker off from contact with other levels of the organization. Communication, like management and the performance of the job itself, became specialized or fragmented.

Division of labor and delegation of authority can be seen clearly in the graphic portrayal of organizational life known as the *organization chart*. It shows vividly the nature and structure of a bureaucracy (Figure 9–1).

In Figure 9–1, the delegation of authority is represented by the vertical dimension. Level A (the top position) has four subordinates, each of whom has five subordinates. Authority is delegated downward and, in this example, each step down in the hierarchy is accompanied by a larger number of subordinates. The degree of specialization or division of labor is represented by the horizontal dimension. Each unit of five positions in Level C is separate (administratively and in terms of function) from the other units on that level.

The chart shows the organization reduced to its component parts, each administered separately, with each higher level of management responsible for coordinating the activities of larger numbers of component parts. Lines of communication are clear. Employees in Level C can communicate upward only through their supervisor in Level B, and receive communications downward in the same way.

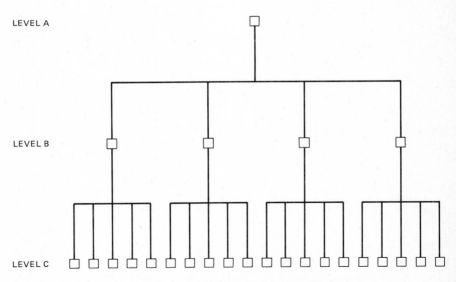

Figure 9–1. A typical bureaucratic organization.

An organization chart also portrays the other bureaucratic dimensions: span of control and structure. *Span of control* refers to the number of people a supervisor controls. There is, of course, a limit to how many subordinates a supervisor can effectively manage. One individual cannot direct the work of two hundred people meaningfully, not without an intervening level of managers, each of whom is responsible for a much smaller number of subordinates. Organizational theorists have focused a great deal of effort on determining the optimum span of control, and although the issue is not fully settled, five to seven subordinates seem to be the most satisfactory.

Structure refers basically to the relative height and width of an organization. The organization in Figure 9–1 is wide in structure but not very tall; that is, its span of control is wide and the levels of authority in it are few. A different structure is shown in Figure 9–2. In this case, the span of control is narrow (no one manages more than two subordinates), and there are many levels of authority. Obviously, organizations with different purposes—such as a manufacturing plant and a research laboratory—lend themselves to different structures. However, the principles of the bureaucratic organization were meant to apply to all organizations, to maximize their productive efficiency.

Organization charts look nice and give some managers the feeling

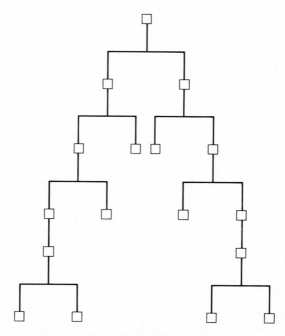

Figure 9–2. A tall organizational structure.

that everyone is in his or her proper place and the mechanism of the organization is running smoothly. However, neat lines and boxes on paper do not always apply to daily operations on the job. There is an organization within the organization—an uncharted complex of informal social groups of workers that can sabotage the most rigid rules of the most dictatorial organization. Often, it is through these informal links that the real work of an organization gets done (or undone).

The major problem with a bureaucratic organization, then, is that no matter how rationally it is designed, how ideal its span of control and structure, how specialized the work, and how well delegated the authority, human beings do not always abide by the formal structure. To explain why they do not, let us examine the criticisms that have emerged over the years against this classic form of organization.

Criticisms of Bureaucracy

The major complaint about bureaucratic organizations is that they ignore human values and needs. They treat employees as blocks on an organization chart, as interchangeable as the machinery they operate. As a result, bureaucracy allows no opportunity for personal growth or self-actualization, both of which are important human motivations.

Individuals are lost in a bureaucracy and have no separate identities. In addition, they have no control over any aspect of work or of the organizational policies that affect the quality of their working life. The ideal employee in a bureaucratic system is docile, passive, and dependent, rather like a child in its relationship to its parents. Decisions are made for them—"for their own good"—because they are not considered capable of deciding for themselves.

Not only are bureaucracies criticized for their stultifying effects on workers but also for their harmful effects on themselves. Just as they prevent personal growth, so do bureaucracies prevent (or minimize) growth on the corporate level. Bureaucracies represent and foster stability, rigidity, and permanence. Therefore, they do not adapt well or quickly to changing social conditions or to technological innovations. New developments are viewed as threats to the orderly structure of the organization, which is more interested in preserving the existing conditions.

Of course, bureaucracies can and do change, but the process of change is slow and difficult. The only way in which change can be introduced is from the top, initiated by the highest leaders. And this change is then imposed by absolute authority from each level of management to the one beneath it. There is no possibility of input from those most directly affected.

In sum, the bureaucratic style of organization, for all of its revolutionary fervor and humanistic intentions, has not been an overwhelming success in terms of satisfying human needs, yet it continues to characterize most business and government organizations today.

Modern Organization Theory

Classic organization theory depicted organizations as systems running automatically, uninfluenced by individual employee-members. The focus was on the functioning total organism (the system) with no consideration of the individuals who comprised the system. It may be analogous to considering the human body solely as a global system, taking no account of the organs of which the body is composed.

Modern organization theory focuses on the individual workers who make up the corporate body. This approach believes that the organization is a reflection and composite of its members and that it is necessary to understand their behavior before attempting to understand the behavior of the organization as a whole. This focus—on the intellectual, emotional, and motivational aspects of human beings—was missing from the classic organizational approach. Thus, topics such as attitudes toward work, job satisfaction, motivation, and psychological aspects of leadership are recognized as being capable of influencing the form and functions of the organization.

This does not mean that modern organization theory ignores the characteristics and needs of the organization as a whole. Rather, these organizational factors are believed to arise from, and be related to, the psychological aspects of the employees (their abilities, characteristics, and needs).

How does modern organization theory apply to reality? To what kind of organization does it lead? We noted that a major criticism of bureaucratic organizations is their tendency to dehumanize workers, to treat them as docile, passive, and dependent. Modern organization theory takes quite a different view of human nature, which is perhaps best summarized by the Theory Y position in McGregor's Theory X/Theory Y formulation (see Chapter 7).

Theory X described a view of human nature that is compatible with the rigid requirements of a bureaucracy. Workers needed a controlling, dictatorial kind of leadership because they were seen as incapable of doing anything on their own. Theory Y, on the other hand, assumed that human beings are highly motivated on their own to seek and accept responsibility in their work. Theory Y also assumed a high level of creativity, commitment, and need for personal growth.

In the Theory Y viewpoint, bureaucratic organizations stifle the individual's high level of motivation and potential for growth. Modern organization theory, building on the work of McGregor and others, holds that the organization must decrease worker dependency, subordination, and submissiveness in order to take full advantage of human potential. Jobs and organizations must be designed less rigidly, allowing opportunity for the workers themselves to determine how best to perform the work. Jobs must be expanded and enriched, increasing the workers' sense of challenge and responsibility. Leadership must become less autocratic and more responsive to input from workers. All members of the organization must be allowed to participate in decision making. Organizations, as a whole, must become more flexible, altering in form and function in response to worker needs and social, technological, and economic forces.

Some of these ideas have been put into practice. In Chapter 8, we noted successful job enlargement programs that have brought a greater sense of freedom to the work place. In Chapter 7, we discussed participatory democracy as a force in organizational leadership. Workers are insisting upon a chance to participate in shaping company policy instead of having to follow orders unquestioningly (and often rebelliously).

In short, the modern organizational style calls for the following: (1) enrichment, enlargement, and expansion of jobs; (2) active worker participation in policy making at all levels (in West Germany and Sweden this already includes the board of directors level); and (3) as a result, greater opportunity for individual expression, creativity, and personal fulfillment.

Conditions for Worker Participation

In order for worker participation to be maximally effective, several psychological and social conditions must be satisfied.[2]

1. Employees must be able to become psychologically involved with the participation. They must fully understand the meaning and the implications of their actions and deal with events and processes in a realistic and objective fashion.

[2] R. Tannenbaum and F. Massarik, "Participation by subordinates." In R. Tannenbaum, I. Weschler, and F. Massarik, *Leadership and Organization: A Behavioral Science Approach* (New York: McGraw-Hill, 1961), pp. 96–100.

2. Employees must be in agreement with the idea of participation. Those who believe that "the boss always knows best" or that they have no business being involved with decision making, will not be highly motivated to participate.
3. Employees must see that the kinds of decisions being considered are personally important and relevant. They must know how their own jobs and the quality of their everyday working lives will be directly affected by the decisions in which they are invited to participate.
4. Employees must be able to express themselves effectively and feel that they are actually contributing to the decision-making process. They must be articulate and possess some experience on which to draw in the matter under consideration.

Another set of conditions for effective participation deals with external conditions that can determine if it is desirable (or possible) to use worker participation in a given situation:

1. Is there sufficient time to permit group decision making? Employee participation in decision making is time-consuming, more so than having a manager make the decision for the group. If a decision must be reached immediately, there may not be sufficient time for the mechanics of group participation.
2. The financial cost of employee participation must not be so high that it will cancel out the advantages. Because employee participation takes time from actual work, the cost of that lost production must enter into the decision to institute or expand worker participation.
3. Employees must feel safe from retribution for their participation. It must be made clear to them that no matter what they say, their rank, salary, and job will not be jeopardized.
4. Employee participation must not threaten to undermine the authority or perceived competence of managers. The fact that employees are participating in decisions that were once made solely by managers must not cause employees to feel that they are now managers, or cause managers to feel that their authority has been taken away.
5. Effective channels of communication must be opened through which employees can readily participate in decision making. These communication channels must be convenient and easy to use.
6. Effective employee participation requires some training so that employees understand the format and the purpose of the participative process.

Examples of Employee Participation

At a coal mining company in Pennsylvania, the workers participated in the redesign of the way in which their work was to be accomplished. In the new approach, work teams were formed that operated without a supervisor. Team members rotated jobs periodically. Supervisors, who no longer had the job of overseeing the work, concentrated on safety. The miners were paid at the highest wage rate but the cost of mining coal dropped by one third.

Workers and management at a company in Tennessee that manufactures automobile mirrors developed a program that allowed workers to go home or to take courses given at the plant if they completed their production quota for the day in less than eight hours. They were paid for the full eight hours regardless of the time they actually worked, as long as they made their quota.

The owner of an appliance store in California gave employees what may be the ultimate in decision-making power. He told them to set their own salaries, number of hours of work each week, and time off. Some employees raised their salaries considerably, but, in return, worked harder than ever before. Some workers took no pay increase at all. Why? One replied, "I don't want to work that hard."

As a result of their full participation in the decisions that directly affected them, the employees in the California appliance store developed a strong sense of responsibility and sensitivity to the business. A fourteen-year employee said, "You have to use common sense; no one wins if you end up closing the business down. If you want more money, you have to produce more. It can't work any other way." Company profits have increased in the five years the plan has been in operation, there has been no employee turnover, little absenteeism or tardiness, and no employee theft (always a problem in retail businesses). In addition, all employees now work fewer hours; they decided that they didn't want to work evenings or Sundays. As a result, the owner closes the store evenings and on Sundays; it turned out that he didn't want to work those hours either.[3]

To demonstrate the extent of the employee participation movement, consider two examples from Western Europe. In an ink-making plant in Denmark, employees met with the engineers and architects who were designing the company's new plant. The employees were given the opportunity of telling the planners how their individual

---

[3] See M. Koughan, "Arthur Friedman's outrage: Employees decide their pay," *Washington Post*, February 23, 1975, pp. C1, C8. Partially reprinted in F. Landy and D. Trumbo, *Psychology of Work Behavior* (Homewood, Ill.: Dorsey Press, 1976), pp. 319–321.

work stations should be designed for greater efficiency, safety, and attractiveness.

In the two years that the new facility has been in use, productivity has more than doubled. In fact, productivity rose 20 per cent at the old plant before the move to the new plant was made, even though a lot of work time was devoted to planning the new facility instead of making ink. Turnover in the new plant was cut from 80 per cent to 10 per cent, and absenteeism, previously as high as 30 per cent, is now almost nonexistent.

One problem did, however, result from the employees' participation: they wanted more of it. Once they had moved to the new facility, the workers in the Danish ink-making plant wanted to be consulted by management on all company decisions. When the company arbitrarily introduced some new equipment, the workers resented not being asked for their advice. An executive said, "Once you start with industrial democracy there is no way of going back." The company now lets employees decide work scheduling and other matters without management control.

An engineering firm in France opened its plant to employee participation from the top level on down. The board of directors is composed of equal numbers of shareholders, managers, and workers. In every unit of the organization there is full and free communication and participation in every decision. All company departments as well as individual work groups operate with autonomy. Employees are consulted on everything from the color of the walls to the design of new products.

The production workers are organized into autonomous groups of five to twelve members. Each group decides on its membership and how its work should be accomplished and in what order the various projects should be undertaken. The group, rather than a supervisor, is responsible for itself and has the power to expel a member who does not do a fair share of the work.

Workers are kept fully informed on every aspect of the organization, including financial matters and the topics discussed at the monthly board of directors meeting.

The company considers education to be an important facet of open communication and of value for increasing originality and creativity. As a result, a portion of the corporate profits is devoted to free courses for employees.

This approach is vastly different from the classic bureaucratic style of organization. But whereas participatory democracy represents a growing movement, it is still the exception in corporate life today. Some people hail the trend as a cure for all organizational ills, but much research is first needed to identify specific aspects of participatory democracy that are responsible for the changes in worker behavior reported thus far. In addition, long-term research is needed to determine how lasting these changes may be. There is not sufficient evidence to conclude that participatory democracy works in all situations. Although it does seem to increase job satisfaction, participatory democracy does not always lead to greater productivity.

There are additional questions about the future of this movement. Will workers, given some degree of participation in decision making, always insist on still greater participation? Will it end in a struggle for ultimate control of the organization or in a new form of dual management?

These questions notwithstanding, the idea of greater worker involvement is an exciting trend in today's world of work.

THE INTRODUCTION OF CHANGE IN ORGANIZATIONS

The classic bureaucratic organization is resistant to change. By emphasizing stability and permanence of structure, bureaucracies are not able to adapt quickly or easily to social and technological changes. Yet organizations, like biological species, must adapt in order to survive. Companies that produced buggy whips went out of business when they did not react to the declining demand for their product. Therefore, organizations must be able to change. How is such change best brought about and how can resistance to change be handled?

When a change is to be introduced into an organization, it is often met with a variety of negative reactions: slowdown in productivity, strikes, hostile and sullen worker behavior, and increased turnover and absenteeism. Whether the change is new equipment, an altered work procedure, revised location and layout of work space, new job titles, or reassignment of personnel, it will usually be met, at first, with some resistance.

This need not always be the case, however. Some organizations are able to introduce changes with the full cooperation and support of the employees. The factor that most determines whether a change will be received positively or negatively seems to be the manner in which the change is introduced. Not surprisingly, allowing employees who will be affected by the change to participate in decisions involving it minimizes the resistance.

In a classic study of this problem, machine operators in a clothing factory were studied for their reaction to a small change in work procedures.[4] The experimenters divided the workers into four groups who differed in terms of how the change was introduced to them. Group I was the no-participation group; the workers were told about the new work procedures but were given no say in the process. In Group II, representatives of the workers met with management to discuss the change. In Groups III and IV, workers were allowed to participate fully with management in implementing the change.

The reaction of Group I to the change was very negative. Production by the members of the group dropped immediately by one third, there were marked expressions of hostility and resentment, and 17 per cent of the group quit within forty days. There was no hostility in Groups III and IV, and none of the workers quit. Production in these groups dropped initially but quickly rose to a level higher than before. Allowing participation through representatives (Group II) was not as effective as full participation by all the workers involved. Clearly, participatory democracy was the best method of overcoming resistance to change, a finding that has been subsequently verified by other studies.

Are these positive effects permanent or do they disappear after the researchers leave? To investigate this question, two psychologists visited a plant four and one-half years after it had undergone a radical change from a centralized, authoritarian, classic bureaucratic organization to a flexible, innovative, fully participative one.[5] The change had been guided primarily by the company president (also a psychologist) and was very successful in terms of productive efficiency and employee satisfaction. The effort is considered a model of how to change an organization effectively.

The visiting psychologists found that the benefits were visible four and one-half years later. In fact, on a number of variables, the effects were even greater than during the period right after the change was first introduced. Table 9–1 shows employee attitudes measured in 1962 before the change was introduced, in 1964 after the change was made, and in 1969 during the follow–up study.

Only two factors (satisfied with supervisor, and plan to stay indefinitely) showed a decline from 1962 to 1969, although these factors are still at high levels.

Other items showed that the general increase in job satisfaction was accompanied by an increase in the workers' concern with production. Also, the company rose from a position of loss in 1962 to one of substantial return on investment by 1964. By 1968 (the last year of record), the company's profits were still increasing.

[4] L. Coch and J. French, Jr., "Overcoming resistance to change," Human Relations, 1(4) (1948), 512–532.

[5] S. E. Seashore and D. G. Bowers, "Durability of organizational change," American Psychologist, 25 (1970), 227–233.

TABLE 9–1

CHANGES IN JOB ATTITUDES

Item	1962 (%)*	1964 (%)	1969 (%)
Company better than most	22	28	36
Own work satisfying	77	84	91
Satisfied with pay system	22	27	28
Company tries to maintain earnings	26	44	41
Satisfied with supervisor	64	54	54
Like fellow employees	85	86	85
Group cohesiveness	25	25	30
Plan to stay indefinitely	72	87	66
Expect future improvement in situation	23	31	43

* Per cent of employees giving favorable responses to questionnaire items about these issues. From S. E. Seashore and D. G. Bowers, "Durability of organizational change," *American Psychologist,* **25**(1970), p. 229. Copyright 1970 by the American Psychological Association. Reprinted by permission.

An organizational change, then, can have long-lasting effects, but these effects are not static. Positive benefits can continue to accrue as a result of the new organizational climate.

These examples illustrate both change in one part of an organization and change in an entire organizational structure. In recent years, attention has been focused on total-organization change. This effort is known as *organizational development* (OD).

OD is a combination of techniques including sensitivity training, role playing, group discussion, and job enrichment. It takes a global or systems approach to an organization, is usually a long-range effort, and operates under a set of assumptions about human nature closely resembling those of McGregor's Theory Y.

OD is usually carried out by consultants called *change agents*. Since they are outsiders, the change agents have the advantage of not being biased by the company's existing social climate and are thus able to view the organization with greater objectivity. Change agents' first task is diagnosis, to find out, through questionnaires and interviews, the organization's present and future problems. They evaluate the organization's weaknesses and strengths, and then work out in considerable detail strategies and techniques designed to solve the problems.

Next in the OD process is the implementation of the recommended strategies, a process known as *intervention,* which begins at the highest management level. Experience has demonstrated that unless organizational changes enjoy the full support of top management, their chances of succeeding are slim.

In actual application, OD varies as a function of the nature of the change agent, the problems facing the organization, and the nature of the organization itself. In other words, OD is flexible in its operation, adapting to the needs of each organizational situation. One generalization can be made: Since most organizations are still classic bureaucracies, OD does serve to free the total organization from rigidity and formality of structure, thereby allowing more flexible and open participation.

THE ORGANIZATION WITHIN THE ORGANIZATION

Within every organization—whatever its style or form—cohesive informal groups develop. Extensive research in social and organizational psychology has shown that these informal work groups have tremendous power in shaping attitudes, behavior, and, consequently, production.

Every group of people that meets periodically, no matter how informal or loosely structured it may be, develops communal norms—a shared set of beliefs, values, and socially acceptable behaviors. In other words, group members come to think and act in similar ways, and this encourages feelings of closeness among them.

In industry, at every level of organizational life, employees band together in informal groups and develop a common set of norms. It is important to remember that these groups are not established by management. They are generally beyond the control of management and they do not appear on organization charts.

What happens when new workers are hired and placed to work in the midst of an existing informal group? In time—usually a very short time—the new workers adopt the characteristics of the group. The group teaches them (in ways sometimes subtle and sometimes direct) their way of thinking and behaving, and demands conformity.

The importance of this for organizational psychology is that the group determines for new employees how they will feel about management and about all other aspects of organizational life. The influence of informal work groups is pervasive, and they are a vital part of the total organizational environment. They can work for or against management by encouraging cooperation and increasing production or by sabotaging management and slowing production.

An Informal Group in Action

For an example of an informal work group, recall the Hawthorne studies. A major finding of this research program was the revelation of the ways in which these groups operate. The existence of informal groups was known thirty years before the Hawthorne studies, but this classic research provided the first empirical evidence on their nature.

The study involved fourteen men working in the bank wiring room of the Western Electric plant who were observed for six months. The observer was present every day and succeeded in gaining acceptance. He was known not to be working for the company and tried to become as much like the workers as possible in speech and behavior. After about three weeks, the workers felt comfortable with the observer and behaved as they had before the observation began.

It was soon noticed that the group had its own standards of behavior and production. The men shared many interests in their conversations, engaged in rough but friendly play or pranks, and were always ready to help one another in their work. They formed a close-knit group and displayed many of the characteristics of a family. They valued the friendship and acceptance of the others and avoided doing anything that might bring disapproval from the group.

The most dramatic impact of the group was its determination of a fair and safe day's level of production. Management had set a standard daily output with an incentive to be paid for meeting and exceeding that level. Thus, a worker could make more money by working faster; management thought this would guarantee maximum production. However, the workers as a group had a different idea about production and had set its own standard that never exceeded the company's level. Believing that if they consistently met or exceeded management's standard, the company would reduce the rate and force them to work harder, the group set a leisurely, easily attainable production rate, willing to forego the temptation of extra money. (And this study was conducted during the Great Depression of the 1930s.)

Some men worked fast in the morning hours, then slowed down during the afternoon; others worked at a slower pace all day. On some days the group completed extra work but saved it for a day when production might be lower. If a worker did not feel well, the others would work harder to take up the slack. Sometimes they reported more production than they had actually accomplished but, over the course of a week, they would plan it so as to achieve their standard.

The men readily admitted to the observer that they could produce more (and thus make more money), but to do so would have defied the group's norms, and the group had effective (and accepted) ways of enforcing the norms. Anyone who worked too slow (unless he was ill) or too fast, was subjected to name-calling ("rate buster," "speed king," "slave"). Deviants were also "binged" (hit hard on the muscles of the upper arm). A new worker quickly learned what was expected—what behaviors would be tolerated and what would not. The group assumed such stature in the workers' daily lives that they considered group acceptance more important than the extra money that could have been earned.

It is interesting that the management of the company was ignorant of the existence of these informal work groups until informed by the researchers.

Nature of Informal Groups

Informal groups exist in virtually every type of organization, setting and enforcing their own standards of behavior and production. They are characterized by intimate face-to-face interactions occurring over an extended period of time. The members must meet frequently in order for the closeness and communality to develop. They have a common identity (such as workers in the same department of the plant) and a central focus. Such groups are not too large since they require direct and frequent personal contact. (Usually, the larger the group, the less personal and direct is the contact among members.)

Most people have a need for affiliation and companionship, and this can be satisfied by the informal group. But the informal work group does more than provide a sense of identity and belonging; it can help workers perform their jobs by defining how to work and how much to work.

The group also protects workers; the strength of numbers can help them resist management demands better than can an individual alone. Thus, there are many reasons why workers may seem loyal to the point of subservience to their informal work group.

The group norms and standards pervade other aspects of life, not just how fast the members work. The group can influence political and racial attitudes, voting decisions, consumer behavior, style of dress, what to eat for lunch, and even where to go on vacation.

Because group membership is so pervasive and satisfies so many needs, individuals place a high premium on being accepted and liked by the other members of the group. As a result, deviant behavior is rarely encountered except with new workers who need a little time to learn the group's ways.

Teaching and enforcing these expectations proceeds in three stages. First, new workers are told what the situation is, what the group does and likes, and, most important, what it will not tolerate. Second, new workers are observed to see how well they are conforming. As with any learning process, people are apt to make mistakes and when this happens the group is ready with a warning and perhaps additional instruction. Third, after an appropriate period of time (the length of which is another group standard) new workers have either conformed or have not and appropriate rewards or punishments are accorded. It has happened that nonconforming workers were made so uncomfortable that they transferred to other departments or quit. Social ostracism—being the lone outcast in a group with which one must spend forty hours a week—is a painful experience that few can tolerate.

The degree of closeness of a group is known as *group cohesiveness*. The greater the cohesiveness, the greater are the power of the group over its members and the pressure on them to conform. Several factors influence cohesiveness. In general, cohesiveness declines as the group gets larger, since there is less opportunity for frequent direct contact and more opportunity for the formation of subgroups or competing groups. Diversity of backgrounds, interests, and life-styles can greatly reduce cohesiveness. A work team composed of employees of similar ethnic and religious background who live in the same neighborhood will be more cohesive than a team composed of diverse ethnic groups, races, or life-styles.

The nature of the work can also influence group cohesiveness. For example, a wage incentive system that rewards on an individual rather than on a team basis can reduce feelings of closeness among group members. Individual reward systems induce competition among workers; team rewards bring about cooperation—everyone works together for a common goal.

Outside pressure or threat affects group cohesiveness. Just as a nation under attack will usually pull together and submerge individual or regional differences, so will a small work group faced with a situation such as an unfair supervisor. Indeed, few things can unite a group faster than shared hatred of a superior.

Another characteristic of informal work groups is leadership. Inevitably, one person emerges as a leader, usually someone who conforms closely to the group's norms. If the leader is effective, however, he or she is capable of changing those norms. Thus, although the organization chart may show that employees work for the company foreman, their own group leader may well have more influence over them.

Informal Groups and Management

There are many opportunities for conflict between the needs and goals of the informal work group and the needs and goals of the organization. In the Hawthorne study, the workers met their own production standard rather than the one set by the company. And, in that example, there was no evidence of hostility toward the company. Had hostility existed, production would probably have been lower or of poorer quality.

If management is to deal effectively with informal groups, it must recognize their existence and try to understand them. Also, supervisors—the representatives of management closest to these groups—must recognize, respect, and, to some degree, accept the group's standards, and must, in turn, be accepted by these informal groups. Supervisors should be both the formal leaders of the departments or sections and informal leaders as well. This is part of the thin line of leadership the first-line supervisors must walk, balancing the needs of the organization with the needs of the workers. If supervisors lose the balance in either direction, they have failed.

A proper rapport between first-line supervisors and informal group leaders is essential since the latter influence the group to either cooperate with, or obstruct, management goals. When cooperation between formal and informal groups can be accomplished, it is usually followed by increases in morale and production, and decreases in absenteeism and turnover.

A pervasive and powerful condition of work, the informal group serves many needs of the workers. It can serve the needs of the organization as well, or it can defeat them.

SUMMARY

All work occurs within some sort of social-psychological organization. Whether the organization is **formal** or **informal,** it dictates ways of behaving, thinking, and feeling to its members. As such, the organization is a powerful influence in the world of work. The field of **organizational psychology** is concerned with the study of various organizational climates and styles and the ways in which these affect the worker on the job.

The two basic organizational styles, **classic** and **modern,** differ in terms of degree of control, rigidity, permanence of structure, and amount of worker participation.

The clearest example of the classic style of organization is the **bureaucracy,** once a humanistic social protest movement against the dictatorial management systems at the beginning of the industrial revolution. Proposed by Max Weber, bureaucracy was intended to be a rational structure in which rules of conduct and lines of authority were rigidly drawn, and in which personal bias and prejudice had no place.

Bureaucracy has four major dimensions: (1) **division of labor** (making jobs simpler and more highly specialized), (2) **delegation of authority** (decentralizing management into small units), (3) **span of control** (number of workers for whom each manager is responsible), and (4) **structure** (height and width of the organization as depicted by an organization chart).

Criticisms of bureaucracies include the charge that they ignore the human element—the worker's values, needs, and motivations. Employees are seen as interchangeable units, passive and dependent on the organization with neither the ability nor the desire to have any say over the conditions of their working lives. Bureaucracies are also criticized for their insistence on rigidity and permanence, making them generally impervious to change. They do not adapt well to changing social or technological innovations.

Modern organization theory, by contrast, focuses on the individual human beings who comprise an organization. It is concerned with the intellectual, emotional, and motivational characteristics of employees. Based on McGregor's Theory Y assumptions about human nature, modern organization theory argues that an organization must enrich and enlarge jobs and workers' opportunities to express their full human potential. To accomplish this, job enlargement, less autocratic leadership, and participation by workers in decision making at all levels of the organization are favored.

Several conditions must be satisfied if **worker participation** in decision making is to be effective: (1) employees must be psychologically involved in participation, (2) employees must be in agreement with the idea of participation, (3) decisions must be viewed as personally relevant to employees, (4) employees must have the ability and experience to express themselves, (5) there must be sufficient time to permit decision making by employees, (6) the cost of participation must not be prohibitive, (7) employees must be safe from retribution, (8) participation must not undermine management, (9) efficient channels of communication must be provided, and (10) employees must be trained in the participative process.

A problem faced by many organizations is employee resistance when a new work method, piece of equipment, or other change is introduced. However, it has been demonstrated that when workers are allowed to participate fully in decisions concerning the change, they will enthusiastically support it. This positive effect of worker participation has been shown to last more than four years after the introduction of a major change.

A series of techniques for successfully introducing large-scale organizational changes is **organizational development** (OD). The process is carried out by consultants (change agents) who diagnose the organization's problems and devise appropriate strategies to eliminate them. The implementation of those strategies is called **intervention,** which operates throughout the organization, usually beginning with top management. Most OD programs, though differing in their particulars, are oriented toward making the organization less rigid in structure and more openly participative.

In every organization, **informal work groups** develop that exert considerable influence on employee attitudes and behavior on the job. Beyond the control of management, these informal groups have their own standards of conduct in regard to production levels and relations with management. Often, the ideals and standards of these groups conflict with those of the formal organization. New employees who do not conform to the group norms may be ostracized.

SUGGESTED READINGS

Bass, B., and Deep, S. *Studies in Organizational Psychology.* Boston: Allyn & Bacon, 1972.

Beer, M. The technology of organizational development. In M. Dunnette, Ed., *Handbook of Industrial and Organizational Psychology.* Chicago: Rand McNally, 1976. Pp. 937–993.

Behling, O., and Schriesheim, C. *Organizational Behavior: Theory, Research, and Application.* Boston: Allyn & Bacon, 1976.

Bowers, D. OD techniques and their results in 23 organizations. *Journal of Applied Behavioral Science,* 1973, **9,** 21–43.

Dalton, G., Lawrence, P., and Lorsch, J., Eds. *Organizational Structure and Design.* Homewood, Ill.: Richard D. Irwin, 1970.

DuBrin, A. J. *Fundamentals of Organizational Behavior: An Applied Perspective.* Elmsford, N.Y.: Pergamon Press, 1974.

DuBrin, A. J. *Casebook of Organizational Behavior.* Elmsford, N.Y.: Pergamon Press, 1977.

Foy, N., and Gadon, H. Worker participation: Contrasts in 3 countries. *Harvard Business Review,* 1976, **54** (May–June), 71–83.

French, W., and Bell, C. *Organization Development.* Englewood Cliffs, N.J.: Prentice–Hall, 1973.

Friedlander, F., and Brown, L. D. Organization development. *Annual Review of Psychology,* 1974, **25,** 313–341.

Hackman, J. R. Group influences on individuals. In M. Dunnette, Ed., *Handbook of Industrial and Organizational Psychology.* Chicago: Rand McNally, 1976. Pp. 1455–1525.

Hackman, J. R., Lawler, E. E., and Porter, L. W. *Perspectives on Behavior in Organizations.* New York: McGraw–Hill, 1977.

Hall, R. *Organizations: Structure and Process.* Englewood Cliffs, N.J.: Prentice–Hall, 1972.

Heller, F. A., and Clark, A. W. Personnel and human resources development. *Annual Review of Psychology,* 1976, **27,** 405–435.

James, L., and Jones, A. Organizational climate: A review of theory and research. *Psychological Bulletin,* 1974, **81,** 1096–1112.

Kolb, D. A., Rubin, I. M., and McIntyre, J. M., Eds. *Organizational Psychology: A Book of Readings,* 2nd ed. Englewood Cliffs, N.J.: Prentice–Hall, 1974.

Kolb, D. A., Rubin, I. M., and McIntyre, J. M. *Organizational Psychology: An Experiential Approach,* 2nd ed. Englewood Cliffs, N.J.: Prentice–Hall, 1974.

Lichtman, C., and Hunt, R. Personality and organization theory: A review of some conceptual literature. *Psychological Bulletin,* 1971, **76,** 271–294.

Margulies, N., and Wallace, J. *Organizational Change: Techniques and Applications.* Glenview, Ill.: Scott, Foresman, 1973.

Payne, R., and Pugh, D. Organizational structure and climate. In M. Dunnette, Ed., *Handbook of Industrial and Organizational Psychology.* Chicago: Rand McNally, 1976. Pp. 1125–1173.

Porter, L. W., and Roberts, K. Communication in organizations. In M. Dunnette, Ed., *Handbook of Industrial and Organizational Psychology.* Chicago: Rand McNally, 1976. Pp. 1553–1589.

Porter, L. W., Lawler, E. E., and Hackman, J. R. *Behavior in Organizations.* New York: McGraw–Hill, 1975.

Pritchard, R., and Karasik, B. Effects of organizational climate. *Organizational Behavior and Human Performance,* 1973, **9,** 126–146.

Schein, E. *Organizational Psychology,* 2nd ed. Englewood Cliffs, N.J.: Prentice–Hall, 1972.

Scott, W. E., and Cummings, L. L., Eds. *Readings in Organizational Behavior and Human Performance,* rev. ed. Homewood, Ill.: Richard D. Irwin, 1973.

Starbuck, W. Organizations and their environments. In M. Dunnette, Ed., *Handbook of Industrial and Organizational Psychology.* Chicago: Rand McNally, 1976. Pp. 1069–1123.

Wieland, G. F., and Ullrich, R. A. *Organizations: Behavior, Design, and Change.* Homewood, Ill.: Richard D. Irwin, 1976.

THE WORK PLACE

We discussed in the last section the effects of the social and psychological climates in which work takes place. The form of the organization, both in its formal and informal structures, the style of leadership, and the motivations of the employees, all influence the levels of productivity and of job satisfaction.

We turn now to a consideration of more tangible factors that form a part of the immediate work place. Work is strongly influenced by physical factors such as the design and layout of a work station; the levels of light, heat, and noise; and also by the number of hours spent working. In addition, the work place can be affected by accidents that occur in the course of a job and by the physical condition of the workers, specifically, if they are under the influence of alcohol or drugs.

You know from your own experience how important the physical environment is in your work. Think of how difficult it is to pay attention to a lecture if the classroom is very hot or the lights are dim, and how hard it is for you to write a term paper if your desk is cluttered with your roommate's clothes or if the room is too noisy.

Many tangible factors in the world of work influence job performance and satisfaction. These factors can lead to poor quality work, irritability, fatigue, boredom, monotony, accidents, and a host of other effects that are detrimental to the quality of working life.

Psychologists have long been interested in these physical aspects of the work place. Research and application efforts have helped to reduce their harmful effects. Industrial psychology has been influential in designing comfortable, safe, and efficient places and tools of work. From high-rise office buildings to assembly lines, psychologists are involved in all facets of the work place, an involvement that will make your own work in the future easier and more productive.

Chapter 10 deals with a number of conditions of work, including the effects of light, noise, temperature, color, and music. The temporal conditions of work—the number of hours worked and how these hours are arranged—are discussed, along with the boredom and monotony produced by some working conditions.

Chapter 11 is concerned with the tools, equipment, and layout of work stations. The field of engineering psychology involves the design of machinery used by human operators, from a factory tool to the cockpit of a jet airplane. The goal of engineering psychology is to provide the best possible coordination and integration of the capabilities and limitations of humans and machines.

Three serious problems that affect the work place—accidents, alcohol, and drugs—are discussed in Chapter 12. Accidents are a major problem in some industries (and in many aspects of life) and psychologists are involved in determining causes of accidents and ways to prevent them. The addictions to alcohol or drugs represent personal tragedies as well as personnel problems. Many organizations try to help addicted individuals, a responsibility in which psychologists are heavily involved.

No matter what kind of work you do, you will see the effects of the work of industrial psychologists as they try to improve the place at which you perform your job.

10

Conditions of Work

INTRODUCTION

We are all aware of the fact that the conditions under which we attempt to accomplish something can greatly influence the efficiency and rapidity of our efforts. Whether we are trying to study, read, change a tire, or work on an assembly line, the immediate environment affects our motivation· to perform the task as well as our actual ability. Is it too hot or too cold? Too noisy or too quiet? Too lonely or too distracting? Is the room or plant depressing in its appearance and inconvenient in its physical arrangement? Is the task boring and repetitive, or demanding and exciting? Can you work in your own way or must you follow the procedures dictated by your supervisor?

These are just some of the conditions that facilitate or hinder workers in the performance of their jobs. A company can select the best employees, train them thoroughly for the job, provide them with top supervisors and an optimal organizational climate—all necessary factors for maximizing production—but, if the physical working conditions are inadequate, production will suffer.

Beginning with the classic Hawthorne studies, industrial psychologists have conducted extensive research programs on all aspects of the physical work environment. Factors such as temperature, humidity, lighting, noise level, and hours of work have been examined in a variety of work settings. Guidelines for the optimal level or range of each of these factors have been established. Much is now known about the work-facilitating characteristics of the physical work environment. There seems little doubt that an uncomfortable work setting can have harmful effects: decreased production, increased errors, higher accident rates, and greater turnover.

When a work setting is made more pleasant and comfortable, production usually increases, at least temporarily. But a serious problem exists for the psychologist and the organization in interpreting any

321

such changes in production. It is difficult to determine precisely what caused the higher production rate. Is it attributable to the new air-conditioning system, or brighter lighting, or the improved sound-proofing (the actual physical changes), or is it because of more subtle psychological factors such as a more positive attitude of the workers toward management for instituting the changes? Perhaps the workers' perceptions of or psychological reactions to the physical changes, and not the changes themselves, cause production to increase and performance to become more efficient. Either way the company is getting what it wants and the workers are happier and more comfortable in the process.

Though it is true that the results might be the same whatever the cause, it is vital that the psychologist and the organization be able to determine precisely the reason for the increased production. For example, suppose it was because of a better attitude on the part of the workers who felt that the company was now interested in them as human beings, not as mere cogs in a machine. If this were the case, it might be possible to influence worker attitudes positively, and thus improve production, through some means other than expensive physical changes in the work environment.

In many industries, there are examples of people working at peak efficiency under seemingly intolerable, or at least uncomfortable, conditions. And, there are many examples of poor production and morale in the most modern, elaborate, and comfortable surroundings. The point is that although the physical conditions of the working environment are important, they are not the whole story. The effects of any physical changes introduced in a plant will be modified or influenced by how the workers perceive and adapt to these changes.

In Chapter 1, in our discussion of the Hawthorne studies, we noted a number of physical changes in the work environment, each of which led to an increase in production. However, when these changes were withdrawn, production still increased. The attitude of the workers was the primary cause of the increased production; improved worker attitudes were brought about by the feeling that management was interested in them as individuals.

One's perception of reality determines behavior, and that perception does not always reflect accurately the objective reality of a situation. For example, one Texas factory provided perfect control of temperature, humidity, and air circulation in its plant. From the day the plant opened, however, the employees complained bitterly about the heat, humidity, and lack of air circulation. A thorough check of the system showed it to be working properly, providing correct temperature and humidity levels for the building.

What was wrong? Why were the employees convinced they felt

too hot and sticky when they could not, in fact, have been? The answer is a function of the workers' perception of the reality of the situation. Most of the employees had been farmers who were not used to spending their days inside a windowless building; they were accustomed to the outdoors and to feeling a breeze. In the factory, the air-conditioning vents were near the fifty-foot-high ceiling so no one could feel the air circulating. A clever and simple solution was to attach long tissue streamers to the vents. Although the workers still could not feel the air circulating, at least they could see that it was doing so, and their complaints stopped.

We discuss several physical aspects of the work environment—from the location of the plant to piped-in music—and we see that such physical changes can affect production but partly because of what these changes mean to the workers. This does not diminish the importance of the physical side of the working environment, but it does suggest that it must always be considered in the light of more subtle and complex psychological forces. Conditions of work also include temporal factors (hours of work, how the hours are arranged, and the number of workdays per week), individual psychological factors (boredom, monotony, and fatigue), and the manner in which the job itself is performed. All of these factors interact to form the immediate physical environment of a job, and this environment helps determine how well or how poorly the work is done.

PHYSICAL CONDITIONS OF WORK

The physical work environment includes everything from the parking facilities outside the plant and the location and design of the building, to the amount of light and noise impinging on an individual's desk or work space. Inadequate parking spaces or a parking lot too far from the building may so irritate employees that their attitudes toward their jobs and employer are negative before they even arrive at their work stations. A factory location inconvenient to reach by car or public transportation, or in an unsafe neighborhood, may also predispose workers to poor morale.

Many manufacturing and business concerns are transferring the plant or office from the downtown section of a city to a suburban location. Corporations can obtain larger quarters, with ample room for expansion, at a much lower cost than in the city. New York City has seen a large number of corporate headquarters move to suburban or rural locations in neighboring New Jersey and Connecticut, or not so neighboring Texas.

323

Although there are economic benefits from such moves, there are also personnel problems, particularly with clerical and secretarial employees. Most of these are young single women who prefer to work and live in the more dynamic city than in the quieter and more remote suburbs. Suburban locations appeal primarily to married people who already live there. Those remaining in the city find they must commute great distances to get to the new plants. Also, in bad weather when roads are dangerous more people experience difficulty getting to work. In the city, public transportation usually continues, if at a slower pace; in the suburbs, most people are dependent on their cars.

Finally, many employees are dissatisfied with suburban locations because they are isolated from the variety of shops, services, and restaurants so readily available in a city. The developers of a new office building in Richmond, Virginia, carefully studied a large group of clerical employees and learned that a working location convenient to services, parking, and public transportation was the single greatest source of concern. It was found that proximity to dry-cleaning facilities was nearly as important as a place to eat, that 85 per cent of the employees studied used the bank closest to their work, and that 60 per cent of the men patronized barber shops near their offices. The people wanted to have these services convenient to their work. The suburban office is often isolated from everything except other offices, so employees cannot combine work with access to necessary services.

Once inside the place of employment, other physical features can create dissatisfaction and frustration. In the Richmond study, the second most important consideration was the ventilating, heating, and air-conditioning system. (In glass-wall buildings, temperatures get uncomfortably hot on the sunny side and far too cool on the shady side.) The most frequently mentioned complaint was having to wait too long for elevators in high-rise office buildings. Other studies have noted numerous complaints about the food in a company facility. Many company cafeterias, intended as a fringe benefit, actually become sources of dissatisfaction.

Another frequent irritant is the number, location, and condition of rest rooms.

All of these factors, none of which involves the actual work itself, can impair productive efficiency on the job. Through poor building location or design, a worker's morale and attitude may be low even before the workday begins.

The location and design of the building are critical for handicapped persons who often are not able to work, not because of lack of ability, but simply because they cannot get to the work station. Steep flights of stairs, aisles and doorways that are too narrow to accommodate a wheelchair, and inadequate restroom facilities have prevented handicapped workers from being employed.

This unfortunate situation has been changing under the impact of the 1973 Rehabilitation Act, which requires affirmative action in employment for the handicapped. In addition to its impact on selection and training programs, this legislation affects building design by requiring the removal of all architectural barriers to the handicapped. All parts of a building must be accessible to those in wheelchairs. This has led to the installation of automatic doors, ramps and elevators, hand-holds, wider doorways, and lower wall telephones.

To enhance the awareness of the problems of handicapped workers, some company managers have spent a day in a wheelchair, experiencing firsthand the difficulties of a handicapped worker in getting around their plant or office. IBM, which has been employing handicapped workers for more than thirty years and which is in the vanguard in redesigning work places, has built ramps, widened doorways, installed a foot-operated door for an employee who could not use his hands, and installed speaker phones for persons who cannot hold a regular phone.

Redesigning the building for the handicapped worker shows how the physical work place can influence not only production but also employment opportunities.

Since the mid-1960s, a new discipline—*environmental psychology*—has sparked a revolution in the design and appearance of work facilities. Combining the talents of architects and psychologists, this field is concerned with all aspects of natural and man-made environments and their impact on human beings.

Consider, for example, research conducted on office design. Only in recent years have the relationships been recognized between the physical aspects of offices and work behavior. The layout of an office can affect communication between and within departments, the flow of work to and from various groups, leader-follower relationships, and group cohesiveness.

A new concept in office design is the *landscaped office,* which originated in Germany and has become popular in the United States. In contrast to private, separate offices, the landscaped office consists of a huge open area (sometimes larger than a football field); there are no floor-to-ceiling walls to divide the area into separate rooms. Instead, all employees—from clerks to corporate officers—are grouped in functional work units each of which is set off from other units by landscaping such as trees and plants, low screens, cabinets, and bookcases.

In addition to being cheaper to construct and easier to maintain, landscaped offices are said to facilitate communication and work flow. Moreover, the openness enhances group cohesiveness and cooperation and reduces psychological barriers between management and employees. Studies of employee reactions to landscaped office design reveal that it has both advantages and disadvantages. Employees find landscaped offices to be more aesthetically pleasing and more conducive to friendships and social relations. Managers find that communication is improved. The major complaints about landscaped offices relate to lack of privacy, noise, and difficulty in concentrating. It has not yet been demonstrated conclusively if employee production increases in landscaped office arrangements.

In addition to studying large-scale questions of work space design, industrial psychologists have conducted extensive research on specific environmental factors including illumination, noise, color, music, and temperature and humidity.

Illumination

It seems like common sense to suggest that the quality of work suffers in the absence of sufficient light. In addition, it is known that continued exposure to inadequate illumination, particularly while reading or performing detailed operations, can be harmful to one's eyesight. Despite this awareness, people still try to read by the light of a twenty-five watt bulb, and industrial employees operate under not much better conditions.

In discussing illumination, several factors are important: intensity, distribution, glare, and the nature of the light source.

Intensity, or level of brightness, is the most common factor associated with illumination. Despite many research studies, there is still no agreement on how bright lighting should be for efficient work. Obviously, the optimal level of intensity varies with the nature of the task to be performed. A job involving the precise manipulation of small component parts—for example, watchmaking or electronics assembly—requires brighter lighting than many other kinds of jobs. Although there is no agreement about ideal levels of intensity, the Illuminating Engineering Society has recommended minimum intensity levels for a variety of work areas, as indicated in Table 10–1.

The amount of contrast between the object being worked on and the general background influences the level of lighting intensity needed for a particular job. The lower the contrast, the brighter should be the illumination. Glare—the amount of light reflected from walls and other surfaces—also interacts with intensity, as does the type of light involved. Although it may be difficult to determine the

TABLE 10-1

RECOMMENDED INTENSITY LEVELS FOR CERTAIN
INDUSTRIAL AND BUSINESS SITUATIONS

Job	Minimum Foot-Candles*
Aircraft manufacturing, supplementary illumination for welding	2000
Assembly, extra fine	1000
Cleaning and pressing industry, inspection and spotting	500
Cloth products, cutting	300
Dairy products, bottle washers	200
Tobacco products, grading and sorting	200
Banks, tellers' stations	150
Candy making, hand decorating	100
Barber and beauty shops	100
Photo engraving, etching	50
Hotels, front office	50
Store interiors, stockrooms	30
Laundries, washing	30
Iron and steel manufacturing, stripping yard	20
Offices, corridors and stairways	20
Airplanes, passenger compartment	5

From *Technical Publication TP-128* (1971), *Foot-candles in Modern Lighting,* General Electric Company, Nela Park, Cleveland, Ohio.

* A foot-candle of light (or standard candle at a distance of one foot) is approximately the brightness produced if a 100-watt bulb were held 10 feet over your head on a completely dark night.

perfect intensity for a particular job, it requires little effort and expense for a company to provide brighter lighting when employees are squinting at their work stations or desks.

Another factor in illumination is the distribution of light in the room or work area. The ideal arrangement is for the light to be uniformly distributed throughout the entire visual field. Illuminating a work area at a much higher intensity than the surroundings causes considerable eyestrain over a period of time. The reason for this is the somewhat natural tendency for the eyes to shift around a room. When a person looks up from a brightly lit area to one more dimly lit, the pupil of the eye dilates. Looking back to the brightly lit area causes the pupil to contract. This constant pupillary activity can cause eyestrain.

That is why, when studying or working at a desk, you should have a ceiling light on as well as the desk lamp focusing on your work. This will give a uniform distribution of light throughout the room.

Similarly, it is less fatiguing to the eyes to have some illumination in the room while watching television, instead of watching in a totally dark room.

Another factor that reduces visual efficiency and promotes eyestrain is glare, caused by light of a brighter intensity than the eye is used to. The brightness comes from the light source itself or from highly reflective surfaces. Studies in laboratory settings have shown that glare produces increased errors in detailed work in as short a time as twenty minutes. Not only does glare cause eyestrain but it can also obscure vision; you may have experienced this when driving at night and confronted with an oncoming car using its high-beam headlights.

Glare can be eliminated in several ways. Extremely bright light sources can be shielded or kept out of the worker's field of vision. Workers could be supplied with visors or eyeshades, such as the type professional gamblers use. Highly reflective surfaces can be eliminated, for example, by painting a high gloss surface with a dull matte finish.

The best way to prevent glare is to provide uniform illumination in the work area in the first place. This is best accomplished through the use of indirect lighting. With direct lighting—bulbs located at various points in the ceiling—the light is concentrated or focused on specific areas, causing bright spots and glare. With indirect lighting, however, no light strikes the eye directly; all light is reflected. Laboratory studies involving a three-hour reading test under indirect and direct lighting show the clear superiority of indirect lighting sources.

Illumination is also affected by the nature of the light source. There are three types most commonly used in homes, offices, and factories: the standard incandescent light bulb, fluorescent lighting, and mercury lighting. Each source offers advantages and disadvantages in terms of cost, brightness, and color. Ordinary fluorescent bulbs create slightly colored light that can give people and some colored objects an unusual appearance. Mercury lamps (often used to illuminate streets and parking lots) create a blue-green color. In jobs where color is important, such as visually inspecting for product defects, the choice of light source is particularly crucial. In sum, the choice of light source must depend on the specific job involved.

In addition to the physical aspects of lighting, there is a psychological component with regard to natural versus artificial lighting. Since so many buildings are being designed without windows, the importance of this consideration is increasing. People who work in some offices express a strong desire for windows, regardless of the adequacy of the artificial illumination. Not only do most workers like to be able to see outdoors but they also believe that natural light is better for their eyes than artificial light. In one study, clerical workers whose desks were far from windows significantly overestimated the amount of natural light they were receiving. This suggests the psychological importance to these workers of having natural light.

Noise

Noise is a common cause for complaint in modern life. In the home, on busy streets, and in the office and factory, we suffer what has been called noise pollution. Noise in these environments makes us irritable and nervous, interferes with sleep, and produces physiological effects including deafness. Whether noise is capable of interfering with productive efficiency on the job, however, is questionable—the evidence is contradictory.

The basic unit for measuring noise is the *decibel* (db), which measures, technically, sound pressure levels. Psychologically, the decibel is a measure of the subjective or perceived intensity of a sound. Zero decibels is the threshold of hearing, the lowest sound that can be heard. Table 10–2 contains sample decibel levels for various familiar

TABLE 10–2

REPRESENTATIVE DECIBEL LEVELS

Source of Noise	Decibel Level
Breathing	10
Whisper (5 ft. away)	30
Average home	50
Conversation at 3 ft.	60
Average automobile at 30 ft.	74
Average factory	80–90
Food blender in kitchen	90
Machine shop	90
Boiler room	90–98
Printing press plant	90–100
Punch press	100
Loud power mower	107
Discotheques, rock concerts	110–120
Snowmobiles	115
Hydraulic press	120
Jet plane at takeoff	150
Rocket launching pad	180

situations. As you can see, we are often assaulted by noises as loud as factories in our own kitchens and backyards.

Certain loudness levels are known to be threats to hearing. For example, a worker who is exposed daily to decibel levels above 80 for a long period of time will undoubtedly suffer some hearing loss. Exposure for short periods of time to levels between 100 and 125 decibels can cause temporary deafness. Short exposure to decibel levels beyond 150 can cause permanent deafness.

In 1971, the federal government established maximum sound levels to which workers may be exposed: 90 decibels for an eight-hour day, 100 decibels for only two hours a day, and 110 decibels for only 30 minutes a day. The Department of Labor has estimated that it will cost private industry more than $10 billion to comply with these standards.

Examining the noise levels for work situations shown in Table 10–2, we find that many factory workers are exposed to dangerous loudness levels. Indeed, this is a source of concern to industry; organizations are faced with hearing damage claims from workers totaling millions of dollars each year. Hearing loss is a recognized occupational hazard for jobs such as riveters, boiler makers, aircraft mechanics, and foundry and textile workers.

The Committee on Environmental Quality of the Federal Council for Science and Technology estimates that the number of workers exposed to unsafe noise levels is at least 6 million, and may be as high as 16 million. The individual hearing loss claims against industry average about $2,000, and more and more workers are becoming aware of their right to compensation for job-induced hearing loss. The potential cost to American industry is staggering. For economic reasons, then, and to comply with federal legislation on noise levels, industry has become noise-conscious.

There may be other physiological costs of high noise levels. Research has shown that when subjects were exposed to noises in the 95–110 decibel range, blood vessels constricted, heart rate changed, and the pupils of the eyes dilated. The constriction of the blood vessels continued for some time after the noise stopped and altered the blood supply throughout the body. It has been suggested that continuous exposure to loud noise could raise the blood pressure and perhaps contribute to heart disease. Loud noises also increased muscle tension.

If these physiological effects were not serious enough, some psychologists have suggested that noise can impair emotional well-being. Those who work in extremely noisy environments are more aggressive, distrustful, and irritable than those who work in quieter surroundings.

A spokesman for a local union of the United Automobile Workers said that some workers preferred the night shift to the day shift because the noise was less at night. Also, night shift workers and supervisors seemed to get along better and to socialize outside of working hours. The opportunity and desire for social interaction on the day shift are reduced because employees in a noisy plant cannot hear each other, are forced to shout, and soon become angry.

Not all kinds of noise are equally annoying or distracting. An important characteristic of noise is whether it is constant or intermittent. The intermittent or irregular noise is much more disturbing than the steady or constant noise. Humans are able to adapt to continuous noises. When a noise is first introduced into our environment, it is disturbing because of its contrast with the relative quiet that preceded it. After a while, however, we may no longer notice the continuous sound. It becomes part of the background because we have adapted to it. For example, when a fan or air conditioner is turned on, we are aware of the sound, but this conscious awareness fades with continued exposure. For the same reason, we no longer hear the noise of the engines on a flight in a jet airliner after a short period of time. We are also able to adapt to intermittent sounds that appear regularly, but noises occurring on a random basis are difficult, if not impossible, to adapt to.

It is important to note that this adaptation may be occurring only at the conscious level. That is, workers may not hear the loud noise of production machinery, but the physiological effects may still be taking place. Hearing suffers, blood vessels constrict, and more energy is required to continue work at the same pace. Although workers are not consciously aware of the noise, these physiological effects, plus the additional energy needed for work, may cause them to feel tired and irritable. Thus, loud noise may exact its toll on the human body even if we consciously adapt to it.

Other characteristics of noise that are potentially disturbing are familiarity, tone, and the necessity of the noise to the job. Research has shown that unfamiliar sounds are more distracting than familiar ones. Workers in a city office building would seldom be aware of the familiar traffic sounds outside the window, but would be distracted immediately if they were to hear the noise of a foghorn. Also, high shrill tones and extremely low tones are much more distracting and annoying than tones in the middle range. Noise seems to be less disturbing if it is a necessary part of work. Secretaries are usually not bothered by the clatter of their typewriters, but a nearby executive trying to read a report may be very disturbed by the same noise.

Thus, all sounds are not equal—some noise is greatly disturbing, some barely noticed, and some peaceful and soothing, such as the sound of the ocean. Also, as with virtually everything, there are in-dividual differences in noise tolerance. One person may not notice the noise that is driving the neighbors berserk. There are people for whom too much quiet is disturbing, such as those who live in the city and find themselves unable to sleep when visiting in the country-side. "The silence," they say, "is deafening."

What are the effects of noise on productive efficiency? We have noted that noise can distract, disturb, deafen, impair physiological functioning, and lead to fatigue. Can it also affect working ability? Because of all the harmful effects of noise, it is usually assumed that noise lowers efficiency on the job. The empirical evidence, however, is contradictory; research has failed to resolve the issue. The question is complicated by factors such as the type of work (a telephone operator may be more distracted by noise than a pneumatic drill operator), the kind of noise involved, and the personal characteristics of the employee.

As noted earlier, it is difficult to determine if changes in production are caused by actual changes in noise level (such as the installation of soundproofing), or to the workers' improved attitudes because they may feel that management has done something for them. Also, if workers realize that they are part of a research study, they may work faster, or slower, than they do ordinarily.

Although it is not possible to conclude that noise definitely leads to impaired performance, certain related findings have some empirical support. For example, it has been shown under laboratory conditions that production decreases slightly following the introduction of noise. After a short period of time, however, production increases and reaches levels beyond the pre-noise level. Of course, the worker must exert extra energy to compensate for the physiological effects of the noise. An artificial laboratory setting with short-term tasks and highly motivated subjects may not accurately simulate conditions found in the factory or office.

Other laboratory studies have shown that the average quantity of work was not affected by intense noise but that the quality of the work was more variable. This occurred with easy and monotonous work, not with difficult and complex tasks.

Studies conducted on the job have shown that whereas noise re-duction did not lead to improvement in production levels, it did lead to a reduction in errors.

Thus, we cannot be certain of the effects of high noise levels on production. However, even if it were shown that noise has no effect on working efficiency, industry still must reduce noise in order to protect the health of employees. Preventing indus-trial noise is an engineering and design problem, but with some items of equipment it is a tremendous challenge. Building quieter machines, particularly for the construction industry, can be very expensive. Also, it has happened that noise reduction was obtained at the cost of reduced efficiency of the equipment. For other types of machinery, mufflers and sound baffles are effective.

One way to prevent noise in adjacent areas of a plant is to move the noisy equipment or to enclose the area with sound-absorbing materials. This does not reduce the noise level for workers who must operate the equipment, but it does prevent others, such as office personnel, from being disturbed by it.

If the noise can't be reduced at its source, the next step is to safeguard the workers through some sort of ear protection such as earplugs, muffs, or helmets worn over the head and ears. Earplugs are the cheapest and easiest means of protection but have not gained wide acceptance in industry, partly because they can be uncomfortable in the process of achieving proper fit. Properly fit and continuously used, however, earplugs can prevent the hearing loss that results from constant exposure to high noise levels. Heavily padded earmuffs are used by persons who work around jet engines, rocket test and launching stations, and other areas of intense noise.

Color

Exaggerated claims have been made about the benefits of the proper color or combination of colors for homes, offices, and plants. Color, it has been alleged, can increase production, lower accidents and errors, and raise morale. Articles in popular magazines tell us that colors can reflect our personalities or change our life-styles. These claims are not supported by empirical evidence, and there is no validity to the purported relationship between the use of a specific color and resulting production or fatigue.

This does not mean, however, that the proper use of color has no place in industry. Color can provide a more pleasant working environment and can aid in safety. For example, color is used in many plants as a coding device. Fire equipment is red, danger areas are yellow, and first-aid equipment is green. This allows such equipment and areas to be quickly and positively identified.

Color can also be used to prevent eyestrain since colors differ in their reflective properties. A white wall reflects more light than a dark one. Thus, the appropriate use of color can make a room seem lighter or darker.

Colors can create differing illusions of size and temperature. A room painted a dark color will seem smaller and more closed in than

333

it actually is. Light-colored walls give the feeling of greater space and openness.

Interior decorators tell us that blues and greens are cool colors and reds and oranges are warm colors. Research studies have not demonstrated any greater tolerance of heat as a function of these different colors, but this illusion persists. It has been said that people behave differently in cool than in warm rooms (defined by color, not temperature). Decorators claim that people are more excitable and animated in a warm room, more relaxed and calm in a cool one. Again, there is little empirical support for this notion.

If a work area is dingy and dreary, repainting it may improve employee morale. A fresh paint job under these circumstances—in any color—may indeed make people happier with their work environment. However, there is little to be said with assurance about the effects of color on human behavior at work.

Music

Since the mid-1940s, there has been a dramatic increase in the number of offices and factories that pipe in music to their employees. As with color, extravagant claims have been made about the effects of music on production and morale. Employees are allegedly happier, work harder, have fewer absences, and are less tired at the end of the workday. A few studies, undertaken by the firms that supply the music, support these claims, but their research leaves much to be desired in terms of thoroughness and competence of design.

Most of the early research on music (conducted in the 1940s and 1950s) indicated that the majority of people liked the idea of music during work and thought it would make them happier and more productive. There has been little research since then. In one of the few recent studies, it was found that the majority of supervisory and nonsupervisory personnel in a government agency felt that background music would have no real effect on the quantity or quality of their work. However, three fourths of the supervisors and non-supervisors said that their co-workers would like music at work. More than 80 per cent believed that background music would make for a more pleasant work environment. Although the supervisors did not believe music would affect their own work, approximately 40 per cent believed it would improve the quantity and quality of the work performed by their subordinates. Nearly 86 per cent of the supervisors believed that their subordinates enjoyed having music during working hours.

These attitudes are important but may vary with the realities of a situation. Other research does bear out the notion that most employees are happier when music is played, but there is not unanimity. About 10 per cent of the employees questioned said they were bothered by music.

There seems to be no valid support for the idea that music will increase production levels for all kinds of work. The effect of music depends, in part, on the nature of the work involved. Research suggests that music may increase productivity on jobs that are reasonably simple, repetitive, and involve units of very short duration such as assembly line work. This type of job is regarded by most people as monotonous and not sufficiently demanding to fully engage the workers' attention. Thus, the music might provide a focus—something to occupy the mind—and cause the workday to pass more quickly and enjoyably.

The situation is different with complex and demanding work. There is no evidence that music will increase production on a difficult job for one very good reason: the complexity of the work demands full and concentrated attention. At the very least, workers would be unable to attend to the music and, if the work were extremely demanding, the music could become distracting and interfering.

Think of the jobs of air traffic controller and assembly line worker at an automobile plant in terms of complexity and demands on the individual. We can understand how music could be soothing and enjoyable to the latter person and annoying or simply unheard by the former.

The effectiveness of music, if any, also depends on the kind of music played. There are individual and group differences in the type of music appreciated. A younger group of workers would probably choose different music than a group of employees over age forty-five. Some studies have reported differences in productive output as a function of various kinds of music (although other studies have failed to confirm this finding). But whatever the effect on production, there is no doubt of the existence of musical preferences. This was demonstrated to the dismay of an employer who allowed groups of workers to play a radio on the job. The inevitable happened—vicious arguments over what kind of music to listen to. Morale fell and the formerly cohesive work units divided into hostile cliques on the basis of musical preference. The distraught employer then allowed more radios to be brought in, but the result was that each group played their radio so loudly that no one heard anything.

Piped-in music (of the Muzak variety) solves the individual choice problem by not allowing any, and, as you can tell from elevators and shopping centers, this music is so innocuous that few people could be offended (and even fewer entertained). Most industrial music is now of the piped-in type.

The effect of music on production is another area in which competent research is needed. Most employees say they like music at work. It may improve production for simple jobs and make some work more pleasant (or less unpleasant), but there are still many unresolved questions.

Temperature and Humidity

We have all experienced the effects of temperature and humidity on our morale, our ability to work well, and even our physical and emotional well-being. The weather and climate affect people in diverse ways. Some of us are happier and have more vitality in cold weather whereas others prefer hot weather. Some are severely depressed by several days of rain whereas others barely notice it.

Our bodies maintain a constant temperature of about 98.6°F. through an elaborate and precise regulatory system. To a great extent, the body is able to maintain this temperature stability despite drastic changes in external temperatures. We help by wearing more clothes in winter and fewer in summer, and by adjusting heating or air-conditioning systems accordingly.

For work that takes place indoors, the temperature and humidity can be properly controlled, assuming the company is willing to spend the necessary money and that the facilities are amenable. A huge steel mill, for example, would be prohibitively expensive to air condition.

Research has established optimal temperature and humidity ranges within which most people feel comfortable. According to heating and ventilation engineers, the most comfortable temperature range is 73°F. to 77°F., and the ideal humidity range is 25 per cent to 50 per cent. These levels apply regardless of the outside temperature and humidity. The expressed temperature preferences of most of us, however, do not agree with these estimates. People seem to prefer somewhat warmer indoor temperatures in winter (69°F. to 73°F.) than in summer (65°F. to 70°F.).

Central control of heat and air conditioning in American homes and work places is a luxury not yet enjoyed by much of the rest of the world. It is not uncommon to find homes and buildings in the industrialized nations of Europe that lack air conditioning although this is changing.

Although most of us work in facilities where temperatures and humidity are controlled, and are not bothered by extremes in weather, there are still many whose places of work are affected by outside temperatures, particularly in summer. How does this affect worker productivity?

The human body can adapt to many conditions: combat, concentration camps, submarines, or space capsules. This adaptability also applies to extremes of weather. Most of us can accept extremely high temperatures and (although it may take up to a week to adapt) can maintain the ability to work in hot and humid weather for long periods of time. For example, shipyard workers in summer can feel the intense heat of the steel decks through heavy shoes. Many people successfully spend their careers under nearly intolerable working conditions (given enough salt tablets and water).

Although we can physically adapt to temperature extremes, can we work as efficiently as under more comfortable conditions? Research in this area is complicated by two additional conditions that interact with temperature to form *effective* temperature. (The thermometer reading is called *absolute* temperature.) These variables—humidity and air movement—are each capable of influencing the other, and all three factors must be considered in combination.

For example, the same temperature can be perceived as both tolerable or intolerable, depending on the humidity. In one research study, subjects judged a temperature of 140°F. to be tolerable when the humidity was low (10 per cent), but intolerable when the humidity was high (80 per cent). Similarly, the rate of air circulation over the skin can affect the tolerability of a particular temperature and humidity level. Air flow facilitates the evaporation of perspiration and thus makes a person feel cooler. A room at 80°F. with 60 per cent humidity but no circulating air is felt to be much less comfortable than the same temperature and humidity levels with moving air.

Research dealing with physical labor has shown that uncomfortable climate conditions can influence the quality and quantity of work performed. Production can fall under extremely hot and humid conditions but, even in the few cases where production remains the same, workers are forced to expend more energy in order to maintain the same output. Other studies have shown that manual laborers must take more frequent rest pauses under hot and humid conditions. These conditions can be better tolerated if there is sufficient air movement. The installation of forced ventilation systems in factories has resulted in higher production levels even though the temperature and humidity have remained the same.

Motivation plays a great part in worker efficiency under extremes of climate. Research conducted by the military has demonstrated that highly motivated men are able to maintain constant work rates under extremes of both heat and cold.

337

Mental work seems to be less affected by heat and humidity than physical labor, at least under laboratory conditions, although some slight effect has been demonstrated outside the laboratory.

It is unfortunate that factory and manual laborers (those most affected by temperature-humidity extremes) are usually the least protected, whereas those working in offices (whose work is less affected) usually are provided with efficient climate control systems.

Where practical, a company's investment in climate control systems for factories and offices would reap the benefits of more comfortable and productive employees. Where it is not feasible to install air conditioning, fans to circulate the air will accrue some benefits. At the very least, a company should provide salt tablets to its workers so that they can replace the salt lost through perspiration.

TEMPORAL CONDITIONS OF WORK

A vital part of the overall work environment is the amount of time spent on the job. The number of hours worked (daily or weekly), and the amount of rest allowed during working hours, are capable of influencing morale and productivity. It seems obvious that a reduction in the number of hours worked per week would bring a corresponding reduction in production; we shall see, however, that this is not always the case. The relationship between number of working hours and production is not necessarily straightforward.

Hours of Work

How long should a person be expected to work each week? Our expectations have changed greatly over the years. At one time in the United States, six-day weeks of 10 and more hours a day were standard. The reduction to a five-day, 40-hour week, now considered standard (considered excessive by some), is a fairly recent development. Overall, there has been a steady decline in the amount of time employees must devote to a job. There is nothing sacred about a 40-hour week; it is not necessarily the most efficient working schedule. For social reasons, and for increased efficiency of the production equipment, workers accept the 40-hour week as the normal condition. In other times, they accepted 48 hours or 60 hours as the standard. Perhaps someday a 20-hour week will be standard and we will wonder how people could have devoted 40 hours each week to a job.

There is another consideration: the tendency to spend as much time as is allowed to complete a task. C. Northcote Parkinson, the

British author and historian, wrote that work will expand to fill the time that is available for it. If workers are expected to complete six units of a product each workday, they will tend to finish six units whether the workday is 12, 8, or 6 hours long.

There is ample evidence that much time is lost in an ordinary workday. A survey of more than 5,000 clerical workers in 10 different companies revealed that of their 37½-hour workweek, no more than 20 hours were devoted to actual work. This staggering finding indicates that nearly half the workweek is lost time to the company; it is actually paying double for the amount of work received. There is a great difference between *nominal* working hours (the prescribed number of hours workers must spend at their desks or machines), and *actual* working hours; the two rarely coincide.

Some of the lost time is scheduled by the company as official rest pauses, but most of it seems to be unauthorized and beyond company control. When workers arrive each morning, it may take a long time for them to actually begin work. They may shuffle papers, sharpen pencils, oil machines (whether or not they need it). During the workday, employees talk socially with co-workers, exceed the length of the lunch break, and take unofficial rest pauses at the water cooler, in the rest room, or by daydreaming.

There is an interesting relationship between nominal and actual working hours: When nominal hours of work are increased, there is a *decrease* in actual hours of work. The longer the workday or workweek, the lower the actual production per hour. This relationship has been demonstrated by considerable research and its validity seems beyond question.

This finding holds even for highly motivated workers. In the early days of World War II in England, that country was trying desperately to hold out against Nazi Germany; patriotic fervor was at a peak. Dangerously low on supplies and equipment, the government increased the workweek in war plants from 56 to 69½ hours. At first production increased 10 per cent, but, very shortly, it fell 12 per cent below the earlier level.

Additional consequences of increasing nominal working hours include marked increases in accidents, illness, and absenteeism. The actual work hours were only 51 out of the 69½-hour week; with the previous 56-hour week, actual work hours were 53. Thus, the workers were less productive with the longer workweek, and these employees were working for their own survival as a nation, which was very much in doubt at the time.

A study conducted in the United States during World War II showed that the seven-day workweek (adopted by many companies during the war) resulted in no more production than a six-day week.

One day of the seven was lost time. The same results apply to peace-time conditions as well.

The relationship between nominal and actual working hours also holds with overtime (when employees are asked to work several hours beyond their normal day for markedly higher rates of pay). Much of this extra time is not productive. Unless there is no alternative, the provision for overtime work is not worth the investment. People adjust to longer hours by working at a slower rate.

If we increase working time and production goes down, will production rise if we shorten the workday or workweek? Some research indicates that the answer is yes. Other studies show that a decrease in nominal work hours has no effect on actual work time; that is, actual working hours remain the same even though the worker spends less total time on the job.

In one case of historical interest (during the 1930s Depression) a plant reduced its nominal working time by 9¼ hours per week, yet actual work time fell only 5 hours. Another plant reduced its nominal workweek by 18½ hours and hourly production increased 21 per cent. Hourly production increases of about 20 per cent have been reported by a number of plants that, in the days before the 40-hour week, cut nominal work time. As to how much the nominal work-week could be reduced, there is no answer yet, but the trend is undoubtedly toward shorter workweeks.

What, then, is the optimal period of time to work? The answer keeps changing. What is normal and most productive at one time may appear excessively long and unproductive 5 or 10 years later. Research studies show the 5-day, 40-hour week to be the most efficient. A typical study compared hourly productivity among groups performing the same job, some for 44-hour weeks and others for 36- and 40-hour weeks; the results favored the 40-hour week. We must, however, examine the context within which these studies were conducted. Virtually all of them were undertaken at the end of the Depression or during World War II, at times when the normal work-week ranged from 48 to 60 or more hours. The same studies conducted today would be in a totally different context. The 40-hour week is now expected—not 50 or 60 hours—and it seems likely that current research would show a workweek shorter than 40 (nominal) hours to be the most effective.

Permanent Part-Time Employment

One trend in working hours is the provision of permanent job opportunities for those who want to work less than the standard 40-hour week. Part-time employment (usually half-time or 20 hours a week) is growing in popularity among both employees and managers. In 1963, 10 per cent of the work force in the U.S. was employed part-time. Today, more than 15 per cent—some 13 million workers—hold part-time jobs.

As noted, full-time employment does not mean that the organization is getting 40 hours of work per week from each employee. And, it is being recognized that some jobs can be accomplished just as well in 20 hours as in 40, particularly writing and research jobs in which there is a great deal of independent work. Also, many lower-level assembly line and clerical jobs can be performed by two persons, each working half-time, as well as by one person working full-time.

Part-time employment is especially attractive to persons who have family responsibilities. By working only half-time, they are able to combine family and career. Handicapped persons often find part-time employment appealing because of their mobility problems. Persons undergoing the midlife crisis (discussed in Chapter 8) welcome part-time employment because it gives them the chance to return to school or to explore other growth opportunities with the extra time provided them. And, some employees prefer part-time jobs simply because they do not want to spend 40 hours a week working in an office or plant. A survey of thirty-five hundred men and women with PhDs showed that 11 per cent of the women and 8 per cent of the men preferred part-time to full-time employment.

The Department of Health, Education, and Welfare found that supervisors of part-time employees were strongly in favor of the concept. A study of part-time caseworkers in Massachusetts showed that those who worked 20 hours a week had a lower turnover and a higher case load contact than full-time employees. Perhaps part-time employees do not take as many unauthorized breaks as do those who work 40 hours a week.

Opportunities for permanent part-time employment are limited but the situation is expected to change in the near future. Congressional hearings have been held on the Part-Time Career Opportunity Act; during these sessions, U.S. Civil Service Commission officials noted that part-time employment is not only an idea whose time has come, but also an idea "begging for attention."

The Four-Day Workweek

Another way to significantly alter the workweek is to reduce it to only four days—a method that is currently enjoying quite a bit of success in the United States.

By the mid-1970s, many factories, offices, and government agencies had changed to a 4-day workweek schedule. This usually involves either 4 days at 10 hours a day (thus maintaining the 40-hour week), or 4 days at 9 hours a day (a 36-hour week with no reduction in pay), and seems to be an idea whose time has come. Union leaders, management consultants, and most of the firms that have tried it are highly enthusiastic.

In most cases, the initiative to shorten the workweek has come not from the union or the employees (as one might expect), but from management for several reasons: the possibility of increased productivity and worker efficiency, an incentive for recruiting and retaining employees, and the hope of reducing absenteeism, which, in many companies, has reached epidemic proportions, particularly on Mondays and Fridays.

Now that the 4-day workweek is being used successfully, some unions and economists believe that it is vital to the country's economic health. Not only might these changes increase productivity but they could also help absorb numbers of unemployed workers. Some believe that the only way to maintain full employment is to have more people working fewer hours each day or fewer days each week.

Converting from a 5- to a 4-day week is difficult and requires flexibility on the part of management. Perhaps this is why smaller firms took the lead in implementing this work schedule. The change requires careful planning and the wholehearted cooperation of the employees. A change of this magnitude cannot be dictated to a company's workers, not if the company expects it to be successful. Management must explain the entire procedure to the workers and allow them time to examine and comment on the new schedule.

One of the first companies to undertake a 4-day workweek was a small Massachusetts firm, Kyanize Paints, employing approximately 200 people. Studies at the plant had shown that more efficient production could be achieved with a longer workday. It was estimated that production would be greater on a 4-day, 9-hour per-day basis than on its present 5-day, 8-hour per-day schedule. Great care and patience were taken in describing to the workers the reasons behind the proposed shift and in explaining what it would mean to them: 3-day weekends, an extra hour of work each day, abolition of formal coffee breaks and of wash-up time at the end of the day, and the same rate of pay for a 4-hour-shorter week. After a 3-month trial period, the union took a vote; 78 per cent of the workers were in favor of the 4-day workweek and so it was made permanent.

The results have exceeded the company's expectations. Production has increased 6 per cent, absenteeism has declined from 3 per cent to less than 1 per cent, morale is extremely high, and there are more job applicants than ever before. The workers feel they have a mini-vacation every week. One said, "The week has been split in two and it's beautiful."

Other companies have reported gains in production as high as 15 per cent, greater cuts in absenteeism, and increased loyalty from their employees. One full day off every week, with no reduction in pay, is an appealing fringe benefit that actively enlists cooperation from employees. The workers in the Kyanize plant, for example, willingly gave up coffee breaks and wash-up time, benefits they had strongly fought for in the past.

That the four-day week has a growing appeal was demonstrated by a recent Gallup poll, which indicated that 45 per cent of men of all ages would like to work on that basis. Wives, however, opposed the new workweek by a ratio of 2:1. Some said that 9 to 10 hours of work each day would be too hard on their husbands. A few said they didn't want their husbands home an extra day each week. Women who work, however, are more favorable to the idea. Finally, a survey taken at 13 companies already on a 4-day week revealed that 92 per cent of the workers liked the new schedule and wanted to stick to it.

Flexible Working Hours

A more radical change in work scheduling is to let employees decide for themselves when they will begin and end the workday. Traditionally, all employees of a firm begin and end the workday at fixed times. This practice was rarely questioned until the late 1960s when several business firms in West Germany, after much study and planning, tried *Gleitzeit* (gliding or flexible hours of work)—called in the United States flextime or flexitime—in order to deal with traffic congestion during rush hours. Under this plan, the workday is divided into four parts, two of which are optional and two mandatory. Employees can report to work any time between 8:15 and 8:45 in the morning and leave any time from 4:45 to 5:15 in the afternoon. The two mandatory periods during which everyone must be on the job are the morning hours from 8:45 until the ½-hour lunch break and the afternoon hours from lunch to 4:45. Thus, everyone must work a minimum 7½-hour workday; the optional maximum is 8½ hours per day.

What determines how long each employee will work each day? This is set up on an individual basis within each department or section, as a function of the company's needs. Thus far, flextime has been very successful and offers several advantages. Rush hour traffic

343

congestion into and out of plants and offices has been considerably reduced; indeed, in some cases it is no longer a problem. Since employees spend less time and energy commuting, they arrive at their jobs more relaxed and ready to begin work promptly. Production increases of 3 to 5 per cent have been reported (at no cost to the companies), and morale improves because employees have more personal responsibility for their work. Also, absenteeism and tardiness are considerably reduced.

The scheduling of flexible working hours has spread rapidly throughout Western Europe. More than half of the West German white-collar work force is now on flextime, as are 30 per cent of the French work force and 40 per cent of the Swiss work force. In Britain, five hundred thousand civil servants and more than eighty private firms have adopted flexible hours of work. The popularity of flexible working hours has been growing in the United States since the early 1970s. Flextime is being used successfully by the Baltimore, Maryland, and Washington, D.C., city governments, Sun Oil, Hewlett–Packard, Sampsonite, Scott Paper, Occidental Insurance, Montgomery Ward's Chicago headquarters and New York buying office, and Westinghouse's Pittsburgh nuclear center.

Flextime programs are also growing in popularity among federal government agencies such as the Library of Congress, the Environmental Protection Agency, the Treasury and Agriculture Departments, and the Civil Service Commission. The widespread use of flexible hours will allow government agencies to provide services to the public for a greater number of hours each day.

Flexible working hours seem to be appropriate for a variety of jobs such as research and development, clerical, and light and heavy manufacturing. In assembly line and shift-work operations, however, flextime is difficult to implement because of the high degree of interdependence among the workers.

When flexible working hours were introduced in the British Civil Service, a great deal of research was conducted on employee and organizational reactions.[1] The results were highly favorable. Most of those interviewed (96 per cent) said that they liked flexible working hours and would not want to return to the fixed-hour system. In addition, 28 per cent of those interviewed believed that the new system improved their satisfaction with their work, and 25 per cent said that it increased the amount of work they accomplished. When asked what features of the flexible hours approach they liked best, the employees listed the following:

[1] J. Walker, C. Fletcher, and D. McLeod, "Flexible working hours in two British government offices," *Public Personnel Management*, **4** (1975), 219.

1. Have a feeling of freedom.
2. Have time for shopping.
3. Able to keep appointments.
4. Easier to travel to and from work.
5. Not possible to be late for work.
6. Can take advantage of good weather.
7. Can store up leave.
8. Can adjust hours if not feeling well.
9. Have time for hobbies.
10. Have time for social life.
11. Can adjust hours according to whether or not busy at work.
12. Have a sense of responsibility.
13. Increases amount or quality of work.
14. Reduces conflict between work and family life.

The flexible approach to work scheduling seems to be a fair and sensible arrangement and offers considerable advantages for both employers and employees.

Rest Pauses

Ever since the Hawthorne studies, the importance of company-provided rest breaks has been widely recognized. Not only have their beneficial effects been amply demonstrated but a more urgent reason also exists for giving employees rest pauses: the employees will take breaks whether or not they are offered. If the time will be lost anyway, the company may as well appear beneficent and supply the rest pauses as fringe benefits.

Research has shown that when authorized rest pauses are introduced, unauthorized breaks decline, although they do not disappear altogether and probably never will. Other potential benefits of formal rest periods are increased morale and production, as well as reduced fatigue and boredom. This is another example of how a decrease in actual working time can result in an increase in efficiency.

Workers engaged in heavy physical labor obviously benefit from rest pauses. Muscles in continuous use tire and become less effective. Periodically resting the muscles is necessary in order to maintain performance levels. Even for more sedentary or mental work, however, the change of stimulation provided by a rest break is helpful; it allows boredom to dissipate and the opportunity to think about something else or to talk with other employees.

Another possible reason for the effectiveness of authorized rest

345

pauses is the improved attitudes of workers toward their employer. When a rest program is introduced, workers may feel that it is an expression of management's concern for them as individuals.

Several factors influence the effectiveness of rest pauses. It must be determined at what time or times of day rest breaks will be most effective, how long they should last, how often they should be provided, whether the company should offer coffee or snacks in an employee lounge or at the work station during rest breaks, or give nothing beyond the break itself. In part, these questions must be answered by a company in terms of each type of job. Workers conducting physical labor outdoors during summer months may need frequent breaks, plus iced water and salt tablets. Workers in air-conditioned offices may need fewer actual breaks but the opportunity to leave their desks for a change of scene.

The details of a rest pause program can usually be worked out on the basis of research on the nature of the job, polling employee preferences, or common sense. The rest pause has come to be an institution. It is expected by new employees and not given up by present employees without a comparable gain in some other area (such as the shorter workweek). In sum, rest pauses are effective, expected, and will be taken anyway, regardless of company rules.

Shift Work

Another temporal condition of work that affects a great many employees is the time of day or night the work takes place. Not everyone works from nine to five. Many companies are in operation more than eight hours each day. Indeed, some operate around the clock and employees must work one of three shifts, usually 7 A.M.–3 P.M., 3 P.M.–11 P.M., or 11 P.M.–7 A.M. Some firms assign individuals to one shift on a permanent basis, whereas others rotate workers, switching them each week or so to a different shift. In most cases, those who work evening or all-night shifts receive extra pay to compensate them for the inconvenience of their working hours.

How do the conditions imposed by shift work affect people? Research conducted in the United States and in Europe has shown that the same workers are less productive on the night shift than the day shift. Absenteeism, however, does not seem to differ from one shift to another.

Not only is production lower during the night shift but the disruption of the normal sleep-wake cycle can also produce physical and psychological effects. Humans develop a *diurnal* rhythm, a regular cyclic patterning of the activities of various bodily organs and glands and the chemical composition of the blood. This rhythm is consistent from one 24-hour period to the next and it means that most of us are more alert and productive during the normal waking hours of the day. When the diurnal rhythm is disrupted, the body undergoes dramatic physical changes. At the very least, it is hard to sleep on the new schedule. The main objection of people who must work at night is this inability to sleep during the day, a difficulty aided by daylight, noise, and the activities of others in the house. In research conducted in West Germany, less than half of the night shift workers studied were able to sleep more than five hours per day. In addition to sleepiness, the workers complained of headaches, difficulties in concentrating, increased errors at work, and ulcers.

There are also social and emotional effects. The family must try to keep the house quiet, and normal household routines are disrupted. Workers are forced to spend less time with the family, normal social life is interfered with, and routine activities such as shopping become difficult to fit into the available waking hours.

There is widespread agreement that if there must be shift work in a plant, fewer problems are encountered with the fixed shift system than the rotating shift system. Persons working permanently on one shift are often able to adjust to a new body rhythm (although it is difficult and the social problems remain). With the rotating system, however, workers must make a new adjustment every week or so, whenever the shift is changed. Thus, they may not be fully adjusted to one schedule before beginning another; before they can adjust to the second schedule, they begin a third. This is a very difficult way to live.

There are ways of alleviating the problems caused by shift work. The most obvious is to employ the fixed shift arrangement; there will still be production and personal problems, but they will be less severe. When the rotating shift system must be used, the changes from one shift to another should be made as seldom as possible (for example, every few weeks instead of every week, as is now often the case).

Better personnel selection can also be an aid to successful shift work; it is known that some people are much better able than others to adjust to new rhythms. Those whose bodies are particularly resistant to diurnal pattern changes should be allowed to work only during the day, for their own good as well as the organization's.

One way to facilitate the change from one shift to another is to lengthen the time off between shift changes. A longer interim period makes the change less abrupt and allows employees to catch up on their rest before starting a new schedule. Also, since the night shift is the most trying for the worker (and the least productive for the company), it could be shortened to make it less stressful and objectionable.

Unfortunately, despite the great amount of information available on the diurnal rhythm and its relationship to productive efficiency, industry has been slow to recognize it and to design work conditions accordingly.

PSYCHOLOGICAL CONDITIONS OF WORK

Other factors that make up the work environment are concerned with the nature of the job itself and its impact on the workers—what may be called the internal environment of the job. In general, we want to know: How do workers feel about their jobs? Do they provide a sense of satisfaction or achievement, or do they make them tired and bored?

As discussed in Chapter 8, the design of the job can influence morale and motivation. Job enlargement (designing jobs to include more duties and responsibilities) has been a successful method of improving morale and motivation. At the other extreme, jobs designed to be so simple that they make no demands upon the worker's intelligence, need for achievement, or even attention (all too common in industry today), result in boredom, monotony, fatigue, and, of course, less efficient production.

The history of job simplification dates from the beginnings of mass production in the early part of the twentieth century. If relatively expensive consumer goods such as automobiles were to be produced in sufficient quantities and at lower costs, old-style production methods —building each unit by hand—would have to be changed. Mass production called for product consistency and standardization so that parts could be interchangeable. It also called for fractionation of the work itself. It was no longer economically or technically feasible for one person to make an entire product; the work had to be divided so that each worker made only a small part of the finished product.

Under the impact of scientific management and time-and-motion studies of work, jobs were fractionated into their smallest possible components. The ideal was to reduce every manufacturing process to the simplest elements that could be performed by a single employee.

Job fractionation and simplification offered advantages to industry and to consumers. It allowed the lowest possible cost per unit produced. When Henry Ford established his assembly line he was able to sell cars at a price within reach of many people who previously could not have afforded them. The same thing soon occurred with other consumer goods. The factory-produced chair in which you are sitting costs considerably less than one handmade by a skilled furniture craftsman. That is another advantage of job simplification: Industry no longer had to rely on skilled craftsmen—the persons who required years of apprenticeship, expected high wages, and were apt to be very independent. The assembly line employed workers with little skill or training; these people could learn an assembly line job quickly. The process also made workers more docile and easier to manage (before the advent of unions). Since they possessed no real usable skills, employees knew they could easily be replaced.

There is no denying that job simplification had a tremendously stimulating effect on the nation's economy. More jobs were available and people had more money to buy the plentiful automobiles and consumer goods. The more people bought, the more factories had to be expanded and that, of course, meant more jobs. Also, new products on the market required additional businesses to sell and service them. Such economic growth could never have taken place if production methods had remained limited to hand craftsmanship. (We are learning, however, that there is a price to be paid for affluence and industrial growth. As we breathe polluted air, search in vain for clean beaches, and get stuck in traffic jams, we may suspect that the price of affluence is higher than we are willing to pay.)

Assembly line workers paid, and are still paying, a high cost for their role in this widespread attainment of affluence. Personal value and meaning of work are destroyed the farther removed workers are from the finished product. The craftsmen who shaped a finished piece of furniture from the raw materials knew the pride and fulfillment of achievement and the challenge of properly using skill, imagination, and intelligence.

Where is the challenge and the satisfaction in making television tuning knobs by machine over and over again, day in, day out? In most cases, the machine makes the part; the worker is simply an adjunct, pressing a button or pushing a lever. Anyone could do it; it has been shown that even chimpanzees can perform many of the production jobs in industry today. All too often assembly line workers do not even know what happens to the part they make or what it has to do with the finished product. Such work has little meaning, provides less satisfaction, and is soon frustrating, boring, and monotonous. Workers become understandably apathetic and uninterested, morale declines, along with the quantity and quality of production. It is easy to understand why we find such poor quality construction in our cars and appliances.

Boredom and Monotony

Two major consequences of job fractionation—boredom and monotony—are important components of the psychological work environment. Boredom, sometimes called mental fatigue, usually results from the performance of a repetitive, monotonous, and uninteresting activity. Boredom can cause a feeling of general malaise—a restless, unhappy, and tired feeling that drains us of all interest and energy. Further, boredom can be caused by many things that once seemed exciting such as reading, watching television, or listening to music.

What is dull and boring for one person may be exciting and challenging for another; this applies even to the assembly line type of fractionated work. Although most people find it boring and monotonous, some do not. And some workers engaged in seemingly challenging work also report boredom and monotony. Motivation is a relevant factor here. The person who is highly motivated to turn out as many units as possible per day will be less bored than a worker who lacks this motivation.

In general, research on boredom shows a resulting decrease in production and greater variability in the work rate. These effects seem to be most severe in the middle of the workday and decrease greatly as the end of the work period approaches.

The observation of individual differences in boredom level led psychologists to investigate personal characteristics to try to identify and predict the boredom-prone individual. Such people, then, should not be hired for monotonous, repetitive jobs, a situation certainly to their ultimate benefit. The research in this area has focused on intelligence and personality. It seems plausible to suggest that the higher a person's level of intelligence, the more likely it is that he or she will be bored by repetitive, nondemanding work. Some research confirms this suggestion; very intelligent people manifest a higher than usual turnover rate in dull, routine jobs, certainly an indication of boredom and dissatisfaction. Persons of lower intelligence are considerably less bored by the same task.

The bored and the not-bored also tend to show differences in personality characteristics. In a study of female workers, those who reported the greatest boredom also evidenced a dislike for routine in any aspect of life, preferred active recreational and leisure pursuits, and were somewhat dissatisfied with their home and personal lives. Those workers who reported much less boredom had a more placid outlook and were generally more satisfied with their lives. Another study revealed that extraverts were more easily bored than introverts. These findings on personality characteristics are of interest but the evidence is not overwhelming. More research is needed before the relationship between boredom and personality can be fully explained.

The obvious problem for industry is how to counteract, prevent, or reduce boredom. Proper personnel selection and placement could effectively prevent boredom. For example, a person with an IQ of

150 should not be placed on an assembly line. But this will not completely eliminate the problem of bored employees because selection and placement techniques are imperfect, and the relationship between personal characteristics and boredom has not been fully established.

A second way of reducing boredom is to enlarge the scope and demands of the job through some form of job enlargement program. For jobs to which this technique can be applied, it has been very successful as an effective motivator and preventer of boredom.

A third method of preventing boredom is to alter the physical, temporal, or social conditions of work. Proper attention to noise reduction, illumination, pleasant colors, and music might counteract the effects of repetitive work. A congenial informal work group can also help. Appropriately scheduled rest pauses have proven effective in helping to alleviate boredom, not because workers on repetitive jobs necessarily need the physical rest, but because they need a change of activity. The greater the change during the rest breaks or lunch hour, the less disruptive will be the effects of boredom.

Other techniques have been used to fight boredom with varying degrees of success. Some companies have tried job rotation—letting workers periodically change to a different activity, sometimes as often as every two hours. Such a practice can only be successful if the alternate activity is not very similar to the original one. If the two jobs are much alike, switching from one to the other will provide little change for the workers. Of course, if the jobs are too dissimilar, extensive training may be required before the worker could make the switch. Some research indicates that job rotation programs lead to a reduction in boredom and to increased job satisfaction, but other studies have failed to confirm this. One interesting finding concerns the attitudes of workers toward job rotation. When asked how they would feel about a rotation system, only 37 per cent of a group of workers thought they would like it. However, 70 per cent of those already involved in a job rotation system reported that they liked it very much.

Another method of counteracting boredom is to teach the workers the value and meaning of their jobs. Greater interest has been engendered among workers who are told how their work (or the part they are producing) fits into the overall plant operation and the finished product. Sometimes, workers of twenty years' experience have no idea how their work relates to the production process as a whole. This kind of awareness can be easily and quickly taught in a few lectures and a tour of the entire plant. When carefully planned and presented, such programs have helped workers develop a new pride in their jobs and a feeling, often for the first time, that their work is

351

important. The programs have also led to increased motivation and, correspondingly, a greater tolerance for repetitive work.

Just because a job is repetitive, it does not follow that it must be boring. An alert, imaginative, and understanding management can prevent boredom and monotony and create interest and motivation instead.

Fatigue

Fatigue is closely related to boredom in its effects on behavior, although the causes of the two conditions can differ greatly. Also, there are really two kinds of fatigue: psychological fatigue (which is similar to boredom), and physiological fatigue, caused by excessive use of the muscles of the body. Although the latter is not a psychological condition of work, it still constitutes part of the internal work environment. Both types of fatigue can cause performance decrements as well as increased errors, absenteeism, turnover, and accidents. Because of its obvious influence on work behavior, fatigue has been the subject of intensive research by industrial psychologists.

Whereas boredom and monotony are basically psychological, fatigue, as noted, has both psychological and physiological components. Prolonged or heavy physical work produces definite and measurable physiological changes in the body. Processes such as heart rate, oxygen consumption, and muscle tension operate at different levels under fatigue. Thus, physiological fatigue can be defined with precision.

The psychological or subjective aspects of fatigue are more elusive in terms of measurement, but no less disturbing to individuals or impairing of their output. We know that when we are excessively tired we experience feelings of strain, irritability, and weakness, and find it difficult to concentrate clearly, think coherently, or work effectively.

On-the-job research shows that the level of production closely parallels reported feelings of fatigue. That is, high reported fatigue is a reliable indicator that production will shortly decline. With most physical work, employees report that they are most tired at the beginning of work in the morning, again just before the lunch break, and finally at the end of the work period. Thus, psychological fatigue does not build up over the course of a work period; it appears and disappears at least three times during the day. This strongly suggests that factors other than the actual work—motivation, for example—play a part in this type of fatigue. It often happens that a person who leaves work at the end of the day feeling exhausted finds that the fatigue suddenly disappears upon arriving home and anticipating a date for the evening. However, regardless of its psychological or motivational components, this fatigue is real to the worker and is still capable of causing a decline in productivity.

Research on physiological fatigue has indicated that greater amounts of physical work can be accomplished when the daily work pace is more gradual. Too rapid a rate of heavy work dissipates the body's energy too quickly so that the worker must then proceed at a slower pace for the rest of the work period. The analogy is made to long-distance runners who must pace themselves so as not to use up all their energy before the distance is covered.

Rest periods are necessary for jobs involving heavy physical labor. Experience has shown that rest pauses should be taken before fatigue has a chance to become complete. The greater the amount of fatigue before the break, the longer the rest period must be. The solution seems to be more frequent rest periods. Also, in order for rest periods to be maximally effective, they must provide total relaxation, not merely a work stoppage. It is the manual laborer, much more than the office worker, who could benefit from comfortable lounges and canteens. Unfortunately, it is usually the case that those who work the hardest physically have the least desirable rest facilities.

There exists a wide range of individual differences in ability to perform physical labor. People differ in physical fitness and general health, and these factors influence how well and how fast they can work. Age is also important; the younger worker is usually better able to maintain a high level of physical labor.

Diet is an influencing variable. Studies of North American eating habits show that youngsters, and others of lower socioeconomic levels, do not have a proper diet because of ignorance of nutritional matters, lack of money, or lack of concern. Most of us eat enough food but often it is not the right kind of food.

Management can take several steps to alleviate physiological and psychological fatigue. Since psychological fatigue is similar to boredom and monotony, the steps suggested in the last section can also be effective in counteracting subjective fatigue. To alleviate physiological fatigue, proper selection of workers for heavy labor, in terms of general health and physical condition, could prevent those for whom the work would be too taxing from entering such occupations. Attempting to get the workers to maintain a steady and somewhat gradual work pace, instead of working at full capacity for short periods, would also be effective. Adequately spaced rest periods are particularly necessary. Providing facilities where workers could relax in comfort, and proper nourishment through a company cafeteria, could also reduce the effects of physical fatigue.

Fatigue seriously interferes with the quantity and quality of all

353

kinds of work. It probably cannot be eliminated entirely, but an enlightened management can keep its effects to a minimum.

SUMMARY

Many aspects of the physical work environment influence job satisfaction and productivity. The focus in this chapter is on three such aspects: physical, temporal, and psychological conditions of work.

Physical conditions of work include a wide range of factors. The location of the place of employment influences employees through proximity to shops, restaurants, banks, and other services. Inadequate heating and air-conditioning systems, elevators, company cafeterias, and rest rooms can also impair efficiency on the job even though they have no direct bearing on the actual job. Handicapped workers are often prevented from accepting certain jobs by design features of buildings that inhibit easy access. Federal legislation now requires the removal of architectural barriers to the handicapped.

Environmental psychology is concerned with the impact of the environment on human behavior. Research has been conducted on the design of offices including the landscaped office, in which people are grouped in functional units with no floor-to-ceiling barriers between them.

In addition to large-scale design problems, psychologists are concerned with specific environmental factors including the effects of illumination, noise, color, music, and temperature and humidity.

With respect to **illumination,** standards exist for determining the desirable intensity levels for different kinds of work place. The distribution of light and glare are also problems that must be considered in the design of proper lighting for work.

Noise is a common problem in many work areas and can lead to temporary or permanent deafness. In an effort to reduce this health hazard, federal legislation has established maximum noise levels to which workers may be exposed. Noise can also produce other physiological effects including increased muscle tension and blood pressure, and constriction of blood vessels. Although noise can be a physical and psychological health hazard, its effects on productive efficiency are not clear.

Color in industry is useful as a coding device, to prevent eyestrain, to create differing illusions of size and temperature, and to improve the aesthetic quality of a work place. Color, however, does not seem to have any bearing on production. The use of **music** at work also seems not to affect productivity, although some employees say they like it. Music can make some work environments seem more pleasant.

Optimum **temperature and humidity** ranges have been established for work places. How comfortable a certain temperature feels depends on the humidity and the amount of air movement. Uncomfortable climate conditions can lower production, particularly on jobs involving physical labor.

Temporal conditions of work include the number of hours worked and the way in which those hours are arranged. Much scheduled work time is lost to unauthorized breaks. In general, when the required number of working hours is reduced, less time is lost and production tends to increase.

Several ways of scheduling work are part-time employment, the 4-day workweek, and flexible working hours. Part-time employment offers opportunities for those who want to combine a career with family, educational, leisure, or other pursuits, and may result in a higher level of productivity. The 4-day workweek has become very popular and apparently results in lower absenteeism and higher morale and productivity. Flexible working hours, in which employees can begin and end the workday when they wish (within a specified time period), also seem to increase production and morale and to lower absenteeism. This schedule gives an added sense of responsibility to workers, and also eases traffic congestion at rush hours.

Rest pauses are taken by employees whether or not officially sanctioned. They are necessary with manual labor in order to rest the muscles and with more sedentary work in order to provide a change of pace and prevent boredom.

Shift work can be very disruptive to the workers' diurnal rhythm and can cause social and psychological problems, especially by forcing workers to sleep when everyone else is awake. Production is lower on the night shift.

Psychological conditions of work deal with the design of the job and its effects on the workers. As a result of scientific management, time-and-motion study, and assembly line manufacturing, most jobs have been simplified or fractionated to the point where they produce boredom and fatigue.

Boredom results from repetitive and monotonous work and can lead to restlessness, tiredness, and lower productivity. Boredom can be relieved by job enlargement, job rotation, improving the conditions under which the work is performed, scheduling rest pauses, and teaching workers the value and importance of their jobs. **Fatigue** can be psychological or physiological and can impair production. Proper selection of workers, attention to diet, rest periods, and proper work pacing can help to alleviate fatigue.

355

SUGGESTED READINGS

Acking, C., and Küller, R. The perception of an interior as a function of its colour. *Ergonomics,* 1972, **15**(6), 645–654.

Bennett, C., and Rey, P. What's so hot about red? *Human Factors,* 1972, **14**(2), 149–154.

Brookes, M. Office landscape: Does it work? *Applied Ergonomics,* 1972, **3**(4), 224–236.

Buisman, B. 4-day, 40-hour workweek: Its effects on management and labor. *Personnel Journal,* 1975, **54,** 565–567.

Dempsey, D. Noise. *New York Times Magazine,* 1975 (November 23), pp. 31+.

Edwards, R. Shift work: Performance and satisfaction. *Personnel Journal,* 1975, **54,** 578–579.

Elving, A., Gadon, H., and Gordon, J. Flexible working hours: It's about time. *Harvard Business Review,* 1974, **52**(1), 18–28, 33, 154–155.

Evans, M. A longitudinal analysis of the impact of flexible working hours. *Studies in Personnel Psychology,* 1975, **6**(2), 1–10.

Eyde, L. *Flexibility Through Part-Time Employment of Career Workers in the Public Service.* Washington, D.C.: U.S. Civil Service Commission, Personnel Research and Development Center, 1975. P-S 75–3.

Flexible working hours. *Personnel Journal,* 1970, **49,** 855–856.

Grayston, D. Music while you work. *Industrial Management,* 1974, **4,** 38–39.

Ivancevich, J. J. Effects of the shorter workweek on selected satisfaction and performance measures. *Journal of Applied Psychology,* 1974, **59,** 717–721.

Kryter, K. *The Effects of Noise on Man.* New York: Academic Press, 1970.

McFarland, R. Understanding fatigue in modern life. *Ergonomics,* 1971, **14**(1), 1–10.

Nemecek, J., and Grandjean, E. Results of an ergonomic investigation of large-space offices. *Human Factors,* 1973, **15**(2), 111–124.

Nord, W., and Costigan, R. Worker adjustment to the four-day week: A longitudinal study. *Journal of Applied Psychology,* 1973, **58,** 60–66.

Poor, R. *4 Days, 40 Hours: Reporting a Revolution in Work and Leisure,* rev. ed. Cambridge, Mass.: Bursk & Poor, 1973.

Simonson, E., and Weiser, P. C. *Psychological Aspects and Physiological Correlates of Work and Fatigue.* Springfield, Ill.: Charles C Thomas, 1976.

Steele, F. I. *Physical Settings and Organization Development.* Reading, Mass.: Addison-Wesley, 1973.

Walker, J., Fletcher, C., and McLeod, D. Flexible working hours in British government offices. *Public Personnel Management,* 1975, 4(4), 216–222.

11

Engineering Psychology

INTRODUCTION

We have discussed several ways in which industrial psychologists contribute to the goals of increasing industrial efficiency, productivity, and job satisfaction. We have seen how the workers with the best abilities can be recruited and selected, how they can be trained for the job in question and supervised and motivated in the most desirable way, and how certain techniques can be used to optimize the work environment and conditions. All of these methods and procedures are time- and research-tested means of aiding the worker in the proper performance of the job.

But there is one aspect of work that has been mentioned only briefly, a factor clearly as influential as any of those discussed: the design of the machines with which workers perform their jobs. The importance of using the right kind of tool, and in the proper way, is evident from your own experience. To hang a picture you could use a doorknob or the heel of a shoe, or a rock to hammer the nail into the wall. All of these would probably work, but you would get the job done in less time and with less aggravation if you used a hammer, the tool specifically designed for your purpose.

Of course, there are many different hammers. You could use one from a child's toy toolbox or a twenty-pound sledgehammer or the standard homeowner's hammer. Again, you could probably accomplish the job with any of those tools but the standard hammer will be the most efficient. Having chosen your tool, you could hold the hammer either near the striking surface or back at the end for better leverage, but one way is more effective than the other.

The point is that a job can be performed in a variety of ways and with more than one tool or object, but, as a rule, there is one best tool and one best way of using it. For the occasional picture hanger this is not too great a problem, but for carpenters who must hammer nails all day, it can be. Providing them with properly shaped hammers of a specific weight, and ensuring that they use them in a certain way, not only allows them to hammer more nails during the work period but also makes the job safer, easier, and less fatiguing.

The same may be said of virtually every industrial job. No matter how well selected, trained, and motivated are the workers, the finished product (and the efficiency with which it is produced) is only as good as the tools or equipment supplied them. This principle applies to everything from hand tools to punch presses to the cockpits of modern airliners.

Equipment must be designed to be compatible with the workers. In a sense, we can think of this as a team operation—a worker and a machine functioning together to perform a specific task that could not be accomplished by either working alone. It is a system—a *man-machine system*—and if the person and the machine are to work in concert, they must be matched to one another, each making the best use of the strengths of the other and, where necessary, compensating for the weaknesses of the other.

This matching of operator and machine is the province of engineering psychology (also called human factors or human engineering). The field is a hybrid of engineering and psychological knowledge. We may formally define it as the science of engineering machinery or equipment for human use, and of engineering human behavior for proper operation of the machines.

Until the 1940s, the design of machinery, equipment, and industrial plants was solely the responsibility of engineers. They made design decisions on the basis of mechanical, electrical, space and size considerations, giving little, if any, thought to the workers who would have to use the machines.

In this situation, the machine was a constant factor, incapable of being changed to meet human needs, so workers had to adapt to the machine. No matter how uncomfortable, tiring, or unsafe the equipment, the operators, as the only flexible part of the man-machine system at that time, had to make the best of it and fit themselves to the machine's requirements.

Adapting the worker to the machine was accomplished by means of time-and-motion study—a precursor to engineering psychology—which analyzed the worker's job to determine how it could best be simplified. (As we see, the early time-and-motion study engineers also made rudimentary efforts at reshaping tools.)

The design of machines by engineers with no consideration for the needs of the people who operated them could not continue indefinitely. The machines were becoming too complex and requiring increasing levels of speed and precision for their proper operation. They were exceeding human capabilities to control them.

What could be done? Selection and training could help, of course, by finding and training people possessing the necessary skills, but that approach is limited by the relatively small numbers of qualified workers. By the time of World War II, the situation had become critical.

Sophisticated war machinery placed great demands upon human capacities, not only upon muscular strength but also higher-level abilities of sensing, perceiving, judging, and rapid decision making. Pilots flying new and faster planes were allowed less time to react, make a decision, and initiate proper action. Equipment such as radar and sonar required new high-level human skills.

For the most part, the equipment worked well, but mistakes were being made: the most precise bombsight ever developed was not bringing about accurate bombing; friendly ships and airplanes were identified incorrectly and fired upon; whales were mistaken for submarines. In short, although the machinery and equipment seemed to function properly, the system—the interaction of the worker and the equipment—did not.

So it was this urgent wartime need that gave rise to engineering psychology (reminiscent of World War I and the beginnings of psychological testing). It was recognized that the capabilities and limitations of human operators would have to be considered in the design of machines in order for the system to function well. Psychologists, physiologists, and physicians found themselves in unusual environments working with engineers in designing aircraft cockpits, submarine and tank crew stations, and even components of uniforms.

As an example of this early work, one large-scale study was concerned with the relationship between the instruments in an airplane cockpit (the various displays and controls) and the pilot's performance. Did the cockpit design and the arrangement of the instruments have anything to do with the ability of the pilot to handle the airplane in different situations?

Mistakes made by the pilots in reading the instruments and operating the flight controls were investigated. The results strongly indicted the design and layout of the controls and displays. Half of the pilots' errors involved confusing one control with another—operating the control to pull up the wheels when they wanted to operate the flaps, for example—a potentially deadly mistake.

The reason for this confusion centered on the lack of consistent or standardized display arrangements from one airplane to another.

A pilot suddenly assigned to a different kind of airplane was confronted with a different cockpit design.

Imagine trying to drive a car in which accelerator and brake pedals are reversed. In an emergency, you would probably step on the brake—at least, where you expect the brake to be—only to find yourself stepping on the gas. This was the situation facing the pilots in World War II. And there were other problems. There was no consistency in the operating characteristics of the aircraft controls. In the same airplane, one control would be switched upward to turn something on, and another switched downward to turn something on. A number of different controls, all with identically shaped knobs, were placed close together so that a pilot who had to look elsewhere for a moment would not be able to discriminate among these controls on the basis of touch alone. Once such problems were recognized, they were corrected in aircraft design, but many pilots were killed because their machines were poorly designed, not from an aerodynamic standpoint, but from the standpoint of the frail human being required to direct, control, and tame so much power.

Since World War II, military equipment has become even more demanding upon the people who must operate it. Aircraft fly at supersonic speeds and fire at planes or missiles they cannot see. How much time does a person have in which to decide to initiate some action, and then to implement the decision? As a rule, not enough; that is, the person must be given help. Computers and other mechanical aids provide information to help make such rapid decisions or, in the case where the alternatives are limited and known, to make them for the human operator.

The growth of engineering psychology has been dynamic, and its practitioners are employed by every area of the military, by defense contractors, by manufacturers of dental and surgical instruments, and by consumer industries. They are also consulted by companies involved in the design of machines used in manufacturing. Not only military equipment has placed increasing demands upon workers, but also factory machinery.

Studies of industrial errors and accidents reveal many examples of machines that are incompatible with the worker's capabilities and habitual ways of responding. An obvious example involves controls designed to operate in ways opposite to the way in which we expect them to operate, the way they have always operated in the past. In the World War II aircraft study, the switches designed to be moved downward to turn something on were contrary to virtually every other "on-off" switch we are used to.

It is similarly annoying (and sometimes painful) to American tour-

361

ists in Europe who find the hot and cold water faucets reversed. You can easily find examples of poor design features in your everyday life—controls that are poorly placed and difficult to reach or dials that are hard to read.

Fortunately, engineering psychologists are working on consumer goods ranging from automobiles and ovens to telephones and type-writers. (Push-button telephones are the result of extensive psychological research into the most efficient arrangement of the buttons.) The phenomenal growth of space exploration has also placed new demands on the skills of engineering psychologists.

Since the field of human engineering is a hybrid, it is not surprising that its practitioners have diverse backgrounds. The membership of the Human Factors Society includes physicians, sociologists, engineers, anthropologists, and other behavioral and physical scientists. More than 50 per cent of the members, however, are psychologists. A number of universities offer graduate and undergraduate degrees in engineering psychology.

TIME-AND-MOTION ANALYSIS

Time-and-motion study was an early attempt to reshape the way workers performed their jobs and to redesign work tools. This field, usually called industrial engineering, can be traced to the beginnings of industrial psychology and its growth has paralleled psychology's attempts to increase the productive efficiency of work. Time-and-motion study and engineering psychology are not synonymous terms or procedures, but they are closely linked, historically and procedurally, and their goals are identical.

The first systematic attempt to study the way in which work was performed occurred in 1898 when an engineer, Frederick W. Taylor, undertook an investigation of the job of shoveling at the Bethlehem Steel Company. He learned that the workers were using shovels of many sizes and shapes and, as a result, the loads lifted by each man ranged from 3½ pounds to 38 pounds. By experimenting with different shovel loads, Taylor determined that the optimum shovel size held 21½ pounds; using this size shovel, the workers were the most efficient. Heavier or lighter loads resulted in a decrease in total daily output. Taylor also introduced shovels of different size for handling different materials—a small one for heavy iron ore and a larger one for ashes. Nowadays such changes sound trivial, but Taylor's work resulted in savings to the company of $78,000 a year. With the new shovels, 140 men could accomplish the same amount of work that had formerly required 500 men. Also, by offering an incentive of higher pay for higher production, the workers' wages increased by 60 per cent.

This was the first empirical demonstration of the relationship between the tools of work and the efficiency with which a job could be performed. When companies realized how much money could be saved through proper investigation of work habits and tools, the field of time-and-motion analysis received a hearty welcome.

The second pioneer in this area was Frank B. Gilbreth, an engineer, who, together with his wife Lillian, a psychologist, did more to promote the growth of time-and-motion study than anyone else. Where Taylor had been concerned primarily with tool design and incentive wage systems, the Gilbreths were concerned with the way in which workers performed their jobs. Their overall goal was to eliminate all unnecessary motion.

It all began when Frank Gilbreth, at age seventeen, was an apprentice bricklayer. On his first day at work he noticed that the bricklayers were engaged in many unnecessary motions in their work. He thought he could redesign the job to make it faster and easier, and within a year, he was the fastest bricklayer on the job. Once Gilbreth convinced his co-workers to try his methods, the whole crew was accomplishing more work than they had ever done before, without being exhausted at the end of the workday.

First, Gilbreth designed a scaffold that could be raised or lowered so that the worker would always be at a level convenient to the work. By analyzing the individual hand and arm motions involved in bricklaying, and making the necessary changes in the way the job was performed, the bricklayers could lay 350 bricks per hour instead of the usual 120. This increase in productivity was brought about not by forcing the men to work faster, but by reducing the number of motions involved in the laying of each brick from 18 to 4½!

The Gilbreths, incidentally, organized their daily lives around the principles of time-and-motion economy and tolerated no wasted motions. Every activity of each member of the family was scrutinized for unnecessary motions. Gilbreth, for example, always buttoned his vest from the bottom up because it took four seconds less than buttoning it from the top down. He used two brushes, one in each hand, to lather his face for shaving, a saving of seventeen seconds. He also tried shaving with two razors, but found that he lost more time bandaging his face than he saved in shaving. The activities of the children were noted on charts so that every minute of the day was as gainfully employed as possible. In spite of this (or perhaps as evidence of increased productivity), they had twelve children, the subject of the book and movie *Cheaper by the Dozen*.[1]

As a result of the efforts of Taylor and the Gilbreths, time-and-motion engineers (or efficiency experts, as they came to be called) studied all types of jobs with the overall goal of reducing to the absolute minimum the number of motions in the performance of a job. Their work revolutionized many jobs, even those in hospital operating rooms. Before Gilbreth analyzed the motions involved in surgery, surgeons had to seek out each tool they wanted to use. Gilbreth urged that a nurse place the required tool in the surgeon's hand, a saving of motion that reduced operating times by as much as two thirds.

The investigations of the efficiency experts provided the most significant results with routine and repetitive work. In a motion study, a worker's individual movements are studied in detail with a view toward modifying or eliminating as many movements as possible. To accomplish this with the greatest precision, motion pictures are taken of job performance and analyzed on a frame-by-frame basis to discover inefficient or wasteful motion.

Through these studies, rules or guidelines for efficient work have been developed. The following is a list of some rules designed to increase the ease, speed, and accuracy of jobs involving manual operations.

1. Minimize the distance workers must reach to get tools, supplies, or operate machines. Reaching motions should be as short as possible.
2. Both hands should begin and end their movement at the same time. Movements should be as nearly symmetrical as possible; for example, the right hand should reach to the right for one item while the left hand simultaneously reaches to the left for another. Such simultaneous movements feel "natural" and do not disturb balance.
3. The hands should always be in motion—never idle—except during official rest periods.
4. The hands should never be given tasks that could be performed more appropriately by other parts of the body, particularly by the legs and feet. Leg muscles are strong and a foot control can often be used, thus relieving the hands of one more operation.
5. Wherever possible, work materials should be held by a mechanical device such as a vise, instead of being held by

---

[1] F. Gilbreth and E. Carey, *Cheaper By the Dozen* (New York: Thomas Y. Crowell, 1948); see also F. Gilbreth, *Time Out For Happiness* (New York: Thomas Y. Crowell, 1970).

the hand. Once again, this releases the hands for another operation.

6. Circular movements of the hands between two points are more efficient than straight line movements, particularly if the movement is made repeatedly and quickly.

7. The work place should be so arranged as to permit workers to sit or stand alternately to perform the job. Thus, the workbench or table should be of sufficient height that the job can be performed while sitting on a high stool or while standing. Alternating positions relieves fatigue.

8. Wherever possible, tools should be combined so as to eliminate the wasteful motions of putting one tool down and picking another up. If the two tools can be combined into one, these motions are dispensed with.

9. Movements should always occur in the direction in which gravity will aid the movement; for example, pulling a heavy weight down instead of pushing it up.

10. Picking up and handling objects should be accomplished in such a way as to require the least amount of precision. Large gross movements are easier, less subject to error, and less fatiguing.

Criticisms of Time-and-Motion Analysis

At first glance, it might seem that these methods of work simplification should have met with enthusiastic acceptance both from management, which receives a greater output, and from labor, whose work is made easier to accomplish. Although management has indeed been delighted with time-and-motion study, the workers have definitely not. Their reaction has been characterized by suspicion and hostility.

Individual workers and organized labor have argued, throughout the years, that time-and-motion studies benefit only the company while adversely affecting the workers. Employees suspect that the only reason for such job analysis is to force them to work faster. They believe that this will lead to lower rates of pay and to dismissals, since fewer workers will be required to maintain the same production level. And it must be noted that this has occasionally been a consequence of time-and-motion studies.

Other worker complaints are that job simplification can lead to monotony, boredom, lack of challenge and responsibility, and an ultimate decline in productivity. As noted in the discussion of job enlargement, many human needs are not being satisfied (in fact, are being thwarted) by the reduction of work to its simplest components.

It is well known in industry that when workers are observed by an efficiency expert, they commonly react by slowing their normal work rate. Too many organizations send industrial engineers to observe a job, often for several days, without informing the workers about the purpose of the time-and-motion analysis and the possible effects the results may have on their jobs. It has been demonstrated (initially by Gilbreth) that employees are much more accepting of time-and-motion studies when management fully informs them of the nature and purpose of the observations. This simple and honest technique usually increases cooperation and the value of the study.

In recent years, criticisms from industrial psychologists and engineers have been directed against certain basic premises of time-and-motion study. They argue that the wide range of individual differences that exists in job abilities and skills negates the idea that there is only one best way of performing a job that is appropriate for all employees. Because of individual differences in physical characteristics and attitudes, the work methods suitable for one employee might not be suitable for another. People are not standardized or interchangeable parts, and to assume that they can and must follow identical work routines is to look upon them as nothing more than machines or robots.

A second professional criticism of time-and-motion study has to do with inadequate sampling. The optimum movement pattern and time for a job are established on the basis of a limited number of observations, usually involving only a small number of the total work force in a specific job category. Of course, if a small number is a representative sample of the work force there would be no problem, but, invariably, it seems that only the best workers already performing the job are studied. The resulting work methods, then, are based on behavior that was desirable for a few superior workers, a sample clearly not representative of the full range of skills and abilities found in the work force.

Also, rarely is an adequate sample of the full workday or workweek studied. For example, a time study might be taken only on Thursday and Friday of a particularly hectic week when workers are more tired and less efficient than normally.

Critics of time-and-motion study also question some of the basic rules of motion listed previously. Recent research suggests that it may not be as efficient to use both hands simultaneously as had previously been thought. Additional research is needed to verify these principles and guidelines.

These criticisms have not been directed against the concept of developing more efficient work methods, but rather against certain weaknesses in the techniques by which work methods have been developed. When these criticisms are taken into account, time-and-motion analysis still can serve to make the worker's job easier and safer, and the company's profits larger.

Many satires and parodies have been written about the notion of judging everything by the criterion of greater efficiency. Suppose, one author noted, we were to undertake a time-and-motion study of a symphony orchestra performance.

For considerable periods the four oboe players had nothing to do. The number should be reduced and the work spread more evenly over the whole of the concert . . . .

All the twelve violins were playing identical notes; this seems unnecessary duplication. The staff of this section should be drastically cut. . . .

There seems to be too much repetition of some musical passages. Scores should be drastically pruned. No useful purpose is served by repeating on the horns a passage which has already been handled by the strings. It is estimated that if all redundant passages were eliminated the whole concert time of 2 hours could be reduced to 20 minutes . . . . In many cases the operators were using one hand for holding the instrument, whereas the use of a fixture would have rendered the idle hand available for other work.[2]

Time-and-motion study is alive and well today, but its use is largely limited to relatively simple and routine tasks such as assembly line jobs. When job operations, equipment, and functions become more complex, a more sophisticated procedure for optimizing work methods and procedures is needed; this is the task of engineering psychology.

MAN-MACHINE SYSTEMS

As we have noted, the early World War II efforts of engineering psychologists were concerned with specific problems of equipment design. Indeed, the field was sometimes referred to as "knob and dial" work because so much of the initial effort was concerned with the proper location and design of individual controls and displays.

As engineering psychology expanded in numbers and expertise, its interests grew to embrace the total relationship between the human operator and the machine. Though still concerned with the design of knobs and dials, engineering psychologists now begin work with an analysis of the task to be performed and a determination of the

[2] "How to be efficient with fewer violins," American Association of University Professors Bulletin, **41** (1955), 454–455.

most effective combination of worker and machine skills to accomplish that task. In other words, engineering psychologists make their input from the earliest stages of a design problem. Instead of being called in, for example, to design and place the pilot's instrument panel components after the airplane has been designed, human engineers now participate in the design of the total airplane as a man-machine system. Problems include the best allocation of functions between the operator and the machine, the kinds of information the operator will need, the kinds of judgments and decisions that will be required, and the quickest and safest way of communicating these decisions to the machine. These are studied in advance and the answers to these questions are used to shape the final design of the machine.

A man-machine system is one in which both components must work together to accomplish the job; neither part of the system is of value without the other. Using this definition, many routine tasks are examples of man-machine systems.

A person pushing a lawnmower is such a system. A person driving a car or operating a drill press is a man-machine system, albeit a bit more complicated. At a more sophisticated level, the Concorde airliner and its required crew of specialists (each responsible for a different part of the operation) constitute a man-machine system.

Even more complex is an air traffic control system at a busy airport. Here the total system includes a number of separate man-machine systems, each an integral part of the whole. If one small part (mechanical or human) fails, all the other parts of the system are affected.

Man-machine systems vary greatly in the extent to which human operators are actively and continuously involved in their operation. In flying an airplane or controlling traffic at a busy airport, operators are an integral part of the total system; their presence is necessary most of the time. Even when an airplane is on automatic pilot, the flight crew must be available to immediately resume control in the event of an emergency.

There are other man-machine systems in which humans interact less continuously. Large-scale production processes such as oil refineries operate with highly automated equipment. No human being is needed to run the machines. But whereas it can be said that automated equipment runs itself, it cannot design, build, or maintain itself. It can't even replace its own light bulb! Human beings are still important components of the system even when they are not directly operating the equipment.

Thus, automation has not diminished the need for engineering psychology. If anything, it has complicated the task of engineering psychologists since they now must deal with new kinds of jobs. Workers required to monitor automated equipment can find the task more fatiguing and boring than actually operating a machine. Monitoring equipment must be designed so as to keep observers alert in order that they can immediately determine when something goes wrong. Also, humans must maintain mechanical systems and so the machines must be designed to facilitate troubleshooting, locating, and replacing defective parts.

The definition and the requirements of man-machine systems remain the same, in principle, regardless of the degree of involvement of the worker with the machine; we are still vital to the system, whatever the degree of automation. (If we should ever develop machines that are able to design, build, and maintain other machines, then we have a problem of a different sort. Perhaps then the machines will produce books about how to engineer human beings to fit the machines' needs!)

Open-Loop and Closed-Loop Systems

There are two varieties of man-machine systems: open-loop and closed-loop. The basic difference between them is their self-correction; that is, whether or not the operation of the machine provides feedback to itself that can then cause a change in its operation.

In the open-loop system, an input enters at a particular point, activates a controlling mechanism, and some sort of activity occurs. This is so, for example, with overhead sprinkler systems installed in many buildings in case of fire. The input is a certain level of heat in the room. When the temperature exceeds this predetermined level, the heat melts a metal plug in the water line, thereby releasing the flow of water (the output).

The system is simple and is not self-regulating. If the room temperature then decreased to below the critical level, the system would not shut itself off; the water would continue to flow until stopped by some external agent such as the owner of the building or the fire department.

A closed-loop system is self-regulating; for example, a building's central heating system. Once the controlling agent—the thermostat—is set at the desired temperature, the furnace turns itself on and off to adjust to temperature fluctuations. The input (the desired temperature) controls the operation of the furnace. When the furnace has run long enough to raise the temperature to the thermostat setting, this new input causes the controlling thermostat to shut the furnace off.

Human beings are self-regulating closed-loop systems. We receive information (inputs) from the environment through the senses. We process the information in some way—storing it for future use, forgetting it because it is trivial, or taking some immediate action (output) on the basis of it.

A man-machine closed-loop system is more efficient than an open-loop system; therefore the latter is seldom used. Figure 11–1 depicts a closed-loop man-machine system. The human operator (the regulator or thermostat) receives input on the status of the machine from the displays. On the basis of that information he or she regulates the machine by initiating some controlling action.

Suppose you are driving your car on a highway at a constant speed. You receive input from the speedometer, process this information, and decide that you are driving too fast. Through the control action of easing your foot off the accelerator, you cause the car to slow down. This decrease in speed is displayed on the speedometer for your information and the process continues.

A driver also receives information from the environment—a sign

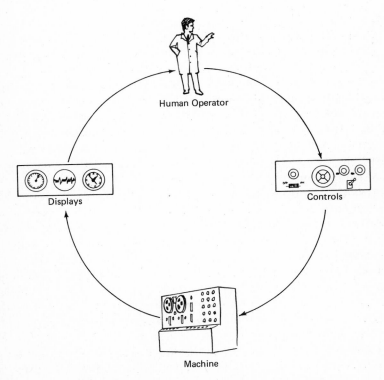

Figure 11–1. Closed-loop man-machine system.

noting a change in the speed limit or a slow car ahead. This information is processed and a change in speed is dictated to the machine. Verification of the changed status of the machine (the new speed) is seen on the speedometer.

Although more complicated, the principle is the same for the most sophisticated man-machine systems, and it is the system as a whole that is the starting point for the engineering psychologist's job.

In designing a man-machine system, there are two broad categories of human engineering considerations; that is, two methods of matching the often conflicting requirements of the worker and the machine. First, there are techniques for designing the physical equipment with which the operator will work. This is properly the province of engineering psychologists. Second, once the system is designed, there are methods of selecting and training persons who possess the abilities to perform the job. This is the province of personnel or industrial psychologists. Both considerations are necessary for efficient performance, but in a complex man-machine system, the problems of equipment design (the so-called hardware problems) are more important.

ALLOCATION OF FUNCTIONS IN MAN-MACHINE SYSTEMS

An initial step in the design of any man-machine system involves making decisions (as many as the complexity of the system requires) about the division of labor between the human operator and the machine. The system requirements (its goals) are nearly always known from the outset. The problem is how to combine the capabilities and the limitations of the two major system components to best fulfill these requirements.

Each step or process in the functioning of the total system must be examined to determine its characteristics, the speed, accuracy, and frequency with which it must be performed, the stress under which it occurs, and the like. When this information is analyzed, it becomes possible to properly match the system requirements with the characteristics of the person and the machine. These matching decisions must also consider information about the number of persons necessary to function as the human part of the system, background characteristics (such as intelligence), and training desired to transform general abilities into specific skills.

These highly complex decisions must be made early in the design process. Their results will help determine the shape and nature of the total system.

There are a number of criteria or guidelines available to facilitate such decisions. Research by psychologists, physiologists, and physicians has revealed much information about human strengths and weaknesses, so we are aware of those functions for which humans are superior to machines as well as those for which humans are inferior. Similarly, engineers (in conjunction with engineering psychologists) are aware of the relative effectiveness of the machines.

In general, humans are superior to machines in performing the following kinds of functions.

1. Detecting through the senses a wide range of stimuli (visual, auditory, tactual, gustatory, and olfactory).
2. Picking out infrequently appearing or low-level stimuli against a confusing background, such as detecting words in radio transmissions containing a lot of static, or detecting blips on a radar screen having poor reception.
3. Sensing, detecting, and recognizing highly unusual or unexpected stimuli in the environment.
4. Being able to remember (or store, in computer terminology) a large amount of information for long periods of time.
5. Recalling (or retrieving) relevant information from the memory storage, particularly very frequent recalling of related information.
6. Being able to use a wide range of past experiences in making decisions.
7. Being able to respond and adapt quickly to diverse situations and emergencies; humans do not require previous programming to meet all situations.
8. Drawing generalizations on the basis of a number of specific observations (inductive reasoning).
9. Exhibiting flexibility in problem solving, including the development of new solutions never before applied to a problem.

Perhaps another advantage of humans over machines is that humans are lightweight and easy to maintain—a great value for the dollar. "Nowhere else can one obtain a self-maintaining computer with built-in judgment, which can be mass produced inexpensively by unskilled laborers who like their work so much." [3]

Human operators bring to the man-machine system a host of remarkable abilities and skills, the more sophisticated of which have not been duplicated in the most expensive, complex, and cumbersome of machines. However, humans also have weaknesses that must be compensated for in the man-machine system.

[3] Quoted in M. D. Dunnette and W. K. Kirchner, *Psychology Applied to Industry* (New York: Appleton-Century-Crofts, 1965), p. 101.

In general, humans are inferior to machines in performing the following kinds of functions.

1. In the range of detection of sensory stimuli; for example, humans cannot detect auditory stimuli beyond frequencies of twenty thousand cycles per second.
2. Long-term monitoring activities, such as watchkeeping or radar observation; human performance is not very reliable over long periods of time.
3. The number of mathematical calculations that can be carried out rapidly without mechanical aids.
4. Retrieving large amounts of data very reliably and quickly.
5. Applying physical force, particularly where precision and continuous application are necessary.
6. Routine, repetitive performance over long periods of time.

Also, human performance is subject to deterioration under conditions of stress or fatigue.

We can readily see which functions are performed better by machines.

1. Machines can detect stimuli such as radar wave lengths and ultraviolet light, which are beyond human sensory powers.
2. Machines can monitor reliably for extremely long periods of time. (The stimulus in question must be programmed or specified for the machine in advance.)
3. Machines such as computers are able to make large numbers of extremely rapid and accurate calculations.
4. Machines can store and retrieve huge amounts of information with an extremely high level of accuracy.
5. Machines can apply greater physical force continuously and rapidly.
6. Machines can engage in highly repetitive activities with no performance deterioration, as long as proper maintenance is applied.
7. Machines do not tire easily.

Lest we begin to feel inadequate and insecure, machines also have weaknesses and limitations.

1. Machines are not very flexible. Even the most sophisticated computer can only do what it is programmed to do. Where adaptability to meet new, rapidly changing circumstances is important, machines are at a disadvantage. They can perform

their prescribed functions well, but can only do what a human operator tells them to do.

2. Machines cannot benefit from past experiences or mistakes. They cannot learn and modify their performance on the basis of experience. Any change in operation must be dictated by a human programmer.

3. Machines are unable to reason or examine various unprogrammed alternatives; machines cannot improvise.

As these lists seem to indicate, it is perhaps naïve to talk (as some futurists do) about redesigning humans out of the system. We can perform certain vital functions that machines cannot. In other cases, we can perform functions at least as well as, and often cheaper than, machines. And, as long as machines lack flexibility and responsiveness, human operators are a necessary component of properly functioning systems.

The problem of function allocation in the design of a man-machine system is not resolved by a designer referring to lists such as these and checking whether a person or a machine can perform the task better. These are guidelines only. There are several considerations beyond the simple superiority of one component over the other. The designer may take note of these guidelines, but they frequently must be modified in the light of other factors.

Some man-machine comparisons are modified by cost. Although it is true that a computer is more efficient than a human at calculating, storing, and retrieving data, it also costs a great deal more. If cost is an important consideration, or if the project budget requires a cutback in expenses, then speed of calculation may have to be sacrificed if a person can do the job almost as well (assuming "almost as well" allows the total system to function satisfactorily).

There may also be social and political considerations, particularly in assigning priority to machines in production facilities. In times of massive unemployment it would be unwise to automate a process that formerly required the skills of a large number of workers. Even though the job may be performed faster and more accurately by machines, is this worth the cost of creating additional unemployment?

The opposite situation of not having enough workers (experienced by some northern European countries) can also influence allocation decisions. Jobs that could be performed quite well by humans must be automated, even though it may cost more to make the finished product. In short, allocation decisions often cannot be based solely on the issue of the superiority of humans or machines for the task.

Their relative superiority must be constantly re-evaluated under the impact of technological innovations and developments. A new machine or process can influence a system already in operation. Until recently, for example, the banking system in the United States required numerous employees to read and sort checks into their proper accounts. For many years, this was a constant in the design of such systems—a human operator was vital to the performance of this task. Today, machines perform these operations by scanning computerized check numbers, thus altering the whole procedure. The system has been redesigned and improved because of technological advances.

The entire allocation question represents a bumpy road full of compromises that must be resolved to the satisfaction of system performance as well as economic, social, and cost considerations. The advantages of selecting one component over the other must constantly be compared with the disadvantages.

This was particularly apparent in the design of vehicles for space exploration. For several reasons (technical, social, and political), the United States space program insisted on using humans in the vehicles. There are obvious advantages to their use (although many argue that just as much information could be collected without a human component in the system). Whereas humans offer certain advantages, the difficulties of keeping them alive in the spacecraft required costly, heavy, and extensive life-support systems—crews had to be provided with an artificial environment in order to survive. Thus, much weight and space had to be added to the total system. This was a great disadvantage, but it was necessary in order to realize the advantages of accommodating humans in the system.

This initial stage of system design—the allocation of functions—is difficult and demanding, but unless all functions have been properly allocated, it is unwise to proceed to the design of the machine itself.

WORK SPACE DESIGN

The effective design of the human operator's work space—whether it is a workbench for electronic part assembly or an air traffic control center—involves certain established principles of design and work economy from the fields of human engineering and time-and-motion study. System analysis of the job and allocation of functions decisions help determine the kinds of tools and equipment needed by human operators to perform their missions in the system. Once the specific items of equipment are determined, the task is to position or arrange them in such a way as to facilitate job performance.

Some of the principles of motion economy discussed earlier serve as guidelines in work space design, and common sense and empirically tested principles are also available.

The first principle of work space design is that all materials, tools, and supplies needed by workers should be placed in the order in which they are to be used so that the paths of the workers' movements are continuous. Also, the knowledge that each part or tool is always in the same place saves the time and annoyance of searching for it.

The second principle is that tools should be pre–positioned so that they can be picked up ready for use. For a job requiring repeated use of a screwdriver, that tool can be suspended just above the work area on a coil spring. When it is needed, workers do not even have to raise their heads to see it—they merely reach up and pull it down in a position ready for immediate use.

The third principle of work space design is that all parts and tools be placed within an easy and comfortable reaching distance. It becomes fatiguing if workers must constantly change positions (either sitting or standing) to reach beyond the normal working area. All work should be able to be accomplished within the maximum reach, as shown in the work assembly station pictured in Figure 11–2. The work activities depicted here can all occur within the confines of the

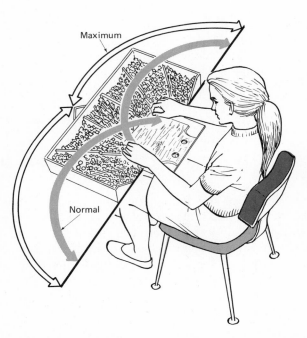

Figure 11–2. Work assembly station. Reprinted by permission from R. Barnes, *Motion and Time Study*, 5th ed. (New York: John Wiley & Sons, 1963), p. 259.

normal arm reach. No movement beyond the maximum reaching distance is ever required. Obviously, the greater the distance the arms are forced to reach, the longer the operation will require. Note too that the bins containing the components for the assembly task are arranged in a semicircle in front of the worker, rather than a straight line. This eliminates excessive reaching that might otherwise have been required; in a straight line arrangement the end bins are farther away.

This semicircular work space arrangement is ideal for any situation involving repeated reaching for several items in a fixed sequence. One research study demonstrated for a large number of workers that shortening the distance to a bin by a mere six inches saved thirty-four thousand hours a year in production time. These results should indicate the importance of proper work space design.

Similar design principles apply to the work space required by a radar operator, or a person seated before a panel or console of lights, dials, and switches, who is monitoring and controlling the operation of complex machinery. Such an operator's console is shown in Figure 11–3. As with the work assembly station, the monitoring console is designed so that operators can see and reach everything necessary

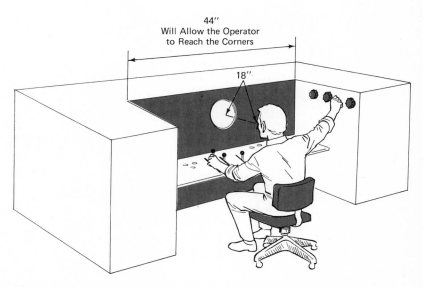

Figure 11–3. Monitoring console work arrangement. From W. Woodson, *Human Engineering Guide for Equipment Designers* (Berkeley, Calif.: University of California Press, 1954), p. 1–37. Copyright © 1954 & 1964 by The Regents of the University of California; reprinted by permission of the University of California Press.

to the successful performance of the task without leaving the chair or even reaching excessively beyond normal seated posture. Studies have shown that average reaching distance is twenty-eight inches. Therefore, all controls, particularly those used most frequently, should be within that distance. Details of shape and arrangement of controls and displays are discussed in the next section.

Important research on work space arrangement has been conducted by a branch of engineering psychology—known as human anthropometry—which is concerned with the measurement of the physical structure of the human body. Complete sets of body measurements have been taken from large populations while at rest and in the performance of various activities: height (standing and sitting), shoulder breadth, back height, seat height, foot and hand length and breadth, chest depth, and so on. These measurements are useful for many aspects of work space design: normal and maximum reaching distances, heights of proper tool and desk arrangement, size and shape of aircraft and automobile seats, and the like. One textbook on human engineering even includes a section entitled, "The Science of Seating," indicating the tremendous amount of research that has been conducted on just this one part of work space arrangement. For jobs that require a sitting position, and for the comfort of passengers, pilots, and drivers, anthropometrists have attacked the problem of seat design with a vengeance.

Relationships Between Work Spaces

We have been concerned with the design of individual work spaces for performing a task. Many jobs involve the interaction of several machines and human operators. A machine that produces one part of a product may pass the finished part on to another machine for the next step in the operation. Two or more people may be required to communicate frequently by voice or mechanical signal, or to pass raw material or parts from one to another. Individual controls may have to be used in sequence; for example, control "B" cannot be activated until control "A" has first been turned on. These interrelationships are *links,* and the method of studying them, with a view to optimizing the various connections, is called *link analysis.* The purpose of link analysis is to determine the number and frequency of the interconnections among system components so that the total work area can be designed to facilitate these connections.

If, for example, an airplane pilot and copilot are in more frequent contact with each other than with any other crew members, their work stations should be situated as close as possible. If certain controls and displays are consulted or used more frequently than others, these should be placed in a position of visual prominence and easy accessibility.

Two approaches to link analysis are observation and interviews with the human operators. The opinions and judgments of employees can be valuable supplements to material obtained by observation. In general, observational methods provide information on frequency of interaction and personal interviews provide an assessment of the importance of these connections.

For very complicated systems, link analyses are usually made by careful study of films taken of the work in progress. This provides a meticulous and permanent record of the various linkages. An eye camera can record the movements of the eyes, including specific points of fixation and length of fixation. Using this mechanism, it has been possible to determine visual links among the displays in an aircraft cockpit during different phases of a flight; that is, which dials were referred to most frequently and for how long during takeoff, landing, and other flight maneuvers. As a result of these studies, the optimum location of six vital visual displays was determined and made uniform for all military and commercial airplanes.

Link analysis can also be performed on systems not yet in operation by means of life-size mock-ups of the system or smaller models. It is more efficient to determine the best linkage arrangement before building the total system than to analyze and subsequently modify one already in operation.

Figure 11–4 shows a system composed of three operators and five machines, and linkages between them. The system has three types of links: control, visual communication, and auditory communication. The numbers 1 to 9 in the small circles represent link values in terms of frequency and importance of the interaction. Part A shows the original arrangement of operators and machines. Some of the distances of high link value (a more frequently used and important connection) are longer than those of low link value; this indicates inefficiency and wasted time. The ideal arrangement, and the whole purpose of link analysis, is to shorten high link value distances as much as possible. The primary guideline is that the higher the link value between two components, the closer these two components should be placed.

Of course, critical distances vary with the nature of the link; that is, whether it is a control, visual, or auditory link. In general, control links should be the shortest of the three, short enough to allow easy and quick access to the control. The best distance for visual links is determined by the size and visibility of the display and the location of any viewing obstructions such as other equipment. For auditory

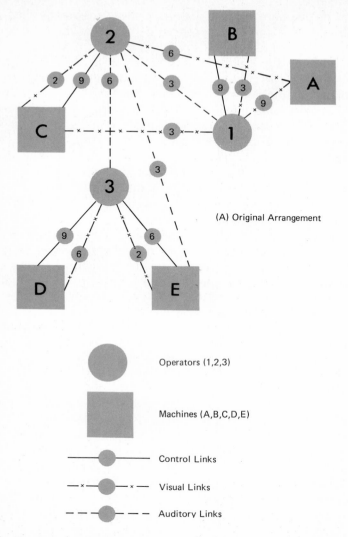

(A) Original Arrangement

Operators (1,2,3)

Machines (A,B,C,D,E)

———————— Control Links

—x——x— Visual Links

— — — — Auditory Links

Figure 11–4. Original and revised systems as a result of link analysis (A and B). From *Human Engineering* by E. McCormick. Copyright 1957, McGraw-Hill Book Company. Used with permission of McGraw-Hill Book Company.

links where amplification aids such as telephone or radio are available, the link distance is not as critical.

Part B of Figure 11–4 shows the revised arrangement of the system components based on the link analysis. High value links have been reduced to the shortest possible distance.

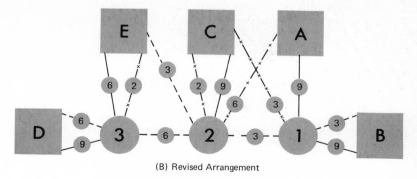

(B) Revised Arrangement

Figure 11–4. (cont'd.)

We have determined the most efficient allocation of functions and the general layout and design of the work space of a man-machine system. We now turn to the details of designing the specific displays and controls for the work station.

PRESENTATION OF INFORMATION TO THE HUMAN OPERATOR

In man-machine systems, operators receive inputs from the machine through one or more physical senses. In driving a car, for example, we receive some information on the operating status of the machine from visual displays (speedometer, temperature indicator, gas gauge), and some from auditory displays (the buzzer that indicates that the key is still in the ignition when the door is open). On an informal basis, we even receive inputs tactually, such as when a poor performing engine causes the car to vibrate.

All three of these senses have been used to present inputs to a human operator, although the visual mode is the most frequently used. One of the earliest decisions, then, concerning the presentation of information is to select the most effective means of communication for various kinds of information. The choice depends on the nature of the information and how it is to be used, the location of the operator relative to the machine, and the characteristics of the specific sense organ.

The visual presentation of information is more appropriate when: [4]

1. The message is difficult, abstract, and lengthy.
2. The information will be referred to at a later time or a per-

[4] A. Chapanis, *Man-Machine Engineering* (Belmont, Calif.: Wadsworth Publishing Co., 1965), pp. 33–34.

manent record is desired (a permanent record of an aural message must be made at the moment of transmission).

3. The environment is too noisy for aural messages.
4. There is no urgency or the aural channels of communication are overloaded.
5. The message consists of many different kinds of information that must be presented simultaneously.

Aural communication of information is more effective when: [5]

1. The information is simple, short, and straightforward.
2. The message is urgent (auditory signals will usually attract attention more readily than visual ones).
3. The environment does not allow for visual communication; for example, dark conditions.
4. The operator's job requires movement to a number of locations (ears can receive messages from all directions).
5. The message deals with a precise moment, such as telling someone when to fire artillery (aural presentation allows for more precise pinpointing of time).

Other conditions can determine the relative effectiveness of these two communication channels, but the previous lists amply demonstrate that situational requirements dictate the choice. We deal mainly with the visual presentation of information since that is the most frequently used mode in man-machine systems.

Visual Displays

One common error made in the visual presentation of input is to provide more information than the operator needs to run the machine. Particularly in the days before the application of human engineering knowledge, instrument panels and display consoles were cluttered with information that served no useful purpose.

For example, most automobile drivers do not need a tachometer to indicate engine rpm; this information will be of little value. It may not be a problem in an automobile, but in an airplane, where large amounts of vital information must be displayed, any useless input only adds to the display problem.

The first question, then, in visual display design is: Is this information necessary to the operation of the system? If the system can function without it, there will be one less item with which to confront

[5] Ibid.

or confuse the already busy human operator. If the information is vital to the operation of the system, the most effective method of displaying it—so that it can be perceived quickly and accurately—must be determined.

Three types of visual displays are commonly used in man-machine systems: quantitative, qualitative, and check reading.

Quantitative displays present quantitative information; that is, a precise numerical value. In situations dealing with speed, altitude, or temperature, for example, the human operator must know the precise numerical value of a condition of the system. A pilot must know if the altitude is ten thousand five hundred feet as dictated by the flight plan. An approximate instead of a precise indication of altitude could lead the plane into the flight path of another aircraft or into the ground in a fog. Five ways of presenting quantitative information, along with their relative reading accuracy, are shown in Figure 11–5.

The open-window type of display was read with the fewest errors. The vertical display was misread more than one third of the time. One variable that may tend to influence reading accuracy is the relative size of the area the observer must view in order to get a reading. In Figure 11–5, the larger the area to be scanned, the greater the errors. However, these results are from an experimental situation in which

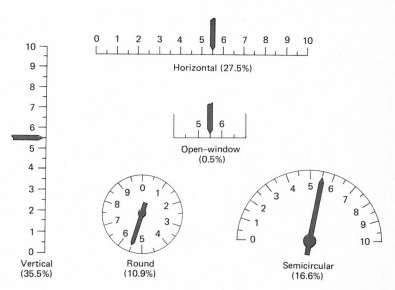

Figure 11–5. Percentage of errors in reading five types of quantitative display. From R. Sleight, "The effect of instrument dial shape on legibility," *Journal of Applied Psychology* **32**(1948), p. 177. Copyright 1948 by the American Psychological Association. Reprinted by permission.

the subjects were required to read the displays in a fixed short period of time. In some situations, the human operator may be able to take more time to read quantitative displays.

Other research has not consistently supported the order of reading accuracy shown in Figure 11–5. In general, however, research indicates that the open-window design does allow for the most accurate readings, particularly when the reading must be made quickly. As to the relative order of accuracy of the other types of quantitative display, the time available in which to read the display appears to be the critical factor.

Many specific design questions must be answered once the type of quantitative display has been chosen. These include the effect on accuracy of the design of the pointer, the size and number of scale markers, the design and location of the numerals, and the separation between the scale markers.

The second type of visual indicators, the *qualitative* displays, are used when a precise numerical reading is not necessary. Again, no more information than is necessary for the operation of the system should be presented. If the operator does not need a precise numerical indication of the status of a portion of the system, no useful purpose is served by presenting it.

Most automobile drivers, for example, do not need to know the precise engine temperature. All most of us want to be sure of is that the temperature is within the safe operating range. This is the case with many components of man-machine systems; it is necessary to know only within what range the system is functioning, and whether the values are increasing or decreasing over time. If drivers see that the engine temperature is rising, they may want to take some corrective action. They do not have to know the precise temperature, but they do need an indication of normal and abnormal operating ranges and whether the temperature is changing over time.

A typical qualitative display is shown in Figure 11–6. Often, the operating ranges are color-coded with the dangerous operating range

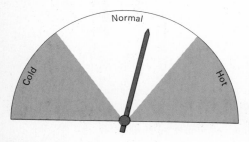

Figure 11–6. A qualitative visual display.

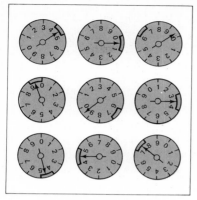

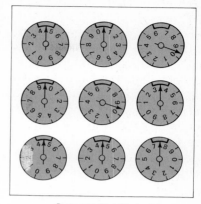

Unpatterned Dial Display   Patterned Dial Display

Figure 11–7. Patterned and unpatterned dial displays. Reprinted by permission from A. Chapanis, W. Garner, and C. Morgan, *Applied Experimental Psychology* (New York: John Wiley & Sons, 1949), p. 151.

(the "Hot" portion of Figure 11–6) shown in red and the safe operating range in green. Such a display not only allows quick and accurate verification of the status of the system but it also reduces the amount of technical information of which the operator must be aware.

When several qualitative displays must be frequently checked, consistent patterning greatly facilitates quick and accurate reading, as shown in Figure 11–7. The placing of the dials so that they always face the same way in the normal functioning range, makes it easier to detect an unsafe reading than in the helter-skelter arrangement (the unpatterned display). The latter forces the operator to look at each dial separately. A quick scanning of the patterned arrangement can usually detect a deviation.

Check reading visual displays tell the operator whether the system is "on" or "off," or is operating normally or abnormally. With an automobile engine temperature gauge, for example, designers have concluded that it is not important to know where in the safe range the temperature is. It is only necessary to know if the engine temperature is safe or unsafe. Can we continue driving the car or must we stop because the engine is too hot?

Oil pressure is another case in which we only need to know if the system is satisfactory or unsatisfactory. This kind of display is sometimes referred to as a "go-no go" display; either the system is in condition to operate (to go) or it is not.

This is the simplest kind of visual display and can be represented by a warning light. When the light is not illuminated the system is functioning satisfactorily, but when the light comes on it indicates a system malfunction serious enough to require immediate corrective action.

There are several considerations in the design of warning lights, especially level of brightness. On a display panel containing several sources of illumination, for example, it is vital that warning lights be at least twice as bright as the background illumination. Location of warning lights is also important. They should be as centrally located as possible within the operator's field of vision. Warning lights placed too far to one side of a console may not attract attention when the operator is attending to other more centrally located displays and controls. Finally, flashing lights have been shown to attract attention much more quickly than continuous warning lights.

Auditory Displays

A less frequently used but still important means of presenting information to human operators in man-machine systems is auditory signaling. Properly designed, an auditory device can be more compelling than a visual presentation for three reasons: the ears are always open but the eyes are not; we can receive auditory information from all directions (we do not have to face a sound in order to hear it, as we must face a visual display to see it); since so much information must be presented visually, that sense is often taxed to capacity in complex systems.

Most auditory signals are used to transmit warning messages and involve buzzers, bells, horns, chimes, or sirens (the latter being the most far-reaching, especially out of doors). Military and commercial aviation make widespread use of auditory warning devices to signal crew members of emergency situations or changes in system performance that require immediate action on their part.

Aside from the obvious necessity of being heard, warning signals should compel instantaneous reaction, be informative, and be easy to discriminate from other signals. Although auditory displays must be loud and compelling, they must not be so loud as to startle the operator or cause pain or hearing damage.

Auditory signals may also be used to transmit more complex information. One example is the shipboard operation of sonar for detection of underwater objects. A high frequency sound is transmitted from beneath the ship through the water. When it strikes a large enough object, it is reflected back to the ship and reproduced as the familiar "ping" sound heard in old war movies.

The job of interpreting the sound (the message or information the sound conveys) is difficult. Intensive training is required to be able to discriminate among the various qualities of a sound. For example, with sonar, if the detected object is moving away from the ship, the reflected sound is of a lower frequency than the transmitted sound. An object moving toward the ship provides a higher frequency of returning sound.

The radio range signals used in air navigation are another example of information transmission by auditory signal. Two directional radio beams at right angles produce the sound. One beam transmits by Morse Code the letter *A* (dot-dash) and the other the letter *N* (dash-dot). When the receiving airplane is flying just between the two crossed beams ("on the beam"), the pilot hears one continuous signal. If the plane is too far to the right or left, the pilot will hear the *A* or *N* signal.

Our auditory sense provides a sensitive indicator of the condition of the machine portion of the system. Through formal signaling procedures such as those described, and through informal signals such as detecting a misfire in an engine, we receive and interpret a variety of information.

Tactual Displays

The communication of information tactually (through the skin senses) is seldom used in man-machine systems. In one form, however, tactual communication is used daily by people throughout the world. Blind persons read through the braille system of tactual displays by passing their fingers over raised dots or points on a flat surface. This can be an efficient and rapid way for them to receive information.

Research has been conducted on the use of dynamic or changing tactual displays to present information to the human operator. One effective technique involves the use of vibrations on the surface of the skin. It has been found that subjects can learn to perceive as many as forty-five distinct tactual sensations through application of the vibrating stimulus to five different areas of the chest, at three different durations, and at five levels of intensity. Subjects learned to receive messages in a language of twenty-six letters, ten digits, and several short words; indeed, this language could be learned as quickly as Morse Code. Trained subjects were able to receive and understand the tactual messages much faster than those trained in Morse Code.

Another example of tactual communication involves the ability of airplane pilots to learn quickly to identify control knobs of different shapes by touch or feel alone. The pilots can then operate these controls without looking at them.

Large-scale tactual communication is not yet in use but its potential for information transmission seems great.

CONTROL FUNCTIONS OF THE HUMAN OPERATOR

In man-machine systems, once human operators have received inputs through the displays and processed the information received, they communicate with the machine through the initiation of some control action. Human operators can transmit control decisions by using switches, push buttons, levers, cranks, steering wheels, foot pedals, and the like.

As is the case with the design and arrangement of displays, decisions must be made with respect to the choice of the controls, their location, and their shape. These decisions will be based in large part on the requirements of the specific task, by what the operator is trying to accomplish or perform. Different kinds of tasks dictate different types of controls.

Thus, engineering psychologists must know in precise terms the nature of the task. Does it involve simply turning on a light or a radio or some other system component, or does it involve a fine adjustment such as selecting one radio frequency from the entire spectrum of frequencies? Does the task require frequent and rapid readjustment of a control, or is one setting sufficient for the completion of the operation? Questions about the amount of force the operator must exert on the control, and about the environmental conditions, must also be resolved. For example, if the control is to be operated outdoors in any kind of weather, will the necessity of wearing gloves interfere with the proper operation of the control? Also, if the control must be operated in the dark, it may require shape coding so as to be easily identified.

Once system designers have answered these questions, they can proceed to select the best control for the particular job. Some general guidelines are available about what type of control is most appropriate for a particular control action. For example, for a task requiring two discrete settings of a control, a hand or foot push button is appropriate. For four or more discrete settings, a group of finger push buttons or a rotary selector switch should be used. For continuous settings, knobs or cranks are preferred.

These are recommendations only; the control choice may have to be modified in the light of other conditions or requirements of the total system.

For proper use, controls must satisfy two additional criteria.

1. *Proper control and body matching.* Although some controls could be activated with the head or the elbow, most of us use only our hands and feet. It is important that no one limb be given too many tasks to perform. Wherever possible, control activation should be distributed among the limbs. The hands are capable of greater precision in control operation, and the feet are capable of exerting greater pressure or force. More control functions should be designed for right-hand operation since the majority of the population is right-handed.

2. *Control-task compatibility.* Where possible, a control action should imitate the movements it produces. Pulling the control column in an airplane to the right pulls the plane to the right; the control movement and the machine movement are parallel. To lower the flaps or landing gear of an airplane, the appropriate controls should move downward. As another example, we usually turn a knob to the right (clockwise) to turn something on. A control that turns to the left to turn something on (to perform the same function) will take a long time to adjust to. Parallel control movements seem the most natural to associate with the resulting machine movements and make the task easier for the operator.

Combining Related Controls

It is simpler and more efficient, in general, to combine controls that perform similar or related operations. There are three control functions on a radio: on-off, volume, and station selection. Yet, there are only two controls. The on–off and volume controls, performing highly related functions, are combined. Not only does control combination reduce the number of separate actions required of the human operator, but it also saves space on the control panel (which, in a complex system, is usually crowded).

Identification of Controls

Controls must be clearly marked or coded to assure their correct and rapid identification. Automobile manufacturers code instrument panels by using pictorial symbols to represent the function of each control (a miniature wiper identifies the windshield wiper switch, for example). On a crowded instrument panel, easily identified controls help minimize potential errors caused by activating the wrong control.

Another useful method of control identification is shape coding. Each knob on a console is of a recognizably different shape. This provides for rapid visual identification of the correct control and allows tactual identification in the dark or when the eyes must focus elsewhere. An efficient means of facilitating identification by shape is to design the control so that its shape represents or symbolizes its function.

The U.S. Air Force, through the results of psychological research, developed a series of shape-coded knobs for use in aircraft (Figure 11–8).

As you can see, some of the controls are more obviously symbolic of their function than others. The landing flap control looks like a landing flap, but, admittedly, it is difficult to design something to symbolize carburetor heat. However, the important point is that each control is unique in touch and appearance, and the control functions can be learned quickly. Standardizing these controls on all aircraft greatly reduces the opportunity for pilot error. Also, it has been demonstrated that these controls can be properly identified even when the pilot is wearing gloves.

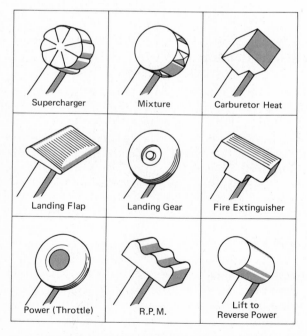

Figure 11–8. Shape-coded controls. From *Human Engineering Guide to Equipment Design* by C. Morgan et al. Copyright 1963, McGraw-Hill Book Company. Used with permission of McGraw-Hill Book Company.

Once the kind and shape of the control have been selected, the engineering psychologist determines the placement of the control on the control panel, and, where appropriate, its relationship to an information display. The location of the control on the operator's console depends primarily on the characteristics of the specific system, but some general design considerations are applicable to most man-machine systems.

A primary requisite for control location is consistency or uniformity of placement. As noted earlier, havoc would be created if the gas pedal were not consistently located to the right of the brake pedal on all types of automobile. The greater the standardization of control arrangement, the easier and safer it is for an operator to work with different models of the same system.

This principle seems to be common sense, yet it took many years of high-level systems analysis before control arrangements achieved some standardization on aircraft instrument panels. There have been several fatal accidents as a result of ignoring this vital and simple rule.

When system requirements call for the sequential operation of several controls, they should be arranged so that they can be activated in a smooth and continuous manner. If five push buttons must be operated, always in the same order, they should be placed in a straight line so that the hand can move quickly and easily from one to another, affording no possibility of their being operated in the wrong sequence.

Controls that are associated with emergency functions should be placed in the normal line of sight where they can be clearly distinguished from other controls, reached quickly, and protected so that they cannot be accidentally activated. The latter is usually accomplished by using a cover or shield that must be raised before the emergency control can be operated.

When displays are associated functionally with controls (such as a dial that must be set by turning a knob), they should be placed as close together as possible. Often, it is desirable to group related displays and controls according to their function. In an aircraft cockpit, for example, all displays and controls involved with the performance of the engines are grouped together. Displays and controls can also be grouped sequentially, in order of use, when that order is consistent.

SUMMARY

Engineering psychology is concerned with the design of the tools and equipment that are used in the performance of work so as to make them compatible with the characteristics of the workers who use them. The field endeavors to blend the limitations and capabilities of operator and machine into a smoothly functioning **man-machine system.** Engineering psychology has grown rapidly since World War II as the machinery of daily life and work have become more complex and difficult to operate.

A precursor to engineering psychology was **time-and-motion study,** which attempted to shape the way in which workers performed their jobs and, to some extent, to redesign the tools of work. Pioneered by Frederick W. Taylor and Frank and Lillian Gilbreth, time-and-motion study focused on tool design, wage incentive systems, and the elimination of all unnecessary and wasted motions. Practitioners of time-and-motion study developed rules for efficient work. Time-and-motion study is not popular with many workers who fear that it will require them to work faster. Other criticisms of time-and-motion study are that people are not alike so there may not be only one best way to perform a job, and that time-and-motion studies are based on inadequate sampling of workers and of time of work.

Whereas time-and-motion study is still applied to routine and simple jobs, engineering psychology is used for more sophisticated jobs involving complex man-machine systems.

There are two types of man-machine systems: open-loop and closed-loop. **Open-loop systems** are not self-regulating; **closed-loop systems** are.

The initial step in the design of a man-machine system is the **allocation of functions** between the human operator and the machine. Each stage and process of the task must be analyzed to determine if it should be performed by a human or by a machine. Humans are superior to machines in detecting a wide range of stimuli, detecting seldom-appearing or low-level stimuli from a confusing background, sensing and recognizing unusual or unexpected stimuli, remembering a large amount of information for a long time, recalling relevant information, using a wide range of past experiences in making decisions, responding and adapting quickly to diverse situations, using inductive reasoning, and exhibiting great flexibility in problem solving.

Machines are superior to humans in detecting stimuli beyond human powers of sensing, monitoring for long periods of time, calculating rapidly and accurately, storing and retrieving large amounts of information, applying physical force, engaging in repetitive tasks with no performance deterioration, and not tiring easily.

Social, political, and financial questions are also involved in the allocation of functions decisions.

Work space design involves some of the principles of motion economy as well as data from human anthropometry (measurements of the physical structure of the human body). There are three general principles of work space design: (1) all materials, tools, and supplies should be located in the order in which they are to be used; (2) tools should be pre–positioned so they can be picked up ready for use; and (3) all parts and tools should be within easy and comfortable reaching distance.

Engineering psychologists are also concerned with the **interrelationships** between work spaces. The effective integration of communications and flow of raw materials and parts from one station to another can be optimized by **link analysis,** an investigation of the number, frequency, and type of interconnection. Link analyses are conducted by direct observation and by interviewing the operators involved.

Another task in man-machine system design is deciding the most effective way to **present information** to the human operator. Visual and auditory senses are most frequently involved, although the tactual sense is occasionally used.

There are three types of **visual display:** quantitative, qualitative, and check reading. A **quantitative** display provides a precise numerical value; a **qualitative** display provides an indication of relative operating conditions; a **check reading** display tells whether a system is operating normally or abnormally, or is on or off.

Auditory displays are used as warning signals and to transmit complex information. They can attract attention more readily than visual displays because the ears are always open and sound can be received from all directions.

Tactual displays (receiving information through the skin senses) are occasionally used. Research has demonstrated that people can be trained to receive a good deal of information tactually.

Controls must be designed to be compatible with the task and with the limitations and capabilities of the operator. They should be combined when they are used to perform similar or related operations, and must be capable of being rapidly and readily identified.

Control identification can be accomplished through the use of pictorial symbols or shape coding.

SUGGESTED READINGS

Adams, J. Research and the future of engineering psychology. *American Psychologist,* 1972, **27,** 615–622.

Alluisi, E. A., and Morgan, B. B. Engineering psychology and human performance. *Annual Review of Psychology,* 1976, **27,** 305–330.

Ayer, N., McNall, P., and Leung, H. Effects of heat stress on performance. *Ergonomics,* 1972, **15,** 681–691.

Biberman, L. M., Ed. *Perception of Displayed Information.* New York: Plenum Publishing Corporation, 1973.

Chapanis, A. On the allocation of functions between men and machines. *Occupational Psychology,* 1965, **39**(1), 1–11.

Chapanis, A. *Man–Machine Engineering.* Belmont, Calif.: Wadsworth Publishing Co., 1965.

Chapanis, A. Engineering psychology. In M. Dunnette, Ed., *Handbook of Industrial and Organizational Psychology.* Chicago: Rand McNally, 1976. Pp. 697–744.

Davis, H. L. Human factors in industry. *Human Factors,* 1973, **15,** 103–177; 195–268.

DeGreene, K. B. *Systems Psychology.* New York: McGraw-Hill, 1972.

Howell, W. C., and Goldstein, I. L., Eds. *Engineering Psychology: Current Perspectives in Research.* New York: Appleton–Century–Crofts, 1971.

McCormick, E. *Human Factors in Engineering and Design,* 4th ed. New York: McGraw–Hill, 1976.

Meister, D. *Human Factors: Theory and Practice.* New York: John Wiley & Sons, 1971.

Niebel, B. W. *Motion and Time Study,* 5th ed. Homewood, Ill.: Richard D. Irwin, 1972.

Parsons, H. M. *Man–Machine System Experiments.* Baltimore: Johns Hopkins University Press, 1972.

Roebuck, J. A., Jr., Kroemer, K. H. E., and Thomson, W. G. *Engineering Anthropometry Methods.* New York: John Wiley & Sons, 1975.

Shephard, R. J. *Men at Work: Applications of Ergonomics to Performance and Design.* Springfield, Ill.: Charles C Thomas, 1974.

Sheridan, T. B., and Ferrell, W. R. *Man–Machine Systems: Information, Control, and Decision Models of Human Performance.* Cambridge, Mass.: MIT Press, 1974.

Singleton, W. *Man–Machine Systems.* Baltimore: Penguin Books, 1974.

Teel, K. Is human factors engineering worth the investment? *Human Factors,* 1971, **13**(1), 17–20. (Teel's answer is yes)

Van Cott, H. P., and Kinkade, R. G., Eds. *Human Engineering Guide to Equipment Design,* rev. ed. Washington, D.C.: Government Printing Office, 1972.

12

Accidents, Alcohol, and Drugs

One aspect of modern industrial life that receives limited publicity is its high level of danger. Accidents occur daily, some involving no more than a bruise or a scrape, and others resulting in permanent disability or death. Industrial safety is a very serious problem. An assistant secretary of the Department of Health, Education, and Welfare described it in these terms: "We are experiencing a national tragedy of occupational injury, disease, and death. The scope of this tragedy, the number of its victims, we can only guess at, and acknowledge that our guess is probably low. . . . Maimed and broken bodies, poisoned lungs and eroded kidneys, workers burned, blinded, or gravely injured in some other way—these are among the regular daily fare of hospitals in every part of the country."

During the peak years of American involvement in Vietnam (1966–1970), more Americans were killed at their jobs than in combat. The nation grieved, and rightly so, for those who died in battle, but there is no national mourning for the thousands of men and women who leave their homes in the morning to go to work and never return because of an industrial accident.

Approximately fifteen thousand people are killed annually in industrial accidents. And the number of disabling injuries, though not fully known, is staggering; an estimated 2.2 million people are disabled each year because of work-related accidents. However, a study by the Bureau of Labor Statistics shows that for each reported disabling injury, ten are not reported. The inevitable conclusion is that as many as 25 million workers sustain injuries each year—one out of every three members of the work force.

The economic cost is also staggering, both to the companies involved and the country as a whole. Billions of dollars are forfeited through lost wages and millions are paid out in worker's compensation and medical benefits. The lost working time because of injuries is now five times greater than the lost working time because of strikes. Yet strikes, like war, achieve national publicity; the worker who loses a leg on the job does not.

The death and disablement toll from work-related disease may be as high or higher than the industrial accident toll. Such illnesses and deaths are more insidious than the sudden traumatic accident because they develop slowly over many years before the worker manifests obvious physical symptoms.

Coal miners, for example, develop a unique respiratory disease called pneumoconiosis, or "black lung," a progressively crippling disorder that reduces life expectancy. Respiratory disease kills five times as many coal miners as it does workers in other occupations. A U.S. senator noted: "Coal miners have been coughing their lives away for 200 years. Any literature you read . . . about coal miners, all through the literature runs the description of a man coughing out his life—a coal miner."

Many chemical industries are fraught with health perils to workers, dangers that are not fully known. As many as 10 million workers are exposed daily to chemicals for which safe thresholds have not yet been established. Nearly 3.5 million people are exposed to asbestos in their jobs, where they face the danger of lung cancer at seven times the national average, as well as a form of pneumoconiosis known as asbestosis. As many as 10 per cent of the country's textile workers are known to have byssinosis, or "brown lung," disease from inhaling cotton dust. Of the six thousand men who have worked in uranium mines, up to one thousand will die of lung cancer because of high levels of radiation exposure.

The list of jobs and industries that expose their workers to unsafe physical working conditions or health hazards is long and depressing. It is a harsh fact that a surprisingly large number of jobs are dangerous to life and limb. The International Agency for Research on Cancer in France studied 196 commonly used chemical compounds and found that 17 of them were known to cause cancer in humans. Of these 17 cancer-causing chemicals, 14 were found in places of work.

Why has so little been done? Who is to blame for these deplorable figures? Employers, politicians, and even the workers' representatives—the unions—must share the blame for this widespread crippling and death. Unions often downgrade safety considerations in order to focus on economic matters. Companies will try to cut costs by not enlarging their safety staffs and by continuing to use obsolete or unsafe equipment. State safety standards are often ineffective and poorly enforced.

For example, in 1970 there were a total of nineteen hundred government safety inspectors for the entire United States. At the same time, there were thirty-three hundred fish and game wardens. Without criticizing fish and game (they have their own problems), it can be suggested that the American worker deserves at least as much consideration and protection.

On December 29, 1970, the Congress finally took action by passing the Occupational Safety and Health Act establishing the Occupational Safety and Health Administration in the Department of Labor, the purpose of which is to assure safe and healthful working conditions by combating industrial accidents and disease. By developing and enforcing federal industrial safety standards, and by sponsoring research into the causes and prevention of accidents and disease, it is hoped that working conditions can be made less dangerous.

Let us consider the general accident picture in the United States. If we include accidents that occur on the highways and in the home, the fatalities dwarf the figures from cancer, heart disease, and other killers. More Americans were accidently killed and injured in the United States during the years of World War II (1941–1945) than suffered death in combat. Each year, approximately 100,000 people are killed in accidents and about 10 million reported injured. Almost half of the deaths result from automobile accidents. The problem of accidents has reached serious proportions and is not receiving the attention that it deserves.

The discussion here is limited to industrial accidents, with a brief mention of highway accidents. Psychologists have conducted many research studies on accidents, focusing on the conditions giving rise to them, the personality patterns of those who seem to have an unusually high number of accidents, and the design of the equipment or machinery involved in accidents.

We cannot assume that industry has totally ignored the problems of accidents and safety; this is not the case. Although some companies may not have done as much as they could have, many have invested considerable time and money for accident prevention programs. Accidents are expensive to employers; they reduce output. Trained workers who have been injured must be replaced, damaged equipment must be repaired, and the morale of a work crew that has suffered the loss of a co-worker must be improved. This all costs money and so companies are understandably concerned with reducing the accident toll. And, it is reasonable to suppose that without industry's present accident prevention programs (however imperfect they may be), the accident toll would be even higher.

Also, safety is not the exclusive responsibility of management. Workers must do their part as well. It has been found that most accidents are caused by the human element, not the machine, and this suggests that workers must take their roles more seriously. For example, the company can provide the best available protective goggles, but if workers won't wear them, they are worthless. As the National Safety Council notes: "Safety is everybody's business." As an employee, a manager, or a driver, safety is your business.

PROBLEMS WITH ACCIDENT STATISTICS

We noted in Chapter 2 that statistics don't lie, but sometimes people who use statistics do distort facts in their favor, backing up their distortions with figures. This is the situation with accident research. The problem is to define an accident precisely, and this is not as ridiculous as it may sound.

How severe must an accident be for it to be included in a company's accident statistics? It seems that different people define accidents in different ways. Suppose a worker drops a heavy barrel—is this an accident? Technically, yes, but whether it would be listed as an accident depends on the consequences, not on the act itself. If the dropped barrel was not damaged, and didn't hurt anyone, the episode won't be recorded as an accident. But suppose the barrel fell on the worker's foot, breaking a few bones—is this an accident? Not necessarily. Many companies would not list this as an accident, even though the worker was hurt and required medical treatment. The injured worker may not be able to walk for a while but, if the company provides a desk job until the worker is better, he or she will not have lost any time from the factory.

Here we have an accident resulting in an injury, yet it may not be included in the accident statistics. The definition of an accident in this case depends on whether the injured worker actually loses time from work. According to the Bureau of Labor Statistics, this distinction keeps many serious accidents from ever being reported.

For example, it has happened that a factory worker has broken a leg—certainly a serious, painful, and annoying accident to the worker who was treated in the company clinic and given some clerical "make work" to perform until the injury healed. Thus, the worker remained on the job, no accident was reported, and the company's safety record remained intact. Was this an accident? Yes, but not for the record.

It was this failure to record all injuries on the job, not just those that kept the worker at home, that led the Bureau of Labor Statistics to the alarming conclusion that for each reported disabling injury there are ten serious injuries not reported. Unreported accidents include eye injuries, broken toes and fingers, and loss of consciousness, but these events are defined as accidents only if they result in lost work time.

Incomplete reporting of industrial accidents makes research into the causes and prevention of accidents more difficult. The available statistics show the results of only a small portion of the accidents and provide little information on the causes. Further, by concentrating on lost-time accidents, the figures provide an inaccurate picture of what has occurred in a particular department or plant.

Industrial organizations like to claim good safety records. A good record shows that a company is doing all it can to promote a safe working environment for its employees. Workers might avoid a company that had acquired the negative public image that follows a high reported accident rate. Higher insurance costs to the company may also be a consequence of higher reported accidents. To achieve a good safety record and, consequently, a good public image, some companies resort to extreme measures such as closed-door accident investigations, inaccurate reporting, and outright distortion of the facts. A union safety chairman in a steel mill stated the following to a U.S. Senate hearing on industrial safety.

The company put a big push on for no disabling accidents for the year, to receive an award. They achieved their goal. We received a nice, beautiful plaque from the National Safety Council. . . .

When we lose a hand, this is not a disabling injury, when we break a leg, this is not a disabling injury. When we have people literally torn apart, receiving hundreds of stitches, and lying in the dispensary for three days, it is not classified as a lost time accident. The company controls all the investigation . . . they have a closed door investigation.

This kind of testimony went on for hundreds of pages as workers from a variety of firms told of the great discrepancy between actual and reported accident rates.

The solution is obvious: all accidents, whatever their severity, must be reported. Also, all accidents must be reported in detail. Only through thorough analyses of past accidents can the same mistakes be prevented in the future and unsafe conditions be eliminated. Lost time accidents are undoubtedly the most severe to the worker and the company, and deserve a major share of attention, but less severe accidents must be studied just as comprehensively. The conditions that lead to an accident today in which a worker merely scrapes a leg could lead to an accident tomorrow in which the leg is lost.

Further, it is important that accidents resulting in no injuries be reported and investigated. The conditions under which a worker drops a heavy barrel are the same whether no harm is done, or the worker breaks a foot, or the barrel rolls down an incline and kills a co-worker. To prevent a recurrence, the worker's behavior and the circumstances of the accident—not just the result—must be studied.

Not all the blame for inaccurate accident reporting can be placed on the company. Sometimes the workers themselves distort the facts. Some employees fail to report minor accidents for fear of acquiring a reputation as careless or accident-prone. Others fear possible punishment because an accident was their fault—they didn't follow accepted operating procedures or neglected to use a safety device.

CAUSES OF ACCIDENTS

The human element—the worker, the driver, the homemaker—seems to be responsible for most accidents whether they occur at the factory, on the highway, or in the home. Thus, factors such as personality, attitude, and general behavior characteristics play an important role in determining the causes of accidents. However, personal factors are not the sole cause of accidents. Conditions of the work environment and the nature of the job itself can also contribute to accidents.

The Physical Environment

Modern technology has created new work environments and machinery that bring new hazards to the workers. For example, high energy sources such as laser beams, once found solely in laboratories for research purposes, are now commonplace for such uses as cutting cloth for the garment industry. Innovative production processes and sophisticated high-speed machinery add considerably to the complexities and dangers of work. We are creating work environments that make fresh demands and require new responsibilities of workers, without, of course, being able to change the workers very much. The evolution in technology proceeds at a faster pace than the evolution of human employees who must understand, operate, and control these advanced machines.

The difficulties in designing a safe working environment grow each year. Workers can and must be trained in safety practices and principles, but training alone does not solve the problem. We must ensure that if workers are doing all they can to protect themselves, they are further protected by properly designed machinery and equipment.

Type of Industry

The frequency and severity of accidents vary as a function of the type of industry and the kind of work being performed. A steel mill provides more opportunities for accidents than does a bank. The more demanding are the physical requirements made upon the worker, the higher is the accident rate. Stressful and tiring work results in more accidents. In general, industries such as construction, mining, lumber and quarry work are high in frequency and severity of accidents. Industries such as aircraft and automobile manufacturing, rubber, warehousing, and communications are usually low.

There are exceptions to these trends. Cement and steel industries report a low frequency of accidents, but when they occur, they are usually quite severe. Electric utility companies report few accidents but these tend to be severe because of the high voltages involved. Retail and wholesale businesses report high accident rates but severe injuries are relatively rare.

Hours of Work

We might suspect that the greater the number of hours worked, the higher the accident rate, but the evidence does not clearly support this idea. Of course, the longer workers are on the job during a workday, the more opportunity they have for accidents, but no evidence indicates that shortening the work period leads to a decrease in accidents. Similarly, there is no support for the notion that lengthening the workday increases accidents. As we noted in Chapter 10, work tends to expand to fill the time available for it, so a lengthened work period usually results in a slower work pace. Thus, the number of accidents per unit of time actually declines, creating the illusion that longer periods of work are safer.

What does seem to make a difference in accident rate is whether the work is performed on day or night shifts. Fewer accidents occur during the night shift, apparently because the artificial illumination provided at night is more effective than the natural illumination conditions during the day. This relationship has been borne out by research comparing the effects of different levels of artificial illumination on accidents during the night shift. The research has shown that accidents tend to increase as lighting becomes less satisfactory.

Lighting

As we know, good lighting can lead to a reduction in the accident rate. One insurance company estimated that 25 per cent of all industrial accidents were caused by poor lighting. Accidents are higher in plants that continue production through dusk, before the lights are turned on. (Dusk is also a time of frequent automobile accidents.) The relationship between level of illumination and accident rate seems firmly established, and a poorly lit work area can be easily corrected by an alert management.

Temperature

The temperature at which work is performed also affects the accident rate. Studies of factory workers have shown that the accident rate is lowest when the temperature is around 68° F. to 70° F. Accidents increase when the temperature varies in either direction, and are particularly frequent under extreme temperatures. Studies carried out in coal mines have shown that at temperatures approaching 85°F., minor accidents were three times more frequent than at lower temperatures (to 62°F.). It seems likely that workers become careless in their work habits under the discomfort produced by high temperatures.

Evidence also suggests that older workers are more affected by temperature extremes than are younger workers. Research has shown, for example, that in hot work environments, older employees are much more likely to have accidents.

Miscellaneous Factors

Several aspects of the work environment were investigated in a now classic study that dealt with more than 250,000 workers in 147 factories.[1] Some of these variables were shown to be related to accident frequency or severity. The following factors were found to be highly correlated with accident frequency.

1. More accidents were reported in plants that tended to lay off workers on a periodic or seasonal basis. Whether this was because of the job insecurity engendered by the layoffs, or the

[1] P. Sherman, W. A. Kerr, and W. C. Kosinar, "A study of accidents in 147 factories," *Personnel Psychology*, **10**(1957), 43–51.

difficulty of keeping trained and experienced workers, is not known.

2. A higher accident rate was found among male workers who had easy access to prostitutes. Why this causes more accidents is not known, but it certainly qualifies as an unusual factor.
3. More accidents were reported in plants that were located near other plants. Perhaps this results in an uglier overall environment or greater difficulties in commuting and parking.
4. The handling of heavy materials (at least 50 pounds) resulted in a higher accident rate.
5. When large numbers of the workers in a plant lived in blighted, slumlike neighborhoods, the frequency of accidents tended to be high.

Two variables were found to correlate with accident severity. First, plants at which managers and workers shared eating facilities reported a lower accident severity rate. It is suggested that this is because of the higher morale of the workers. Second, those factories that had employee profit-sharing plans had fewer severe accidents. Later research studies report evidence that workers who share in their company's profits are generally better motivated.

There are, then, numerous factors in the physical work environment that directly cause accidents, or lower morale and motivation to the point where the resulting carelessness leads to an accident. More attention should be paid to these physical factors since some of them —lighting and temperature, for example—can be easily maintained at optimal levels.

Equipment Design

Another aspect of the physical work environment related to accidents is the design of the equipment or machinery used on the job. Too often, equipment is planned for the convenience of the design engineer, or along aesthetic lines, without due consideration of the limitations and capabilities of the worker who has to use it. Locating a "stop" button where it is difficult to reach, for example, can have deadly consequences if the machine must be shut down immediately. Poor placement of switches and other controls, inadequate warning lights for system malfunction, and dials that are difficult to read, can all lead to accidents. The proper matching of the machine with the capabilities of the operator is the province of engineering psychologists (Chapter 11). Their work on equipment design has been very effective in accident prevention.

Also important in the design of safe machinery is the development of built-in safety devices and other aids to prevent accidents. Safety devices must not interfere with the actual operation of the machine, but function, for example, to keep a worker's hand away from sharp moving parts or to automatically cut off the power supply and stop the machine in an emergency.

Over all, the human element is the most important causal factor in accidents. Proper attention to equipment design and to the work environment can help reduce the frequency and severity of accidents. It is probably true, however, that no piece of equipment or machinery can be made completely foolproof.

Personal Factors

Psychologists have conducted much research on the relationship between personal characteristics or abilities and accidents. Success has been mixed, partly because the complex interrelationships of some variables make it difficult to interpret the results clearly. There are also confounding variables, such as self-selection in taking a job initially and remaining on the job for any length of time. If a job is known to be dangerous, certain people will not even apply for it. When, for example, psychologists wish to study the personality characteristics of construction workers who have had several accidents versus those who have not, the task is made more difficult by the factor of self-selection; only workers who possess specific personality traits may be working in that job.

Self-selection also applies to the length of time employees remain on a job. If there is danger involved in the task, then many workers (those who are afraid, have had too many accidents, or have been disabled on the job) will not stay very long. If psychologists wish to compare more experienced with less experienced workers in terms of accident rate, they may find themselves dealing with workers who differ in more ways than just length of work experience; those workers who have remained on the job have been self-selected in terms of lower levels of fear or susceptibility to accidents.

These difficulties do not mean that research on personal causes of accidents is impossible, only that great care is necessary in the design and interpretation of such studies.

Intelligence

It seems reasonable to expect intelligence to correlate negatively with accident rate; we would expect less intelligent workers to have more accidents than more intelligent workers. However, the evidence does not clearly support this idea. Some studies suggest that intelligence is related to accident-free behavior only in certain kinds of jobs, for example, those requiring a high degree of judgment (as opposed to those involving repetitive manual labor).

Health and Physical Condition

It is well documented that health is related to accidents. The evidence shows that employees who are in poor health or have had frequent illnesses tend to be highly susceptible to accidents.

Physical disabilities—assuming that the workers' general health is good and that they are assigned jobs commensurate with their abilities —do not necessarily predispose workers to accidents. Indeed, handicapped workers are usually highly motivated to work well and safely, often more so than nonhandicapped employees. Assuming proper placement, accident rates among the handicapped are lower than accident rates for able-bodied workers.

One physical defect that is related to accidents is poor vision. On the highway as well as in the factory, tests have shown that people who have fewer accidents generally have better vision. One investigator gave vision tests to a large group of machine operators and compared their test performance with the number of past accidents. Of those who passed the vision test, only 37 per cent had experienced accidents in the previous year. Of those who failed the vision test, 67 per cent had had accidents in the previous year.

Except in extreme cases, a company's medical department can identify and correct vision problems, and in terms of accident rate (and probably productivity as well), it would be worthwhile to do so. A few companies provide free periodic vision examinations for their employees and recommend corrective action where necessary. In cases incapable of correction, workers with poor vision could be placed in less hazardous jobs in order to reduce their accident potential. Excessive use of alcohol or drugs can increase susceptibility to accidents. This is amply documented in automobile accident records; half of all automobile accidents can be traced to excessive drinking.

Fatigue

Fatigue causes a decline in production and an increase in accidents. Indeed, research has shown a close relationship between accident frequency and production level. During a typical 8-hour workday, periods of production increase are accompanied by decreases in accidents. In a 10-hour workday, a sharp rise in the accident rate during the last two hours has been reported in some industries, presumably because of fatigue.

Work Experience

A lower level of on-the-job work experience tends to result in a higher accident rate. Studies have shown a decrease in accidents over the period from the beginning of a new job to one and one-half years later. In one study, new workers averaged seventy-seven minor mishaps on their first day of work, but on the next six workdays the accident figure dropped to approximately 13. Thus, there is a need for comprehensive safety training before the worker actually begins the job. It is not enough to train new workers in the specific skills and abilities required for successful performance of their jobs. They must also learn safe work rules and proper attitudes toward safety. In comparing groups of workers that had received safety training with those given no such training, the first group experienced many fewer accidents in their early days on the job.

The relationship between accidents and long-term work experience is not as clear. Although studies have reported fewer accidents among workers who have greater experience, these findings are biased by the self-selection factor discussed previously. Workers who have had numerous accidents may have been fired or transferred to other jobs, or quit to search for safer work. Therefore, we cannot conclude that longer work experience by itself leads to a reduction in accidents. The decrease in accidents for experienced workers may be caused by the fact that those who had more accidents may have dropped out. It also could be because of age (see the following).

Proper research on accidents as a function of job experience does not involve simply the comparison of a low experience group with a high experience group. The psychologist must study the accident records of a group of workers over a period of time, beginning with their early employment. When this is done for one or two years, the results support the suggestion that more experienced workers have fewer accidents. Studying the same group of workers over 10 to 20 years, however, is extremely difficult because of the changes in work methods, equipment, and conditions that can take place during so long a period. In the face of marked differences in conditions of work, it is not meaningful to compare accident rates in one time period with accident rates many years later.

Age

The relationship between age and accidents is similar to the relationship between experience and accidents because of the high correlation between age and experience. Older workers have spent more time on the job and so are more experienced than younger workers. Because of this interaction of age and experience, studies comparing the accident rates of different age groups are complicated by the self-selection problem.

Other factors that may interact with age are health and attitude. As a rule, the state of health, as well as specific abilities such as vision and hearing, deteriorate with advancing age. Perhaps counteracting this factor are the greater job knowledge and more highly developed job skills evidenced by older workers. Older persons' reaction time or eye-hand coordination may no longer be as good, but by virtue of their greater experience, they may have a fuller command of the nuances and demands of the job. Younger workers' attitudes toward safety, as well as toward other aspects of the job, may tend to be less serious than those of older employees.

With these considerations in mind, and noting the influence of job experience, it is possible to conclude that older workers have fewer accidents than younger ones. Again, it must be stated that age alone may not be the single determining factor in accident rates, but rather one that represents a constellation of variables.

Although the frequency of accidents declines with age, the severity of accidents increases. When older workers do have accidents, they are likely to be more severe in terms of their physical consequences and time lost from the job.

Personality Characteristics

One popular belief in the field of accidents and safety is that persons who tend to have a great many accidents possess a unique set of personality characteristics that clearly distinguish them from those persons who have few accidents. Research has not consistently supported this contention but there is some evidence to suggest that people who have a high number of accidents have some similar personal characteristics.

One study revealed that a group of workers with high accident rates were excessively ambitious and revengeful and, at the same time, afraid and fatalistic. The low accident group did not display these characteristics to the same degree. Other research has suggested that accident repeaters are less emotionally stable, are hostile toward authority, are high in anxiety, do not get along well with others, and have erratic work histories.

It must be emphasized that the relationships between personality characteristics and accident frequency are not very strong. Most of them appear only when groups scoring extremely high and low on personality variables are compared. There is no basis for concluding that the high accident repeater has a personality clearly different from that of the accident-free individual.

However, emotional factors are of some consequence in accidents; accidents seem to vary as a function of a person's temporary emotional state. For example, the person who is angry with a spouse or boss, or with the anonymous driver who cuts ahead on the highway in the morning, or who is anxious about money matters or family affairs, is likely to be less attentive on the job and therefore more susceptible to accidents.

In studies comparing emotional state and accident frequency, results show many fewer accidents when workers are happy and content than when they are angry, frustrated, or worried. One group of factory workers studied were reported to be depressed nearly 20 per cent of their time at work. Regardless of the reasons for the depression, the findings clearly revealed that more than 50 per cent of the accidents that occurred during the time of the study took place during this negative emotional period. (Production is also affected by transitory emotional states, decreasing during emotional lows.)

Thus, temporary emotional states, more than general personality patterns, seem to be causal factors in accidents. Workers subjected to the stress of an unhappy homelife or other personal or job-related problems are more susceptible to accidents on the job (and, of course, on the highway). Identification of employees undergoing such strains, followed by effective counseling, could help to reduce accidents.

ACCIDENT PRONENESS

The theory of accident proneness—that certain people are more likely than others to have accidents—has been popular for many years. Its simplicity and apparent potential for reducing accidents have made it attractive. According to proponents, it is only necessary to measure the characteristics of those who have large numbers of accidents and then use these measurements as predictive devices. That is, those who scored high on these factors could be placed in jobs where there are few opportunities for accidents to occur; high-risk jobs would be given to those scoring low on accident proneness tests.

The theory rests on the assumption that most accidents are caused by or involve the same few people. It is also assumed that accident-prone individuals are likely to have accidents regardless of the situation. Whatever they are doing, the theory states, accident-prone individuals are likely to have an accident while doing it. Studies have shown, for example, that 10 per cent of a work group had 50 per cent of the accidents. Some people in the group had no accidents, whereas others had a number of accidents; therefore, the latter are accident prone.

Is it reasonable to assume, however, that all people in a group are expected to have the same number of accidents, and, further, that any deviation from this expectation (those few people who have more accidents than others) is the result of accident proneness? Critics of the theory believe that these assumptions are false.

One frequently overlooked factor is that the number of accidents in a group for a given period of time is likely to be smaller than the number of people in the group. If 100 workers in a department had 50 accidents in one year, it is possible that no more than 50 workers had accidents, in which case 50 per cent of the group caused 100 per cent of the accidents. And this assumes that each person had one accident—hardly accident proneness. Yet, it is possible for an investigator to conclude that since these 50 persons had all the accidents while the other 50 had none, the former group must be accident prone.

Similar reasoning could be applied if 25 workers in the group each had two accidents during the year. Random factors or equipment failures could have caused the accidents to happen to these particular workers and not to the others. In the following year, these 25 people may have no accidents. Interpretation of such statistics is fraught with potential error.

An effective way to test the accident-proneness theory is to compare accident records of the same individuals for two different time periods, thus determining if the same people had repeated accidents. Psychologists have made such comparisons, and the resulting correlations have not been high. This suggests that a person's past accident record is not a valid predictor of the future record.

A noteworthy finding involves a second look at a set of accident statistics that had originally been interpreted as supporting the accident-proneness theory. In analyzing driving records of nearly thirty thousand persons, it was found that less than 4 per cent of them accounted for more than 36 per cent of the accidents in a six-year period. This seemed to suggest that a small group was involved in a large number of accidents; if they could be prevented from driving, the accident rate would be cut by more than one third.

The same statistics were reanalyzed by comparing the accident records for the first three-year period with those for the second three-year period. This time it became clear that the accidents did not involve the same drivers during the two time periods. Those identified as safe drivers during the first three-year period (having had no more than one accident), accounted for more than 96 per cent of all the accidents in the second three-year period. This is highly damaging to the theory of accident proneness: If those who had most of the accidents during the first period had been predisposed to accidents by some unique set of personal characteristics, then they should have had the majority of the accidents during the second period. They did not.

Although the accident-proneness theory still has ardent supporters, it no longer enjoys the credibility it once did. Recent evidence does suggest that some people might be predisposed to have more accidents in certain situations; some workers will have a high number of accidents in one type of work but not in another. Accident proneness may be specific to the situation and not a general tendency in all situations. This specificity limits the predictive value of the theory.

A final argument against accident proneness involves the assumption that the characteristics of high accident repeaters are distinct from those who have few accidents. As noted in our discussion of personality and accidents, the research does not strongly support this contention.

ACCIDENT PREVENTION

There are several steps and procedures by means of which an organization can undertake a campaign designed to prevent or reduce accidents.

Reporting and Analyzing Accidents

First, detailed and accurate data on past accidents in the organization must be accumulated. Surely the best way to develop protective and preventive measures against future accidents is to find out what went wrong in the past. Accident data from different firms, and from various departments and activities within the same firm, can be analyzed to determine particularly dangerous industries and operations so that greater attention can be focused on them. It is probably true that an accident program is no better than the quality and thoroughness of its accident reports. All accidents, no matter how minor any personal injury, should be reported.

An accident report should contain the following information:

1. Precise time and location of the accident. Many aspects of a job, as well as overall working conditions, can change during a workday, especially from one shift to another. These background factors must be thoroughly understood since they may have contributed to the accident.

2. Type of job and the number of employees performing it. Specifics of the job classification and required operating procedures should be known, as well as the number of people performing that job. It is important to determine how many employees in the same job have had accidents in a given period of time.

3. Personal characteristics of the accident victim. Age, health, and job experience are influential factors in accident behavior. This information, plus psychological test and background data available from selection procedures and supervisors' ratings of performance efficiency, should all be reported in as much detail as possible.

4. Nature and cause of the accident. The accident report should describe exactly what led up to the accident, what happened to the worker(s), and, if applicable, damage to equipment. The cause, if known or suspected—such as equipment failure, careless operating procedures, or failure to use safety devices— should be noted.

5. Results of the accident. Specific damage to equipment, raw materials, and the manufacturing process should be described. If a personal injury resulted, a detailed medical report of the extent of the injuries, treatment, and prognosis for recovery should be included.

Proper Design of the Work and Its Environment

Although most accidents are caused by the human element, the physical work environment can provide hazards and potential sources of accidents. For example, a poorly designed machine or work area often leads to what is defined in an accident report as a human error, but which is an error that could have been prevented through proper equipment design.

This aspect of accident prevention, the engineering phase, is probably the single most important aspect of a safety program. No matter

411

how much is known about past accidents, or how well trained and motivated are the workers to avoid accidents, if the equipment is unnecessarily dangerous, accidents are likely to occur. Machinery and work areas designed for safety may also serve to increase workers' confidence and allay apprehensions about accidents.

As far as the work environment is concerned, the illumination must be adequate for the job tasks, and the temperature maintained at a comfortable level. The work area should be kept clean and orderly; accidents have been traced directly to poor housekeeping. Oil or grease spots on the floor and equipment cluttering stairways have directly caused expensive and injurious accidents that could easily have been prevented.

Proper maintenance of all operating machinery is also a safety aid. A machine allowed to function improperly, or one that has been repaired incorrectly, often causes accidents.

First-aid equipment, fire extinguishers, and other safety accessories should be conveniently placed throughout a work area and painted in such colors as to be easily identified. Time lost in searching for a fire extinguisher, for example, greatly increases the seriousness of the accident.

We discussed the importance of properly designed production machinery and noted that it must be compatible with the capabilities and limitations of the operators. Controls that are hard to reach or require unusual force to operate, or dials and displays that are excessively complicated and so easily misread, are obvious design mistakes that are ready sources of accidents.

Emergency controls must be easily accessible and quickly operated. A machine designed so that if a worker gets a hand caught, the shut-off control is difficult to reach, is an open invitation to a serious accident. Safety engineers and engineering psychologists are now aware of these design dangers.

The design of safety aids and devices is a crucial part of the engineering phase of accident prevention. Perhaps no machine safety device can be made totally foolproof but it is possible to come close. Two general principles apply to the design of safety devices. First, the machine should not function unless the safety device is in place or in operation. A punch press that will not work unless the hand guard is in place is as safe as possible. In this case, the worker is forced to manually engage the hand guard in order to operate the machine. If the press were designed to operate whether or not the hand guard was in place, a lazy or careless worker might decide it isn't worth the effort to swing the guard into place each time, and lose a hand as the result.

Second, the safety device must not interfere with production. If the installation of a safety guard on the punch press means that fifteen fewer units will be produced each day, management and the incentive-paid worker will be dissatisfied. Also, the safety device should not cause the employee to work harder or to engage in additional operations in order to maintain the same production level. The frustration and possible fatigue induced by such extra effort may in themselves lead to accidents.

There are, then, several steps a company can take in the proper design of the equipment and the work environment in order to reduce the possibility of accidents. Although the engineering phase is vital to the success of an accident prevention program, the program may not be totally effective unless the workers are carefully trained and sufficiently motivated to work safely.

Training for Accident Prevention

The training phase of an accident prevention program focuses on specific safe job skills and attitudes toward safety. Neither aspect is fully effective alone; both on-the-job behavior and attitudes must be oriented toward reducing accidents. Workers may be well aware of the safest way to operate the equipment but if their attitude toward safety is negative, this job knowledge alone may not protect them from harm. Similarly, a positive attitude will not prevent accidents if employees do not know the rules for safe operation of their equipment.

With respect to job skills, inexperienced workers are highly susceptible to accidents during the initial period on the job. Research studies have shown that training in the safe way of performing a work task leads to a reduction in accidents for new employees.

Most company training programs devote some time to safety matters. Special dangers and potential hazards of the job are pointed out and information presented on the nature, causes, and results of past accidents. The company's rules for safety on the job are taught, as are the location of emergency first-aid equipment and the medical facility. It is not unusual, for particularly dangerous jobs, to teach employees the principles of first aid. Safety training, however, should not stop when employees begin work. Most companies continue some form of safety training throughout an employee's career. Systematic safety inspections are frequently made and safe working habits continually checked upon. Publicity campaigns designed to maintain safety awareness are periodically launched.

Further, when accident rates are observed to increase, retraining is often put into effect. Sometimes, experienced employees become careless or forgetful of safety procedures so a refresher course is required. Some firms periodically offer safety retraining programs to all employees, regardless of the accident rate. The goal is to maintain in employees a constant awareness of safety and a continuing interest in safe working habits. Generally, firms that continue safety efforts in systematic and thorough fashion have been rewarded with substantial reductions in lost hours of work. The money thus saved usually more than pays the cost of the safety training programs.

A key role in any successful safety training and awareness program is played by the foremen. Many companies pay special attention to their safety training. More than any other level of management, foremen, because of their close daily association with workers, must be alert to unsafe working conditions and practices. They are in the best position to remind employees of safe working habits and to arrange for proper maintenance of machinery and the work environment.

Foremen are also in the best position to advise the safety engineer on weaknesses in the safety program, and to suggest to the training department when retraining might be advisable. The best safety training program will be less than maximally effective if foremen do not follow it up by insisting on adherence to safe working procedures. Further, foremen, by example and instruction, can maintain proper motivation toward safety. If foremen display a lack of concern for safe procedures, certainly the workers will not be concerned about them.

However, foremen cannot be expected to display proper awareness of safety problems unless their superiors do also. Tolerance of sloppy accident reporting, and a negative or even neutral attitude toward safety on the part of higher management, neither encourages nor reinforces foremen to attend to the problem. All levels of supervision must demonstrate to subordinates that safety is everybody's responsibility. Only with such broad support will training programs be most effective.

Safety Publicity Campaigns

In order to motivate employees to follow the safe working practices they have been taught, many organizations engage in publicity and promotional campaigns. Bright, attractive posters are located throughout the plant, booklets on safety are distributed, charts noting accident-free days are displayed, and safety contests (companywide or nationwide) are conducted.

Posters are the most frequently used technique but their effectiveness depends on the kind of message displayed. Negative themes

("Don't do this,") coupled with gruesome scenes of mangled bodies ("or this is what will happen") are particularly ineffective. These fear-oriented appeals create resentment and even anger toward the company as well as toward the message itself. The most effective safety posters stress positive themes such as "Wear Hard Hat in This Area," or "Hold On to Railing." They should be attention-getting through the use of bright colors, sharply defined lettering, and visible placement. The effect of safety posters on behavior has rarely been studied but results have shown increases in safety practices within six weeks after the introduction of posters into the plant.

Booklets of instructions and safety rules do not seem to be very effective, no matter how widely they are distributed. It is relatively simple to make sure that all workers in a factory receive a booklet. It is far more difficult to make them read it. In truth, such booklets are rarely read.

Safety contests can be an effective device for maintaining an interest in safety. Some contests reward workers on an individual basis for accident-free work over a given period of time. Other contests operate on a group basis where the work crew or department receives an award if it remains accident-free for a period of time. Another approach pits one department against another to see which has fewer accidents per unit of time. Nationwide contests are sponsored by organizations such as the National Safety Council.

Contests serve to make workers more conscious of safe operating procedures and thus result in a reduction in accident rates. Unfortunately, this awareness does not usually last much longer than the life of the contest. One possible solution is to have continuous contests, changing the awards frequently enough to maintain interest.

A disadvantage of safety contests is that they may pressure workers, foremen, or executives to suppress the number of reported accidents. However, incomplete accident records will be self-defeating in the long run since successful accident prevention programs depend on accurate and complete statistics.

If any one of these steps to accident prevention—analyzing past accidents, optimizing work conditions and equipment, training employees in safe working procedures and attitudes, and continually promoting safety awareness—is ignored, the safety program as a whole will suffer.

AUTOMOBILE ACCIDENTS

For anyone who reads a daily newspaper, it is impossible to be unaware of the tragically high automobile accident toll in the United

States. Since the development of the automobile as a means of transportation, nearly nineteen million Americans have died on the nation's highways—almost three times the number of deaths recorded in all of our wars combined.

Workers are more likely to be injured or killed while driving to work than when they are on the job. Until 1974, between 50,000 and 60,000 people were killed in car accidents each year. When the highway speed limits were reduced to 55 miles per hour (an outgrowth of the 1974 energy crisis), the death rate dropped by more than 9,000 per year. This demonstrated what everyone already knew; accidents are less likely to be fatal when they occur at slower speeds. It is also known that the type of road influences the frequency of accidents. Freeways and interstate highways have the lowest accident rate, and four-lane undivided highways have the highest accident rate. Thus, speed and highway design are two factors that can influence the carnage caused by automobile accidents.

Another factor in automobile safety is the design of the automobile so as to minimize the chances of injury or death when an accident occurs. Spurred by consumer advocate Ralph Nader, cars have been redesigned to reduce the effects of the so-called "second collision," the colliding of the occupants with internal parts of the car during the period immediately following a collision.

In 1966, the federal government enacted the National Traffic and Motor Vehicle Safety Act, aimed at the automobile and tire manufacturers, with the goal of instituting industrywide safety standards. Since that time, automobiles have been equipped with several safety innovations: safety lap belts and shoulder harnesses, head rests, collapsible steering columns, padded instrument panels, pneumatic bumpers, and other devices designed to minimize personal injury in a crash. These changes have been beneficial, but they are directed not toward reducing the number of accidents but rather their severity— a worthy endeavor but perhaps incomplete.

Most of the effort made in the area of automobile safety has been in terms of the design and engineering of the machine. There has been little legislative attempt to correct what so much psychological research has shown to be the major cause of automobile accidents: the driver.

The Committee on Highway Safety Research of the National Academy of Sciences stated that as much as 90 per cent of all highway accidents are caused by human error. Research by insurance companies has suggested that most automobiles involved in accidents seem to have been in good mechanical condition prior to the collision (although admittedly this is difficult to determine).

Consider the results of a detailed investigation in Michigan of 435 traffic deaths. The findings revealed that 89 per cent of the accidents could be traced directly to a violation of some traffic law. Alcohol was involved in 44 per cent of the fatalities. (In a similar study in Miami, Florida, alcohol was involved in 55 per cent of the traffic deaths.) Other contributing factors in the Michigan traffic deaths were poor judgment, inexperience, and excessive speed.

Subsequent research supports these findings and provides additional information. The following list summarizes the major findings of automobile accident investigations:

1. Excessive speed accounts for almost half of the deaths and injuries.
2. Driving under the influence of alcohol is a contributing factor in about half of the fatality cases. This finding is consistent and it is to the continuing shame of state legislatures that there are few really punitive laws against drunken driving. In most cases, even repeated offenders are allowed to continue to drive. In contrast, European countries with swift and heavy penalties for drunken driving have markedly reduced their traffic death rates.
3. Drivers under age twenty-five and over age sixty-five have more than their share of accidents.
4. The most dangerous time to drive is between 4:00 and 6:00 P.M. when it is dusk and people are rushing to get home from work.
5. Weekends, particularly Saturday, are also unsafe times to drive.
6. Drivers who are characterized as aggressive, socially irresponsible, and emotionally unstable have more accidents than those who lack these characteristics.

In sum, automobile accidents are largely attributable to age, alcohol, and attitudes. These factors are all amenable to change, but little has been done.

Studies also show that students who volunteer for driver education courses in school have better attitudes toward driving than those who do not. Police department clinics, set up in some cities for accident repeaters, seem to be of some value in changing attitudes and motivating safe driving behavior. Intensive publicity and law enforcement campaigns are also effective, but not for very long periods of time.

Can accident behavior be predicted on the basis of psychological tests or driving records? Unfortunately, past driving records seem to be of little value in predicting future driving behavior. Some studies have shown that drivers who have had several accidents in one time period are accident-free at a later time. There is at best only a slight relationship between individual accident rates in two different time periods.

417

A variety of psychological and psychomotor tests have been administered to drivers to determine if the results correlate with subsequent driving behavior. Tests of visual acuity, reaction time, intelligence, attitude, and psychophysical abilities have all been given, but the results have been disappointing.

Nevertheless, it is possible to conclude that the causes of most accidents are psychological and thus not capable of correction by engineering. Redesigning the automobile can change what could have been a fatal accident to a minor one (if occupants use the provided seat belts and shoulder harnesses, for example), but it cannot prevent the majority of accidents from occurring. Only "redesigning" the driver's behavior and attitudes will reduce the frequency of accidents, but altering motivations is a long-term and exceedingly difficult task.

ALCOHOLISM IN INDUSTRY

Throughout the United States, there are approximately 6.5 million known alcoholics; the actual figure is no doubt higher. The U.S. Public Health Service considers alcoholism one of the four major health threats, along with heart disease, cancer, and mental illness. Although the country as a whole has begrudgingly admitted its alcoholic problem, it has been slow to react in terms of treating alcoholism as a disease, rather than a symptom of low will power or degeneracy. Some cities, however, have made great strides in the treatment of the problem drinker, no longer jailing alcoholics but instead arranging for their treatment.

The American Medical Association has published a *Manual on Alcoholism,* incorporating the medical community's current thinking about the problem and its treatment. Alcoholism is defined as an illness characterized by an inability to control the consumption of alcohol such that intoxication is the inevitable result once drinking has begun. Medically, then, alcoholism is an addiction, a pathological drug dependence that is harmful to health and that interferes with normal functioning.

Unlike many health threats, alcoholism can be successfully treated through a variety of methods. It has been shown that as many as 75 per cent of all alcoholics can be rehabilitated.

With so many chronic alcoholics among the population, it follows that many of them are working in industry or government where their drinking can interfere with performance on the job. Yet it was not until the 1960s that North American industry began to accept the fact that there were alcoholics in its employ. Now, industry is gradually coming to assume responsibility for trying to rehabilitate alcoholic workers.

Scope of the Problem

It is estimated that approximately 8 per cent of the American work force are alcoholics. The cost to the nation's economy and to employers is put in excess of $15 billion a year. Employers of alcoholic workers are plagued by tardiness, excessive absenteeism, increased errors, growing inefficiency, and, often, the eventual loss of an employee in whom much money and training may have been invested.

The problem exists at all levels of corporate life. Most alcoholics in our society are not "skid row" derelicts, according to the National Institute on Alcohol Abuse and Alcoholism. Indeed, more than 70 per cent of the known alcoholics live in good neighborhoods and are professional, semiprofessional, or managerial workers. More than 50 per cent of all alcoholics are college graduates or have attended college.

As noted, there is a growing recognition of this problem on the part of employing organizations. The Department of Labor now advises its U.S. Employment Service offices throughout the country to consider alcoholics as handicapped and to treat them as disadvantaged workers in helping them find employment. Labor unions have undertaken extensive campaigns to warn members of the dangers of the excessive use of alcohol and have organized rehabilitation programs. Many large corporations try to help alcoholic employees through company-sponsored programs.

Effects of Alcoholism on the Job

It is popularly believed, particularly by alcoholics, that drinking will not affect their behavior at work, and that no one will notice any difference in the way they perform their jobs. This is decidedly untrue —the deteriorating effects of excessive drinking are evident almost immediately. However, at the beginning stages of alcoholism, it requires a trained observer to notice the changes.

Behavioral changes occur gradually but after three to five years of steady drinking, the employee's performance and efficiency have deteriorated so greatly that they become obvious to any alert supervisor. The general downward path of an alcoholic's behavior is portrayed graphically in Figure 12–1. The right-hand column lists the definite visible signs of altered job performance during the first few

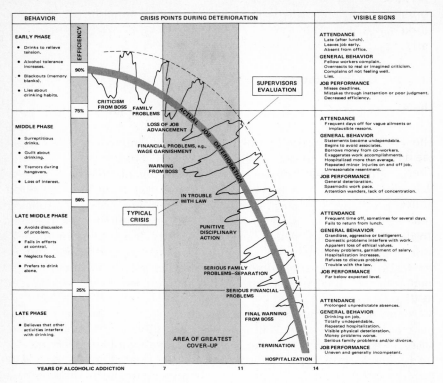

Figure 12–1. Deterioration in behavior and job performance of an alcoholic as a function of time. © 1967 Doyle Lindley, Bechtel Corporation, and reproduced by permission. See also A. Carding, "Booze and business," *Administrative Management*, **30**(1969), p. 21.

years of drinking: excessive absenteeism, long lunch breaks, lies, mistakes, reduced efficiency, and so on. In the middle phase of the drinking problem, we see gross changes in behavior that can no longer be overlooked. By this time, the alcoholic has usually been given at least one warning from superiors and is no longer considered for promotion.

Finally, as the job deterioration curve shows, everything goes downhill for the alcoholic—family life, reputation, financial stability, and, of course, the job. Ironically, yet understandably, each crisis precipitated by drinking is yet another reason to continue drinking, so a vicious cycle is established that, unless help is offered and accepted, leads to failure in every sphere of life and to jail, hospitalization, or an early death.

Because of the effects of alcoholism on job performance and efficiency, the problem must be faced. When a worker's superiors continue to ignore excessive drinking, thinking they are helping the worker, they are actually only prolonging the difficulty. Help at an early stage is vital to an alcoholic's recovery.

The Alcoholic Executive

The plight of the alcoholic employee is tragic and costly, but when the alcoholic is an executive, the cost to the company is even greater. There are no exact figures on the number of alcoholic executives but it is clear that they constitute their proportionate share of all alcoholics in the world of work. When a company loses an executive because of a drinking problem, it has lost someone in whom it had invested a great amount of money to train, whose salary was high, and whose responsibilities, judgment, and decision-making ability were important to the success of the organization. Business and management publications speak in circumspect tones about one of the most disastrous business mergers of all time—a merger that had been arranged by a high-level executive while intoxicated.

Executives at all levels are called upon daily to make important decisions and those persons who are under the influence of alcohol are no longer equipped to exercise decision-making skills. Usually, it is not the younger executive (whose responsibilities are not as great) who is prone to alcoholism. Rather, the National Council on Alcoholism has reported that the problem is greatest among executives between ages thirty-five and fifty, their years of primary value to the company.

Alcoholic executives, more than factory workers, are adept at concealing their problem for a longer period of time. They work in an environment in which drinking is an accepted and sometimes necessary part of the workday. Many private offices have their own bars, and it is not unusual for executives to have several drinks before and during lunch.

Another aid to drinking executives are secretaries, who are often willing and able to cover up for executives' indispositions. Thus, with no one observing executives (in the way in which production workers are always visible to superiors), and with secretaries to make excuses for them, alcoholic executives are able to escape detection longer than their counterparts on the assembly line.

There is one final comfort for executives who drink—they are not as likely to be fired as are factory workers. The alcoholic executives' chances of being ignored or given a make-work job are much greater; whereas management has finally recognized the problem of alcoholism on the factory floor, it is somewhat reluctant to admit that it exists in the neighboring executive office.

Rehabilitation of Alcoholics in Industry

Alcoholics can be rehabilitated and, fortunately, industry's interest in helping its drinking employees has increased in recent years. More than three hundred American corporations and federal government agencies sponsor formal alcoholic rehabilitation programs, and more companies join this list every year. Concerned firms include Allis-Chalmers, DuPont, Eastman Kodak, Consolidated Edison, and the Kemper Insurance Group.

The Oldsmobile division of General Motors Corporation recently ordered alcoholic employees to seek a cure or be fired from their jobs. Studying those who sought help, a Michigan State University research project found a 30 per cent decrease in sickness benefits, a 56 per cent decrease in leaves of absence, and an 82 per cent decrease in job–related accidents.

There is some feeling of corporate humanitarian responsibility to help alcoholic employees, but the major reason for the interest in rehabilitation is pragmatic: by rehabilitating rather than firing alcoholic employees, a company saves money in the long run. The president of one major corporation said: "the most expensive way to handle alcoholic employees is to fire or ignore them, and the most profitable and effective way to handle them is to help them to recover."

It is interesting that industry may be able to offer a much greater motivation for alcoholics to seek help than can families or friends—that is, their job. Many psychologists and physicians who work with alcoholics agree that the fear of losing their jobs may carry more weight with alcoholic workers than any cajoling or threatening from spouses, or even the danger of an early death. To alcoholics, keeping the job may be the last defense against admitting that they have a problem. When that defense is jeopardized, the motivation to seek or accept help is usually great.

How do rehabilitation programs in industry work? Most of them seem to follow the three-step process suggested by the National Council on Alcoholism.

1. Education of managers and supervisors. The purpose is to convince these leaders that alcoholism is not a moral or ethical issue but rather a medical problem—an illness or disease that can be cured.

2. Early detection of alcoholic workers by supervisors who should be instructed about what symptoms and behavioral and performance changes to look for. Early detection improves the chances of recovery.
3. Referral of alcoholic employees for help. Some companies utilize their own medical and psychological staff to treat alcoholics. Others send workers to outside (often live-in) clinics. Most organizations provide for treatment on company time and continue the workers' salaries while they are undergoing treatment.

A very useful method of treatment involves other employees who are members of Alcoholics Anonymous. This organization is extremely effective in dealing with the problems of alcoholism because its members have all experienced the illness and know all too well what it is like.

Although there is controversy about the success of organizational rehabilitation programs, the efforts are expanding. Many companies stress early detection of alcoholic workers and have set up formal training programs for supervisors to teach them to recognize those behaviors that signal alcoholism.

There is some evidence (although it is not very strong at present), to suggest that reformed alcoholics are better workers. Their performance no longer suffers from their drinking, and they may realize that this is their last chance, and thus put forth extra effort. However, even if their job performance weren't better than it was before rehabilitation, the company still has reclaimed trained and experienced workers who otherwise would have been lost to themselves and to the organization.

When 8 per cent of a company's employees suffer from a disabling illness, someone must help. Whatever their motivation, it is refreshing to see industry assume this responsibility.

THE DRUG PROBLEM IN INDUSTRY

In the late 1960s, drug abuse became a serious and visible problem, particularly among the nation's youth. In high schools and colleges, as well as among servicemen, drug taking approached epidemic proportions. Estimates of high school and college students taking some drug ranged from 30 to 60 per cent. It was inevitable that drug use should also become a problem at work. There was no reason to suspect that people who used drugs would suddenly stop when they graduated from school or got out of the army and found jobs. Therefore, seemingly overnight, industry found itself with a serious drug problem.

By 1971, the problem had become severe enough for the American Management Association to hold its first seminar on drug abuse, and for management and labor to become alarmed. Although the number of drug addicts (or even occasional users) does not approach the number of alcoholic workers in industry, drug use on the job remains a serious problem that is likely to grow.

Scope of Drugs in Industry

No figures are available on exactly how many drug users are currently employed in American business and industry. One study surveyed eighty companies and found that seventy-five of them had some problem with drug abuse. The five companies not affected were small concerns with mostly older employees. In another survey of fifty companies in New York City, forty-five of them reported incidents involving drugs. One of these firms spent $75,000 in one year to replace drug-addicted workers. Another company reported a 20 per cent drop in performance as a result of drug use.

Whatever the actual incidence of drug use in the world of work, it is serious enough for many employing organizations to take steps to deal with it. For example, a recent survey of municipal governments found that 59 per cent of the agencies had instituted some sort of preemployment screening to detect drug users. Some 20 per cent of the city governments had established guidelines to deal with the drug problem, and more than 34 per cent of them had established drug abuse education programs. An additional 25 per cent indicated plans to establish them.[2]

Labor unions, justifiably concerned about the physical condition of their workers, are conducting workshops for local unions. The United Auto Workers issued a formal appeal for intensified research efforts into the causes and cures of drug use, and is working closely with management to deal with the problem. The AFL-CIO conducted a national survey of their membership on drug use and reached the following conclusions.

1. The great majority of drug users are employees in the eighteen to thirty age bracket, and most are between eighteen and twenty. However, drug use is spreading to other age groups.

[2] F. A. Malinowski, "Employee drug abuse in municipal government," *Public Personnel Management*, **4** (1975), 59–62.

2. The greatest drug abuse problem is in the service trades, offices, and retail stores. Less drug use (although it does exist) is found in the garment, meat packing, and automobile industries.
3. Drug use in industry has spread to all racial and ethnic groups but is found mostly in black, Mexican-American, and Puerto Rican groups.
4. Drug use in industry is confined largely to the major cities of the east and west coasts. It is less of a problem in smaller towns in other sections of the country but it is spreading.

The problem is not limited to factory workers but appears in offices, advertising agencies, and on Wall Street in New York City where users are white, middle class, and older, not youthful members of minority groups.

Stimulants or pep pills are used extensively in the trucking industry and other kinds of work, where a person must stay awake and alert for long periods of time.

The current trend seems to indicate that drug abuse could become an even greater problem in industry than alcohol in terms of the disruptive effects on production and efficiency. Aside from the question of the legality of drugs, drug users are potentially more dangerous to a firm than are alcoholics for another reason. Alcoholics rarely proselytize or try to get friends and co-workers to share the joys of alcohol, but drug users frequently attempt to "turn others on." Drug addicts will actively try to hook others in hopes of selling them drugs and thus financing their own habits.

Effects of Drug Use on the Job

Behavioral effects vary with the kind of drug taken. Generally, the new user exhibits marked changes in behavior such as deterioration in attendance habits, work quality, personal hygiene, and manner of dress, as well as flare-ups in temper, a tendency to borrow money, and the wearing of dark glasses. There is also likely to be impairment in judgment and reflexes, sluggishness of movement, dilation or contraction of the pupils of the eyes, bloodshot eyes, and, in extreme cases, needle marks on the arms or elsewhere.

Obviously, these behavioral changes influence on-the-job performance and efficiency. Also, depending on what there is to steal in the company, drug use can lead to an increase in thefts by workers who are trying to support the expensive drug habit. In short, drug users become marginal employees who are an administrative and economic burden to management and potentially harmful to the morale

425

and safety of other employees. Particularly in hazardous occupations, drug users, like alcoholics, can be a menace to themselves and to their co-workers.

How Does Industry Meet the Problem?

Organizations are reacting to their drug problems in several ways. They are enlarging security departments, using undercover agents, screening applicants for past drug use, and firing users immediately upon detection. A growing number of companies are engaging in educational and rehabilitation programs. For the most part, however, industry assumes a hard line with the user and a harder line with the addict.

The first step taken by many companies is a simple and direct statement to employees and job applicants about their policy concerning drug use and the consequences for violating that policy.

The second step is careful screening of all job applicants. Personnel departments look attentively for gaps in employment history, less than honorable military discharge, and the physical signs of drug addiction. Urinalysis is being used as a screening technique at some plants, although it is legally and ethically controversial. Further, it is expensive, time-consuming, and unreliable. One company using urinalysis rejected 25 per cent of its applicants in one year; it later found out that 25 per cent of those who passed the screening test had used drugs before their employment.

The third step, and the most difficult of all, is to detect present employees who are using drugs. One large firm hired an ex-addict to work in various parts of the plant where he spotted drug users and eventually broke the drug ring. A large telephone company hired private detectives who joined the work force and found a drug ring operating out of a men's room. The use of undercover agents, although potentially dangerous, has been successful in breaking up drug groups in several plants.

What do organizations do with drug users when they are exposed? The company that hired the ex-addict had drug users and pushers arrested on the job, in full view of other employees.

Most companies differentiate between occasional users of soft drugs and addicts or pushers of hard drugs. If occasional users have a good performance record, and if they agree to undergo treatment, some companies will arrange for medical help and, in a few cases, even pay for it. If users refuse help they are immediately fired. Some companies have set up their own treatment facilities but most rely on outside rehabilitation centers. Many firms, however, fire the occasional user and would not knowingly hire such persons. Drug pushers are arrested as quickly as plant security personnel can identify them and call the local police.

The attitude of understanding and sympathy that characterizes industry's treatment of alcoholic workers is only beginning to be extended to drug users. Alcoholism is viewed as more socially acceptable than drug addiction. Also, many companies feel a greater obligation to alcoholics because they are usually older workers in positions of responsibility who have been with the company a long time. "That's a lot different," one executive said, "from a kid of seventeen who walked in yesterday."

The consensus among business executives is that the drug problem in industry will become more severe as greater numbers of young people find employment. Just as the army has been forced to rehabilitate its drug addicts, so, too, will many employing organizations.

SUMMARY

Accidents on the job result in approximately fifteen thousand deaths and as many as 25 million injuries every year. In addition, workers may be subject to disease contracted on the job such as pneumoconiosis or black lung disease, byssinosis or brown lung disease, and many forms of cancer. To try to counteract industrial accidents and disease, the U.S. Congress passed the Occupational Safety and Health Act, which has established, and tries to enforce, industrial safety standards. If we add those killed in household and automobile accidents to those killed on the job, the accident toll rises to one hundred thousand victims a year.

One problem with accident research is that many employing organizations distort their **accident data** through incomplete recording, in an effort to keep safety records intact.

There are several causes of accidents; some relate to the physical environment in which work takes place and others to workers' personal characteristics.

Aspects of the **physical work environment** that affect accident rates include (1) type of industry (industries such as mining, construction, and lumber are more dangerous than others); (2) temporal working conditions (although the total number of hours worked is not related to accidents, when the work is performed is important; for example, fewer accidents occur during the night shift than during the day shift); (3) lighting (poor lighting seems to be associated with a higher accident rate); (4) temperature (accidents increase when temperatures rise above 70°F. or fall below 68°F.); (5) equipment design (the absence of built-in safety devices and poor design of machinery can increase accidents); (6) miscellaneous factors (plants that lay off workers on a seasonal basis or are located near other plants have higher accident rates; plants whose employees live in slum areas have higher accident rates).

The **personal factors** in accidents that have been studied include (1) intelligence (there seems to be no relationship between intelligence and accident rate); (2) physical condition and health (both factors, particularly poor vision, contribute to accidents); (3) fatigue (fatigue is closely related to accident rate); (4) work experience and age (although there are complicating variables, older workers with more job experience generally have fewer accidents than younger workers who are new to the job); (5) personality characteristics (although accidents seem to vary as a function of a person's temporary emotional state, they do not seem to be related to general personality patterns).

The concept of **accident proneness**—that some people are more likely to have accidents than others—is a popular notion but one that enjoys little experimental support.

An organization can take a number of steps to try to **prevent accidents** from occurring: (1) complete reporting and analysis of all accidents—each accident must be investigated thoroughly and reported in detail so that comparative accident data can be studied; (2) proper design of the work and its environment—work areas must be well lighted, clean, and orderly; machinery must be well maintained and designed to be compatible with the capabilities of the workers; safety devices must not interfere with production and must be designed so that machinery will not operate unless they are in place; (3) training for accident prevention—workers and supervisors must be trained not only in specific job skills but also in attitudes toward safety; (4) safety publicity campaigns—these campaigns can be useful, but only if they stress positive themes.

A great deal of research has been conducted on **automobile accidents.** As many as 90 per cent of them are caused by human error. Most accidents can be traced to age, alcohol, or attitude. Although design changes in automobiles and lower speed limits can reduce the severity of injuries once an accident has occurred, changing the behaviors and attitudes of drivers seems to be the only way of reducing the number of accidents.

Alcoholism in industry affects 8 per cent of the work force and is responsible for tardiness, absenteeism, increased errors, inefficiency, and much human misery. Although alcoholism is a problem among all levels of employee, it is particularly costly to organizations when it occurs among executives. Industrial and governmental employers try to help alcoholic workers through rehabilitation programs, education of managers, and early detection of alcoholics.

Drug use in industry, though not as serious a problem as alcoholism, is increasing. Drug use occurs mostly among eighteen to thirty-year-olds, in service trades, offices, and retail stores, in the major cities on both coasts, and among minority group members.

Employing organizations are beginning to institute rehabilitation programs, but many drug users are fired and drug pushers are arrested. In general, industry treats drug users more severely than it treats alcoholics.

SUGGESTED READINGS

A new approach to treating alcoholism. *Business Week,* 1975 (September 8), 83–84.

American Management Association. *Helping the Alcoholic Employee.* New York: American Management Association, 1973.

Anderson, R. *OSHA and Accident Control Through Training.* New York: Industrial Press, 1975.

Ashford, N. *Crisis in the Work Place: Occupational Disease and Injury.* Cambridge, Mass.: MIT Press, 1976.

Barrett, G. Public policy and the prediction of accident involvement. In K. Wexley and G. Yukl, Eds., *Organizational Behavior and Industrial Psychology.* New York: Oxford University Press, 1975. Pp. 629–634.

Boley, J. *A Guide to Effective Industrial Safety: How to Reduce Costly Injuries and Accidents.* Houston: Gulf, 1977.

Chambers, C., and Heckman, R. *Employee Drug Abuse: A Manager's Guide for Action.* Boston: Cahners, 1972.

Chiles, W., and Jennings, A. Effects of alcohol on complex performance. *Human Factors,* 1970, **12,** 605–612.

Forbes, T. W., Ed. *Human Factors in Highway Traffic Safety Research.* New York: John Wiley & Sons, 1972.

Hammer, W. *Occupational Safety Management and Engineering.* Englewood Cliffs, N.J.: Prentice-Hall, 1975.

Kane, K. Corporate responsibility in the area of alcoholism. *Personnel Journal,* 1975, **54,** 380–384.

Kenyon, W. Alcoholic at work. *Personnel Management,* 1974, **6,** 33–36.

MacBeth, J., and Wiegand, J. Alcoholism: A rehabilitation program that works. *Supervisory Management,* 1975, **20,** 2–6.

Malinowski, F. Employee drug abuse in municipal government. *Public Personnel Management,* 1975, **4,** 59–62.

Margolis, B. L., and Kroes, W. H., Eds. *The Human Side of Accident Prevention: Psychological Concepts and Principles Which Bear on Industrial Safety.* Springfield, Ill.: Charles C Thomas, 1975.

Peterson, D. *Safety Supervision.* New York: American Management Association, 1976.

Presnall, L. What's wrong with alcoholism control programs? *Personnel,* 1970, **47**(March), 38–43.

Rogers, R., and Colbert, J. Drug abuse and organizational response: A review and evaluation. *Personnel Journal,* 1975, **54**, 266–271.

Scher, J. *Drug Abuse in Industry: Growing Corporate Dilemma.* Springfield, Ill.: Charles C Thomas, 1973.

Sharma J., and Vardhan, H. On-the-job safety: It's up to the supervisor. *Supervisory Management,* 1975, **20**, 35–39.

Shaw, L., and Sichel, H. S. *Accident Proneness.* Elmsford, N.Y.: Pergamon Press, 1971.

Signori, E., and Bowman, R. On the study of personality factors in research on driving behavior. *Perceptual and Motor Skills,* 1974, **38**, 1067–1076.

Stellman, J. M., and Daum, S. M. *Work is Dangerous to Your Health: A Handbook of Health Hazards in the Workplace and What You Can Do About Them.* New York: Pantheon, 1973.

CONSUMER PSYCHOLOGY

Not everyone works for an organization, but all of us are consumers of the products and services of a great many organizations. We buy automobiles, cosmetics, food, and appliances; we vote for political candidates and for issues; we respond to appeals from charities and pressure groups. And we are constantly bombarded by communications from all these organizations—messages from industry, government, or individuals urging us to behave in one way or another. We are influenced by thousands of advertising appeals that appear on television screens, highway billboards, and the pages of our magazines and newspapers.

Consumer psychology is concerned with the interactions between consumers and organizations that affect us all. Advertisers spend billions of dollars each year to influence us, and most of the persuasive techniques they practice were devised by psychologists.

Consumer psychology is also important to you as an employee, particularly if you work for a company that produces consumer goods and services. If people don't buy what your company makes, it will not be in business for long.

Chapter 13 deals with the major facets of the producer-consumer interaction: the research methods of consumer psychologists, the nature of advertising, television programming, and the importance of packaging, product image, and sex in product promotion. On the consumer side, we discuss buying behavior, brand loyalty, and the effects of personality, social class, ethnic group membership, and age.

13

Psychology and the Consumer

One of the most visible areas in which psychology contributes to organizational life today involves the relationship between the producers of goods and services and the consumers. No matter how high the level of production or the quality of a company's products, the company will not be successful unless the public is made aware of the product and persuaded to buy it. Thus, a company's survival depends on its ability to promote, advertise, and market its product.

There are several critical steps in the development of an efficient and high quality production process, and the influence of psychology is important at each step: in selecting and training the work force; in developing effective leadership, motivation, and job satisfaction; and in designing the tools, equipment, and work space for safe and efficient production. A failure at any of these steps can spell failure for the organization. However, the perfect work force operating under ideal conditions cannot survive if the consuming public does not buy the finished product. There have been many instances of fine products and worthy organizations failing because consumers ignored them in the marketplace.

For a product, a service, or even a political candidate to sell, people must be made aware of it and persuaded that they should (indeed, must) have it. This function of persuasion is accomplished by the branch of industrial psychology known as consumer psychology. Psychologists are aided in this endeavor by professionals from other disciplines. To fully understand the complexities of the potential consumer requires the skills of sociologists, economists, and statisticians, as well as copywriters, account executives, film makers, and the host of other talents employed by advertising agencies.

Although psychologists may be only a part of the marketing, ad-

433

vertising, and promoting effort, their contribution is unique. They bring to the field a methodology, specific research tools, and the general principles of human behavior gleaned from laboratory and clinical research. The methodology is, of course, the rigorous scientific method, with its controls and experimental safeguards applied so successfully in the laboratory and on the factory assembly line. As noted in Chapter 1, psychologists study human behavior objectively, whether the individual is taking a test, performing a job, or purchasing a new car. In each case, what the person does—how he or she behaves—can be observed and analyzed systematically to determine the nature of the behavior. Once the behavior is understood, it is possible to manipulate the environmental stimuli so that people will work faster, more safely, and with greater satisfaction, or will choose one make of car over another.

Psychologists have developed a number of research tools to enable them to analyze and understand human behavior. These techniques—personality tests, attitude questionnaires, public opinion polls and surveys—developed for use in the laboratory or the clinic, are also useful in the marketplace. The principles that underlie the construction and application of an attitude questionnaire hold, whether it is used to measure job satisfaction or cereal brand preferences. Because of their experience in observing, measuring, and recording human behavior in such a variety of situations, psychologists are also able to develop new research techniques, in response to specific needs.

Another contribution of psychologists to consumer psychology is the application of the established principles of human behavior. From a century of study of basic human processes of perception, learning, motivation, and personality, psychologists have learned a great deal that can be applied to people in the marketplace. For example, the research on conditions that facilitate learning can aid in the design of an advertising campaign, the goal of which is to have consumers learn and retain the advertising message so that they are led to a specific product on a supermarket shelf. Basic principles of human perception can help in promoting the attention-getting value of an advertisement or of the package in which the product is presented. Social psychological research has revealed factors that make for greater persuasibility of a communication or message.

Consumer behavior has been of interest to industrial psychologists since the beginnings of the field. Indeed, industrial psychology was formally launched by the work of Walter Dill Scott on advertising and selling. The Division of Consumer Psychology of the American Psychological Association (Division 23) includes more than three hundred psychologists and is growing every year. In addition, many psychologists work in this area but do not hold membership in the division.

Vital to industry, and necessary for the continuing growth of the economy, consumer psychology is also of practical importance to you as a consumer. Consider all the products you have purchased. What led you to buy one brand of deodorant over another? What convinced you in the first place that you needed a deodorant? Unless you have a real problem (like people constantly avoiding you), you were probably convinced by constant exposure to advertisements. This is something you must have, you were told, to be "nice to be near," to get married, or to get a promotion.

As to the specific brand you purchased, that too was probably decided on the basis of the advertising appeal or the "image" represented by the product, the attractiveness of the package, or its location on the drugstore shelf (this, too, is a carefully planned aspect of a promotional campaign).

Billions of dollars and thousands of hours are expended by companies each year in the effort to get you to notice, want, and purchase their products. It is important to you, then, both as a member of an organization making products, and as a consumer, to understand the principles and practices of consumer psychology.

SCOPE OF CONSUMER PSYCHOLOGY

The study of consumer psychology is growing rapidly, more so now than at any other period in its history. In the years between 1968 and 1972, more articles were published in the area than had been published in all the years before 1968 combined. As many as ten thousand articles on consumer psychology were published between 1967 and 1976.[1] There seems to be no way of escaping the influence of consumer psychology. Pick up a magazine, turn on the radio or television, drive down a highway—almost everywhere you will be bombarded by advertising messages. It is estimated that the average American is exposed to as many as fifteen hundred ads every day, through one medium or another. These ads may try to sell you dog food or detergent, and exhort you to join the army or vote for Candidate X, or persuade you to donate money to medical research or the college of your choice. Of course, no one can adequately attend to so many messages, nor should we, if we want to maintain our

[1] J. Jacoby, "Consumer psychology: An octennium," *Annual Review of Psychology*, **27** (1976), 331.

sanity. Many ads are blocked out because they are not perceived. In fact, more than fourteen hundred of the daily messages are not received at all. Most people are able to react to only about a dozen of them. But whether or not we see or hear these messages, they are there, cluttering the media. Even if we remain unaware of specific ads, we are most certainly aware that the process of advertising is going on all around us.

Another indication of the scope of consumer psychology is that increasing numbers of Americans are serving as subjects in consumer research. Our buying, viewing, and travel habits are constantly being scrutinized by consumer researchers. We are approached at home, in shopping centers, at the theater, and questioned about the products we use, the programs we watch, or the purchases we plan to make. Sample soaps are delivered to every home in a certain district; if we buy the product when the sample runs out, this is reflected in the area's sales figures. Thus, we are probed and peeked at through consumer research to determine our likes and dislikes, then prodded or provoked by the advertising messages designed on the basis of this research.

Some advertising practices have acquired (and deserve) a negative reputation, but much of the advertising to which we are exposed is informative and instructive. We can save money by reading the sale ads in the local newspaper, or learn about product differences (where these differences are real, not merely verbal) by reading descriptive advertising literature.

Critics of advertising argue that most people are offended and insulted by advertisements, particularly by those on television, but apparently this is not the case. Surveys show that only a minority (5–14 per cent) hold unfavorable attitudes toward advertising. As many as 41 per cent have favorable attitudes.

But whatever our personal judgment about the credibility, usefulness, and morality of advertising, the fact of its existence on a huge, and increasing, scale cannot be denied. We will be better equipped to cope with advertising if we understand what advertisers want to do and how they attempt to do it.

Let us consider some of the functions of the consumer psychologist. Manufacturers must inform and instruct the public about the nature of their product. Potential buyers must know what the product does, why it performs better than its competitor, and how much it costs. There are more than three hundred thousand brand name products of all types on the market today. In a typical supermarket, for example, over seven thousand different products are available. In the face of such formidable competition, manufacturers must ensure that their products can be readily recognized, identified, and associated with. The typical buyer will purchase the item that sounds or looks familiar over one that is unknown.

But communication should not be solely from producer to consumer. A two-way communications link must be established. Manufacturers must be constantly alert for changes in the demand and preference for their products. Ignorance or delayed awareness of such changes can mean losing out to a competitor. Manufacturers must be sensitive to the nature of the market, and capable of responding quickly to changes by modifying an advertising campaign, a package design, or the product itself.

The task of defining a potential market is accomplished through in-depth studies of consumer needs, desires, buying habits and attitudes. And these consumer characteristics are influenced by factors such as age, education, and socioeconomic level. This type of market information affects product packaging, displaying, and advertising, and also determines production schedules and distribution facilities. Product demand is subject to seasonal variations, general economic and political conditions, and technological innovations in related areas.

Therefore, consumers must continually be studied and industry kept aware of their likes, dislikes, fears, desires, prejudices and whims. A primary law of survival in the marketplace is to produce what people want to buy; this information is determined only through sound research.

Once the nature and composition of the market for a product have been delimited, consumer psychologists must determine how to effectively reach that market. This is the area of advertising. The type of advertising appeal that will produce maximum sales, and the medium through which the advertising should be presented, depends on the nature of the market.

A luxury automobile or sailboat will only be purchased by a certain segment of the population, and the advertisements must be geared to their level of sophistication and taste, and be presented in media known to reach them. More potential buyers for these products will read a magazine such as *The New Yorker* than *Popular Mechanics*. Similarly, the image created by the ad will not be the same for a $10 watch as for a $500 watch. Many products fail or succeed on the basis of the compatibility of the advertisement with the product market.

Often the product market compatibility issue can be decided by a product testing program. By releasing a new product (or an improved version of an existing product) to a limited group of people before its release to the general public, it is possible to determine reactions to and acceptance of the product. Often, this method allows deficiencies to be perceived and corrected before widespread distribution.

In essence, consumer psychology deals with the complex relationship between buyers and sellers. If sellers are to be successful, they must know their buyers, how to appeal to them, and how to persuade them to buy the product. This knowledge comes only through patient, thorough, and expensive research. The scope of consumer psychology is broad, but its effectiveness is limited by the quality of the underlying research.

RESEARCH METHODS IN CONSUMER PSYCHOLOGY

Several research methods are used by consumer psychologists in their continuing studies of markets, product preferences, and other aspects of consumer choice behavior. In general, much of the research involves the application of the standard psychological research techniques (discussed in Chapter 2), but additional methods have been developed for special purposes.

Consumer research is conducted in a variety of settings—university laboratories, private homes, street corners, shopping centers, as well as laboratories established by some advertising agencies. Wherever the research is conducted, and whatever technique is used, the studies should be performed under the same rigorous and objective conditions required of all psychological research.

Survey and Polling Methods

Most research that deals with consumer preferences, buying behavior, or reactions to new products or television programs is conducted by some form of survey or public opinion poll. The basic premise underlying the use of surveys is simple: most people can and will articulate their feelings, reactions, opinions, and desires, when asked about them.

This assumption holds whether we are trying to determine a person's reactions to a new peanut butter or to a presidential candidate, and is supported by much research involving careful, thorough, and precise questioning of representative samples of the population whose opinions are at issue. We have only to recall how accurately most pre-election public opinion polls have predicted election results, or how successfully many new products have been introduced on the basis of market testing, to know that the survey method often does work well.

However, there have also been failures to accurately predict election results, and new products that have faded into obscurity. Part of the difficulty is the complex and changeable nature of consumers, who may, for example, tell an interviewer on Friday that they will vote Republican and then vote Democratic on Tuesday because of a sudden downturn in the stock market. Or the respondents who say that they drink imported beer, but if the interviewer could open their refrigerators or follow them to the store, it would be found that they actually drink a much cheaper brand. They told the consumer researcher that they preferred the more expensive product because they thought it would make them look better. Garbage can searches have revealed that people actually drink more than twice the amount of beer and liquor than they report to interviewers. Similarly, when people are asked about their debts, they tend to underestimate the dollar amounts. Thus, we tend to change our minds or tell interviewers what we think will give us a higher status—and on such vagaries elections are lost and manufacturers go bankrupt.

These problems, though capable of distorting research results, are not a fault of the survey method but rather of the diversity, or perversity, of human nature. Of course, improper utilization of research methods can also render the results useless. A poorly constructed questionnaire administered to a nonrepresentative sample will do more harm than good, but again, that is not a fault of the technique itself.

(Specific considerations in developing and applying the survey method are discussed in detail in Chapter 2.)

In-Depth Methods

People may misrepresent themselves to interviewers when asked for their opinions or questioned about the products they use. Because of this potential source of distortion, some consumer psychologists believe that it is not fruitful to ask persons directly for their reactions or attitudes. They contend that the direct question as asked may differ from what the respondents actually heard. For example, by asking what brand of beer a person drinks, we are, in effect, asking what kind of person he or she is. The respondent may not feel that consumer researchers are asking merely about beer preference. Rather, they are really asking: "Do you drink the cheap stuff or the expensive, high status, snob appeal brand?" Critics of the survey method say that we cannot uncover true human motivations and feelings by asking direct questions that allow the respondents to distort their feelings.

To probe deeper motivations, in-depth procedures are thus advocated, such as projective techniques (the Rorschach, Thematic Apperception Test, or sentence completion test, for example). The theory behind the use of these techniques is the same whether they are applied for selection purposes or for the evaluation of a new product. Presented with an ambiguous stimulus such as an inkblot, it is assumed that personal needs, values, and fears will be projected into the act of interpreting the stimulus.

Aside from the procedural and methodological differences between the survey and in-depth approaches, there is a basic difference in the results. The survey method is essentially a counting procedure; it tells the researcher how many people say they use, or will buy, a certain product. The in-depth methods provide information on why people use or buy a particular product. Because of the emphasis on motivation, the in-depth approach is sometimes called *motivation research*.

A classic example of the in-depth approach in consumer research is the instant-coffee study conducted in 1950, an attempt to determine basic attitudes toward Nescafé.[2] Instant coffee was, at that time, a new product that met with a good deal of consumer resistance. To find out why, the direct survey approach was tried first. Respondents were asked, "Do you use instant coffee?" If they said no, they were asked what they disliked about it. The researchers suspected that the reasons given by the majority of the non-instant-coffee users concealed other hidden motivations, so then the indirect, in-depth approach was attempted.

A shopping list was shown to two groups of women (fifty in each group), and they were asked to describe the personality of the housewife who would make up such a list. The shopping lists were identical except that one list included instant coffee and the other included a "real" coffee (Table 13-1). The approach is a projective technique designed to reveal the respondents' inner feelings about the person who would use either type of coffee. The respondents are not asked directly to reveal their own feelings (at least as they perceived the situation), but, in reality, they projected their own feelings in their characterization of the fictitious shopper.

On the basis of the type of coffee used (since the other items on the shopping lists were the same), the fictitious shoppers were given totally different personalities by the respondents. Almost half of them described the woman who bought instant coffee as a lazy housewife who failed to plan household purchases and schedules well. She was described as a spendthrift by 12 per cent, and as not being a good wife by 10 per cent.

The "real" coffee shopper was described in much less negative terms. No one characterized her as a spendthrift or a poor wife; only a minority described her as lazy.

The descriptions of the two shoppers in this research study ap-

[2] M. Haire, "Projective techniques in marketing research," *Journal of Marketing*, **14**(April 1950), 649–656.

TABLE 13–1

SHOPPING LISTS IN INSTANT-COFFEE STUDY

List 1	List 2
1 can Rumford's Baking Powder	1 can Rumford's Baking Powder
2 loaves Wonder bread	2 loaves Wonder bread
bunch of carrots	bunch of carrots
Nescafé instant coffee	1 lb. Maxwell House Coffee (Drip Ground)
Pound and a half of hamburger	Pound and a half of hamburger
2 cans Del Monte peaches	2 cans Del Monte peaches
5 lbs. potatoes	5 lbs. potatoes

Adapted from M. Haire, "Projective techniques in marketing research," *Journal of Marketing,* **14** (April 1950), 649.

parently reveal why instant coffee took so long to be accepted. The unflattering image of the synthetic coffee user was a projection of the consumers' own feelings about the product. Perhaps people were slow to accept instant coffee because they were afraid of being thought of as the lazy kind of person described in the in-depth study.

In the initial consumer survey that asked people directly why they didn't like instant coffee, most respondents said they didn't like the flavor. But the real motivation may have been that they would feel lazy, failing in their household duties, and wasteful by buying instant coffee—the kind of information difficult to elicit in the direct and formal questionnaire or interview.

The in-depth approach to the study of consumer motivation has received both favorable and unfavorable publicity. Theoretically, the in-depth approach offers the same advantages as projective tests for personnel selection; that is, the ability to reach unconscious levels of motivation, to determine feelings and desires that could not be reached by direct objective tests and questionnaires. However, many psychologists suggest that this does not work in reality. Further, projective tests have a record of low reliability and validity. Even the most highly trained and experienced clinical psychologists often disagree on the interpretation of projective test results. And this is true even in a clinical setting where the practitioner may devote a great deal of time to a patient, and may supplement projective test results with other tests and examinations. If the method is of doubtful validity in a clinical setting, it must be even more questionable in consumer psychology where the practitioner is often less skilled and devotes less time to securing results.

There have been fruitful uses of projective techniques in consumer research. The successful introduction of the hardtop convertible automobile was made on the basis of consumer attitudes and feelings determined by the in-depth approach. Unfortunately, the advertising industry does not publicize failures, so it is difficult to determine precisely how successful this technique has been.

BEHAVIORAL STUDIES IN CONSUMER PSYCHOLOGY

In both consumer surveys and in-depth research methods, the focus is on opinions, feelings, and motivations; in short, on how people say they react to and feel about certain products or experiences. Although these data can be useful in the study of consumer psychology, the methods share one basic weakness: they describe (however accurately) only what people *say* they will do. These expressed intentions do not always coincide with actual behavior.

Some consumer studies do show a positive correlation between expressed intention and actual behavior, but many others do not. As noted, people sometimes tell an interviewer that they prefer one brand of a product but buy another brand.

Because of this frequently observed discrepancy, many consumer psychologists believe that the most accurate way to investigate consumer behavior is to observe that behavior. Whether in a laboratory or a shopping center, the focus is on what people do when purchasing a product or expressing a preference for one brand over several others.

Purchasing Behavior

Common sense suggests that the best test of the acceptance of a new product, or of a new advertising campaign for an existing product, is actual sales figures. Surely, if sales for a toothpaste increase by 21 per cent in the six months following a new advertising approach, we can conclude that the campaign is successful.

Unfortunately, since all the variables capable of influencing sales were not controlled, we cannot conclude with certainty that the advertising campaign was solely, or even partially, responsible for the boost in sales. The company's aggressive sales staff may have arranged for more prominent counter display of the toothpaste during the six-month period; this factor alone could be responsible for the higher sales, independent of the new advertising. Or a competitor may have been criticized in a government report for using a new ingredient alleged to be harmful, thus throwing business to all other toothpaste manufacturers.

The point is that sales records can reflect factors other than the one being considered, and without adequate control over all possible influencing variables it is impossible to explain exactly what affected the sales figures.

A more direct way of investigating actual purchasing behavior is to place observers at various points throughout shops or supermarkets. Although expensive and time-consuming, this technique offers several advantages, in addition to providing an accurate record of actual buying behavior.

One study conducted in a supermarket determined which family member bought a particular product and who (if other family members were with the shopper) may have influenced or determined the purchase. The study also showed how many people bothered to compare prices of competing products, or studied the packages for information other than price. Also, the extent to which brand choices seemed to have been decided before entering the store (selecting a particular brand without hesitation or consideration of other brands) was revealed.

Thus, useful information on actual purchasing behavior can be obtained from on-the-spot observations, but the technique has limitations in addition to the expense and time involved. The method tells what is being purchased, but not why the consumer is choosing that brand over another. The question of motivation must still be pursued by the survey or in-depth approaches.

Another limitation is the problem of adequate sampling of shopping behavior. Stores in different locations—for example, inner city versus suburban—attract different clientele with varying needs and income levels. The nature of the shopper can vary in the same store at different times of the day or week. People forced to shop evenings and weekends may make different purchases than those free to shop during the day. The problem can be dealt with by making observations in different neighborhoods and at various shopping hours, but this greatly increases the cost of the study.

A final limitation is the lack of suitable experimental control over all possible influencing variables. (This is a weakness of all types of observational research studies.) In observing shopping differences between an urban and a suburban supermarket, for example, it is difficult to determine if the differences are a function of social, economic, or ethnic composition of the clientele, of the different product layouts in the stores, or of the availability of some products and not others. Specialty items may not be stocked at stores in low-income neighborhoods; it cannot be determined, therefore, if the product doesn't sell in that situation because of its cost or simply its lack of availability.

These limitations do not negate the usefulness of the research method, but they do call for special attention in the design and conduct of the investigation.

Brand Identification and Preference Research

Research dealing with the ability of consumers to recognize or identify specific product brands is widespread in consumer psychology. The behavior being studied—preference, rather than actual purchase—is amenable to study under well-controlled laboratory conditions. Thus, we can have greater confidence in these results than in the results of some observational studies. Even when brand preference studies are conducted under natural conditions, such as in a shopping center, it is relatively easy to control all relevant influencing variables.

Much brand preference research focuses on consumers' ability to discriminate among competing brands of a product. For example, when all recognizable cues are removed—the product's name or distinctive package or container—can a person distinguish between one kind of cola and a competing brand? This research usually demonstrates that people cannot discriminate among brands. Several studies dealing with cola drinks have shown that people cannot identify the best-known products by taste, once distinctive packaging characteristics were removed. Even people who said they would drink only Coca-Cola were not able to distinguish that product from other cola drinks. Similar results have been found for competing brands of cigarettes, whiskey, beer, and margarine. Apparently, with some products, consumer preferences and brand loyalty are caused by factors other than the intrinsic qualities of the product itself.

It is essential in brand identification research that subjects be exposed to the various brands in blindfold fashion, with beverages served in identical bottles, product names taped over, and any other distinguishing characteristics, such as a unique cigarette filter tip, disguised in some way.

Consumer preference studies are also concerned with testing new products to determine customer reaction in advance of a product's release to the market at large. For example, studies have been performed on the tactual sensations or "feel" of various clothing fabrics, preferences for shapes of sponges, and perceived crispness of breakfast cereals in different packages. One study showed that consumers believed bread to be fresher when enclosed in a plastic bag than in wax paper alone. Without tasting or feeling the bread itself, consumers judged freshness solely on the basis of the wrappings.

These studies can control all variables likely to affect preference except the one under investigation. Such careful research, using subjects representative of the intended market, can provide manufacturers with much information about the reaction to their products. In addition, testing can detect deficiencies or undesirable features that can be corrected before the product is released for sale.

Testing Advertisements

A major research activity of consumer psychologists is testing the effectiveness of advertising and promotional campaigns. The tremendous amounts of money spent by business firms on advertising make such research necessary for several reasons: (1) to determine, by pretesting advertisements, their acceptability and effect, before the ad is actually used; (2) to ascertain if a current advertising campaign is reaching the intended audience; (3) to find out if the message transmitted in the ads is the same one being received by the audience; (4) to learn how many of the people in the audience are really attending to the ad. Whether an ad is tested in advance of use or when a campaign is already under way, there are several specific techniques to determine its effectiveness.

The most direct approach is to *ask respondents* for their personal reactions to an ad. People are asked, for example, if the ad really makes them want to buy the product, if they believe the ad, or which of two ads for the same product is the more interesting or attention getting.

A requirement of this method is that the sample consist of a representative group of the same people for whom the product is intended. Using bachelors or elderly people to pretest an ad for baby food may not be wise, since their reactions can be expected to differ from those of a young couple expecting their first child.

A frequently used technique of testing advertising effectiveness is the method of *aided recall*. Designed for any ad in any medium, the method attempts to assess the memorability of an advertisement. Shortly after an ad has appeared in a magazine or been televised, a cross section of consumers is questioned about whether they read that issue of the magazine or saw the program in which the commercial appeared. If they did, they are asked if they read or saw the commercial in question. Those who did see the ad are asked to tell as much of its selling message as they can remember. During this recall, the interviewer asks specific questions about various aspects of the ad, thus "aiding" the recall.

Another technique for testing the effectiveness of specific advertisements is *recognition*. People who have seen a particular television program or magazine are shown copies of ads that appeared therein and asked questions about them: Did the respondents remember seeing the ad? Did they remember the name of the product? Had they read at least half of the written part of the ad when they first saw it?

There is an unfortunate weakness in the recognition method, which is not present with the recall method. People will sometimes say that they have seen an ad, even if they have not. This tendency was verified by using ads in the recognition test that had not yet appeared. Thus, it is possible to detect this kind of response faking.

Laboratory approaches to measuring advertisement reaction use elaborate electronic apparatus. An *eye camera* films the eye movements and fixations of subjects who are able to move their heads freely and read magazines at their own pace, turning the pages at leisure. The film record of eye movement provides much useful information, such as which of several ads on the same page attracted attention first or held attention longest, what feature of an ad did a person look at first, in what sequence did the eye explore the various parts of an ad, and how long did the person look at an ad.

Another useful instrument is the *tachistoscope,* which permits short-term exposure of a visual stimulus. The device can be useful in pretesting ads; it makes it possible to determine how much information a person can perceive and recall on the basis of a very short exposure to an ad. Through research using the tachistoscope, it is possible to determine the maximum amount of information that can be presented in an ad.

Another laboratory technique for evaluating advertisements involves physiological measuring devices such as the *galvanic skin reaction recorder,* which makes a gross measure of emotional arousal. It would be ideal to measure a person's emotional reactions to different kinds of ads, but the device is not that reliable, and much conflicting data have appeared from such studies.

A more promising method records the amount of *pupil dilation* in response to a visual stimulus. When the eyes see something that interests the person, the pupils dilate slightly, enough to register on the recording apparatus. The pupils contract when the eyes view uninteresting material. This approach has the capability of accurately measuring level of interest; it does not tell how much people say they are interested (that can be faked), but how much they actually are interested. Pupil size cannot be voluntarily controlled by the respondents.

Another way of measuring the effectiveness of advertising is with operant conditioning techniques. By using a machine called CONPAAD (Conjugately Programmed Analyses of Advertising),[3] researchers can determine how positively reinforcing various commercials are. By pressing a foot pedal, consumers determine whether or not a commercial shown on a screen in front of them stays on or fades out. It is assumed that the commercials that are more reinforcing elicit a higher rate of responding (pressing the foot pedal) than commercials that are less reinforcing. By responding at a faster rate, the subject maintains a brighter picture and a louder sound. Research has demonstrated that the technique is very reliable and valid, correlates highly with verbally expressed preference, and provides precise quantitative results.

Some consumer psychologists argue that these laboratory and field approaches provide some useful information on how people may feel about an ad, but that the only meaningful test is whether the ad results in increased sales. We noted the limitations of using sales figures as a criterion of success, but a more experimental approach—*sales tests*—is designed to reduce these deficiencies. It is a test in the sense of exerting experimental control over all influencing variables.

A sales or advertising campaign is introduced in selected cities or geographic areas. Other areas, chosen to be as similar as possible in all respects to the test market areas, serve as controls; the ads are not seen in the control areas. Assuming comparability of test and control areas, any resulting increase in sales in the test areas must be attributable to the advertising alone.

The major advantage of this approach is the control, which can produce conclusive results. The psychologist is not measuring interest in an ad, or what people say they remember about an ad, or how much their pupils dilate when they see it, but whether they actually go out and buy the product solely on the basis of the advertising. Further, the experimental controls assure that purchasing behavior is not caused by extraneous variables that operate independently of the advertising.

This approach to advertising effectiveness is desirable, but it, too, has limitations. An adequate sales test requires great expense, considerable time to arrange, and precise accounting of what large numbers of people do and do not purchase during the period of the study. Another limitation involves the control areas. By not exposing people in the control areas to the new advertising, the manufacturer may lose sales to competitors.

In spite of the difficulties and expense, increasing numbers of ad-

---

[3] L. Winters and W. Wallace, "On operant conditioning techniques," *Journal of Advertising Research,* **10** (1970), 39–45.

vertising agencies are undertaking sales tests because they offer the most accurate method of gauging the impact of advertising effectiveness on the basis of its most important goal—increasing sales.

A means of testing magazine and newspaper advertising is through the use of *coupon returns*. For the most part this is used to gauge reader interest, not actual buying behavior, except in those cases where the coupon is sent to the manufacturer to purchase a product. In most cases, however, coupons are used to get a sample, a brochure, or to enter a contest. When the inducement to return the coupon is especially attractive, there is the danger of people responding in the absence of any real interest in the product itself. There are also those who will return virtually any coupon, simply because they like to receive mail. There is no way of knowing how many coupon returns are from habitual coupon clippers and how many are from people genuinely interested in the product.

The technique of coupon return is in widespread use by many companies. What it may indicate is the attention-getting value of the ad and the attractiveness of the inducement to clip the coupon. Except in the relatively rare case of mail order sales on the basis of coupons, this method does not provide a measure of the effectiveness of an ad in increasing sales.

There are, then, a variety of methods available to measure the impact of advertisements. Despite the great effort expended in pretesting and posttesting ads, there are still advertising campaign failures. Usually, assuming a worthwhile product, these failures are not an indictment of the methods themselves, but of their improper implementation by people insufficiently trained to carry them out, or companies unwilling to pay for sound research.

TELEVISION PROGRAMMING RESEARCH

Millions of dollars are spent annually to develop television programs that will attract and hold a sizable portion of the viewing audience. Each fall, the widely touted new season opens and the networks compete for the considerable prizes of the advertising dollar. The fact that so many "new and exciting" programs are canceled long before the end of the viewing season (September–October to March–April) attests to the frequency with which television executives are unable to select winning programs.

There are research techniques available that can help to decide in advance of actual programming how successful a new series may be.

Also, audience reaction, once a series is under way, can be reviewed periodically. Finally, there are methods to determine not only the size of the audience for a particular program but also its composition. This information is particularly important to sponsors as it will influence the design of commercials.

Predicting Reactions to New Programming

Sometimes, before a program or series is put on the air, a representative sample of viewers is invited to view a pilot film of the series. The usual procedure is for the viewers to communicate their reactions continuously throughout the program. Viewers are given a control device with two push buttons. When they are indifferent or neutral toward a scene, they don't press either button, but when they like a scene, they press the appropriate button and when they dislike a scene, they press the other button.

Each control device is linked to a recorder so that a permanent record of the individual reactions is made for detailed analysis. The advantage of this approach is that it provides a minute-by-minute, scene-by-scene evaluation of all parts of a program, not just a single judgment on the entire program. By analyzing total audience reaction, it is possible to get an overall response to the program as well as the detailed reactions. This can lead to changes in specific scenes of the program before its release to the general public.

This is an excellent technique for predicting program acceptance, assuming that the subjects are a representative sample of the viewing audience. Subject sampling is a crucial factor; if it is not done correctly, all other experimental controls and precautions may be negated.

Determining Audience Size and Reactions

There are several techniques to measure the ratings of television programs. The simplest and most direct is a personal interview survey by mail or telephone. Mailed questionnaires suffer from a low rate of return and the impossibility of determining how those who do respond might differ from those who do not.

Telephone surveys are frequently used and follow one of two basic approaches: (1) the interviewer asks the respondents about their television viewing during a recent time period, such as the previous day —for example, what programs were seen and which family members watched each program; (2) the interviewer asks respondents what program, if any, is being watched at the moment of the telephone call.

A mechanical technique that eliminates many of the sources of error found in any survey uses a recorder installed in the homes of a viewer sample. The device, unobtrusive and silent, makes a permanent record of exactly when the television set was on and to what channels it was tuned over the course of a day. This kind of device is used to determine the Nielsen ratings, which provide the basis for deciding whether programs will be continued or dropped. Although it provides an accurate record of channel choice for all programming periods, it does not tell which viewers are watching a particular program. Indeed, it cannot tell if anyone is watching. Some people leave a television set on much of the time as a baby-sitter for infants or because they like some sound in the house.

Another technique for assessing audience size and personal reactions to television programs involves a monthly television quotient (TVQ). Each month, members of a consumer panel composed of a representative sample of viewers fill out a questionnaire covering all network programs shown during the month, even those the viewers did not watch. The respondents rate each program on a six-point scale, from "one of my favorites" (1) to "never seen" (6). A TVQ is calculated for each program by dividing the number of respondents awarding the program a (1) rating by the number of respondents giving a (6) rating. It is possible to compute a TVQ for the total viewing audience, as well as separate scores for different segments of the audience (by age or sex, for example).

The results can provide information to determine better scheduling of programs. Frequently, a program many people say they like will not get many viewers simply because it is shown at the same time as a more popular program. When this is the case, moving the program to a different time slot will usually increase the viewing audience. The TVQ, since it measures attitudes toward programs rather than viewing behavior, is thus a valuable guide to television programming.

THE SELLER

This section deals with the efforts of the sellers of goods to encourage, persuade, stimulate, or manipulate you, the consumer, so that you will buy their products. These numerous activities can be summed up by the label *advertising,* and we examine some of the techniques, tricks, and problems of this sometimes devious art, recognizing also its level of success.

Nature and Scope of Advertising

The influence of advertising can be seen all around us every day. There are more than 4 million firms in the United States, ranging from the corner hardware store to the Fortune 500 corporations, and nearly all of them engage in some form of advertising. There are more than four thousand advertising agencies that handle about one fourth of all the money spent on advertising each year.

Approximately 75 per cent of the money spent on advertising is devoted to the six major media: newspapers, television, direct mail, magazines, radio, and outdoor (billboards), in that order of intensity. We may sometimes forget that radio and television programming, and most newspapers and magazines, are supported primarily by the advertising dollar. Television viewers do not pay for the expensive programs they watch; without advertising revenue, this programming could not be made available without charge.

The overwhelming majority of advertising is the *direct sell* type, oriented toward an immediate response on the part of the consumer. Most newspaper and local radio advertising is of this kind, offering sales, coupons, and special purchases.

A second category of advertising is designed to create consumer *awareness* of a new product or model, or an improved product, package, or price change. This type of advertising tries to reinforce the product's brand name. Since so much of our purchasing behavior is by brand name, companies spend great sums of money to try to establish and maintain the name of their company or product in the public's awareness.

The third category of advertising attempts to establish an *image* for a product, service, or organization. Many products cannot be distinguished from one another in terms of ingredients or quality, so advertisers try to create distinguishable differences in terms of the image or symbol the product represents. For example, an automobile must do more than provide transportation. It must, through its image, make the owner feel younger or sportier or higher in status. The president of a large cosmetics firm said, "In the factory we make cosmetics; in the store we sell hope." And a professor continued, "It is not cosmetic chemicals [people] want, but the seductive charm promised by the alluring symbols with which these chemicals have been surrounded—hence the rich and exotic packages in which they are sold, and the suggestive advertising with which they are promoted." [4]

Included here is institutional advertising for which the goal is to

[4] T. Levitt, "The morality (?) of advertising," *Harvard Business Review,* **48**(July 1970), 85.

convince the public that an organization is a good neighbor and community benefactor. An example of this is the campaign conducted by an oil company to promote, not their products, but highway safety.

There are three goals of any advertising campaign.

1. To produce an awareness of and knowledge about a company, product, or service.
2. To create a positive regard and preference for the product.
3. To stimulate a desire for and action toward the product; in other words, to purchase it.

Advertising Appeals

The major way in which an advertisement can satisfy these goals is in terms of its appeal; that is, what it promises to do for the potential purchaser. Which human needs or motivations does the product promise to satisfy? We have many drives: innate or primary ones for food, water, shelter, safety, and sexual satisfaction; and a variety of learned or secondary drives that vary from one culture or subculture to another, or from one person to another.

Thus, not all segments of the population have a similar need for achievement or for affiliation or for status. These drives depend on a person's past experiences; the experiences of a child growing up in Beverly Hills, California, foster a different set of adult needs than the experiences of a child growing up in Harlem.

To sell their products, advertisers must gear their messages toward satisfying the right needs, but this is difficult to do because of the group and individual differences in needs as well as the complexity of human motivations.

It is not difficult to determine in many ads the appeal that is being made. A mouthwash or shampoo virtually guarantees that its user will be hungrily sought after by the opposite sex. An after-dinner drink being consumed by an expensively dressed couple in a country club assures the drinker of enhanced status and prestige.

Advertisers continually study consumers to determine these motivations and to slant their messages accordingly. Often, such studies result in a drastic change in the advertising appeal. For example, the theme of an advertising campaign for a well-known household cleaner was its cleaning speed—consumers were told that it worked faster than any other product. Consumer research reported that people who were using the product rarely said they did so because of its alleged speed. Instead, more than half the users said they bought the product because it was gentle to their hands. The wrong appeal was being used, and the situation was quickly remedied.

A choice must be made about the manner in which any appeal should be formulated. Should the message indicate that something pleasant will happen to you if you do use the product (a *positive* appeal), or should it show that something unpleasant will happen if you don't use the product (a *negative* appeal)? For example, what is the best way to market a deodorant soap? Do you portray men and women sitting home alone—with no dates or friends—because they don't smell good or fresh or clean? Or do you show them at a party, or even getting married, all because they used the correct product?

The negative appeal has been shown to be effective for certain kinds of products. The negative appeal does not work, however, when the consequences are overly unpleasant, such as showing pictures of horrible automobile accidents in a campaign to promote safe driving. These advertisements distract people from the message.

A standard approach combines both appeals, first showing the negative consequences of not using the product, and then showing the benefits when the consumer began using the product. Both positive and negative appeals can be effective, then, depending on the product being promoted and on the personal characteristics of the consumer market for that product.

Trademarks

A trademark familiar to most of the consuming public can greatly facilitate advertising effectiveness because it serves as a shorthand symbol of the feelings and images associated with the product through past advertising. Key aspects of the product can come to be identified with and exemplified by the trademark. Most trademarks are simply the name of the product, for example, Coca-Cola, Kleenex, Xerox.

When a trademark is well established in the consumer's vocabulary, it alone—without any other advertising message—can stimulate the person to recall the product and its image.

Often, a distinctive slogan ("I'd walk a mile for a Camel," "When it rains, it pours") will become so associated with past advertising and the trademark that it assumes the characteristics of the trademark alone. An advertising format can also become inseparably identified with a trademark and can likewise take on its characteristics.

Consumer psychologists have devoted considerable research to the effectiveness of trademarks and brand names (often the two are synonymous), concerned primarily with their ease of identification and with their meaning. How quickly they can be recognized is usually studied by means of the tachistoscope, flashing trademarks briefly (perhaps 1/50th of a second) to the subjects to determine what names and symbols can be most readily identified.

Trademark meaning can be studied by using the free association technique in which people respond with the first word that comes to mind when presented with a trademark or brand name as the stimulus word.

This research can be of great value by informing manufacturers how recognizable the product name is, and what that name means to the consuming public. Often, such tests lead to a modification in a trademark to make it a more effective advertising cue.

Sometimes a trademark can be so effective that it comes to stand for all brands of a certain type of product. For example, "kleenex" is now used to mean any kind of facial tissue, and "xerox" any kind of photocopier. When this happens, the company can lose its ready identifiability and share of the market.

Product Image

An integral aspect of advertising is the establishment of a product's image. What ideas, thoughts, and feelings are associated with the product's "personality"? The development of a successful product image—one with which people will want to identify—has frequently brought companies from obscurity to prosperity. Indeed, the image of a product can be far more important in selling than the nature of the product itself.

Take the example of Marlboro cigarettes. When first introduced, their packaging and advertising were oriented toward an elegant and essentially feminine personality. Consumer response was not spectacular. In hopes of boosting sales, a new advertising campaign was launched to change the image. Cowboys, ranchers, and other rugged-looking outdoor men, sporting tattoos and riding horses were used in the advertisements. The Marlboro Man in Marlboro Country became part of our lives and sales soared.

A little-known shirt manufacturer became a success overnight by using an image based on a distinguished-looking man wearing an eye patch. The image of urbanity and sophistication greatly increased the · sales of Hathaway shirts.

The most difficult problem in the development of a product image is not the transmission of the image to the public, but the determination of what that image should be. What will attract potential buyers to one make of automobile or refrigerator or sportswear rather than another? What kind of product personality should be stressed?

454

There are several methods for studying product image. One technique involves *group interviews* with selected samples of consumers in which they are questioned in detail about their perception of and feelings toward various products. This in-depth approach attempts to elicit hidden feelings—positive and negative—about the products in question.

A more objective approach involves the *adjective checklist*. People are asked which of a number of descriptive adjectives or phrases characterize their feelings about a particular product. A variation of this approach asks people to apply each adjective in the checklist to one of several products or to their conception of the type of person who would buy those products.

Based on this research, advertisers can decide which qualities to stress (and which to ignore) in developing an image for the product.

The Package

Another important aspect of an advertising and promotional campaign for a product is its package. This is the part of the product that customers see at the critical moment of decision prior to purchase. When looking for a box of cookies on the supermarket shelf, and confronted by a dizzying array of competing brands, shoppers may not remember the commercial they saw the previous night on television. At the moment of purchase, the package may well be the deciding factor.

The old saying about not being able to judge a book by its cover may be true, but we still tend to make decisions on that basis. How often do we evaluate people on the basis of their clothes or their car? We all tend to categorize others based on their "cover." We make similar judgments about many of the things we buy. Psychologists have found many examples where consumers' attitudes about a product are based not on the quality of the product, but on the wrapping or package in which it was presented.

In one study, two groups of people were asked about the taste of coffee. One group was served coffee from a modern electric coffee maker and the other group was served from an antique coffee urn. The antique urn group rated the coffee much better tasting than the modern coffee maker group. And the coffee itself? The same in both cases. The container from which the coffee was poured influenced the way in which the people perceived its taste.

In another study, pills of two different sizes were shown to groups of patients and doctors, and they were asked to rate the potency of the drug contained in the pills. Both groups insisted, on the basis of size, that the larger pill was the more potent. In fact, however, the larger pill was less than half as strong as the smaller pill.

According to a well-known consumer psychologist, a properly designed package must satisfy six criteria.[5]

1. Convenience. The package must hold just the right amount of the product to satisfy the average user's needs. It should not be too bulky or heavy.
2. Adaptability. The package must fit the space in which such a product is normally kept. For example, medicine bottles should not be too large for a medicine cabinet.
3. Security. The package must assure consumers that the product is of high quality.
4. Status or prestige. Consumers must feel that the package enables them to express something about themselves. A worthy or desirable personal quality must be stimulated by the package.
5. Dependability. The package must cause consumers to feel that they can depend on the product and its manufacturer.
6. Aesthetic satisfaction. The design, shape, and color of the package must be aesthetically pleasing.

Overall, the packaging must reinforce the image or personality of the product established by the advertising. A cologne advertised for the virile man should not be packaged in a pink tube with fancy lettering, but in a box with bright bold colors.

The design and matching of package and product can be determined through careful research on consumer reactions to existing as well as new packages. Consumers can be asked to examine a package, and then to free associate—to tell whatever comes to mind when they see the package—and this research can determine the positive or negative images elicited by the package. Survey and in-depth procedures can also be used to determine packaging impact and preference.

Sex in Advertising

The use of attractive men and women and seductive fantasies are prominent in advertising. Such illustrations are used to sell everything from spark plugs to perfume. Since the approach is so frequently used,

---

[5] E. Dichter, "The man in the package." In S. H. Britt, *Consumer Behavior in Theory and in Action* (New York: John Wiley & Sons, 1970), pp. 356–360.

it is natural to assume that its effectiveness as a sales technique has been established beyond question.

However, its value has been accepted on faith alone, with little research support. The research that has been conducted is not optimistic. Sex appeal in ads does seem to have a high attention-getting value for both men and women. Studies of consumers looking at magazines show that, of a variety of ads on a single page, most people immediately look at the one that contains an element of sex. But what then? Research has shown that ads featuring provocative pictures of women are read more often by women than by men. Men are attracted to this type of illustration, but women read the message along with it. In many cases, this means that the wrong audience is reading the message; usually the attractive woman was included in the ad to seduce men into reading the message.

A similar phenomenon occurs with ads using pictures of attractive men; the messages are more often read by men than by women. Once again, the wrong audience is reading the message.

Even more discouraging is evidence suggesting a very low recall rate for messages accompanying sexy illustrations. One company tried two ads, each with a coupon to return. One ad featured a young woman in a bikini; the other did not. The coupon return was much higher from the ad without the illustration.

Laboratory research verifies the field observations. In one study, male subjects were shown a number of ads, some with and some without sexy illustrations. They were then shown the same ads with the brand names deleted and asked to identify the product or advertiser. When questioned again, twenty-four hours after seeing them, there was no difference in recall for the sexy and the nonsexy ads. After seven days, however, they had forgotten significantly more of the sexy than the nonsexy ads.

In sum, the wrong audience reads the messages accompanying sexy ads and, although many people enjoy looking at the illustrations, they don't remember the advertising messages that accompany them.

Introducing a New Brand

One frequent business activity is the introduction of new brands of a product. Every year, there seem to be new brands of toothpaste, cigarettes, and breakfast cereal, among many others. Some of these new brands succeed and become well established in the marketplace. Others, for a variety of reasons, fail and are withdrawn from the market. And some new brands do not even reach the public; they are doomed by the results of test-market research.

Introducing new brands is an expensive and risky operation. Some 70 per cent of all new products do not go beyond the test-market stage. An unknown percentage fail (unknown, because companies do not generally talk about their failures), even when they had succeeded in the test marketing. Companies spend a great deal of time and money on research that they hope will lead to the development of new products, but only 20 per cent of that effort is successful.

In order to find out why some new brands succeed and others do not, one hundred new food products were studied.[6] Half of them were successful and half were not. Some interesting and significant differences were found between the successes and the failures. Of the successful new brands, 74 per cent offered better quality or performance at the same or even higher prices than competing brands. There was a high correlation between the success of a new brand and its degree of difference from existing brands. Most successful new brands offered an obviously new appearance, or performance, in a way that was immediately apparent to consumers. Most successful brands represented a dramatically new idea.

On the surface, then, it may seem simple to ensure the success of a new brand: offer consumers better value, make sure the product is noticeably different from competing products, and be the first with a new idea. Apparently, most new brands do not meet these criteria.

Success of Advertising Campaigns

We turn now to the most important question of all for the seller: Is the advertising, on which so much money is spent, really effective? Let us consider the success of large-scale advertising campaigns first. Unfortunately, in many cases, neither the advertising agency nor the company whose product is being promoted really knows how successful an advertising campaign has been. Further, when success (or lack of it) is known, it is often kept secret from anyone not directly involved with the company. Understandably, companies do not want to broadcast their failures or have competitors learn of a new technique that has been enormously successful.

Some advertising campaigns have been evaluated. One study—an analysis of 135 campaigns described by the agencies as highly successful—tried to determine the specific objectives established by the companies and advertising agencies for each campaign, and if the campaign met these objectives.[7] Specific objectives were measured by

[6] J. H. Davidson, "Why most new consumer brands fail," *Harvard Business Review*, **54**(2) (1976), 117–122.

[7] S. H. Britt, "Are so-called successful advertising campaigns really successful?" *Journal of Advertising Research*, **9** (2) (1969), 3–9.

the following criteria: (1) was the basic message of the campaign well defined? (2) was the target audience delimited? (3) were the intended effects of the campaign predetermined? (4) were criteria for evaluating the campaign's success established?

Of the 135 advertising campaigns studied, 64 per cent met the first three criteria, but less than 2 per cent satisfied the fourth. Only two campaigns had established any criteria to measure success.

How well did the campaigns meet any previously set objectives? In 69 per cent of the cases, the so-called proof of success touted by the advertising agency was not at all related to previously set objectives.

These campaigns were chosen for analysis precisely because they were alleged to be successful. Under careful scrutiny, most of them turned out to lack any real evidence of success.

Specific goals must be established in advance of an advertising campaign, along with the means of measuring goal satisfaction. In the absence of well-defined objectives, there is no way to determine how worthwhile the campaign was.

In another large-scale attempt to measure the effectiveness of an advertising campaign, 108 products advertised in eight countries over a period of ten years were analyzed. It was found that a 1 per cent increase in advertising expenditures yielded an average of 0.25 per cent increase in sales. Additional increases in the amount of money spent on advertising yielded diminishing returns; in other words, doubling the advertising budget never doubled sales.

Advertising was found to create preferences for a particular brand but the effect was modest. Overall, the companies studied did obtain a positive return for their advertising investment, but the return was hardly spectacular.

Other attempts to measure the success of advertising have been more limited, concerned not with a total promotional campaign but with a single type or style of ad. One study involved mailing thirteen different advertisements to two randomly selected groups of women. One group received an ad every week for thirteen weeks and the other group received an ad every four weeks for a year. The goal was to determine how the differential rate of advertising exposure would affect recall of the ad. In telephone interviews, the consumers were aided in their recall by mention of the product, and were then asked specific questions about the ad: what did it look like, what did it say about the product, where had they seen it (to determine if they remembered those ads that were sent to them).

More concentrated exposure to the ads—receiving them every week—yielded a higher rate of recall (63 per cent) than receiving them every four weeks (48 per cent). A second finding related to

TABLE 13–2

USE OF ADVERTISEMENTS
FOR VARIOUS PRODUCTS

Item	Ads Used (%)
Shoes	9
Personal accessories	12
Apparel	23
Home furnishings	26
Large appliances	42
Small appliances	43
Toys	46
Auto accessories	50
Furniture	52

forgetting, which occurred at a surprising rate. For the weekly exposure group, the 63 per cent recall rate had dropped by half after four weeks, and by two thirds after six weeks. However, increasing the amount of advertising exposure decreased the forgetting. In other words, the more frequently the subjects saw the ads, the better they remembered them.

Another research study designed to test the success of advertising dealt with the use of advertising in shopping. A group of 506 women who had made a shopping trip within one month for something other than food, houses, or automobiles, were interviewed extensively about that shopping trip. In order to be included in the sample, a consumer had to have shopped for an item costing more than $5. The group selected had made a total of 891 purchases during the month in question. Only 24 per cent of the purchases were made on the basis of information from some form of advertising. Overall, advertising seemed to have been of limited assistance in the shopping activities.

However, when advertising was related to the type of product purchased, it had been used in more than half the cases for some items and less than 10 per cent for others. Table 13–2 shows the use of advertisements for various products.

Apparently, for items on which shoppers have the greatest amount of personal information (shoes, personal accessories, and apparel), they have little need for the information supplied by advertising. For infrequently purchased items, there was greater reliance on advertising messages.

Another variable correlated with the use of advertisements was price. The more expensive the purchase, the greater the recourse to advertising information (although it did not exceed 50 per cent, even for the most expensive items).

Comparing shoppers who relied more heavily on advertising with those who did not revealed differences in shopping behavior. Those who made greater use of ads were better informed about the nature of the products they were buying, shopped at more than one "favorite" store, and were much more concerned about price.

These few representative studies about the success of advertising indicate how such research is performed and what aspects of advertising are being investigated. It is impossible to give a simple answer to the question, "Is advertising effective?" The answer is both yes and no. Under certain conditions, for certain products, and with certain types of people, some advertising is effective. For other conditions, products, and people, advertising seems to be of little value.

The only definitive statement to be made about research on advertising effectiveness is that there must be more of it. Too many advertising campaigns are undertaken in the absence of specific goals and are praised as successful in the absence of supporting empirical evidence.

THE CONSUMER

As the previous data indicate, consumers do not use advertising for all of their purchases. Not everyone is persuaded by appeals to buy a particular brand, or even that they need that kind of product or service. Personal characteristics of consumers, as well as their social class or ethnic group, can provide a more powerful impetus to buy a particular product than any amount of advertising.

Buying Habits and Brand Loyalty

Many products that are purchased periodically are bought on the basis of habit. Habitual behavior occurs in nearly everything we do, and there is no reason it should not appear in our shopping behavior as well. Habits represent routine and easy ways of responding to complex situations. Decisions do not have to be made, and alternative behaviors or products do not have to be examined or considered. Once we have decided a product is of sufficient quality for our needs, it is simpler to continue to buy that particular product, especially if it is frequently purchased (such as a food product).

461

To demonstrate how powerful habits can be in shopping, one study had a supermarket change the way in which canned soups were displayed on the shelf. The soups had been grouped by brand, but were changed to an alphabetical arrangement by type of soup. Signs explained the new alphabetical arrangement but they did not prevent a great deal of confusion. More than 60 per cent of the customers were fooled by the new arrangement. Habit led them to the space on the shelf where they had always obtained the same brand of soup. Half the customers, questioned after they had purchased soup, said that the soups had been stocked in their usual order and were surprised to find the wrong cans in their shopping basket. Only one fourth of the customers were able to cope with the new arrangement. Nothing about the product's packaging or advertising had been changed, only the location on the supermarket shelf.

Habits lead human behavior in consistent and narrow paths. Once established, it is difficult for an advertising campaign to change them. Also, buying habits seem to persist for a very long time. One study found that a high rate of brand preference persisted over a twelve-year period. Of a group of subjects, initially contacted between ages seven and seventeen, and again twelve years later, one third were found to prefer the same products and brands. These results reinforce the importance to advertisers of establishing brand preferences and loyalty in childhood. Once caught, a person may remain loyal to a particular brand for many years.

It is difficult to determine precise differences between buying habits and brand loyalty; both are defined in terms of repeat purchase behavior. Both can make shopping easier in that the consumer, having selected an agreeable brand, need no longer consider alternative products. No matter whether repeat purchasing behavior is called brand loyalty or buying habit, the result is that the consumer is relatively impervious to advertisements for competing brands.

Personality Characteristics

Much research in consumer psychology has been directed toward defining the personal characteristics of those who use certain products, prefer particular brands, or choose to attend to particular media. If manufacturers know how the people who use their products differ from those who do not, they will be able to design their advertising campaign to take advantage of the distinctive characteristics of their customers.

Information on age, intelligence, personality, or other characteristics of users is immensely valuable in advertising. Similarly, personal characteristics of readers of different magazines or viewers of different television programs tell advertisers where to place their messages for maximum effectiveness in reaching potential buyers.

For example, one study administered an objective personality test to a sample of nine thousand people and correlated the test scores with consumer behavior. It was found that cigarette smokers scored much higher than nonsmokers on needs for sex, aggression, and achievement. Among smokers, those who used filter cigarettes differed from those who used nonfilter cigarettes; filter smokers were higher on dominance and achievement, and nonfilter smokers were higher on aggression and need for independence. You can understand how useful this information could be to a manufacturer planning to market a new filter cigarette. Knowledge of the personality characteristics of the market will help determine the most effective advertising appeals.

Another consumer study measured three aspects of interpersonal behavior—compliance, aggressiveness, and detachment—in a group of male consumers, and correlated these scores with product preference. No differences were observed with cigarette brand preferences, but 60 per cent of the compliant and aggressive people were nonsmokers, whereas 68 per cent of the detached people were smokers.

With other products, the study found that compliant people were more likely to use a mouthwash, to buy Dial soap, and to use Bayer aspirin than other brands. Aggressive people preferred Van Heusen shirts (which stresses aggressiveness in its ads), Old Spice deodorant, after-shave products, and manual razors. The only difference in consumer behavior found with detached people was that they were much more likely to drink tea than were the other two personality types. No detectable differences among the three types of consumers were found for hairdressing, toothpaste, beer, or gasoline.

Not all investigations of personal characteristics have revealed such differences. Some studies have reported no personality differences among those who prefer one brand over another, or between users and nonusers of various products. Of course, some products or brands may appeal to such a diverse population of consumers that no consistent personality differences among them exist. Also, some personality tests are deficient in terms of reliability and validity, and this can account for the lack of positive findings.

Price

The price of a product can be an important influence on buying behavior, often independent of advertising or of a product's quality.

Consumers frequently use price as an index of quality on the assumption that the more an object costs, the better it must be. Many consumers automatically reach for the product with the higher price. Some manufacturers capitalize on this belief and charge a higher price than their competitors for a product of equal quality. Studies have shown that identical products, differing only in price, will be judged solely by their price; the most expensive product is rated as the highest in quality.

Another aspect of price in the marketplace is that some consumers don't seem to consider price when shopping for certain items. Observations of supermarket shoppers reveal that most of them do not look for price information when buying breakfast cereals. Also, it has been found that many shoppers are unaware of the current prices charged for certain products. For other products, however—such as Coca-Cola or their preferred brand of coffee—shoppers can accurately report the current price.

A popular technique to gain sales, when introducing a new product or a new package for an existing product, is to charge a low price for a period of time as an "introductory offer." The theory behind this is that shoppers will continue to purchase the product out of habit when the price is later raised to the level of competing products. In practice, however, this does not seem to work. Sales are high during the introductory offer period (higher than for the same product selling at its usual price in other stores), but when the price is raised, sales drop sharply and remain lower than in stores that charged the usual price from the outset.

Another aspect of product pricing deserves mention. Often, shoppers are unable to determine which of several brands of a product is the best buy because of different package weights or sizes. Is Brand X that sells for $1.82 for a six-ounce package cheaper than Brand Y at $2.89 for eleven ounces? Observations have shown that most shoppers cannot make these comparisons and find the lowest price.

The use of unit pricing, which presents cost-per-serving or cost-per-item information, is growing in supermarkets and may, in time, eliminate this problem.

Social Class and Ethnic Group Characteristics

Considerable research in sociology and social psychology has confirmed important and predictable differences in values, attitudes, and behavior among people of various social classes. The way in which people raise their children, the neighborhood and type of house they live in, their political attitudes, their prejudices, all vary from lower to middle to upper class.

In view of major differences in life style and values, it might be suggested that there are also differences in consumer behavior. For a product to be successful, it must be promoted in such a way as to appeal to the social class which represents its best market. Advertising a Rolls-Royce in *Family Circle* magazine (sold in the supermarket) would be a poor matching of a product with its potential market.

In one study of consumer behavior and social class, more than one thousand female department store customers were interviewed about various aspects of their shopping behavior. The results were compared with their social class (based on occupation, neighborhood, income, and level of education of the head of the family).

Upper-class shoppers used newspaper ads as an aid to shopping much more frequently than did lower-class shoppers. Only 39 per cent of those in the lowest social class looked at newspaper ads; 91 per cent of those in the highest social class did so. Those in the higher classes made many more shopping trips over a year than did those in lower social classes.

Upper class shoppers preferred department stores and seldom went to discount stores. Half of the lower class shoppers also shopped in department stores, but more of them shopped in discount stores as well.

It must be noted that many social class consumer differences, once readily identifiable, have now become somewhat blurred. Incomes in the lower and middle classes have been rising, and increased affluence (and easy credit) offers the opportunity to emulate the upper classes in buying behavior. Also, many truly wealthy people (particularly of the "old family money" type), tend not to display their wealth; for example, driving smaller, older cars, and putting elbow patches on the old tweed jacket. On the other hand, people who are striving for social acceptance would never be seen in such cars or clothing.

Although social class differences are disappearing to some extent, it is still possible to differentiate among consumers in terms of product and brand preference by social class membership.

Another characteristic that can be used to distinguish among consumers is the ethnic group to which they belong. Blacks, Jews, Italian-Americans, Mexican-Americans, Puerto Ricans, Orientals, and others, all have distinct preferences for certain kinds of products, as demonstrated by substantial consumer research.

Blacks, as a group, constitute approximately 11 per cent of the population of the United States, but in the large cities often make up more than 90 per cent of the residents. The fact that this represents a large market with a lot of purchasing power has been widely recognized by advertisers since the 1960s. Studies have demonstrated differential purchasing behavior for black and white consumers. For example, blacks buy more than 50 per cent of all the Scotch whiskey sold in the United States and almost half of the grape soda. In addition, they consume substantially more cooked cereals, cream, rice, frozen vegetables, and syrup than whites. Also, they purchase higher priced cars than whites with comparable incomes.

A major area of consumer preference difference among ethnic groups is in food purchasing. Studies conducted in New York City among Italian, Jewish, black, and Puerto Rican families showed that second-generation Italian and Jewish women were antagonistic toward processed and packaged foods; fresh foods were preferred over canned and frozen foods. Black women, while showing some preference for fresh foods, were generally more accepting of packaged foods. Puerto Rican women combined their traditional foods with a variety of packaged foods. Of the four groups, Puerto Rican women were the least reluctant to try new food products. Jewish and Italian women rated frozen food dinners extremely low, and black women somewhat higher; the greatest sales of frozen food dinners were to Puerto Rican women.

Such preferences obviously influence food sales in ethnic neighborhoods and determine what food products local stores must stock.

The same hierarchical rating holds true for another convenience food: cake mixes. The white Protestant majority of the population has accepted virtually all new food innovations to a degree much higher than any of these minority groups.

Thus, not only advertising but distribution of food products must conform to ethnic considerations. As individual families become more assimilated into the larger culture and move out of their ethnic neighborhoods, their food preferences may undergo a change, but within the ethnic enclaves, eating habits can still be predicted with some accuracy.

The Youth Market

Manufacturers and advertisers know that a significant portion of the consuming public are teenagers and children, and this has had a strong effect on production and advertising.

Young consumers are a rich target for advertising; they spend a great deal of money every year, at least for some products (for example, tapes and records, clothing, and cosmetics). Not only is today's youth affluent (compared to past generations) but they also differ in other respects.

Consumer research shows that more young people are going to college than in past generations and this exposure to higher levels of education has important implications for their consuming behavior. Many of them are less interested in buying products for the alleged prestige or status. They seem to place a greater emphasis on value, quality, durability, and service. In short, they may be more sophisticated and demanding consumers.

Advertisers have found that standard techniques and approaches do not work with adolescent consumers and they have been forced to try new methods and messages. Research has shown that three advertising themes have been successful in appealing to the youth market: humor, candor, and simplicity. Treating the product in a light and humorous fashion, admitting to imperfections, and simplifying ads, have proven to be effective.

It is important for advertisers to sell to the youth market, but it is even more important to persuade teenagers that a particular product is the best on the market. The earlier brand loyalty is instilled, the longer the person will be a steady customer.

Young children actually purchase few items on their own, but they influence many purchases made by their parents. Therefore, much advertising is directed toward children between the ages of five and thirteen. Teenagers make many purchases on their own, but they also encourage their parents to buy things, from a new breakfast cereal to a new car.

Children are encouraged to become consumers as early as possible. Studies have shown that most children have begun some form of consuming behavior by age seven. Initially, children mimic their parents' buying behavior, and later, that of their peer group. Social psychologists report that by the time children are eleven years old, their consumer behavior patterns are similar to those of adults.

Marketing to children employs several techniques: placing products that appeal to them on the lower shelves in the supermarket, cartoon commercials on children's television programs, and distributing free in schools pencils, coloring books, or book covers emblazoned with a product's name.

A substantial portion of the advertising directed toward children appears on television. These commercials have generated a great deal of controversy. Many complaints about the ethics of such advertising have been voiced by parents and consumer groups. Congressional hearings have frequently been held on the issue.

There is no disagreement about the effectiveness of television as a medium for reaching children with advertising messages. Approximately 25 per cent of the population—more than 50 million people—are under the age of thirteen, and this large audience spends more time watching television than it spends in school. The commercials that they see on television seem to be effective. Both laboratory and observational studies report that television commercials increase children's motivations to acquire many of the products displayed.

Studies also show that by age five, children have developed negative attitudes toward commercials, attitudes that increase as children grow older. First, they become annoyed with commercials and, later, they come to distrust them. "They're all lies," a ten-year-old told a group of researchers. By ages seven to ten, children will reject misleading advertising, feeling that they are being cheated; by then they have learned that many advertising claims are false.

However, children also come to realize that these misleading commercials are socially acceptable, and thus begin to believe that society sanctions a good deal of hypocrisy. This conflicts with the moral principles they have been taught. By ages eleven or twelve, children have begun to accommodate or accept adult values (for example, cheating on income tax returns, lying by politicians, deception by advertisers) and, as a result, develop cynicism. Thus, television advertising plays an important and potentially harmful role in the socialization of our children.[8]

Despite the negative attitudes induced by television commercials, such advertising does accomplish its intended task. In one study, a group of children complained about television commercials, but more than 50 per cent of them said they had purchased, or persuaded their parents to purchase, the products shown in the "distasteful and deceiving" commercials.

Perhaps, in time, we may fully learn one of the oldest lessons in history: *caveat emptor*. Let the buyer—of ideas, policies, values, theories, research findings, and products—beware.

SUMMARY

Consumer psychology affects all of us. It influences the products we buy and use, the success of the economy, and the survival or failure of the companies for which some of us may work. We are constantly being bombarded with advertisements and frequently being studied to determine their impact.

[8] See T. G. Bever, M. L. Smith, B. Bengen, and T. C. Johnson, "Young viewers' troubling response to TV ads," *Harvard Business Review*, **53**(6) (1975), 109–120.

Consumer psychologists use a variety of research methods; some of these are standard psychological tools, which are also applied in other areas of industrial and organizational psychology, and some are developed specifically for the study of consumer behavior. The most frequently used method is the **survey,** in which (through questionnaires and interviews) feelings and attitudes on a variety of topics are investigated. Another method is the **in-depth approach,** which uses projective techniques to attempt to probe hidden motivational aspects of product choice and use.

Consumer psychologists also use **behavioral studies** to investigate how people actually behave in consumer situations. Techniques to study consumer behavior include observations of actual purchasing behavior, research on brand identification and preference, and testing of advertisements by various methods and equipment such as the eye camera and tachistoscope.

Consumer psychologists conduct much research on **television programming** to help develop programs that will attract large audiences. The television networks continually study audience reactions and characteristics for different programs. Panels of representative viewers are used to screen programs in a studio and record their reactions, or watch them at home and respond to mail or telephone surveys. Another method maintains a mechanical record of when a television set is turned on and off, and what channel is selected, for a sample of viewers' homes.

There are three kinds of advertising: direct sell, to create an image for a product or an organization, and to create consumer awareness of a new product.

There are three goals of an advertising campaign: to make consumers aware of, and knowledgeable about, a product; to create a preference for the product; and to get consumers to buy the product. One way to accomplish these goals is through the advertising appeal, based on the kind of human need or motivation the product is designed to satisfy. Appeals can be either positive or negative.

Trademarks can become effective advertising aids, as can product **image** (the "personality" of a product—the thoughts and feelings it produces). The **package** in which the product is presented is also an important selling aid, and it can be very influential at the actual moment of purchase.

Sex in advertisements is a common technique that attracts people to the ads but doesn't seem to influence how much of the advertising message they will remember.

Introducing a **new brand** of a product is a risky operation that fails more often than it succeeds. For the greatest chance of success, a new brand must offer consumers better value, be noticeably different from its competitors, and be the first with a new idea.

Research has shown that advertising campaigns are not always successful. They seem to work for certain products, under certain conditions, and with certain people, but not for other products, conditions, and people.

Several factors influence the consumer. **Buying habits** and **brand loyalty** can render buyers immune to advertising for products other than those to which they are loyal. Personal characteristics, social class, and ethnic group membership can determine the products that people buy and use, as can the product's **price.** It has been found that some consumers associate higher price with higher quality, some don't examine prices for certain products, and others have great difficulty determining the unit price of a product.

Much advertising is oriented toward young people, who represent a large and growing market for certain products. Both adolescents and children seem to be influenced by television advertising, even though children learn by the age of five to distrust commercials.

SUGGESTED READINGS

Aaker, D., and Day, G., Eds. *Consumerism: Search for the Consumer Interest,* 2nd ed. New York: The Free Press, 1974.

Alpert, M. Personality and the determinants of product choice. *Journal of Marketing Research,* 1972, **9**(1), 89–92.

Barry, T., and Hansen, R. How race affects children's TV commercials. *Journal of Advertising Research,* 1973, **13**(5), 63–67.

Bennett, P. D., and Kassarjian, H. H. *Consumer Behavior.* Englewood Cliffs, N.J.: Prentice-Hall, 1972.

Bever, T. G., Smith, M. L., Bengen, B., and Johnson, T. C. Young viewers' troubling response to TV ads. *Harvard Business Review,* 1975, **53**(6), 109–120.

Blackwell, R. D. *Contemporary Cases in Consumer Behavior.* New York: Holt, Rinehart and Winston, 1976.

Bloch, C. E., and Roering, K. J. *Essentials of Consumer Behavior.* New York: Holt, Rinehart and Winston, 1976.

Blum, M. L. *Psychology and Consumer Affairs.* New York: Harper & Row, 1977.

Cadbury, N. When, where, and how to test market. *Harvard Business Review,* 1975, **53**(3), 96–105.

Callahan, F. Advertising's influence on consumers. *Journal of Advertising Research,* 1974, **14**(3), 45–48.

Chevalier, M. Increase in sales due to in–store display. *Journal of Marketing Research,* 1975, **12**(4), 426–431.

Cohen, J. B., Ed. *Behavioral Science Foundations of Consumer Behavior.* New York: The Free Press, 1972.

Courtney, A., and Lockeretz, S. A woman's place: An analysis of the role portrayed by women in magazine advertisements. *Journal of Marketing Research,* 1971, **8**(February), 92–95.

Davidson, J. H. Why most new consumer brands fail. *Harvard Business Review,* 1976, **54**(2), 117–122.

Dichter, E. *Packaging: The Sixth Sense.* Boston: Cahners, 1975.

Donohue, T. Effect of commercials on black children. *Journal of Advertising Research,* 1975, **15**(December), 41–47.

Engel, J. F., Kollat, D. T., and Blackwell, R. D. *Consumer Behavior,* 2nd ed. New York: Holt, Rinehart and Winston, 1973.

Farley, J. U., Howard, J. A., and Ring, L. W., Eds. *Consumer Behavior: Theory and Application.* Boston: Allyn & Bacon, 1974.

Goldberg, M., and Gorn, G. Children's reaction to television advertising. *Journal of Consumer Research,* 1974, **1**(2), 69–75.

Howard, J. A., and Ostlund, L. E. *Buyer Behavior.* New York: Random House, 1973.

Jacoby, J. Consumer psychology as a social psychological sphere of action. *American Psychologist,* 1975, **30,** 977–987.

Jacoby, J. Consumer psychology: An octennium. *Annual Review of Psychology,* 1976, **27,** 331–358.

Jacoby, J., Szybillo, G. J., and Berning, C. K. Time and consumer behavior: An interdisciplinary overview. *Journal of Consumer Research,* 1976, **2**(4), 320–339.

Kassarjian, H. H., and Robertson, T. S., Eds. *Perspectives in Consumer Behavior,* rev. ed. Glenview, Ill.: Scott, Foresman, 1973.

Katona, G. Psychology and consumer economics. *Journal of Consumer Research,* 1974, **1**(2), 44–51.

Lambin, J. What is the real impact of advertising? *Harvard Business Review,* 1975, **53**(3), 139–147.

Lessig, V. Consumer store images and store loyalties. *Journal of Marketing,* 1973, **37**(4), 72–74.

McNeal, J. U. *An Introduction to Consumer Behavior.* New York: John Wiley & Sons, 1973.

Martineau, P. *Motivation in Advertising: Motives That Make People Buy.* New York: McGraw-Hill, 1971.

Noble, V., Comp. *The Effective Echo: A Dictionary of Advertising Slogans.* New York: Special Libraries Association, 1970.

Nuckols, R. C. On the reproduction of consumer psychologists. *Professional Psychology,* 1976, **7,** 609–617.

Peretti, P., and Lucas, C. Newspaper advertising influences on consumers' behavior by socioeconomic status of customers. *Psychological Reports,* 1975, **37,** 693–694.

Reynolds, F. D., and Wells, W. D. *Consumer Behavior.* New York: McGraw-Hill, 1977.

Scitovsky, T. *The Joyless Economy: An Inquiry Into Human Satisfaction and Consumer Dissatisfaction.* New York: Oxford University Press, 1976.

Scott, R. *The Female Consumer.* New York: Halsted Press, 1976.

Sheth, J. N. *Models of Buyer Behavior: Conceptual, Quantitative, and Empirical.* New York: Harper & Row, 1974.

Venkatesan, M., and Losco, J. Women in magazine ads: 1959–1971. *Journal of Advertising Research,* 1975, **15**(5), 49–54.

Villani, K. Personality/life style and television viewing behavior. *Journal of Marketing Research,* 1975, **12**(November), 432–439.

Ward, S., and Robertson, T. S., Eds. *Consumer Behavior: Theoretical Sources.* Englewood Cliffs, N.J.: Prentice-Hall, 1973.

Winter, F. Laboratory measurement of response to consumer information. *Journal of Marketing Research,* 1975, **12**(4), 390–401.

INDEX

473